HOW TO PASS the Washington Real Estate Exam

2nd Edition

Published by the NATIONAL REAL ESTATE INSTITUTE

14949 N.E. 40th Street, Suite 300
Redmond, Washington 98052
(206)881-2517 / 1-800-221-9347

PRINTED IN THE UNITED STATES OF AMERICA
ISBN: 0-915799-42-1

Cover photograph by Brian Wilson

Table of Contents

Section One: Your Real Estate License

Section Two: Real Estate Math

Section Three: Review Questions

Section Four: Sample Examinations

Section One
Your Real Estate License

1. Instructions for License Applicants

Qualifications

Washington law requires you to meet certain qualifications before you can apply for your salesperson or broker's license. These qualifications are set forth below:

Salesperson's License

1. Age — you must be 18 years or older.
2. Experience — none required.
3. Residency — you must be a resident of the state of Washington.
4. Education — you must have successfully completed a thirty clock hour course in real estate fundamentals. (You may take the exam before you have completed this course, but it must be completed before you apply for your license.)
5. You must pass the salesperson's examination.
6. You must pay the appropriate license fee.

Broker's License

1. Age — you must be 18 years or older.
2. You must have a high school diploma or its equivalent.
3. Experience — you must have at least two years experience as a full time real estate salesperson in Washington (or another state with comparable requirements) in the previous five years. Alternatively, the experience requirement may be met if you can satisfy the Director of the Department of Real Estate that you are otherwise qualified by reason of practical experience in a business related to real estate. You must submit a completed employment affidavit with your application.
4. You must be able to furnish proof of completion of at least 90 clock hours of real estate courses, including one course in brokerage management, and one course in real estate law. Each course must be at least 30 clock hours. Courses must be

completed within the five years prior to applying for the examination. (Proof of the 90 clock hours must be included with the exam application as the licensing division does not maintain records of individual courses completed by the licensee.)

5. You must pass the broker's examination.
6. You must pay the appropriate license fee.

Application for the Exam

1. Complete an Examination Application.
2. Determine the appropriate fee for the application. (A list of fees can be found at the end of this section.) Money orders or checks should be made payable to the "State Treasurer." **Do not send cash.**
3. If applying for the broker's exam, obtain transcripts of the required courses.
4. If applying for the broker's exam, you must submit the appropriate Employment Verification Form.
5. Mail the completed form, appropriate fee, transcripts and Employment Verification Form (if applicable) to:

   State of Washington
   Department of Licensing
   Real Estate
   P.O. Box 247
   Olympia, Washington 98504

   You may submit two exam fees if you want. The double fee will result in your being automatically scheduled for the next examination if you don't show up at the exam or fail to pass it. If you pass the first exam, the second fee will be applied to your first license fee at the time of license application. **There is no walk-in testing.**
6. Examinations are given on a monthly basis. You will be assigned to the next available examination. As soon as your application is processed, study materials (for first-time applicants) and an admission ticket will be mailed to you.
7. You may not apply for your license until after you have received your exam results. After you pass the examination, you have one year from the date of that examination to apply for a license. If you fail to apply within the one year period, you will have to take and pass another exam before you can get your license.

The Examination

General Information. The real estate exam is taken in one four hour session. Each exam is broken down into two sections, a national section and a Washington section. There are 140 multiple choice questions on the salesperson's exam (100 in the national portion and 40 in the state portion) and 150 multiple choice questions on the broker's exam (100 in the national portion and 50 in the state portion).

Test Centers. Examinations are scheduled in the following locations: Bellevue, Bremerton, Centralia, Midway, Mount Vernon, Pasco, Lynnwood, Spokane, Tacoma, Vancouver, Wenatchee, and Yakima.

Notification of Exam Results. Your exam results will be mailed to you. **Results will not be given over the phone.** To pass the salesperson's exam, you must answer **70%** (98) of the questions correctly. To pass the broker's exam, you must answer **75%** (112) of the answers correctly. If you pass, you will receive an application for a license.

Content of the Exam. The content of each exam covers **four major fields of real estate subject matter**: property ownership, transfer, and use; brokerage and laws of agency; valuation and economics; and finance. Approximately 10% of the questions require mathematical computations. The following list of subtopics is for informational purposes only and should not be considered totally inclusive.

I. Property Ownership, Transfer, and Use

A. Nature of real property
   1. Definitional elements of types of property
   2. Methods of legal description

B. Parties dealing with interests in real property
   1. Capacity
   2. Individuals
   3. Corporations
   4. Partnerships

C. Land titles and interest in real property
   1. Fee simple, ownership in severalty
   2. Life estate, tenancy in common, tenancy by the entireties
   3. Leasehold interests

D. Special interests relating to real property
   1. Easements
   2. Mortgages and mortgage clauses

E. Special relationships between persons holding interests in land
   1. Fixtures
   2. Priorities of liens
   3. Encroachments
   4. Restrictions
   5. Mechanic's liens
   6. Attachments and transfer of real estate

F. Acquisition and transfer of real estate
   1. Contracts and agreements
   2. Options
   3. Deeds

4. Adverse possession
5. Court action

G. Public land use control
1. Planning and zoning
2. Property taxation
3. Eminent domain
4. Water rights
5. Health and safety codes in building

II. Brokerage and Laws of Agency

A. Real estate agency
1. Nature of distinctions between types of agents
2. Creation of agency relationships
3. Duties of agent toward principal
4. Duties of agent toward third parties
5. Duties enforced by licensing authorities
6. Rights of agent in relation to principal(s)
7. Termination of agency

B. Federal fair housing laws

C. Federal Real Estate Settlement Procedures Act

D. Property management
1. Management contracts
2. Rentals and leases
3. Repairs and maintenance

III. Valuation and Economics

A. Concepts and purposes of appraisal
B. Appraisal techniques
C. Depreciation
D. Principles of real property value
E. The appraisal process
F. Economic trends
G. Neighborhood analysis
H. Site analysis and valuation
I. Gross rent multiplier
J. Principles of capitalization
K. Market data approach
L. The appraisal report
M. Real estate economics and trends in land use

IV. Finance

A. Mortgage lending agencies
B. Government mortgage institutions
C. Mathematics of financial practice

D. Federal truth-in-lending legislation
E. Principles of finance

Obtaining Your License

After passing the examination, you will be sent a salesperson's or broker's license application. This form must be completed and returned along with the appropriate fee and proof of completion of required courses (for salesperson's exam). You have **one year** from the date of the exam you passed in which to apply for your license.

Licenses are issued for **one year**. Regardless of the date it was issued, your license will expire on your next birthday (this is if the licensee is a natural person; if the licensee is a corporation, the license expires on December 31). When renewing a salesperson's license for the second time, you must submit proof of completion of 30 clock hours of approved real estate courses. A list of approved courses is available from the Licensing Division.

Fees

Real Estate Broker:

Exam Application/Examination	$50.00
Reexamination	50.00
Original License	50.00
License Renewal	50.00
Late Renewal	75.00
Duplicate License	15.00
Certification/License History	25.00
Name or Address Change	15.00

Real Estate Broker - Branch Office:

Original License	$40.00
License Renewal	40.00
Late Renewal	60.00
Duplicate License	15.00
Name or Address Change	15.00

Real Estate Salesperson:

Exam Application/Examination	$35.00
Reexamination	35.00
Original License	35.00
License Renewal	35.00
Late Renewal	55.00
Duplicate License	15.00
Certification/License History	25.00
Name or Address Change	15.00

2. *Suggested Study Technique*

Step 1: Complete Your Course of Study

This book is designed to test the knowledge you have already acquired through completion of a Fundamentals of Real Estate course. A thorough and up-to-date text, *Fundamentals of Washington Real Estate,* also published by the National Real Estate Institute, is recommended for this course of study. *Fundamentals* covers in considerable detail 95% of the topics you will find in these sample tests and on the state exam itself. A thorough understanding of the materials in *Fundamentals* makes passing the real estate exam a near certainty.

Step 2: Review the Math Section

The math section in this book deals with the type of problems known to be on the state license exam. Review this section carefully before you attempt any of the sample problems or exams.

The primary purpose of this math section is to develop in more detail the principles explained in the math chapter in *Fundamentals of Washington Real Estate.* A secondary purpose is to familiarize the student with a broader range of math problems, including some problems of greater complexity than those found in *Fundamentals.* Upon completion of the exercises contained in this math section, the student should be well prepared to answer any math question found on the state exam, as well as handle with confidence the many math problems that come up in the day to day practice of real estate.

Just a word on pocket calculators — if a calculator is not already an important part of your personal and business life, it will soon be. To the practicing real estate agent, the pocket calculator has become an invaluable tool. Calculators that range in price from $10 to $75 enable today's agents to quickly and accurately solve mathematical problems ranging in difficulty from the simple to the complex. Commission, interest, amortization, proration and depreciation problems are easily handled if the agent 1) knows the appropriate formulas and 2) understands how to operate the pocket calculator.

To the license applicant the pocket calculator is a terrific aid because Washington allows its use during license examinations. Questions that used to consume valuable time and bewilder license applicants should now represent the easy part of the examination.

Step 3: Work Through the Sample Exam Questions

The sample exam questions are arranged according to topics for easy review (the topics correlate to the chapters found in *Fundamentals of Washington Real Estate.*) As you test yourself on each topic, you can determine the specific areas you may need to spend more time on. Then go back to the chapters in your *Fundamentals* text and review the material again. When you can successfully answer 85% - 90% of the questions on each topic, you will be ready to move on to the sample exams.

Step 4: Take the Sample Exams

In the final week before the exam, you should be devoting **90% of your study time to reviewing the sample examinations**. Each sample exam is designed to be as similar to a state exam as possible. Since each exam has the same number of questions as the state exam, time yourself to see if you can comfortably answer all the questions in the four-hour time period. If you run out of time on the first exam, don't panic. That's why there's more than one sample exam. Each sample exam you take should make you more familiar with the material and more comfortable with the test-taking process.

The last exam is a sample broker's exam. Even if you are taking the salesperson's exam, we recommend that you take this exam as well. The questions are slightly more difficult and if you can master this exam, you should be well prepared to take the salesperson's exam.

3. Successful Examination Techniques

Be prepared. By using this book, you are practicing one of the keys to succesfully taking and passing an examination: preparedness. However, once the time arrives to take the test, you can improve your chances of success even more by using a few simple techniques.

Be relaxed. Get a good night's sleep before the day of the exam. Arrive at the test site early so you are not rushed. Wear comfortable clothing and bring a sweater if there is a chance the exam site will be chilly.

Be confident. You've prepared for this test, and you can and will pass. Do not become discouraged if you cannot answer some of the questions; you don't need a perfect score.

Follow directions. Read the test directions carefully and be sure you understand them. If you have questions, ask the test moderator. When filling out your answer sheet, be sure to give all the information requested, and RECORD YOUR ANSWERS IN THE PROPER LOCATION.

Read the questions first. You should read each question thoroughly before you look at the possible answers. You may wish to cover the answers with your hand or a piece of paper while you read the question. If you jump ahead to answers, you may miss a key word or phrase in the question. For example, many questions ask you to choose the answer that is NOT a true statement. Be on the lookout for key words that can change the meaning of the question, words such as NOT, EXCEPT, BUT, etc.

Skip the tough questions. As you work your way through the exam, ignore those questions which are very difficult, or which you simply find impossible to answer. Don't waste time on the hard questions until you have answered all of the easy ones. Then you can go back and work on the more difficult questions if you have the time. (When you skip a question, remember to skip a space on your answer sheet too.)

Eliminate wrong answers. If you know that a particular answer is wrong, cross it out in your question book. You run less of a risk of making a careless error if you work "backwards" in this fashion, eliminating all the wrong answers in order to find the right one. Also, if you skip a question and come back to it later, you will need to spend less time on it the second time around if you have already eliminated some of the wrong answers by crossing them out.

If you don't know, guess. There is no penalty for a wrong answer. If you find that you simply don't know the answer to a question, you have at least a 25% chance of getting it right just by guessing (as opposed to no chance at all if you don't put down any answer). You can improve your odds even more if you have eliminated one or more of the answers. For example, if you know that answers (a) and (b) are incorrect, but you don't know whether (c) or (d) is correct, your chances of guessing correctly are 50-50.

Budget your time. There are always a few people who finish the exam in half the allotted time. Nine times out of ten, these people are not "geniuses," they have simply given up. Don't rush to be the first one done with your exam. In fact we recommend that you use all the time available to you. If you have answered all the easy questions, work on the hard ones. If you have answered all the hard ones too, guess at the impossible ones. Finally, double check your answers and your answer sheet to make sure everything is correct and in the right place.

Answer every question. If it comes down to the wire and you still have not answered all the questions, guess at the remaining ones. Remember, it is better to guess than to leave an answer blank.

Section Two
Real Estate Math

1. Introduction

Math is a fundamental tool used by real estate licensees in all aspects of their profession. When you become a licensee, you will be using math to compute loan amounts, closing costs, commissions and the square footage of property. Because math is such a vital part of the real estate profession, a fair portion of the real estate license exam is made up of math problems.

The primary purpose of this math section is to develop in detail, through explanations and exercises, the basic arithmatic principles you will need to know. Upon completion of the problems contained in this section, you should be well prepared to answer any math question found on the state exam, as well as handle with confidence the many math problems that come up in the day to day practice of a real estate professional.

Approach to Solving Math Problems

While the prospect of mathematical computations arouses fear in the hearts of many of us, the math principles you will need to know are actually very basic. Solving math problems can be simplified by using a step-by-step approach. The most important step is to thoroughly understand the problem. You must know what answer you want before you can successfully work any math problem. Once you have determined what it is you are to find (for example, interest rate, loan-to-value ratios or amount of profit), you will know what formula to use.

Then you must choose the correct mathematical formula. The formulas you will most likely be using will be explained in this chapter.

The next step is to substitute the numbers you know into the formula. In many problems you will be able to substitute the numbers into the formula without any additional steps. However, in many other problems, it will be necessary to take one or more preliminary steps, for instance, converting fractions to decimals.

Once you have substituted the number into the formula, you will have to do some computations to find the unknown. Most of the formulas have the same basic form (A = B x C). You will need two of the numbers (or the information that enables you to find two of the numbers) and then you will either have to divide or multiple them to find the third number, the answer you are seeking.

The Basic Mathematical Formula

Though it may not seem like it, the formulas we apply when solving routine real estate math problems are the same ones we use over the course of an ordinary day, for instance, when balancing the check book or budgeting for groceries. The numbers may be larger and the situations different, but the formulas are the same.

To illustrate the basic mathematical formula, let's solve this simple equation:

2 x 3 = ?

Most of us learned our multiplication tables (at least 1 through 10) in the third or fourth grade, so we can quickly answer the above problem without too much trouble:

2 x 3 = 6.

But what if we are looking for something else: *? x 3 = 6.*

Again, you know without picking up a pencil that the answer is two. But what is significant here is that we have transformed a multiplication problem into a division problem: *6 ÷ 3 = 2.* Likewise, if the question is *2 x ? = 6,* the problem is solved by division: *6 ÷ 2 = 3.*

Now let's work the same kind of problem but use larger numbers: *186 x 1,412 = ?*

The answer is *186 x 1,423 = 262,632.* If we rearrange the equation, we get *? x 1,412 = 262,632*

Answer: *262,632 ÷ 1,412 = 186*

The numbers above are larger than *2 x 3 = 6,* but the formula is the same. In the first instance we have a simple multiplication problem; in the second and third instance we have simple division problems. Now let's look at some typical real estate math problems.

2. *Percentage Rate Problems*

The basic formula for a percentage rate problem is: the percentage of the total equals the part, or percent x total = part.

$\% \times T = P$

Let's look at some real estate math problems using this formula:

1. A lender made an $86,000 loan at 13% interest. What is the annual interest?

$\% \times T = P$
$13\% \times \$86{,}000 = ?$
$.13 \times 86{,}000 = \$11{,}180$

or

2. A lender made a loan at 13% annual interest which yielded $11,180. What was the loan amount?

$\% \times T = P$
$13\% \times ? = \$11{,}180$
$11{,}180 \div .13 = \$86{,}000$

or

3. A lender made a loan of $86,000 which yielded $11,180 annual interest. What was the interest rate?

$\% \times T = P$
$? \times \$86{,}000 = \$11{,}180$
$\$11{,}180 \div 86{,}000 = 13\%$

Now let's compare the real estate math equations with our initial simple equation.

$2 \times 3 = ?$	$\$13\% \times 86{,}000 = ?$
$2 \times 3 = 6$	$.13 \times \$86{,}000 = \$11{,}180$
$? \times 3 = 6$	$? \times \$86{,}000 = \$11{,}180$
$6 \div 2 = 3$	$\$11{,}180 \div \$86{,}000 = .13$
$2 \times ? = 6$	$13\% \times ? = \$11{,}180$
$6 \div 2 = 3$	$\$11{,}180 \div .13 = \$86{,}000$

As you can see in the above examples, the formulas are the same:

- if the unknown in the equation is on the **right**, it is a **multiplication** problem;
- if the unknown is in the **center** or to the **left**, it is a **division** problem.

Different Circumstances, Same Formula

Even if the circumstances change, the formulas do not. For example:

1. A lender made a $95,000 loan which yielded $8,250. What was the interest rate?

or

2. A real estate broker sold a house for $95,000 and earned a commission of $8,250. What was the commission rate?

or

3. An investor earned $8,250 from an investment of $95,000. What was the investor's rate of return?

or

4. Based on an apartment's annual net income of $8,250, an appraiser estimated the property's worth to be $95,000. What capitalization rate did she use?

The circumstances in each of the above problems are different and may appear to require different solutions. But they don't — in every instance the formula is the same.

? x 3 = 6 | *? x $95,000 = $8,250*
6 ÷ 3 = 2 | *$8,250 ÷ $95,000 = .086842 or 8.7%*

Problems involving percentages or rates (e.g., interest rates, commission rates, rates of return, etc.) can almost always be solved by a variation of the *2 x 3 = 6* formula. Invariably, percentage rate problems are made up of three parts: two known parts and one unknown part. Armed with two of the three piece "percentage rate puzzle," it is easy to find the missing part.

Arranging the Equation in the Proper Order

Many students have trouble arranging the numbers that make up a *2 x 3 = 6* equation in the proper sequence. For example, you know that a bank made a $48,000 loan and collected $5,280 in annual interest. You want to discover the interest rate. You know the two necessary numbers to solve the problem and you know how to plug them into the percentage rate formula:

% x T = P
? x $48,000 = $5,280

Because the unknown number is on the left, you know you must rearrange the formula into a division problem. But in what order should they be arranged? If you have an aptitude for math, you will easily determine the proper sequence. But such an inclination, like the ability to carry a tune or paint a picture, is not possessed by everyone. Fortunately, while you may not instinctively know how to set up the problem properly, you can do it easily by following the steps outlined below.

Step 1: Set up the equation by the "x" and "=" signs. (The *x* always comes before the *=sign; ____ x ____ = ?)*

Step 2: Using the percentage formula, plug in the numbers you know:

% x T = P
? x $48,000 = $5,280

Step 3: The unknown quantity always goes after the equal sign. In this case it is the interest rate that is unknown. So we must rearrange the equation so that the interest rate portion of the equation comes after the equal sign. Remember that when the unknown factor is on the left side of the equal sign, the problem becomes a division problem: ____ ÷ ____ = *? (interest rate).*

Step 4: Use the appropriate variation of the *2 x 3 = 6* formula to determine the proper sequence of numbers.

? x 3 = 6	*? x $48,000 = $5,280*
6 ÷ 3 = 2	*$5,280 ÷ $48,000 = .11 or 11%*

Exercise: A real estate broker negotiated the sale of a property. The commission was $7,150. The commission rate was 5%. What was the sales price?

Step 1:

Step 2:

Step 3:

Step 4:

Solution:

Step 1:		*x*		=	
Step 2:	*.05*	*x*	*?*	=	*$7,150*
Step 3:		÷		=	*? (total unknown)*
Step 4:	*$7,150*	÷	*.05*	=	*$143,000*

Sales price: $143,000

Profit or Loss Problems

A variation of the typical percentage rate problem is the profit or loss problem. An example of a profit or loss problem is shown below:

Example: Jones bought a property and sold it nine years later for $92,000. This represented a 23% profit. What did Jones originally pay for the property?

The formula for solving this problem is the same as for any other percentage rate problem:

2 x 3 = 6
2 x ? = 6
1.23 x ? = $92,000

As you probably noticed, the figure placed in the equation is not .23 (23%) but 1.23 (123%). This is because the selling price ($92,000) is 123% (not 23%) of the original purchase price. Jones sold the property for 123% of what was originally paid for it. If the property would have sold for 23% of the original price, Jones would have sustained a substantial loss.

1.23 x ? = $92,000
$92,000 ÷ 1.23 = $74,977

Look what would happen if you placed .23 in the equation instead of 1.23:

.23 x ? = $92,000
$92,000 ÷ .23 = $400,000 (incorrect)

In the question it is stipulated that $92,000 represented a profit. Jones could hardly have paid $400,000 for the property, sold it for $92,000 and claimed a profit.

At this point, many of us might ask: "Why can't we just take 23% of $92,000 and subtract it to find the original purchase price?"

Because we are looking for 23% of the unknown (original purchase price) and not 23% of $92,000.

$92,000 x .23 = $21,160
$92,000 - $21,160 = $70,840 (incorrect)

Now let's try a loss problem. Suppose Abernathy sold Blackacre for $69,000, which was 17% less than the purchase price. To find out the original purchase price, your equation would read as follows:

.83 x ? = $69,000
$69,000 ÷ .83 = $83,133

As you might have guessed, you always **add or subtract the percentage of gain or loss from 100%.**

If you buy and sell for the same price, you receive 100% of what you paid for the property. If you sell for an 11% profit, you receive 111% of what you paid for the property. If you sell for an 11% loss, you get 89% of what you paid. For the sake of working a profit or loss problem, add the percentage of profit to, or subtract the percentage of loss from, 100%.

Quiz
Percentage Rate Problems

1. Jones paid $98,500 for his home in 1987, but lost his job one year later and was forced to sell the property quickly. Acting under pressure, he settled for 9% less than what he had paid one year earlier. What was the selling price?

   a. $88,000
   b. $90,411
   c. $89,635
   d. $86,841

2. Mary bought a small apartment in 1984 for $142,000. In late 1987, she sold it for $163,655. What was her percentage of profit?

   a. 12.5
   b. 13.23
   c. 14.61
   d. 15.25

3. Carmaechal bought a rental home four years ago. Recently he accepted an offer of $119,500 for the property because it represented a 25% profit over the original purchase price. What did he first pay for the property?

   a. $90,150
   b. $95,600
   c. $89,625
   d. $93,500

4. Jones bought an apartment building two years ago. Under her management, monthly income from the apartment has gone up from $4,500 to $6,300. What is the percentage of increase?

   a. 71%
   b. 35%
   c. 40%
   d. 120%

5. First National loaned Smith $73,500. The year interest payments amounted to $7,715.50. What was the interest rate charged on the loan?

   a. 10.5%
   b. 11%
   c. 9.5%
   d. 10%

6. On the sale of his house, John took back a second mortgage for $15,000, with payments of interest only at 10.5% per annum during the first three years. How much interest will John receive in the first year?

   a) $131
   b) $1,575
   c) $1,500
   d) $4,725

7. If property values have incresed by 27% over the past five years, what is the current value of a home that sold for $92,000 five years ago?

   a) $119,000
   b) $127,000
   c) $116,840
   d) $72,441

8. A $20,000 investment yielded $3,000 in profit during the first year. What was the percent of return on the investment?

   a) 15%
   b) 17%
   c) 20%
   d) 30%

Answers to Precentage Problems

1. c) $98,500 x .91 = ?
   $98,500 x .91 = $89,635

2. d) ? x $142,000 = $163,655
   $163,655 ÷ $142,000 = 1.1525
   1.1525 = .1525 or 15¼% profit

3. b) 1.25 x ? = $119,500
   $119,500 ÷ 1.25 = $95,600

4. c) ? x $4,500 = $6,300
   $6,300 ÷ 4,500 = 1.40
   1.40 = .40 or 40% increase

5. a) ? x $73,500 = $7,715.50
   $7,715 ÷ 73,500 = .105 or 10.5%

6. b) .105 x $15,000 = ?
   .105 x $15,000 = $1,575

7. c) 1.27 x $92,000 = ?
   1.27 x $92,000 = $116,840

8. a) ? x $20,000 = $3,000
   $3,000 ÷ $20,000 = ?
   $3,000 ÷ $20,000 = 15%

3. Interest Problems

Annual Rates

Most interest problems involve calculating simple interest over a period of time. Interest rates are almost always annual rates. Thus, unless otherwise stated, if a lender quotes an 11% rate of interest, he or she means 11% per year. However, sometimes an interest problem will refer to semi-annual, biannual, semi-monthly or bimonthly interest payments. You should know what each term means.

Semi-annual: twice a year
Biannual: also twice a year
Semi-monthly: twice a month
Bimonthly: once every two months

30 Day Months; 360 Day Years

Ordinarily, interest calculations are based on **30 day months** and **360 day years.** This means that with respect to interest computations there are no 28 or 31 day months. This is done merely to simplify calculations.

Simple Interest

Most interest problems involve **simple interest**. Simple interest is the interest paid only on the principal amount of the loan and not on accumulated interest. Most personal and real estate loans call for simple interest.

Compound interest ("interest on interest") is interest paid on both the principal and the accumulated unpaid interest. For example:

First year
12% (rate) x $115,000 (loan) = $13,800 (interest)

Second year
12% (rate) x $128,800 ($115,000 + $13,800) = $15,456 (compound interest)

Unless the problem specifies that the interest is compound, it is always presumed to be simple interest.

Computing Annual Interest

To determine annual interest you need only multiply the amount of the debt by the annual interest rate.

rate of interest x principal loan amount = interest amount
r x p = i
12% (rate) x $115,000 (loan) = $13,800 (annual interest)

If you wanted the monthly interest you would divide annual interest by 12 (months).

$13,800 ÷ 12 = $1,150 (monthly interest)

To determine the daily interest cost you divide the annual interest by 360 (days) or the monthly interest by 30 (days).

$13,800 ÷ 360 = $38.33
$1,150 ÷ 30 = $38.33

Basic Interest Problems

Let's start with a relatively easy interest problem.

Example: Jones borrowed $12,400 at 13½% interest. How much interest did Jones pay?

Formula: *r x p = i*
.1350 x $12,400 = $1,674

But the problem might be posed a little differently.

Example: Jones obtained a loan at 13½% interest. After one year Jones had paid $1,674 in interest. What was the loan amount?

Formula: *r x p = i*

2 x ? = 6	*.135 x ? = $1,674*
6 ÷ 2 = 3	*$1,674 ÷ .135 = $12,400*

Once again, it's the *2 x 3 = 6* formula. Another way to present the problem is as follows:

Example: Jones borrowed $12,400 and paid $1,674 annual interest. What was the interest rate?

Formula: *r x p = i*

? x 3 = 6	*? x $12,400 = $1,674*
6 ÷ 3 = 2	*$1,674 ÷ $12,400 = 13½%*

Occasionally, the problem will be complicated with a preliminary problem.

Example: Jones borrowed $12,400 and paid the loan back after 90 days. Interest paid during that period was $418.50. What was the loan's interest rate?

Since the problem gives you amount of interest for a 90 day period, but asks for the annual rate of interest, the preliminary problem is to determine the amount of annual interest. If interest calculations are based on a 360 day year, 90 days would be one-fourth of a year. Therefore:

$418.50 (¼ annual interest) x 4 = $1,674 (annual interest)

Once you have the annual interest, the rest is easy.

? x 3 = 6	*? x $12,400 = $1,674*
6 ÷ 3 = 2	*$1,674 ÷ $12,400 = .135 or 13½%*

Computing Daily and Monthly Interest

Earlier it was explained that annual interest divided by 360 (days) equals the daily interest, or divided by 12 (months) equals the monthly interest. This information can be very useful in solving certain problems.

Example: Your buyer seeks a temporary loan in the amount of $62,000 to help finance the purchase of a home. Her present home has been sold and the sale is expected to close in 45 days. She plans to use the proceeds from the sale to repay the temporary loan. You locate a lender who is willing to make the loan at 14¾% interest. Your buyer wants to know how much interest she will have to pay over the 45 day period.

Solution:
1. .1475 (rate) x $62,000 (loan) = $9,145 (annual interest)
2. $9,145 ÷ 360 = $25.40 (per day interest charge)
3. $25.40 (per day charge) x 45 (days) = $1,143 (interest payable)

If the closing was delayed 4 days and it took your buyer 49 days to repay the loan, how much interest did she pay?

49 x $25.40 = $1,244.60

Example: Jones borrowed $98,500 for five years with interest only payments. After 18 months, she pays off the loan and learns that during this period she has paid $21,054.38 in interest. What was the interest rate?

Solution:
1. *Determine monthly interest charge*
   $21,054.38 ÷ 18 = $1,169.69 (monthly interest)
2. *Multiply monthly interest by 12 for annual interest*
   12 x $1,169.69 = $14,036.28 (annual interest)
3. *? x 3 = 6*　　*? x $98,500 = $14,036.28*
   6 ÷ 3 = 2　　*$14,036.28 ÷ $98,500 = 14.25%*

Quiz
Percentage and Interest Rate Problems

1. What is the annual interest rate on a $16,000 loan when the required interest payments are $160.00 per quarter? At least:
   a. 6%, but less than 7%
   b. 5%, but less than 6%
   c. 4%, but less than 5%
   d. 3%, but less than 4%

2. An FHA borrower secured a loan in the amount of $57,250 to purchase a home. This loan was based upon 97% of the first $25,000 of the purchase price and 95% of the remaining balance. The purchase price of the property was most nearly:
   a. $59,737
   b. $54,397
   c. $57,890
   d. $60,120

3. Jones purchased a property for $200,000, paying 25% in cash and obtaining a purchase money loan for 75% of the purchase price. After 10 years, the property had doubled in value. Disregarding any equity build-up on the purchase money loan, what is Jones' initial cash investment now worth?
   a. $120,000
   b. $250,000
   c. $100,000
   d. $200,000

4. Mr. Adams and Mr. Hart each borrowed $75,000, using their homes as security. Mr. Adams' loan was for 20 years and Mr. Hart's loan was for 30 years. Adams' payments were $865.37, including 12¾% interest. Mr. Hart's payments were $815.03, including 12¾% interest. If both loans were paid over their full terms. Adams' interest payments would be approximately what percentage of the total paid by Hart?
   a. 36%
   b. 61%
   c. 39%
   d. 164%

5. A few months ago, a real estate investor purchased a property for $50,000. He made a $4,000 downpayment and assumed a $36,000 trust deed against the property. No principal or interest payments are required during the first year. Soon after he resells for double the original purchase price. What is each dollar of his original cash investment now worth?
   a. $10.00
   b. $11.00
   c. $1.00
   d. $9.00

6. An investor paid $36,000 for a four-unit apartment house. Each apartment rents for $85 per month. The investor figures that by good management a profit of 45% of gross rentals could be made. If this is true, what rate of return will the investor realize on her investment?
   a. 11.33%
   b. 5.5%
   c. 5.06%
   d. 5.1%

7. The annual income from a property with a $120,000 building is $9,600. This represents a 6% return on the total investment. The indicated value of the land is:
   a. 50% of the building value
   b. 33% of the building value
   c. 25% of the building value
   d. 20% of the building value

8. An owner of an apartment building containing 20,000 square feet of living space wants to carpet 60% of the living space. If the carpet costs $6.00 per square yard, the total cost of carpeting would be most nearly:
   a. $8,000
   b. $13,333
   c. $15,050
   d. $72,000

9. Craft, who needed $3,000 to buy a new car, hired Broker Denton to negotiate a loan for him. Craft gave the lender a note for $3,600 secured by a second deed of trust against his home. The note was payable $77 per month including 10% interest per annum over a 3-year term. Craft signed a mortgage loan disclosure statement which showed that he would receive an estimated $3,000 from the completed transaction. The total principal amount which Craft must pay to the lender is:
   a. $3,600
   b. $3,000
   c. $3,100
   d. $3,492

10. There are five units in a condominium. Jones paid $12,600; Smith paid $13,500; Adams paid $13,750; Able paid $14,400; and Clark paid $15,250. There is a $1,800 annual maintenance fee and each owner must pay a proportionate share based upon the ratio of his or her unit purchase price to the total purchase price of all units. Mr. Jones' monthly share will be approximately:

a. $28.12
b. $27.17
c. $36.00
d. $32.40

11. If the value of a property is estimated to be $190,000 and the net income is $13,680, the capitalization rate must be:

a. 7.2%
b. 6.5%
c. 7.5%
d. 7%

12. An investor purchased property for $10,000 a few months ago, paying $1,000 in cash, with the seller taking back a trust deed for the balance of the purchase price. Soon thereafer, she sold the property for $20,000 before any payments had been made on the trust deed note. Under these circumstances, each dollar invested was worth.

a. $100.00
b. $11.00
c. $1.10
d. $10.00

13. An investor held a 5-year Trust Deed and Note which was recently paid in full at 7.2% interest per annum. If the total interest received from the borrower was $4,140, what was the approximate original amount of the loan?

a. $11,500
b. $57,500
c. $29,700
d. $5,900

14. In connection with a personal loan, a borrower paid $100 interest during a 90-day period. If the loan amount is $5,000, what was the interest rate?

a. 8%
b. 10%
c. 5%
d. 11%

15. Mr. Painter owns a parcel of land which is valued at $10,000. There is an existing first deed of trust in the amount of $9,000 which bears an annual rate of interest of 6%. Painter receives an 8% return on the property value after the standard operating expenses have been deducted. What would the return on his investment be?

a. 80%
b. 8%
c. 26%
d. None of the above

16. After deducting a $140.00 escrow fee and a commission equal to 6% of the sales price, the seller receives $13,584. What is the selling price?

a. $14,540
b. $14,440
c. $12,770
d. $14,600

17. Investor purchased a property for 20% below the listed price and later sold the property for the original listed price. What was the percentage of profit?

a. 25%
b. 40%
c. 10%
d. 20%

18. Astor sold his residence which was free and clear of any liens. Deductions made in escrow amounted to $215.30 plus a broker's commission of 6% of the selling price. The selling price was the only credit item. Astor received a $15,290 check from escrow. The selling price was most nearly:

a. $16,495
b. $16,430
c. $16,200
d. $16,266

19. A bank agreed to lend a property owner a sum equal to 66⅔% of her property's appraised value. The interest rate charged on the amount borrowed is 15% per annum. The first year's interest amounted to $9,500. What was the value placed on the property by the bank?

a. $75,000
b. $85,000
c. $100,000
d. $95,000

20. Adams bought a property for $15,000, paying $2,000 cash and the balance on a $13,000 note. At the end of the first year, before any payments were made on the note, she sold the property for twice the amount paid. Each dollar of original investment would be worth:

    a. $7.50
    b. $11.00
    c. $8.50
    d. $6.50

21. How much money must be invested at 6% interest to generate an income of $125 per month?

    a. $50,000
    b. $25,000
    c. $20,000
    d. $9,000

22. Smith borrowed $750 and signed a straight note bearing interest at the rate of 6% per annum. If he paid $67.50 interest during the life of the note, what was its term?

    a. 20 months
    b. 24 months
    c. 18 months
    d. 12 months

23. A beneficiary is collecting interest-only payments on a first deed of trust. If the first payment of interest was $245, what is the loan balance if the interest rate is 12½% per annum?

    a. $20,000
    b. $23,520
    c. $24,260
    d. $25,000

24. If the total amount of interest paid over a five year period came to $5,450 and the annual rate of interest was 8.4%, what was the original amount of the loan?

    a. $12,976
    b. $15,000
    c. $11,000
    d. $9,550

25. An investor bought two lots for a total of $3,000. Later he divided the lots into three lots and sold each for $2,400. His percent of profit was:

    a. 240%
    b. 140%
    c. 40%
    d. 20%

26. A husband and wife own a retirement lot in a resort area. The annual taxes on the property are $400.00. If the total taxes do not exceed 1% of the full cash value of the property, the "full cash value" would be:

    a. $40,000
    b. $20,000
    c. $80,000
    d. $10,000

Answers to Percentage and Interest Problems

1. c) Convert quarterly payments to annual payments ($160 x 4 = $640)
? x $16,000 = $640
$640 ÷ $16,000 = 4%

2. a) .97 x $25,000 = $24,250
.95 x ? = $33,000
$33,000 ÷ .95 = $34,737
$25,000 + $34,737 = $59,737

3. b) $200,000 less $50,000 (25% initial cash investment = $150,000 loan
$200,000 x 2 = $400,000 present value
$400,000 - $150,000 = $250,000 present value of initial cash investment

4. b) Adams will made 240 payments (20 yrs x 12 months) of $865.37
$865.37 x 240 = $207,688.80
$207,688.80 - $75,000 loan = $132,688.80 (interest)
Hart will make 360 payments (30 yrs x 12 months) of $815.03
$815.03 x 360 = $293,410.80
$293,410.80 - $75,000 loan = $218,410.80 (interest)
? x $218,410.80 (Hart) = $132,688.80 (Adams)
$132,688.80 ÷ $218,410.80 = .6075 or 61%

5. b) $40,000 x 2 = $80,000 sales price
$80,000 - $36,000 = $44,000 equity
$44,000 ÷ $4,000 (cash investment) = $11 value of each dollar invested

6. d) $85 (unit rent) x 4 (units) = $340 monthly rent
$340 x 12 (mos.) = $4,080 gross annual rent
$4,080 x .45 = $1,836 profit
$1,836 profit ÷ $36,000 = .051 or 5.1%

7. b) .06 x ? (property value) = $9,600
$9,600 ÷ .06 = $160,000 property value
$160,000 - $120,000 (building) = $40,000 land value
$40,000 ÷ 120,000 = .3333 or 33%

8. a) .60 x 20,000 = 12,000 sq. ft. to be carpeted
12,000 sq. ft. ÷ 9 (convert to sq. yards) = 1,333.33 Sq. Yards
1,333.34 x $6.00 = $8,000.04

9. a) Craft signed a promissory note for $3,600 and that is the principal amount to be paid. The rest of the information is not relevant to the question.

10. b) $12,600 + $13,500 + $13,750 + $14,400 + $15,250 = $69,500 total purchase price of all units
$12,600 ÷ $69,500 = .18 or 18%, which is the ratio of Jones' unit price to total purchase price of all units
$1,800 (maintenance fee) x .18 = $324 (Jones' annual share)
$324 ÷ 12 = $27 (Jones' approximate monthly share)

11. a) ? x $190,000 = $13,680
$13,680 ÷ $190,000 = .072 or 7.2%

12. b) $20,000 resale price - $9,000 (trust deed) = $11,000 equity
$11,000 ÷ $1,000 = $11 present value of each dollar invested

13. a) $4,140 ÷ 5 = $828 annual interest
7.2% x ? = $828
$828 ÷ .072 = $11,500 loan amount

14. a) $100 x 4 = $400 annual interest
? x $5,000 = $400
$400 ÷ $5,000 = .08 or 8%

15. c) .08 x $10,000 = $800 gross return
$9,000 x .06 = $540 interest paid
$800 - $540 = $260 (net return)
$10,000 - $9,000 = $1,000 invested
? x $1,000 = $260
$260 ÷ $1,000 = .26 or 26%

16. d) .94 x ? = $13,724 ($13,584 + $140)
$13,724 ÷ .94 = $14,600

17. a) .80 x 100% = 80%
80% x ? = 100%
100% ÷ 80% = 1.25 or 125% or 25% profit
Example:
$100,000 (asking price) x .80 = $80,000 (sales price)
$80,000 x ? = $100,000 (resale price)
$100,000 - $80,000 = $20,000 profit
$20,000 ÷ $80,000 = .25 or 25%

18. a) .94 x ? = $15,505.30 ($15,290 + $215.30)
$15,505.30 ÷ .94 = $16,495

19. d) Determine the loan amount first:
.15 x ? = $9,500
$9,500 ÷ .15 = $63,333 loan amount
Relate loan amount to appraised value
.6666 x ? = $63,333
$63,333 ÷ .6666 = $95,009 value

20. c) $15,000 x 2 = $30,000 sales price
$30,000 - $13,000 = $17,000 equity
$17,000 ÷ $2,000 (cash investment) = $8.50 present value of each dollar invested

21. b) $125 x 12 = $1,500 annual income
.06 x ? = $1,500
$1,500 ÷ .06 = $25,000 investment

22. c) Determine annual interest:
.06 x $750 = $45 annual interest
$67.50 ÷ $45 = 1.5 year term of loan
1.5 years = 18 months

23. b) .125 x ? = $2,940 ($245 x 12)
$2,940 ÷ .125 = $23,520

24. a) $5,450 ÷ 5 = $1,090 annual interest
.084 x ? = $1,090
$1,090 ÷ .084 = $12,976

25. b) 3 x $2,400 = $7,200
? x $3,000 = $7,200
$7,200 ÷ $3,000 = 2.4 or 240%
Investor sold lots for 240% of what was paid for them; the profit is 140%

26. a) .01 x ? = $400
$400 ÷ .01 = $40,000

4. Area and Volume Problems

At some point in your exam you will probably be asked to compute the area of a lot or building. Area is the total surface as measured in square units, e.g., square feet or square yards. You may also have to measure the volume of something, like a building, which is the amount of space occupied in three dimensions, referred to as the cubic contents, e.g., cubic feet or cubic yards.

How to Find Areas

Rectangles. A rectangle is a four-sided figure with four right angles. The **opposite** sides are equal in length and parallel to each other.

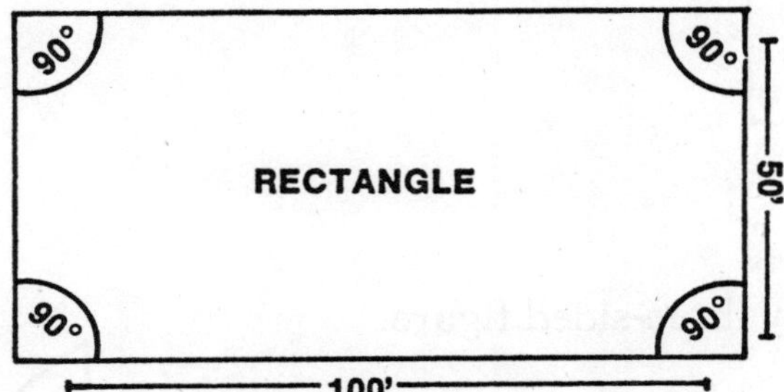

Formula. To find the area of a rectangle, multiply the length of one side of the rectangle by the length of an adjoining side. For example:

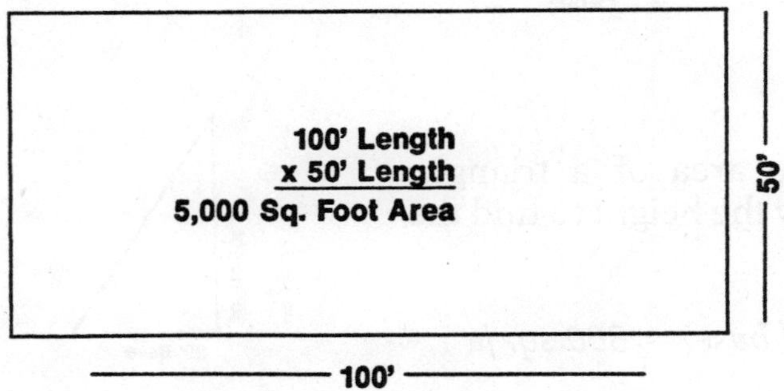

Keep in mind, in a real estate problem the rectangle will likely be an area of land or a building and the length of any given side will probably be referred to as the **width, frontage, depth**, etc.

Square. A square is a four-sided figure with four right angles. All sides are equal and parallel to each other.

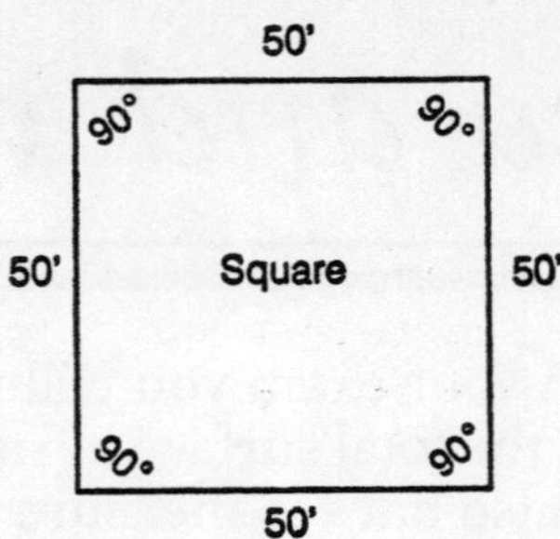

Formula. As with a rectangle, to find the area of a square, multiply the length of one side by the length of an adjoining side. For example:

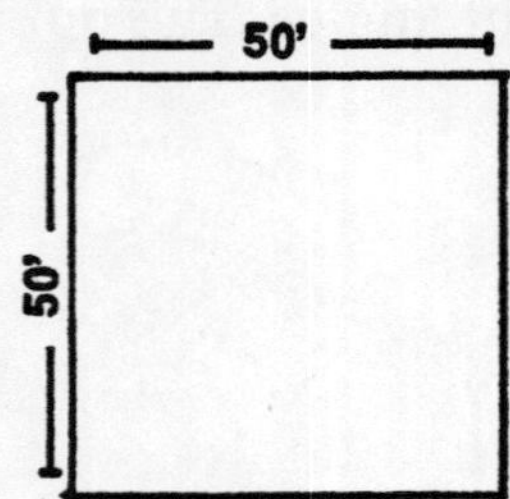

50' x 50' = 2,500 sq. ft.

Triangles. A triangle is any three-sided figure.

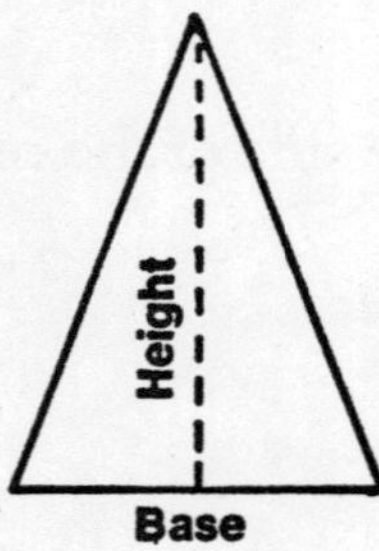

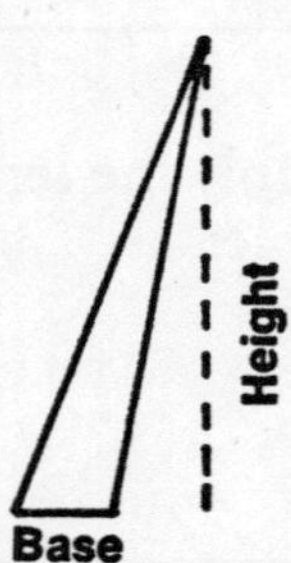

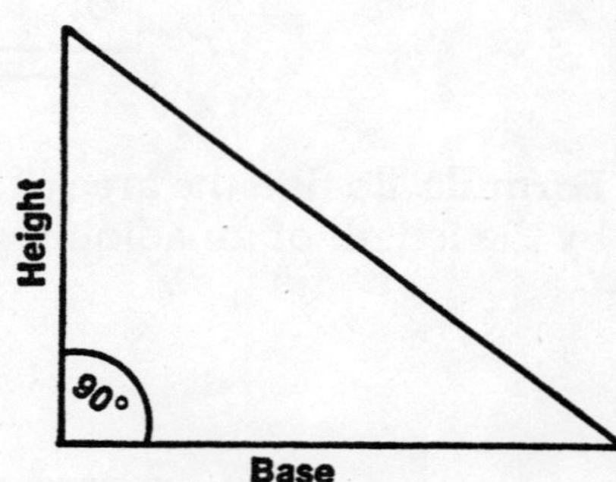

Formula. To find the area of a triangle, multiple ½ the base by the height to find the area. For example:

30' (height) x 10' (½ of base) = 300 sq. ft.

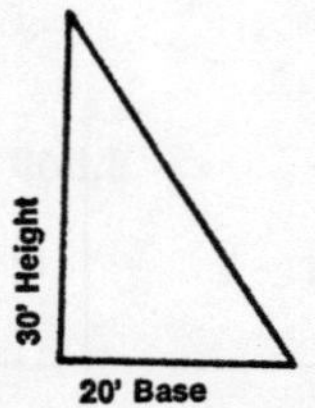

Trapezoids. A trapezoid is a four-sided figure with two sides that are parallel to each other and two sides which are not. The parallel sides are unequal in length, but the non-parallel sides are equal in length. For example:

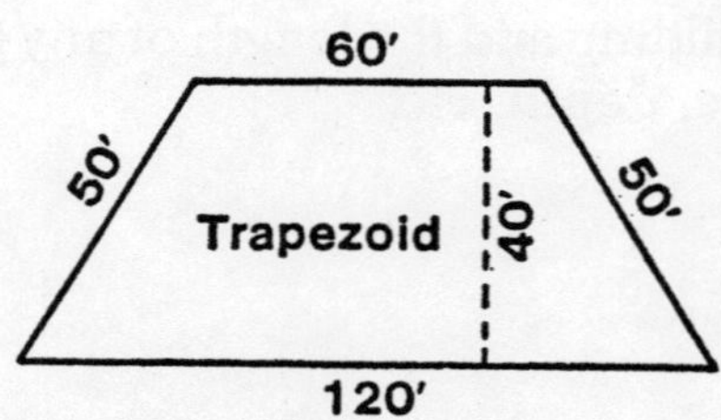

Formula. The average of the parallel sides is multipled by the height to determine the area. For example:

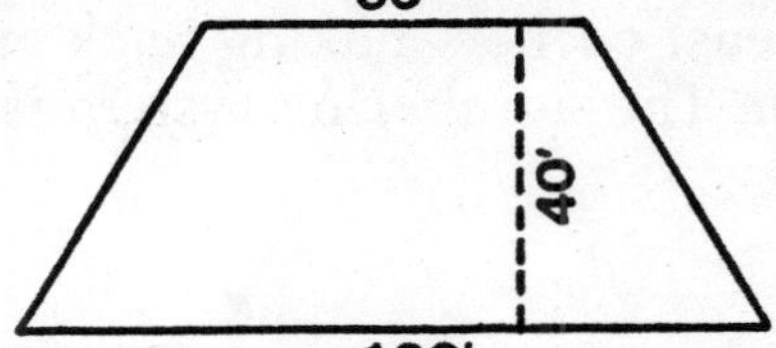

60' + 120' = 180' ÷ 2 = 90

90' average x 40' height = 3,600 sq. ft.

Finding the Missing Dimension

In many cases, you are given the area and one of the dimensions and are asked to compute the missing dimension.

Example: The area of a rectangle is 4,000 square fee. The base is 80'; what is the height?

4,000 Sq. Ft.

?

80'

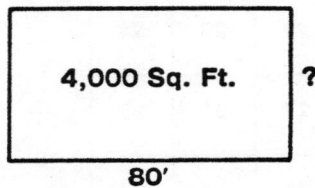

Solution: Using the always handy *2 x 3 = 6* formula, you can quickly determine the answer. To find the solution to the above problem simply divide the area by the known dimension:

4,000 sq. ft. ÷ 80' = 50' missing dimension

Missing Dimension - Right Triangles. If the area and either the base or height of a right triangle is known, the missing dimension can be computed by dividing the area by half of the known dimension. For example:

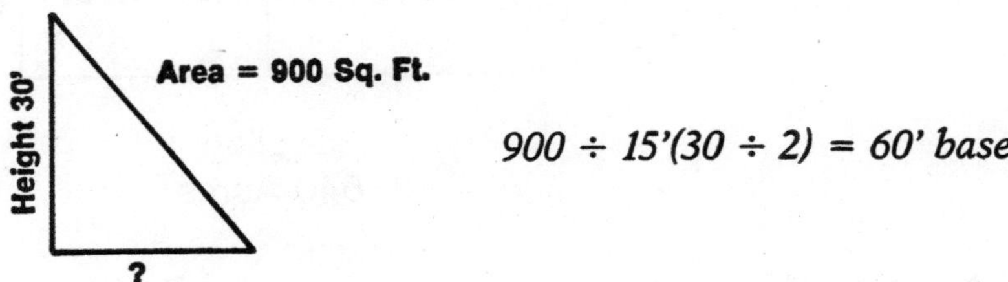

900 ÷ 15'(30 ÷ 2) = 60' base

Solving Area Problems Involving Government Survey Legal Description

The government survey system is also called the **rectangular survey** system, or simply the **township and range** system. The basic unit of measurement in the government survey system is the **township**, an area of land six miles square (36 square miles)

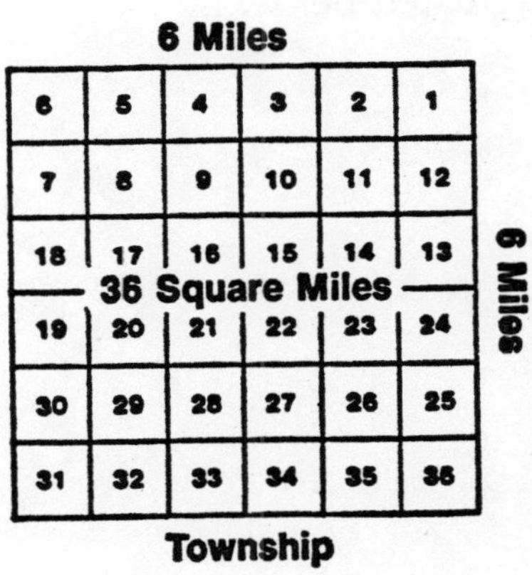

A township is divided in **36 sections**. Each section is 1 mile by 1 mile. The sections are numbered as indicated below. As you can see, the numbering scheme begins in the northeast corner snaking back and forth until it ends with section 36 in the southeast corner. The numbering system is the same for every township.

Township Divided Into Sections

NW —1 Mile— NE

6	5	4 640 Acres	3	2	1
7	8	9	10	11	12
18	17	16	15	14	13
19	20	21	22	23	24
30	29	28	27	26	25
31	32	33	34	35	36

6 Mile (sides); —1 Mile— (right side)

SW SE

One section of land contains **640 acres.** Each section can be divided in a number of ways. For instance, here it is shown divided into quarters. A quartersection contains **160 acres.**

NW¼ 160 Acres	NE¼ 160 Acres
SW¼ 160 Acres	SE¼ 160 Acres

Section
640 Acres

The SE¼ of section 27 contains 160 acres and is situated in a standard township as indicated below:

21	22	23	24
28	(27, SE¼ shaded)	26	25
33	34	35	36

As previously mentioned, a section can be subdivided into smaller parcels. In this diagram, a parcel is divided in ¼ of a quarter section. How many acres does the parcel contain?

Answer: 40 acres; ¼ of a quarter section (160 acres) is 40 acres.

20	21	22	23	24
29	28		26	25
32	33	34	35	36

Locating the Described Land

To locate land described by government survey, **start at the end of the description and read backwards** to the beginning. Let's use the following description as an example.

> *The N½ of the SE¼ of the SW¼ of section 12, township 7 north, range 3 east, Mt. Diablo meridian.*

1. The first step is to locate the meridian. If a government survey description failed to include the meridian, it would be defective. The Mt. Diablo meridian is in central California.

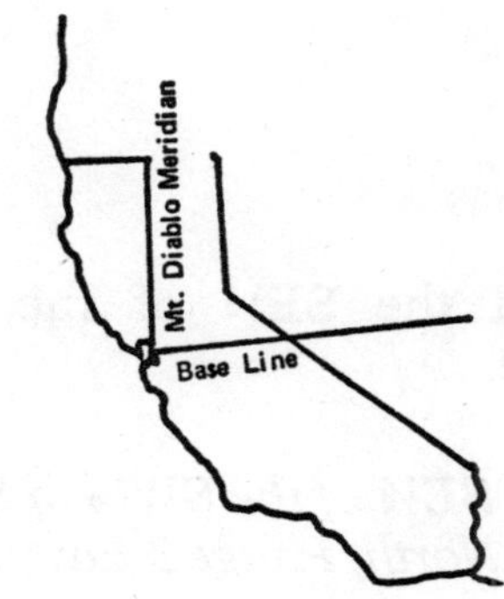

2. Next identify the correct township by counting seven townships north of the baseline and three east of the meridian.

The N½ of the SE¼ of the SW¼ of Section 12, ***Township 7 North, Range 3 East,*** *Mt. Diablo meridian.*

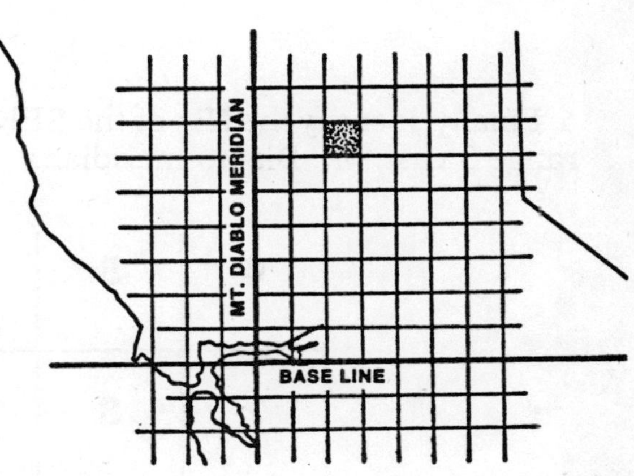

3. Locate Section twelve.

The N½ of the SE¼ of the SW¼ of ***Section 12****, Township 7 North, Range 3 East, Mt. Diablo meridian.*

6	5	4	3	2	1
7	8	9	10	11	12
18	17	16	15	14	13
19	20	21	22	23	24

4. Find the SW¼ of section twelve.

The N½ of the SE¼ of the ***SW¼*** *of Section 12, Township 7 North, Range 3 East, Mt. Diablo meridian.*

4	3	2	1
9	10	11	
16	15	14	13

5. Then find the SE¼ of the SW¼ of section twelve.

The N½ of the ***SE¼*** *of the SW¼ of Section 12, of Township 7 North, Range 3 East, Mt. Diablo meridian.*

4	3	2	1
9	10	11	
16	15	14	13

6. Finally, identify the **N½** of the SE¼ of the SW¼ of section twelve in township 7 north range 3 east, Mt. Diablo meridian.

6	5	4	3	2	1
7	8	9	10	11	
18	17	16	15	14	13

Determining Number of Acres

Determining the number of acres in a government survey description is relatively simple. There are always 640 acres in a section, so start with the portion of the description that refers to the section and work backwards to the beginning. It is so easy you can do the calculations in your head.

> **Example:** *The N½ of the E½ of the NE¼ of the SW¼ of the NE¼ of section 13, township 15 north, range 10 east, Humboldt meridian.*

The township and range numbers and the name of the meridian are irrelevant to your computations. There are 640 acres in any section, including section 13, and that is all you need to know.

(2½ acres) (5 acres) (10 acres) (40 acres)
North½ of the East½ of the NE¼ of the SW¼ of the
(160 acres) (640 acres)
NE¼ of section 13 (remainder of description irrelevant to computations)

As you can see, there are 2½ acres in the described parcel. The answer was achieved in seconds. To determine the number of square feet in the parcel, multiply the number of acres by 43,560 (square feet in an acre).

43,560 sq. ft. in acre x 2.5 acres = 108,900 sq. ft. in parcel

Caution: Very often a parcel will be situated in two sections. For example, "the southeast quarter of section 14 and the northeast quarter of section 22." When this happens, the acreage contained in each section is computed separately and then added together.

(160 acres) (160 acres)
The SE¼ of section 14 **and** *the NE¼ of section 22*

160 acres in section 14
+ 160 acres in section 22
320 acres in described parcel

Another variation of an area problem that pertains to government survey descriptions is where the described parcel is entirely contained within one section but is situated in more than one quarter section. For instance, "the South ½ of the Northwest ¼ **and** the Northeast ¼ of the Southwest ¼ of Section 11."

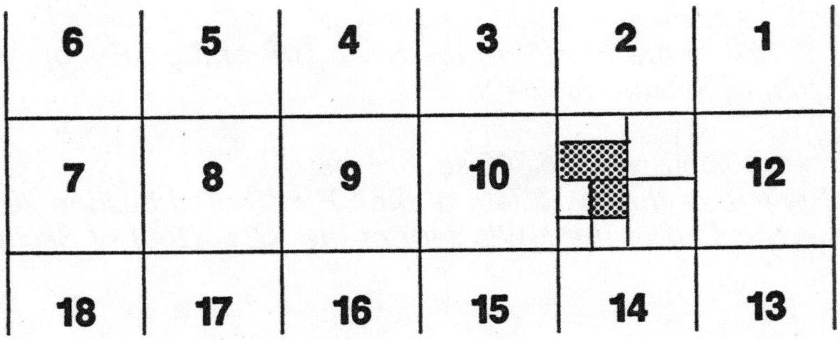

6	5	4	3	2	1
7	8	9	10		12
18	17	16	15	14	13

How many acres are in the described parcel?

(80 acres) (160 acres) (40 acres)
The South ½ of the Northwest ¼ and the Northeast ¼ of
(160 acres) (640 acres)
the Southwest ¼ of Section 11.

80 acres
+ 40 acres

120 acres in the described parcel

The key in both of the preceding examples (parcel situated in more than one section or more than one quarter section) is the word "and" in the body of the description. The word "**and**" divides the description into parts which must be computed separately and then added together.

Exercise: Find the number of acres contained in the following descriptions. Convert the acres into square feet.

1. *The NE¼ of the SW¼ of the NW¼ of Section 6.*

2. *The W½ of the SW¼ of the NW¼ of the NW¼ of Section 22.*

3. *The S½ of the E½ of the SW¼ of the SE¼ of the NE¼ of Section 31.*

4. *The SE¼ of the SW¼ of the SE¼ of Section 20 and the N½ of the NW¼ of the NE¼ of Section 29.*

5. *The S½ of the SE¼ of the SW¼ of the NW¼ and the E½ of the NE¼ of the NW¼ of the SW¼ of Section 5.*

Answers:

1. *10 acres x 43,560 = 435,600 square feet*
   The NE¼ (10) of the SW¼ (40) of the NW¼ (160) of Section 6 (640).

2. *5 acres x 43,560 = 217,800 square feet*
   The W½ (5) of the SW¼ (10) of the NW¼ (40) of the NW¼ (160) of Section 22 (640).

3. *2½ acres x 43,560 = 108,900 square feet*
   The S½ (2½) of the E½ (5) of the SW¼ (10) of the SE¼ of (40) the NE¼ (160) of Section 31 (640).

4. *30 acres x 43,560 = 1,306,800 square feet*
   The SE¼ (10) of the SW¼ (40) of the SE¼ (160) of Section 20 (640) ***and*** *the N½ (20) of the NW¼ (40) of the NE¼ (160) of Section 29 (640).*

5. 10 acres x 43,560 = 435,600 square feet
The S½ (5) of the SE¼ (10) of the SW¼ (40) of the NW¼ (160) **and** *the E½ (5) of the NE¼ (10) of the NW¼ (40) of the SW¼ (160) of Section 5 (640).*

Exercise: Find the number of acres contained in the shaded areas in the sections below.

1.

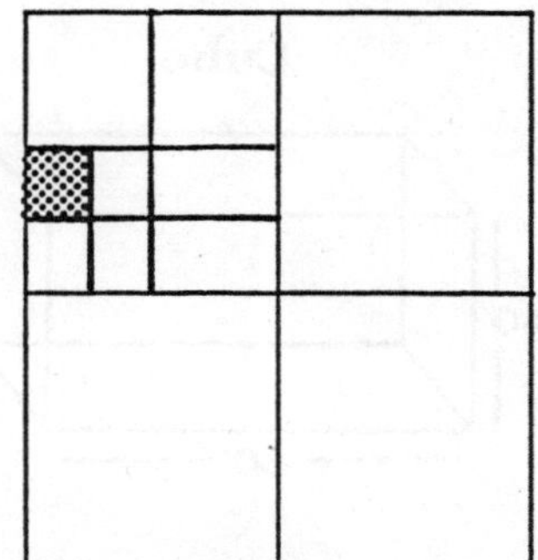

2.

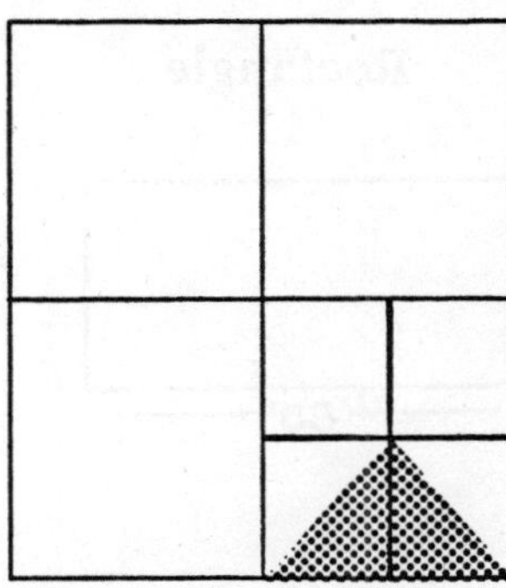

3.

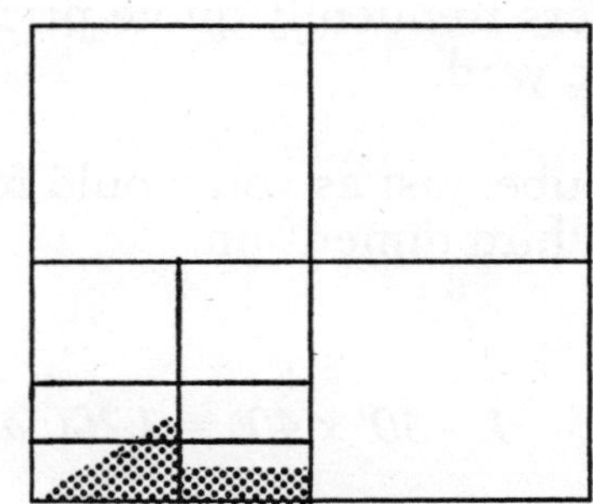

4.

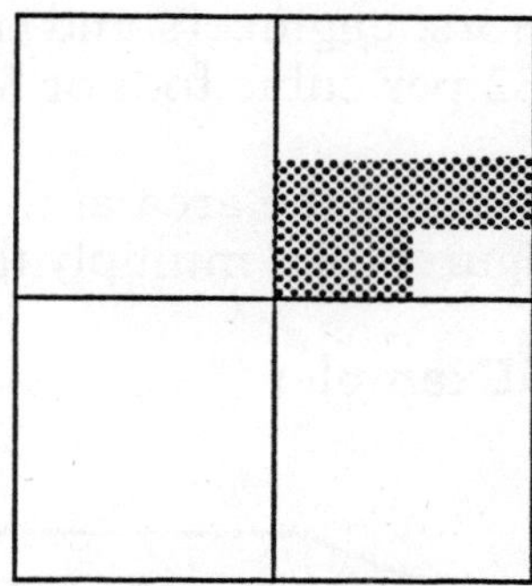

Answers

1. 10 acres. It is the NW¼ of the SW¼ of the NW¼ of the section.

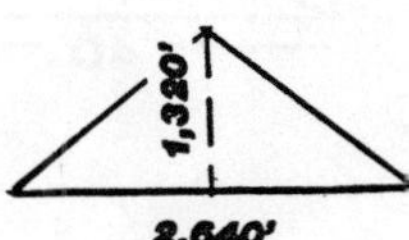

2. 40 acres. The triangle has dimensions of 2,640 x 1,320. Half the base times the height: 1,320 x 1,320 = 1,742,400 square feet; divide by 43,560 = 40 acres.

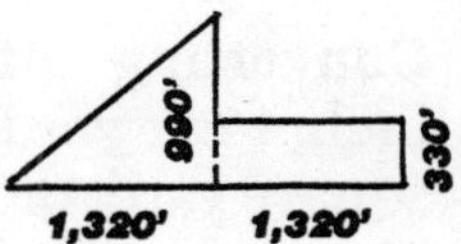

3. 25 acres. There is one triangle and one rectangle. Half the base times the height for the triangle: 660 x 990 = 653,400 square feet; divide by 43,560 = 15 acres. Base times the height for the rectangle: 1,320 x 330 = 435,600 square feet; divide by 43,560 = 10 acres. 15 acres + 10 acres = 25 acres.

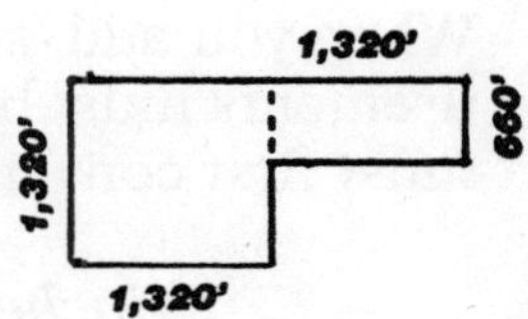

4. 60 acres. There is one square and one rectangle. 1,320' x 1,320' = 1,742,400 square feet; divide by 43,560 = 40 acres. 1,320' x 660' = 871,200 square feet; divide by 43,560 = 20 acres. 40 acres + 20 acres = 60 acres.

How to Find Volumes

Volume is always in cubic measurements. When recalling the difference between area and volume, think of the surface of one of a box's sides (area) and the airspace contained within the box (volume).

Unlike squares or rectangles, which have two dimensions, cubes are three-dimensional.

Example:

Rectangle

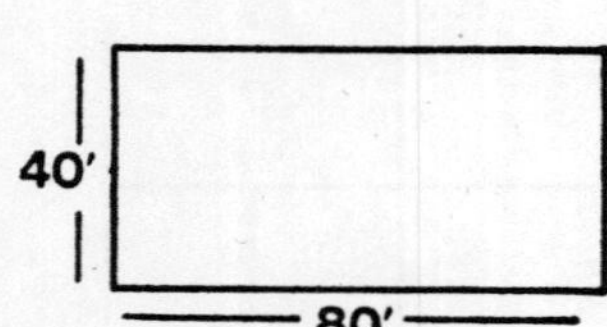

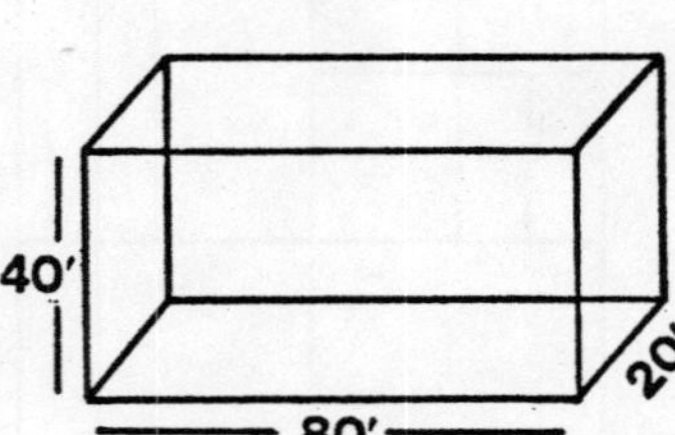

Contractors, engineers and material suppliers frequently quote prices in cubic terms, e.g., $6.82 per cubic foot or $21.84 per cubic yard.

Formula. Find the area at the base of the cube, just as you would for any two-dimensional figure, then multiply the area by the third dimension.

Example:

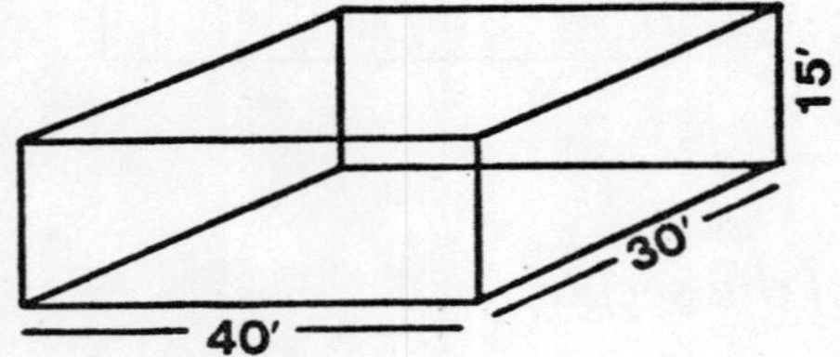

1. *30' x 40' = 1,200 area*

2. *1,200 area*
   x 15 3rd dimension
   18,000 cubic ft. volume

Converting Different Measures. Real estate practitioners measure **distances** by the inch, foot, yard, or mile. **Areas** are usually measured by the square inch, square foot, square yard, or square mile. **Volumes** are measured by the cubic inch, cubic foot, or cubic yard.

When you add, subtract, divide or multiply for distances, areas or volumes, the measurements must be identical. For example, you cannot multiply 12 inches by 6 feet. You must first convert one or the other (inches to feet or feet to inches).

12 inches x 6 feet = 1 foot x 6 feet = 6 square feet

Measurements.

Length:

12 inches = 1 foot
3 feet = 1 yard
5,280 feet = 1 mile

Area:

12 inches x 12 inches (144 square inches) = 1 square foot
3 feet x 3 feet (9 square feet) = 1 square yard
208.71 feet x 208.71 feet (43,560 square feet) = 1 acre
5,280 feet x 5,280 feet = 1 square mile

Volume:

12 inches x 12 inches x 12 inches = 1 cubic foot
3 feet x 3 feet x 3 feet (27 cubic feet) = 1 cubic yard

Example: ACME Concrete is employed to lay a sidewalk in front of the new ABC Bakery Shop. The sidewalk is to be 5 feet wide, 15 yards long and 6 inches deep. How many cubic feet of concrete will be required to finish the sidewalk?

Answer: You can't multiply feet by yards by inches, so some conversions must be made before calculating the answer:

5 feet x 45 feet (3 x 15 yards) x .5 (½ foot/6 inches)
5 feet x 45 feet = 225 sq. feet (area)
225 feet x .5 = 112.5 cubic feet (volume)

Area and Volume Problems Often Preliminary. Frequently, identifying the area or volume of something is only a first step towards solving a real estate math problem. In fact, more often than not the answer being sought involves money. For instance, in the preceding example, the question might have been, "If the concrete costs $1.50 per cubic foot, what would be the total cost of the sidewalk?"

5 feet x 45 feet = 225 sq. feet (area)
225 sq. feet x .5 feet = 112.5 cubic feet (volume)
112.5 x $1.50 = $168.75

Converting Square Yards and Cubic Yards. As indicated earlier, a square yard is 3 feet by 3 feet, a cubic yard is 3 feet by 3 feet by 3 feet.

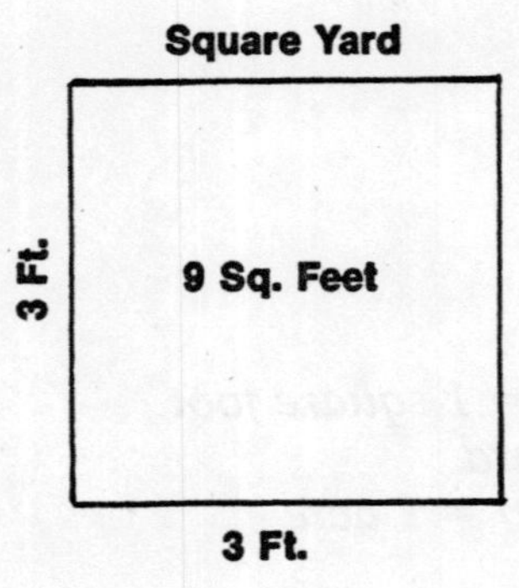

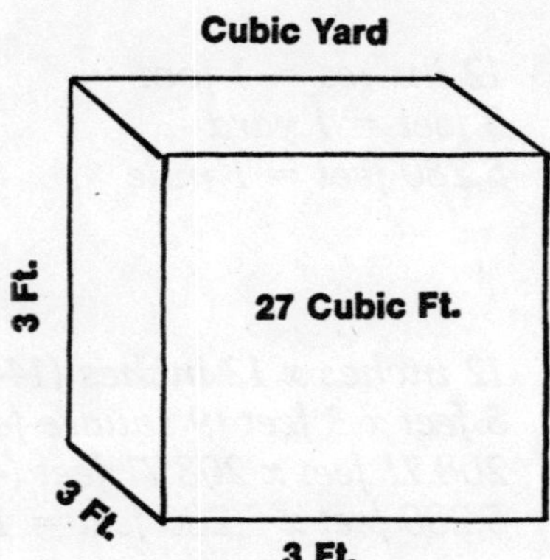

Conversions from square feet to square yards or cubic feet to cubic yards, and vice versa, are relatively simple.

1. Square feet to square yards. To convert square feet to square yards, simply divide by 9.

> **Example:** Foss owned a building which contained 12,640 square feet. How many square yards did it contain?
>
> *12,640 square feet ÷ 9 = 1,404.44 square yards*

2. Square yards to square feet. To do the reverse, convert square yards to square feet, multiply by 9.

> **Example:** Jones sold a building that had a roof surface area of 712 square yards. How many square feet were contained on the roof's surface?
>
> *712 square yards x 9 = 6,408 square feet*

3. Cubic feet to cubic yards. To convert cubic feet to cubic yards, divide by 27.

> **Example:** Johnson received a quote from an excavation contractor for the removal of 14,826 cubic feet of soil. How many cubic yards of soil were to be removed?
>
> *14,826 cubic feet ÷ 27 = 549.11 cubic yards*

4. Cubic yards to cubic feet: For this conversion, multiply by 27.

> **Example:** Smith purchased 1,842 cubic yards of land fill. How many cubic feet were included in the land fill?
>
> *1,842 cubic yards x 27 = 49,734 cubic feet*

Quiz
Area and Volume Problems

Area Problems

1. A building has a floor space that measured 24' x 30'. If the walls are 6" thick, how many square feet would the building take up?

   a. 720 square feet
   b. 775 square feet
   c. 735 square feet
   d. 732 square feet

2. To identify the number of square feet in a square 40-acre parcel, you would multiply which of the following dimensions?

   a. 5,280' x 5,280'
   b. 1,320' x 1,320'
   c. 660' x 660'
   d. 2,640' x 2,640'

3. If a salesperson sold a parcel with 500 front feet at $400 a front foot and was to receive 40% of the broker's 6% commission, the salesperson would receive?

   a. $3,200
   b. $4,800
   c. $12,000
   d. None of the above

4. "Beginning at a point located 45' from the southwest corner of the intersection of 10th and Main Streets, follow a line due east 500', thence at a right angle due south 735', thence at a right angle due west 599', thence back to the point of beginning," is a legal description which contains approximately how many acres?

   a. 9
   b. 7
   c. 10
   d. 8

5. A parcel of land, which is rectangular in shape, has a canal running diagonally from one corner to the other. It divides the land into two equal lots. One lot measures 550 feet across and has a depth of 840 feet. Approximately how many acres are contained in the entire parcel?

   a. 4.7
   b. 8.3
   c. 5.3
   d. 10.6

6. The number of linear feet on each side of an acre of land that is almost square would be closest to:

   a. 199'
   b. 208'
   c. 255'
   d. 290'

7. What is the approximate square footage of the house in the drawing?

   a. 2,200
   b. 1,655
   c. 1,433
   d. 1,615

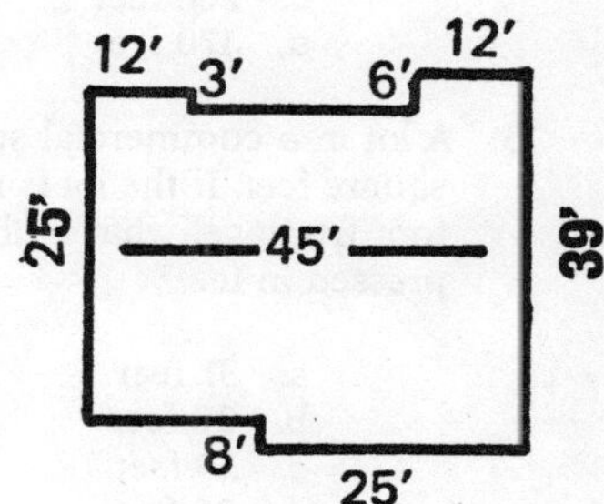

8. How many acres are contained in the triangle illustrated below?

   a. 30
   b. 40
   c. 20
   d. 10

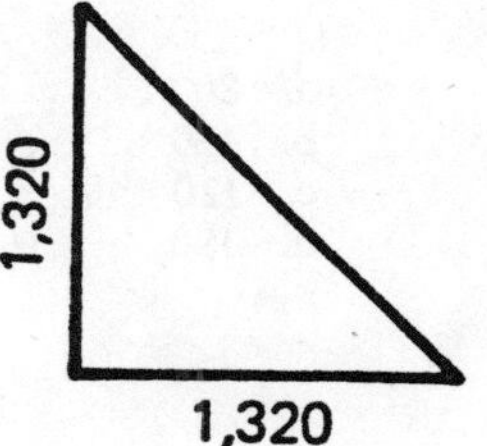

9. A parcel of land 660 feet wide by 1,320 feet deep totals:

   a. 40 acres
   b. 30 acres
   c. 20 acres
   d. 10 acres

10. 1,320 feet by 1,320 feet is:

    a. 80 acres
    b. 20 acres
    c. 40 acres
    d. 60 acres

11. An investor paid $193,000 for a lot on which he intended to build an apartment complex. If the lot was 200 feet deep and cost $4.40 per square foot, the cost per front foot was:

    a. $960
    b. $440
    c. $220
    d. $880

12. A rectangle shaped lot contains 45,100 square feet and has a depth of 410 feet. The owner wants to add onto the lot by buying the two lots on each side of it. If each adjoining lot contains 12,300 square feet, what will be the combined front footage of all three lots after the purchase?

a. 210 feet
b. 130 feet
c. 200 feet
d. 170 feet

13. A lot in a commercial subdivision contains 1,320 square feet. If the lot is rectangular and has a 45-foot frontage, what is the depth of the lot as expressed in feet?

a. 31 feet
b. 28 feet
c. 29 feet
d. 30 feet

14. The number of acres in the parcel of land illustrated below is:

a. 80
b. 160
c. 120
d. 180

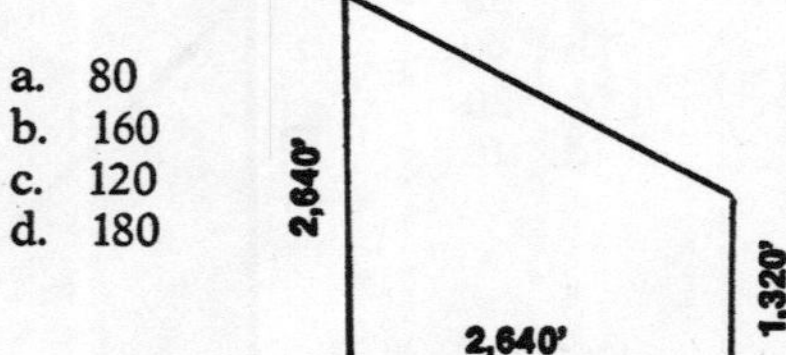

15. An individual owns a corner lot that measures 100 feet by 100 feet. She wants to install a six foot sidewalk within the lot limits along the two sides bordering the streets and cement costs $1.70 per square foot. What will the sidewalk cost?

a. $1,020.21
b. $2,040.00
c. $2,816.46
d. $1,978.80

16. Hinckle owns a parcel of land ¼ mile wide and ½ mile long. He wants to clear a 50' wide area the length of the property plus 3 evenly divided 50' wide areas across the parcel. If he is charged $60 per acre to clear this strip, what will it cost?

a. $455
b. $540
c. $444
d. $450

17. Smith purchased a ¾ acre lot with a depth of 110 feet, for the purpose of subdividing it into 82.5' wide parcels. Before doing so, she elected to acquire the adjoining parcel which contained the same depth but had only ⅔rds as much land. The cost of the second parcel was $1,400. She plans to divide the two parcels and sell them for $750 per lot. If on resale she nets 50% profit over what she paid for the parcels initially, what was the cost of the first parcel?

a. $3,100
b. $1,600
c. $3,000
d. $2,500

18. A lot that measures 1,740 feet by 1,740 feet represents approximately how many acres?

a. 60
b. 70
c. 50
d. 40

19. A square acre of land is divided into four lots of equal dimensions. The depth of each lot is approximately 209 feet. What is the total front footage of each lot?

a. 218 feet
b. 50 feet
c. 52 feet
d. 55 feet

20. Mr. Carlson owned a parcel of land free and clear of any liens. The property consisted of 397,440 square feet. Recently he decided to sell all of the property, except a 60' x 90' segment which he would keep for his own use. He received $1,250 per acre for the land that was sold. What was the sales price?

a. $9,375.00
b. $7,091.00
c. $11,250.00
d. $8,461.12

21. A road that runs the full length of the south half of a section is one side of a rectangular parcel. If the parcel contains 3 acres in area, its width is nearest to:

a. 40 feet
b. 30 feet
c. 50 feet
d. 20 feet

22. How many linear feet of single-strand wire would be necessary to fence the parcel described as the NW¼ of the NW¼ of the NW¼ of section 6?

a. 1,230
b. 2,640
c. 5,280
d. 660

23. How many acres of land would be contained in the following? "The N½ of the W½ of the W½ of the NW¼ of Section 5 and the E½ of the NE¼ of the NE¼ of Section 6."

a. 60 acres
b. 50 acres
c. 40 acres
d. 20 acres

24. If an easement for a road runs across the entire south side of a section and the total area covered by the easement is four acres, the width of the road would be:

a. 45'
b. 35'
c. 55'
d. 25'

25. What is the total area contained in the following description? "The S½ of the SE¼ of Section 15 and the NE¼ of the NE¼ of Section 22 and the W½ of the NW¼ of Section 23."

a. 220 acres
b. 240 acres
c. 160 acres
d. 200 acres

Volume Problems

1. A two-story commercial building measures 46' x 80' at its base. The height of the first story is 16' and the height of the second story is 14'. Replacement cost of the first story is calculated at $4.40 per cubic foot; the second story cost is $3.20 per cubic foot. Based on the above, the replacement cost of the building would be:

a. $518,144
b. $329,728
c. $416,211
d. $423,936

2. How many board feet of wood are there in a board that is nine feet long and four inches by four inches?

a. 8
b. 6
c. 12
d. 4

3. How many cubic yards of cement are there in a driveway 30' x 34' x 4"?

a. 1224
b. 408
c. 15
d. None of the above

4. What is the replacement cost of the driveway if the concrete slab 4" thick costs $15.00 a cubic yard with labor totaling $272.00?

a. $460.85
b. $838.67
c. $4,320
d. $7,072

5. How many square feet of concrete would be required to construct a sidewalk 6" deep and 7' wide around the outside of a 60' x 90' corner lot?

a. 1,099 square feet
b. 1,050 square feet
c. 1,001 square feet
d. None of the above

6. How many board feet of lumber in a piece 2" x 4" x 12'?

a. 12 board feet
b. 8 board feet
c. 6 board feet
d. 4 board feet

Answers to Area and Volume Problems

Area Problems

1. b) The 6 inch walls add 1 foot to the base and 1 foot to the height (see illustration).

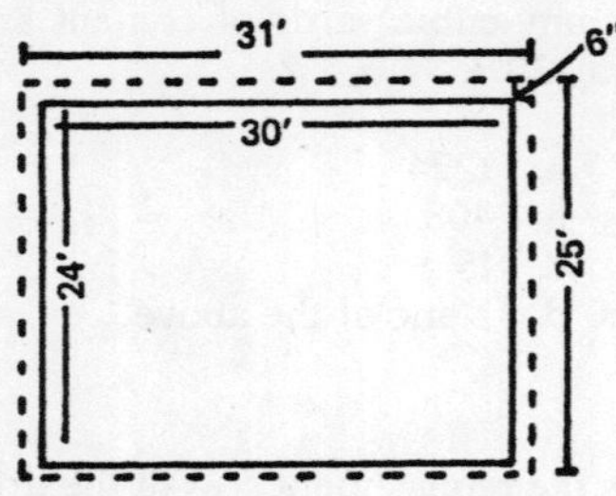

25' x 31' = 775 sq. feet

2. b) 40 acres (see illustration below)

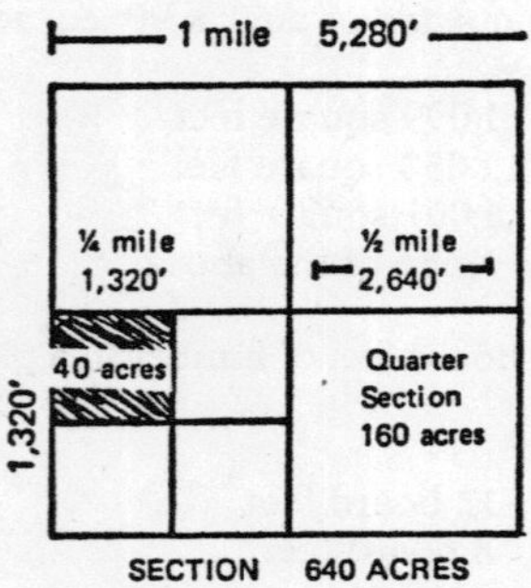

3. b) 500 x \$400 = \$200,000 (sales price)
\$200,000 x 6% = \$12,000 (commission)
\$12,000 x .40 = \$4,800 (salesperson's share)

4. a) Divide the parcel into a rectangle and a triangle as indicated below. Compute the area of the rectangle, the area of the triangle, add them together and divide by 43,560.

735' x 500' = 367,500 sq. feet
735' x. 49.5 = 36,382.5 sq. feet
367,500 + 36,382.5 = 403,882.5 sq. feet in parcel
403,882.5 ÷ 43,560 = 9.27 acres

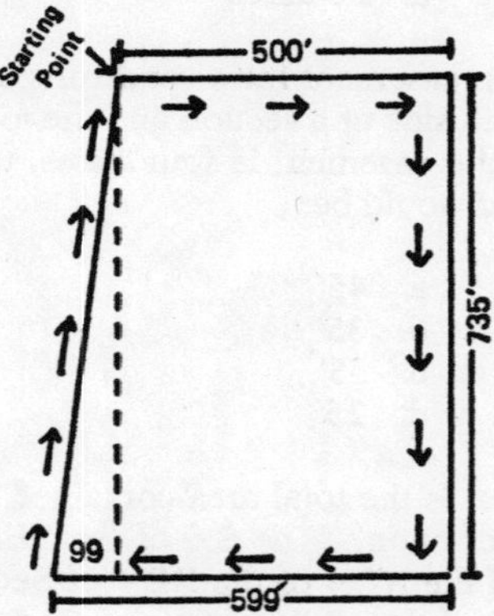

5. d) With or without the canal, the two parcels form a rectangle with dimensions of 550' x 840'.

840 x 550 = 462,000 sq. ft.
462,000 ÷ 43,560 = 10.6 acres

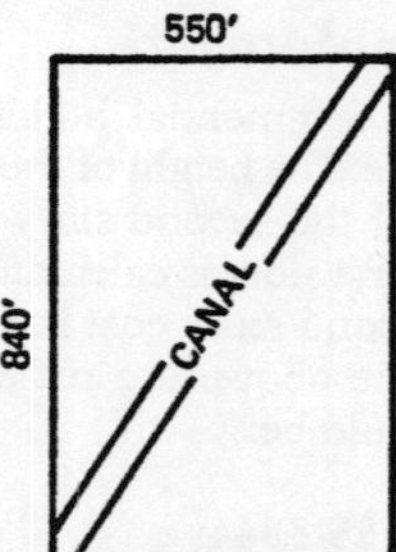

6. b) An acre that is square is 208.7' by 208.7'

7. c) 1,433 square feet. By drawing dotted lines as indicated below, you can form four rectangles with known dimensions:

3' x 12' = 36 sq. ft.
6' x 12' = 72 sq. ft.
8' x 25' = 200 sq. ft.
25' x 45' = 1,125
Total = 1,433 sq. ft.

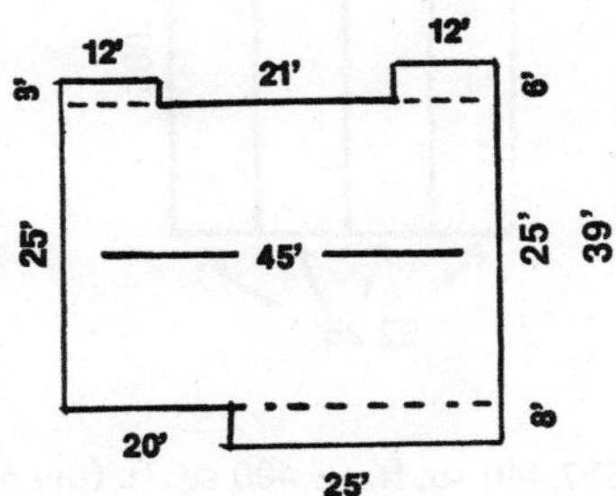

8. c) ½ base times height
660' x 1,320' = 871,200 sq. ft.
871,200 ÷ 43,560 = 20 acres

9. c) 660' x 1,320' = 871,200 sq. ft.
871,200 ÷ 43,560 = 20 acres

10. c) 1,320' x 1,320' = 1,742,400 sq. ft.
1,742,400 ÷ 43,560 = 40 acres

11. d) 1. Determine the area of land: $193,000 ÷ $4.40 = 43,864 sq. ft.
2. Determine front footage: 43,864 ÷ 200' = 219.32 front foot
3. $193,000 ÷ 219.32 = $879.99 or $880 per front foot

12 d) You have a large rectangle with a total area of 69,700 sq. ft. (12,300 + 45,100 + 12,300). Presuming the depth of all three lots is the same (410'), the frontage can be determined by dividing area by depth.
69,700 ÷ 410 = 170 frontage

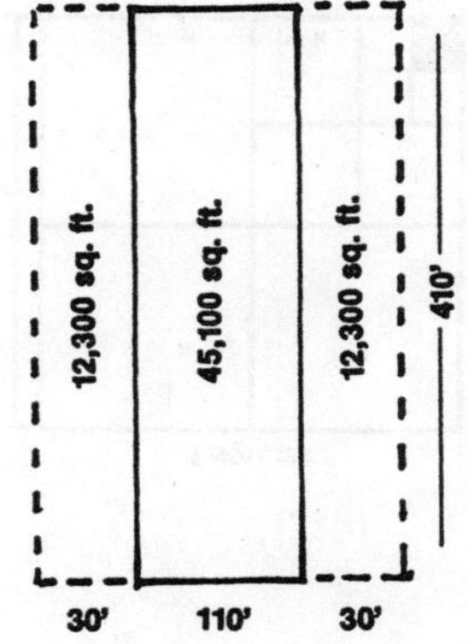

13. c) Area divided by frontage equals depth.
1,320 ÷ 45 = 29.33 depth

14. c) Once again, divide the parcel into a rectangle and a triangle, compute their areas, add them together and divide by 43,560.

2,640 x 1,320 = 3,484,800 sq. ft.
2,640 x 660 = 1,742,400 sq. ft.
3,484,800 + 1,742,400 = 5,277,200 sq. ft.
5,227,200 ÷ 43,560 = 120 acres

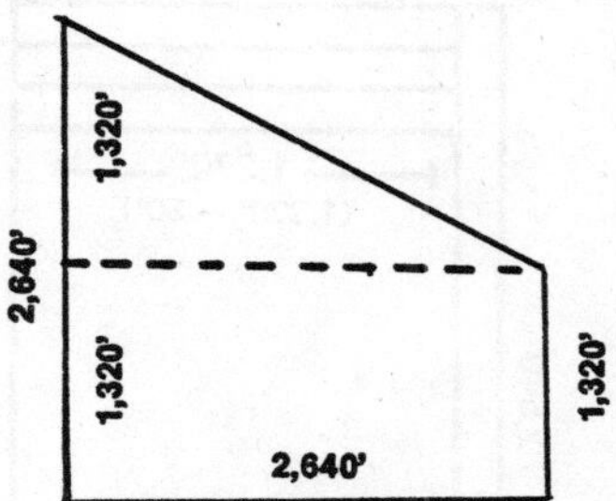

15. d) By looking at the illustration you can see that the dimensions of the sidewalk are 6' x 94' and 6' x 100.
6' x 100' = 600 sq. ft.; 6' x 94' = 564 sq. ft.
600 sq. ft. + 564 sq. ft. = 1,164 sq. ft.
1,164 x $1.70 = $1,978.80

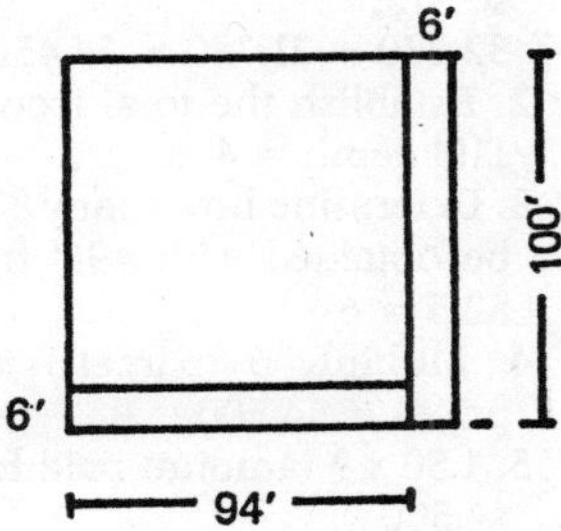

16. c) Again, as you can see from the illustration, the lengths of the "3 evenly divided" areas across the parcel should only be 1,270' (not 1,320) because of the 50' wide strip that is cleared for the length of the property.

50' x 2,640' = 132,000 sq. ft.
150 x 1,270 = 190,500 sq. ft.
132,000 + 190,500 = 322,500 sq. ft.
322,500 ÷ 43,560 = 7.40 acres
7.40 x $60 = $444

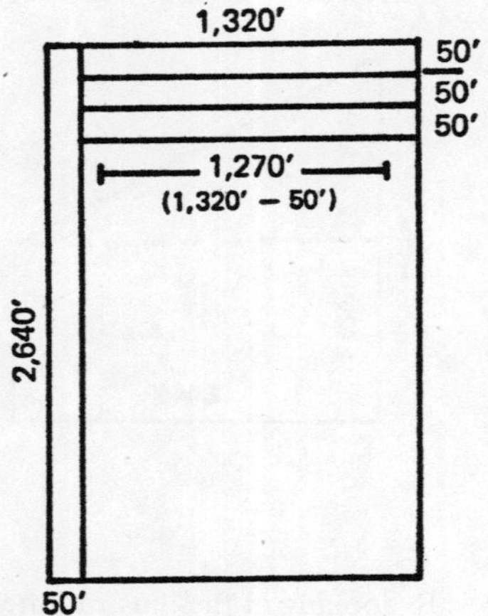

17. b) 1. Establish the area of the two parcels: the first parcel is ¾ acre (43,560 x .75 = 32,670 sq. ft.); the second parcel is ⅔ of the first parcel (32,670 x .6666 = 21,780 sq. ft.);
32,670 + 21,780 = 54,450 total sq. ft.
2. Establish the total frontage (54,450 ÷ 110' depth = 495'
3. Determine how many 82.5' parcels can be obtained with 495' frontage (495 ÷ 82.5 = 6)
4. Multiply 6 (parcels) x $750 (selling price) = $4,500
5. 1.50 x ? (amount paid for the 2 lots) = $4,500
6. $4,500 ÷ 1.50 = $3,000 (amount paid for the two lots)
7. $3,000 - $1,400 (cost of second lot) = $1,600 (cost of first lot)

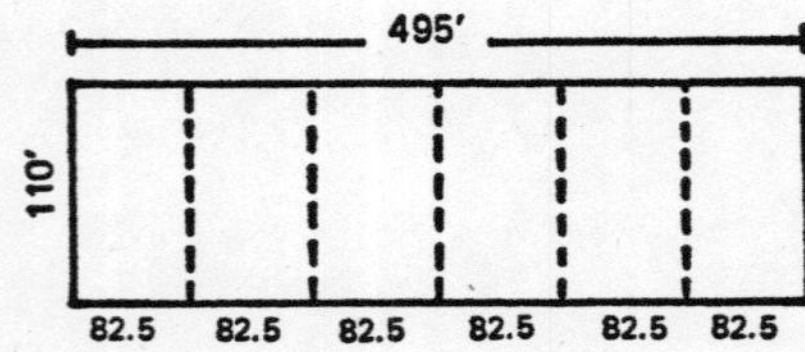

18. b) 1,740 x 1,740 = 3,027,600 sq. ft.
3,027,600 ÷ 43,560 = 69.5

19. c) Since the parcel is square, the width must also be 209'. Divide 209' by 4 = 52.25.

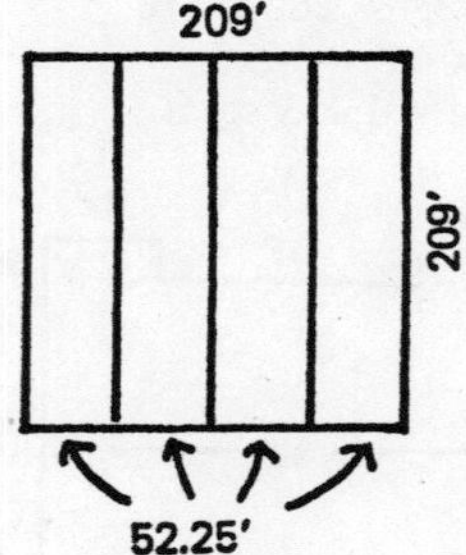

20. c) 397,440 sq. ft. - 5,400 sq. ft. (the 60' x 90' segment) = 392,040 sq. ft. that was sold.
392,040 ÷ 43,560 = 9 acres
9 x $1,250 = $11,250

21. c) You have the length of the rectangle, 2,640, and the area (3 x 43,560), 130,680 sq. ft.
130,680 ÷ 2,640 = 49.5 width

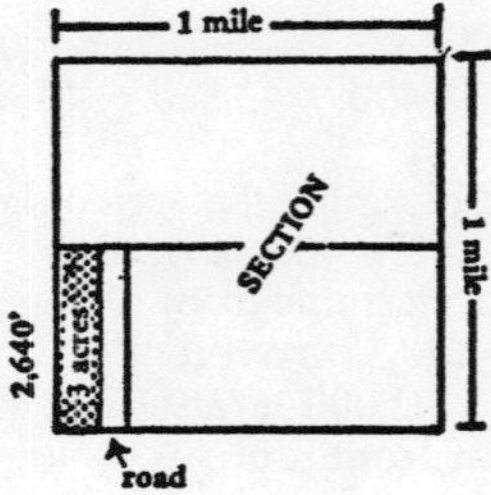

22. b) The described parcel is 1/8 mile on each of its 4 sides. 4 x 1/8 = 4/8 or ½ mile or 2,640'

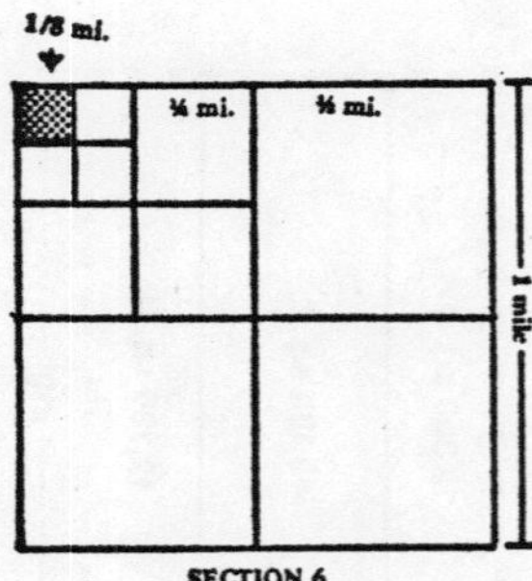

23. c) (20) (40) (80)
The N½ of the W½ of the W½ of the
(160) (640) (20)
NW¼ of Sections 5 AND the E½ of the
(40) (160) (640)
NE¼ of the NE¼ of Section 6.

20 acres + 20 acres = 40 acres

24. b) 1. 4 x 43,560 = 174,240 sq. ft. area
2. 174,240 ÷ 5,280' = 33' width
This is the closest answer.

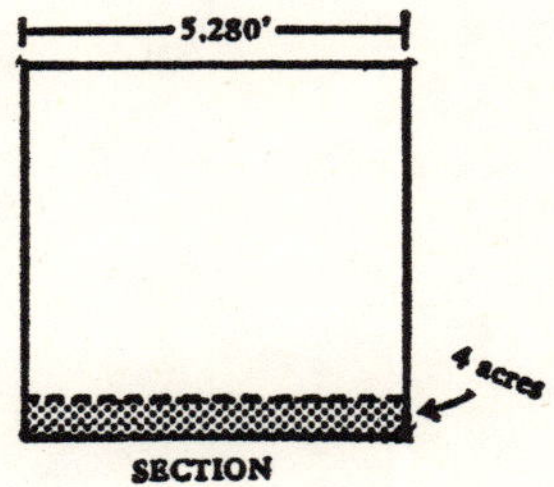

25. d) (80) (160) (640)
The S½ of the SE¼ of Section 15 AND the
(40) (160) (640)
NE¼ of the NE¼ of Section 22 AND
(80) (160) (640)
the W½ of the NW¼ of Section 23.

80 acres + 40 acres + 80 acres = 200 acres

Volume Problems

1. d) Determine area of first floor and multiply by the height.
46' x 80' = 3,680 square feet
3,680 sq. ft. x 16' = 58,880 cubic feet on first floor
Second floor area the same as first floor: 3,680 sq.ft.
Multiply by height: 3,680 x 14' = 51,520 cubic feet

Multiply cubic feet on each floor by respective costs and add together:
58,880 x $4.40 = 259.072
51,520 x $3.20 = 164,864
$423,936

2. c) A board foot of lumber is any combination of three dimensions totalling 144 cubic inches (e.g., 12" x 12" x 1").

Convert 9 feet to inches: 9' x 12" = 108"
108" x 4" = 432 sq. inches x 4" = 1,728 cubic inches
1,728 ÷ 144 = 12 board feet

3. d) 30' x 34' = 1,020 sq. ft. x ⅓' (convert inches to feet) = 340 cubic feet
340 ÷ 27 = 12.59 cubic yards

4. b) Refer to the previous problem. 12.59 cubic yards x $15 = $188.85
$188.85 + $272 (labor) = $460.85

5. a) You multiply 67' x 7' because there is an additional 7' at the corner due to the width of the sidewalk. Then you multiply 90' x 7'
67' x 7' = 469 sq. ft.
90' x 7' = 630 sq. ft.
1,099 sq. ft.

The 6" depth referred to in the question is irrelevant because you were asked for square feet rather than cubic feet.

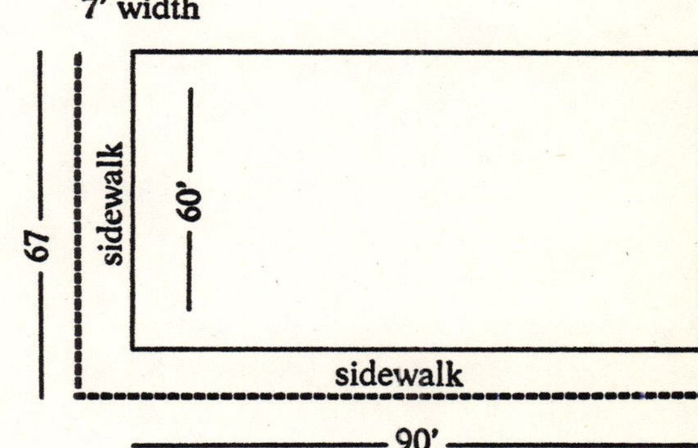

6. b) 2" x 4" = 8 sq. inches x 144 inches (convert feet to inches) = 1,152 cubic inches

1,152 ÷ 144 (cubic inches in a board foot) = 8 board feet

5. Commission Problems

Most commission problems are solved through the use of the *2 x 3 = 6* formula.

Example: Broker Jones sells a home for $82,000 and a 6% commission. What is the amount of the commission?

2 x 3 = ?
$82,000 x .06 = ?
$82,000 x .06 = $4,920

Example: Broker Jones earns a commission of $6,150, which was 7% of the selling price. What was the selling price?

? x 3 = 6
? x .07 = $6,150
$6,150 ÷ .07 = $87,857

Example: Broker Jones sells a home for $118,000 and earns a $7,080 commission. What was the rate of commission?

2 x ? = 6
$118,000 x ? = $7,080
$7,080 ÷ $118,000 = .06 or 6%

The arithmetic involved when computing commissions is usually quite simple. However, a commission problem can appear more difficult if the circumstances surrounding the problem are unfamiliar to us or if the problem contains information we do not recognize as irrelevant.

Example: Broker Herold negotiates a five-year lease calling for monthly payments of $2,850. The commission rate is 5%. What is the amount of the commission?

$2,850 x 60 (months) = $171,000
$171,000 x .05 = $8,550 commission*

** Lease commissions are usually based on the full amount of the lease (e.g., total lease payments over 5 years).*

Example: Broker Wells negotiates an eight year warehouse lease calling for payments of $4,200 a month. The agreed commission was 6% for the first two years, 3% for the next three years and 1% for the last three years. What was the amount of the commission?

$4,200 x 24 (months) = $100,800 x .06 = $6,048
$4,200 x 36 (months) = $151,200 x .03 = $4,536
$4,200 x 36 (months) = $151,200 x .01 = $1,512
Commission $12,096

Example: Broker Henderson listed a property for $162,000. Salesperson Smith from ABC Realty sold it one week later for $141,000. The commission was 7% and the two offices agreed to a 50/50 split. ABC Realty had an agreement with Smith to pay 28% of its share of the commission. How much did Smith receive?

$141,000 x .07 = $9,870 total commission*
$9,870 x .50 = $4,935 to ABC Realty
$4,935 x .28 = $1,381.80 to Smith

** The asking price is irrelevant. The commission is based on the actual selling price.*

Quiz
Commission Problems

1. A lot was sold for $14,500 and the seller paid a commission of 6% of the selling price. If the listing salesperson received 25% of the total commission and the selling salesperson received 35%, the selling salesperson received:

   a. $394.50
   b. $264.50
   c. $304.50
   d. None of the above

2. A real estate salesperson sold a lot for $31,000. If the broker's commission was 6% and the salesperson was to receive 45% of the total commission for selling the property, the salesperson would receive:

   a. $1,001.00
   b. $1,860.00
   c. $959.95
   d. $837.00

3. An owner listed her home at a price which would leave her $18,800 after she paid the broker a 6% commission. If the broker sold the property at the listed price, how much commission would be paid?

   a. $1,200
   b. $1,064
   c. $1,088
   d. $1,193

4. Mr. Smith listed a lot for sale for $18,300. The broker later presented an offer to Mr. Smith for much less than the listed price. Mr. Smith and the broker discussed the situation and agreed to counteroffer at 6% below the asking price provided the broker agreed to reduce her commission by 16⅔%. Initially the broker's commission was to be 6% of the sales price. What would the seller receive for his property assuming the only deduction from the selling price would be the broker's commission?

   a. $16,170
   b. $17,202
   c. $18,300
   d. $16,300

5. You sell a home for $100,000. The listing calls for a six percent commission on the sale. If your broker splits the commission 60/40 (40% for you), how much will you receive?

   a) $6,000
   b) $4,000
   c) $3,600
   d) $2,400

6. A broker earned a commission of $7,500 on the sale of a house. If the commission rate was 6%, what was the sales price?

   a) $125,000
   b) $100,000
   c) $130,000
   d) $150,000

7. A broker earns a commission of $6,650 on the sale of a property for $95,000. What is the rate of commission?

   a) 5%
   b) 6%
   c) 6.5%
   d) 7%

Answers to Commission Problems

1. c) $14,500 x .06 = $870 commission
$870 x .35 = $304.50 commission to selling salesperson (% paid to listing salesperson irrelevant)

2. d) $31,000 x .06 = $1,860 total commission
$1,860 x .45 = $837 to salesperson

3. a) ? x .94 = $18,800
$18,800 ÷ .94 = $20,000
$18,800 is 94% (100% - 6%) of $20,000
$20,000 - $18,800 = $1,200

4. d) $18,300 x .94 (asking price less 6%) = $17,202 (sales price)
$17,202 x .06 = $1,032.12 (6% of sales price)
$1,032.12 x .83333 (100% - 16.6666%) = $860.10 (broker's commission)
$17,202 - $860.10 = $16,341.90 (net to seller)

5. d) .06 x $100,000 = ?
.06 x $100,000 = $6,000 total commission
.4 x $6,000 = ?
.4 x $6,000 = $2,400

6. a) .06 x ? = $7,500
$7,500 ÷ .06 = ?
$7,500 ÷ .06 = $125,000

7. d) ? x $95,000 = $6,650
$6,650 ÷ $95,000 = ?
$6,650 ÷ $95,000 = 7%

6. Amortization Problems

To amortize a loan is to structure the payments of principal and interest so that they will retire the debt completely at the conclusion of the loan term.

How Amortization Works

Payments made on amortized loans include both principal and interest. In the early years of a long-term real estate loan the majority of the payment is interest, and only a small part is applied to the principal. Nonetheless, with each payment the loan balance is lowered by the principal portion of the payment and the next month's interest is calculated on the reduced balance.

Example: A $110,000 loan at 12½% is amortized over 30 years. The monthly payment is set at $1,173.98. The interest portion of the first payment is $1,145.83

$1,173.98	*total payment*
- 1,145.83	*interest payment*
$28.15	*portion of 1st payment applied to principal*

The debt is thus reduced by $28.15

$110,000.00	*original loan*
- 28.15	
$109,971.85	*loan balance before second payment*

The amount of all succeeding principal and interest payments will remain constant throughout the term of the loan, but since the debt is reduced with each payment, the interest portion diminishes steadily while the principal portion increases. In the last years of the loan, since the debt is significantly lower, most of each payment is principal with only a small part being applied to interest.

Calculating Principal and Interest Portions of Each Payment

There are two quick and easy ways to determine loan balances. The best way is to purchase and learn to use a pocket calculator that has the capacity to compute loan balances as quickly as you can feed it the necessary data — original loan amount, interest rate, term and age of loan. The second way is to refer to printed amortization (loan progress) charts that can be obtained from most lenders. You cannot take loan progress charts into a license examination.

You can solve amortization problems without the help of a sophisticated calculator or loan progress charts, but the process is more time consuming. In order to compute a loan balance after a specified number of payments, you must know (1) the loan balance,

(2) the annual interest rate and (3) the total principal and interest payment. This data will be contained in a license examination question. A typical examination question will be answered to help explain the amortization process.

Amortization Formula

Example: Abernathy obtained a $67,500 30-year loan at 11¾% interest. The principal and interest payments were $681.35. After making just three payments, she was transferred and had to sell the home. What was her loan balance after three payments?

Step 1: Calculate the interest for the initial loan amount.

$67,500	*initial loan*
x .1175	*(11¾%)*
$7,931.25	*annual interest*

Step 2: Determine the monthly interest.

$7,931.25 ÷ 12 (months) = $660.94 monthly interest

Step 3: Deduct the monthly interest from the monthly principal and interest payment.

$681.35	*principal and interest payment*
- 660.94	*interest portion of payment*
$20.41	*principle portion of payment*

Step 4: Subtract the first principal payment from the original loan amount.

$67,500	*original loan amount*
- 20.41	*1st principal payment*
$67,479.59	*principal balance after 1st payment*

You repeat this four step process as many times as necessary to solve the problem. Our sample problem called for the loan balance after the third payment, so you repeat the process two more times.

Remember, the **interest portion of the next payment is based on the declining principal balance.** Thus, the interest for the second payment is computed on the basis of the $67,479.59 balance after the first payment.

Amortization procedure continued...

Step 1: Calculate the interest for the balance after the first payment.

$67,479.59	*loan balance after 1st payment*
x .1175	
$7,928.85	*annual interest*

Step 2: Determine the monthly interest.

$7,928.85 ÷ 12 = $660.74 monthly interest

Step 3: Deduct the monthly interest from monthly principal and interest payment.

$681.35	*principal and interest payment*
- 660.74	
$20.61	*principal portion of payment*

Step 4: Subtract the principal portion of payment from the loan balance after the first payment.

$67,479.59	*balance after 1st payment*
- 20.61	
$67,458.98	*balance after 2nd payment*

Now repeat the process one more time.

Step 1: Calculate the interest for the balance after the second payment.

$67,458.98	*balance after 2nd payment*
x .1175	
$7,926.43	*annual interest*

Step 2: Determine the monthly interest.

$7926.43 ÷ 12 = $660.54 monthly interest

Step 3: Deduct the monthly interest from the monthly principal and interest payment.

$681.35	*principal and interest payment*
- 660.54	
$20.81	*principal portion of interest*

Step 4: Subtract the principal portion of the payment from the loan's balance after the second payment.

$67,458.98	*balance after 2nd payment*
- 20.81	
$67,438.17	*balance after 3rd payment*

Obviously the amortization process is tedious in the absence of loan progress charts or the more sophisticated pocket calculators, and the likelihood of an examination question asking for a loan balance after the third or fourth payments is minimal.

Example: How much interest will Abernathy pay over the entire 30-year loan term?

Answer: Multiply the monthly principal and interest payment by the number of months contained in a 30-year loan for the total principal and interest payments, then deduct the principal loan amount. The difference is the interest.

1.

30	*years*
x 12	*months*
360	*months in loan term*

2.

$681.35	*monthly P & I payment*
x 360	
$245,286	*total P & I payments*

3.

$245,286	*total payments*
- 67,500	*loan amount*
$177,786	*total interest payments*

Quiz
Amortization Problems

1. A second trust deed of $1,000 was to be paid in annual installments of $300 plus 9% interest, with a balloon payment of the balance at the end of the third year. The loan balance after the second annual installment had been paid was:

   a. $400.00
   b. $424.00
   c. $515.60
   d. $561.10

2. A $5,000 land contract of sale is payable on a principal reduction plan of $50 per month with interest at 10% per annum. Based on these figures, how long will it take to amortize the loan?

   a. 100 months
   b. 7 years
   c. 10 years and 8 months
   d. The answer cannot be determined

3. Jim Carlson, a licensed real estate broker, obtained an offer from Ms. Green on a vacant lot for $6,000 on the following terms: $2,000 down with the balance secured by a purchase money trust deed and note, payable at $70 per month, including interest at 7.2%. The offer was accepted by the seller. What is the loan balance after the first three monthly payments?

   a. $3,861.17
   b. $3,790.00
   c. $3,466.83
   d. $3,186.18

4. If a purchase and sale agreement called for the buyer to execute a second trust deed in favor of the seller in the amount of $2,500, payable at $30 per month, including interest at 8%, the first month's principal payment would be:

   a. $16.67
   b. $30.00
   c. $20.00
   d. $13.33

5. The following information pertains to an exclusive authorization and right to sell:
   Ending at noon on June 5, 1987. Selling price: $85,000 including ww/cpts and drapes. Terms: $28,000 cash or more. Buyer to assume existing 1st deed of trust and note of approximately $57,000 payable in monthly installments of $447.51 including 9% interest, with all unpaid principal and interest due and payable in full on March 1, 1993, or upon resale of the property, whichever comes first.

   If the property was sold on May 10, 1987, what would the seller's loan balance be at the time of sale if the listing was signed by the seller April 27, 1987 and all payments including taxes are current?

   a. $56,979.99
   b. $56,982.44
   c. $57,552.49
   d. $56,552.49

6. If a note in the amount of $112,450 specifies monthly payments over a period of 30 years at 11.3% interest per annum, what is the first month's interest payment?

   a. $1,016.12
   b. $1,058.90
   c. $1,082.41
   d. $998.72

7. Mr. Jones purchased a home and financed it with a 1st deed of trust and note in the amount of $20,000 payable at $143.90 per month, including 7.2% interest. Five years later, he sold the home for cash. The loan balance at the time of sale was $18,000. There was a prepayment penalty of 2% of the original loan amount. Based only upon the figures provided, how much did the loan cost Mr. Jones if he sold his property for $20,000?

   a. $7,034
   b. $8,634
   c. $9,034
   d. $9,067

8. Ms. Adams bought a home for $75,000. She paid $15,000 cash and financed the balance for 30 years with amortized payments of $529.36 per month including 10.2% interest. If all payments were made when due, what is the percentage of interest costs to the original purchase price?

   a. 154%
   b. 57%
   c. 75%
   d. 174%

9. A house cost $120,000. The cash downpayment was $25,000. The purchaser executed a first deed of trust for the balance of the purchase price payable at $896.83 per month including interest at 11% per annum for 30 years. The interest cost for this loan is what percentage of the selling price?

   a. 169%
   b. 69%
   c. 190%
   d. 59%

Answers to Amortization Problems

1. a) The key to this question is the term "plus interest," which tells you that the $300 principal payments do not include interest. There are two annual principal installments made in the amount of $300, plus interest. $1,000 - $600 = $400

2. a) Again, the question specifically states that the contract is based on "a principal reduction plan of $50 a month." $5,000 ÷ $50 = 100 months

3. a) $6,000 - $2,000 = $4,000 trust deed
$4,000 x .072 = $288 (annual interest)
$288 ÷ 12 = $24 (1st month's interest)
$70 payment - $24 interest = $46 1st month's principal
$4,000 - $46 = $3,954 balance after 1st payment
$4,954 x .072 = $284.69 annual interest
$284.69 ÷ 12 = $23.72 2nd month's interest
$70 - $23.72 = $46.28 2nd month's principal
$3,954 - $46.28 = $3,907.72 balance after 2nd payment
$3,907.72 x .072 = $281.36 annual interest
$281.36 ÷ 12 $23.45 3rd month's interest
$70 - $23.45 = $46.55 3rd month's principal
$3,907.72 - $46.55 = $3,861.17 balance after 3rd payment

4. d) $2,500 x .08 = $200 annual interest
$200 ÷ 12 = $16.67 1st month's interest
$30 - $16.67 = $13.33 1st month's principal payment

5. a) The seller would have made one principal and interest payment between the date of the listing (4/17) and the date of sale (5/10).
$57,000 x .09 = $5,130 annual interest
$5,130 ÷ 12 = $427.50 interest portion of May payment
$447.51 - $427.50 = $20.01 principal portion of May payment
$57,000 - $20.01 = $56,979.99 new loan balance

6. b) $112,450 x .113 = $12,706.85 annual interest
$12,706.85 ÷ 12 = $1,058.90

7. a) $143.90 x 60 (mos.) = $8,634 principal and interest payments over 5 years
$8,634 - $2,000 (principal paid) = $6,634 interest
$20,000 (original loan) x .02 (prepayment penalty) = $400
$6,634 + $400 = $7,034 cost of loan

8. d) $529.36 x 360 (mos.) = $190,569.60 total principal and interest payments
Loan amount is $60,000 ($75,000 - $15,000)
$190,569.60 - $60,000 = $130,569.60 interest paid over term of loan
$75,000 (purchase price) x ? = $130,569.60
$130,569.60 ÷ $75,000 = 1.74 or 174%

9. c) $896.83 x 360 (mos.) = $322,858.80 total principal and interest payments
Loan amount is $95,000 ($120,000 - $25,000)
$322,858.80 - $95,000 = $227,858.80 interest paid over term of loan
$120,000 (purchase price) x ? = $227,858.80
$227,858.80 ÷ $120,000 = 1.898 or 190%

7. Discounting Loans - Points

To discount a loan is to deduct interest in advance from the face amount of the promissory note. For example:

$50,000 loan at 12% interest with a 5% discount

$50,000	*loan amount*
x .05	*discount rate*
$2,500	*amount of discount*

In the above example, the borrower would sign a promissory note calling for repayment of $50,000 at 12% interest, and yet the actual amount received from the lender would only be $47,500 ($50,000 - $2,500). The discount amount ($2,500) would be additional profit for the lender.

Discounts are commonplace in loan transactions today. In the past they applied almost exclusively to FHA and VA transactions, but are now used regularly in connection with conventional loan transactions as well. The effect of points is to increase the lender's yield over and above the interest rate stated in the promissory note.

When a lender discounts a loan, it is sometimes referred to as **charging points.** The term "point" is a contraction of the larger term, "percentage point." Each point represents 1% of the loan amount. If a lender charges six points, the loan is discounted by 6%. Sometimes the loan origination fee, which is the handling charge assessed by the lender at the time the loan is made, is also referred to in terms of points (i.e., a 2% loan fee might be referred to as two points.)

Another type of "discounting" a loan occurs when the lender sells the loan to a third party investor. For instance, Seller Brown sold her home and took back a second mortgage on her property from Buyer Smith in the amount of $10,000. Now Brown needs some cash and decides to sell the second mortgage to Mortgage Investments, Inc. However, Mortgage Investments, Inc. will not pay Brown the entire face value of the second mortgage, but will discount it in order to take into account transaction costs, risk of default and profit. Mortgage Investments may offer to pay Brown only 60% of the face value, or $6,000. From Brown's point of view, $6,000 is better than no cash at all, so she accepts the offer. Brown's mortgage has been "discounted" by 40%.

Quiz
Discounting Loans

1. The Johnsons sold their home and had to carry back a second trust deed and note of $5,310 at 11½% interest. If they sold the note for $3,823.20 before any payments had been made, the discount rate came to:

   a. 54%
   b. 25%
   c. 72%
   d. 28%

2. Mr. Clay is interested in purchasing a loan that bears 14½% interest for one year with the unpaid balance due at the end of that year. The borrower is to pay $296.04 per month for twelve months. Mr. Clay plans to offer the beneficiary 60% of the face value of the loan. If this is a straight loan, how much should Mr. Clay offer?

   a. $13,500
   b. $14,100
   c. $14,650
   d. $14,700

3. A bank customarily charges four points on their loans and then later sells these loans at a 3.5% discount. If the bank received $14,475 when it sold one of its loans at the discounted rate, what was the original amount of the loans?

   a. $14,500
   b. $15,000
   c. $15,500
   d. $14,900

4. A $5,000 note is to be paid off at the end of twelve months. It bears an interest rate of 6% per annum and is purchased by an investor for $4,500. What is the rate of return on the principal amount invested?

   a. 16%
   b. 17.8%
   c. 20%
   d. 10%

5. Mary sold her house and took back a note for $4,200, secured by a second deed of trust. She promptly sold the note for $2,730. This represents a discount of:

   a. 65%
   b. 55%
   c. 35%
   d. 28%

6. It is generally noted that 6 discount points equal 1% interest. What can the seller be expected to pay on a $24,000 FHA loan at 9% if comparable conventional loans bear interest at the rate of 9¾% and the lender wants to increase the effective yield of the FHA loan to that of the conventional loan?

   a. $2,400
   b. $1,080
   c. $240
   d. None of the above

7. Able purchased a 2nd deed of trust and note for 80% of its $1,500 face value. The loan was scheduled to fully amortize in one year and called for payments of $131 per month, including 9% interest. If Able held the note for the full year, and the borrower paid according to the terms of the contract, what was the yield on Able's original investment?

   a. 25%
   b. 29%
   c. 35%
   d. 31%

Answers to Discount Problems

1. d) $5,310 x ? = $3,823.20
$3,823.20 ÷ $5,310 = .72 or 72%
$3,823.20 is 72% of $5,310, which means the note was discounted by 28%.

2. d) A straight note calls for payments of interest only.
$296.04 x 12 (mos.) = $3,552.48 annual interest
? (loan amount) x .145 = $3,552.48
$3,552.48 ÷ .145 = $24,499.86 or $24,500 loan amount
$24,500 x .60 = $14,700 discounted amount

3. b) If a lender discounts a loan by 3½ points (3½%), he is actually advancing 96½ cents on the dollar.
? (loan amount) x .965 = $14,475
$14,475 ÷ .965 = $15,000 loan amount

4. b) $5,000 - $4,500 = $500 discount
$5,000 x .06 = $300 interest
$4,500 (amount paid for note) x ? = $800 ($500 + $300)
$800 ÷ $4,500 = .1777 or 17.8%

5. c) $4,200 x ? = $2,730
$2,730 ÷ $4,200 = .65 or 65%
$2,730 is 65% of $4,200
Discount rate is 35% (100% - 65% = 35%)

6. b) 6 points = 1%
4½ points = ¾% (6 points x .75 = 4½ points)
$24,000 x .045 = $1,080

7. d) $1,500 x .80 = $1,200 amount paid
$131 (payment) x 12 (mos.) = 1,572
$1,572 (collected) - $1,200 (paid) = $372 profit
$1,200 x ? = $372
$372 ÷ $1,200 = 31% return

8. Capitalization Problems

Capitalization is a method of appraising real property by converting into present value the anticipated future net income from the property. The **capitalization rate** is the rate used in the capitalization method or income approach to appraising property. The capitalization formula is:

property value x capitalization rate = net income

$$V \times R = I$$

To an appraiser the unknown quantity in the equation is usually the property value. The appraiser can identify the net income by analyzing, among other things, the property's income and expense statement. The capitalization rate can be selected by direct comparison, which is the most common method, by the band of investment or summation methods (see "Selecting an Interest Rate" in the appraisal chapter in *Principles of Real Estate*). With the capitalization rate and net income in hand, the appraiser can, with acceptable accuracy, estimate the value of the property.

Example: An appraiser determined a 12 unit apartment house was netting approximately $92,000 annually. By direct comparison she concluded 11% was a competitive capitalization rate. What is her estimate of the property's value?

Answer: $V \times R = I$

$? \times .11 = \$92,000$

$\$92,000 \div .11 = \$836,364$

You probably recognized the $2 \times 3 = 6$ formula. In the above case, the unknown is the equivalent of 2.

$? \times 3 = 6$	$? \times .11 = \$92,000$
$6 \div 3 = 2$	$\$92,000 \div .11 = \$836,364$

Suppose the value of the property and the net income are known but the capitalization rate is unknown.

Example: An appraiser determined a property's net income was $57,000 and on the basis of this estimated the property's value to be $456,000. What capitalization rate did the appraiser use?

Answer: $V \times R = I$

$2 \times ? = 6$	$\$456,000 \times ? = \$57,000$
$6 \div 2 = 3$	$\$57,000 \div \$456,000 = .125$
	or 12½%

Annual Figures

Frequently capitalization questions will be compounded by the use of monthly rather than annual figures.

> **Example:** A property generates $1,650 net income a month. Using a capitalization rate of 10½%, what is the value of the property?

All figures, including earnings and expenses, must be converted to annual figures. **No exceptions.**

Answer: *$1,650 x 12 (mos.) = $19,800 annual net income*
? x .105 = $19,800
$19,800 ÷ .105 = $188,571

Income Property Operating Statement

Refer to "The Income Approach to Value" in the appraisal chapter of *Principles of Real Estate* for an explanation of earnings and expenses as they relate to the capitalization process. In some instances, capitalization questions might present preliminary problems (such as determining net income) before the primary problem (estimating the property's value) can be answered.

> **Example:** A 36 unit apartment house is under appraisement. 20 of the units rent for $350 a month; 10 rent for $425 a month; the remaining 6 rent for $450 a month. The property's annual taxes are $28,800. Utilities are estimated $2,416 a month. The annual insurance premium is $5,300. Maintenance expenses run consistently around $1,850 a month. The cost of managing the property is $37.50 per unit per month. The appraiser determines by market analysis that a 6% bad debt/vacancy factor is realistic and by the same method concludes a 9¼% capitalization rate is a competitive rate. What will be the estimate of value?

Answer: Convert all the numbers to annual figures, and from the gross income deduct the bad debt/vacancy factor and operating expenses to arrive at the net income. Then divide the net income by the capitalization rate for the estimated value.

Step 1: Determine gross income

$350 x 20 units x 12 mos. = $84,000
$425 x 10 units x 12 mos. = $51,000
$450 x 6 units x 12 mos. = $32,400
Gross income $167,400

Step 2: Determine annual expenses

Utilities: $2,416 x 12 mos. = $28,992
Maintenance: $1,850 x 12 mos. = $22,200
Management: $37.50 x 12 mos. x 36 units = $16,200

Step 3: Determine bad debt/vacancy factor

$167,400 x .06 = $10,044

Step 4: Determine net income

Gross income	*$167,400*
Less bad debt/vacancy	*- 10,044*
Effective gross income	*$157,356*
Less operating expenses	
Property taxes	*$28,800*
Utilities	*28,992*
Insurance	*5,300*
Maintenance	*22,200*
Management	*- 16,200*
Net income	*$55,864*

Step 5: Calculate value

$55,864 ÷ .0925 = $603,935 estimated value

NOTE: Principal and interest payments on a mortgage or trust deed, also called **debt service payments**, are not deducted from gross earnings to determine net income because principal and interest payments are not considered operating expenses. After identifying net income and capitalizing it into the property's value, deduct the principal and interest payments from the net income to determine the **cash flow**.

Capitalization Rate and Value

If the capitalization rate goes up, the value goes down and vice versa. The capitalization rate is, in part, influenced by the **degree of risk** presented by the investment property. In its simplest form a capitalization rate is an interest rate, and if the risk is high the capitalization (interest) rate will go up. Conversely, if the risk is low the capitalization rate will go down.

For examination purposes, the degree of risk is usually reflected in the quality of an income producing property's tenants.

Example: You are asked to appraise two buildings that are side by side. Both are approximately the same size and condition and generate the same amount of money. One has a hardware store for a tenant, the other is leased by the U.S. Postal service. To which one will you likely give the higher value estimate?

The answer is the building with the Postal Service tenant. Why? Because the Post Office is the more stable and reliable of the two tenants.

Let's presume both buildings generate $31,800 a year net income. But, because the hardware store is a lower quality tenant you decide to use a 10% capitalization rate with the hardware store and only a 9% rate with the Post Office building (the lower the risk, the lower the capitalization rate). Look at how the different capitalization rates affect the buildings' values.

Post Office: ? x .09 = $31,800
$31,800 ÷ .09 = $353,333 value

Hardware Store: ? x .10 = $31,800
$31,800 ÷ .10 = $318,000 value

Quiz
Capitalization Problems

1. An appraiser was appraising a rented single-family residence. Another similar home in the immediate neighborhood recently sold for $84,000 and was renting for $525 per month. If the property being appraised rents for $575 per month, the value set by the appraiser would most nearly be:

   a. $97,500
   b. $118,000
   c. $108,000
   d. $92,000

2. Jones wants to make an investment in real property and is considering buying a vacant lot on which she will build a structure which will house a hardware business. This represents an accurate projection of the highest and best use of the land. The improvements will cost $150,000. The rental income will be $2,500 per month and the estimated annual expenses are $6,000. If the appraiser uses a 12% capitalization rate, what can Jones reasonably expect to pay for the land?

   a. $36,000
   b. $60,000
   c. $50,000
   d. It would not be profitable for her to build

3. An income property was appraised for $100,000 using a 6% capitalization rate. If an appraiser used an 8% capitalization rate the value of the property would be:

   a. $85,000
   b. $75,000
   c. $90,000
   d. $70,000

4. A 20-unit apartment building was valued at $250,000 using a 10% capitalization rate. A new owner bought the property and raised each apartment's rent by $10 per month, without an increase in the operating expenses. If he used a 12% capitalization rate, the property would now be worth approximately:

   a. $260,000
   b. $240,000
   c. $230,000
   d. $220,000

5. The real property taxes on an income property increased $900 in one year. All other expenses and income remained the same. Using a 10% capitalization rate, the value of the property would change by which of the following amounts?

   a. $90 decrease
   b. $9,000 decrease
   c. $900 decrease
   d. There would be no change in value

6. An investment property is appraised at $400,000 with a net income of $36,000 and a 9% capitalization rate. What would be the value of the property if you used a 12% capitalization rate?

   a. $423,000
   b. $450,000
   c. $300,000
   d. $250,000

7. Mr. Adams owns an income property in which he deducts $27,000 in operating expenses from his gross income. If the operating expenses are 30% of the gross income, the value of the property, using 12½% capitalization rate, is:

   a. $504,000
   b. $270,000
   c. $216,000
   d. $397,000

8. Mr. Able invested in a 20-unit apartment building several years ago. Recently, a new freeway was constructed near the property. Because of the closeness of the freeway Able estimates that he loses $200 a month in rent. If comparable buildings in the area are figured at a capitalization rate of 12%, what is the monetary loss in value to the property?

   a. $2,400
   b. $20,000
   c. $2,000
   d. $24,000

9. An apartment building's operating statement reveals the following:
   Annual gross income - $10,000
   Vacancy factor - 10%
   Annual operating expenses - $4,000
   Principal and interest payments per month - $250
   Using a 10% capitalization rate, what is the property's value?

   a. $20,000
   b. $30,000
   c. $50,000
   d. $60,000

10. A property is valued at $200,000 using a capitalization rate of 8%. If the appraiser used a 10% rate, the estimated value would be:

    a. $160,000
    b. $150,000
    c. $120,000
    d. $180,000

11. The value of a 20-unit property has been determined to be $240,000. An analysis of the market has confirmed that the owner would be justified in applying a 10% capitalization rate when anticipating the property's net income. Should the owner increase the gross rentals $10 per unit per month and experience no increase in the expense of operation and should the capitalization rate be advanced to 12%, what would be the estimated value of the property?

    a. $264,000
    b. $240,000
    c. $220,000
    d. $200,000

12. Johnson bought an apartment building with 24 apartments. In 1987, all the apartments were rented for $85 and there were no vacancies. In 1988, Johnson rented the apartments for $95 each but experienced a 10% vacancy factor. Which of the following statements is true?

    a. both years were equal
    b. more was earned in 1988
    c. more was earned in 1987
    d. less was earned in 1988

13. The income of an improved property is $16,000 and this amounts to an 8% return on the current value. If the improvements are valued at $120,000 and have an economic life of 50 years, the value of the land is:

    a. $20,000
    b. $40,000
    c. $30,000
    d. $80,000

14. A prospect is considering the purchase of an income property. The property's operating statement shows $94,500 in expenses deducted from gross income to arrive at the net income. The deductions amount to 60% of the gross income. If an appraiser uses a 12½% capitalization rate, what is the value of the property?

    a. $620,000
    b. $504,000
    c. $196,000
    d. $182,000

15. Jones owns an income property in which $47,000 was deducted from gross income for operating expenses. If the operating expenses are 30% of gross income, the value of the property, using a 12½% capitalization rate, is:

    a. $804,000
    b. $496,000
    c. $877,336
    d. $396,000

Answers to Capitalization Problems

1. d) This is actually a "gross multiplier" problem. The gross multiplier method is an income method often applied to residential properties.
$84,000 (value of comparable) ÷ $525 (monthly rent) = 160 monthly multiplier
$575 (subject prop. rent) x 160 = $92,000 subject property value

2. c) $2,500 x 12 = $30,000 annual income
$30,000 - $6,000 = $24,000 net income
$24,000 ÷ .12 = $200,000 value of entire property
$200,000 - $150,000 = $50,000 land value

3. b) $100,000 x .06 = $6,000 net income
$6,000 ÷ .08 = $75,000

4. c) $250,000 x .10 = $25,000 net income
Increase rent for 20 units by $10 each = $200 a month or $2,400 a year
$25,000 + $2,400 = $27,400 increased rent
? x .12 = $27,400
$27,400 ÷ .12 = $228,333 new value

5. b) The $900 increase in taxes reduced the net income by that amount. Losses are capitalized like income: divide the loss in earnings by the capitalization rate for the loss in value.
$900 ÷ .10 = $9,000 value lost

6. c) $400,000 x .09 = $36,000
? x .12 = $36,000
$36,000 ÷ .12 = $300,000
If the capitalization rate increases and the income stays the same, the value decreases.

7. a) Determine the gross income with the following formula:
? x .30 = $27,000 expenses
$27,000 ÷ .30 = $90,000 gross income
$90,000 - $27,000 = $63,000 net income
? ÷ .125 = $63,000
$63,000 ÷ .125 = $504,000 value

8. b) Capitalize losses as you would income
$200 x 12 = $2,400 annual loss
$2,400 ÷ .12 = $20,000 value loss

9. c) Gross income $10,000
- vacancy factor $1,000
- operating expenses $4,000
Net income $5,000
$5,000 ÷ .10 = $50,000 value
(Do not deduct principal and interest payments to determine net income.)

10. a) $200,000 x .08 = $16,000
? x .10 = $16,000
$16,000 ÷ .10 = $160,000 new value

11. c) $240,000 x .10 = $24,000 net income
20 x $10 = $200 increase per month, $2,400 per year
$24,000 + $2,400 = $26,400 revised income
$26,400 ÷ .12 = $220,000 revised value

12. b) 1987: $85 x 24 x 12 = $24,480 annual income
1987: $95 x 24 x 12 = $27,360 annual rent
$27,360 x .90 (100% - 10% vacancy) = $24,624 annual income

13. d) ? x .08 = $16,000
$16,000 ÷ .08 = $200,000
$200,000 - $120,000 = $80,000 land value

14. b) ? x .60 = $94,500 expenses
$94,500 ÷ .60 = $157,500 gross income
$157,500 - $94,500 = $63,000 net income
$63,000 ÷ .125 = $504,000 value

15. c) ? x .30 = $47,000 expenses
$47,000 ÷ .30 = $156,667 gross income
$156,667 - $47,000 = $109,667 net income
$109,667 ÷ .125 = $877,336 value

9. *Profit and Loss Problems*

If a property sells for more than it originally cost, it has been sold for a profit. If it sells for less than it originally cost, it has been sold at a loss. The formula for determining profit or loss is:

value before x percent of profit or loss = value after
VB x % = VA

In profit and loss problems, **100%** is a key figure because it represents the value of a property before profit or loss, usually the price paid for the property.

Example: Smith sold her property for $50,000, which was 100% of what she paid for it. How much did she originally pay for the property?

value before x 100% = $50,000
$50,000 ÷ 1.00 = $50,000 value before

Now let's change the details a little. (Remember that the percent of profit is added to 100% and the percent of loss is deducted from 100%)

Example: Smith sold her property for $83,000 which was 25% more than she paid for it. How much did she originally pay for the property?

	VB x % = VA
? x 3 = 6	*? x 1.25 (100% + 25%) = $83,000*
6 ÷ 3 = 2	*$83,000 ÷ 1.25 = $66,400 value before*

As you can see, once again we are working with the *2 x 3 = 6* formula. Watch what happens if Smith sells for a loss.

Example: Smith sold her property for $88,000 which amounted to a 10% loss. How much did she originally pay for the property?

VB x .90 (100% - 10%) = $88,000
$88,000 ÷ .90 = $97,778 value before

Quiz
Profit and Loss Problems

1. Smith bought a property for $16,500. Now she intends to sell the property and figures her selling expenses will total 12%. If this is true, how much would Smith have to obtain for her property to just break even, not realizing a loss or gain?

   a. $18,480
   b. $14,520
   c. $19,800
   d. $18,750

2. A lot sold for $16,350, which was 9% more than its original cost. The original cost was:

   a. $14,715.00
   b. $14,878.50
   c. $15,000.00
   d. $16,000.00

3. A husband and wife sold their home for $17,200. This represents 9% more than what they paid for it. The original cost of the home was most nearly:

   a. $15,825
   b. $15,800
   c. $16,000
   d. $15,652

4. A homeowner sold her house for $23,000, which represented a 15% profit over what she had originally paid for the house. What was the original price of the home?

   a. $27,000
   b. $19,550
   c. $20,000
   d. None of the above

5. Sarah purchased some land for $62,000 and later sold it for a 15% profit. What was the sales price?

   a) $71,300
   b) $72,200
   c) $73,100
   d) $74,000

6. Honus realized a loss of 8% when he sold his property for $141,000. What did he originally pay for the property?

   a) $151,261
   b) $152,280
   c) $153,261
   d) $153,280

7. Twenty years ago, Luann paid $80,000 for her property. What is the percent of increase in the property's value if it is now worth $225,000?

   a) 345%
   b) 245%
   c) 365%
   d) 281%

Answers to Profit and Loss Problems

1. d) ? x .88 = $16,500
   $16,500 ÷ .88 = $18,750
   $16,500 is 88% of $18,750

2. c) ? x 1.09 = $16,350
   $16,350 ÷ 1.09 = $15,000

3. b) ? x 1.09 = 17,200
   $17,200 ÷ 1.09 = $15,799.82 or $15,800

4. c) ? x 1.15 = $23,000
   $23,000 ÷ 1.15 = $20,000

5. a) $62,000 x 1.15 = ?
   $62,000 x 1.15 = $71,300

6. c) ? x .92 = $141,000
   $141,000 ÷ .92 = ?
   $141,000 ÷ .92 = $153,261

7. d) $80,000 x ? = $225,000
   $225,000 ÷ $80,000 = ?
   $225,000 ÷ $80,000 = 2.81 or 281%
   increase

10. Depreciation/Appreciation Problems

Appreciation is a rise in value or price. The term depreciation has different uses, but in any case it means some kind of loss in value due to any cause. To an appraiser, depreciation will represent an **actual loss in value** that will affect the appraised value of the property. To an accountant, depreciation is a **hypothetical loss in value** that affects an owner's financial status and has income tax consequences.

For examination purposes, you will find land and improvements can depreciate or appreciate at different rates and that most of the problems will involve **straight line depreciation**, which means that the property depreciated in equal annual amounts during its useful life.

Example: The useful life of a building is 20 years. The building will depreciate at a rate of 1/20, or 5% each year.

100% ÷ 20 years = 5% annual rate of depreciation

Exercise: solve the following problems.

1. A home has an estimated useful life of 40 years. What is its annual rate of depreciation?

2. A warehouse has an economic life of 15 years. How much will it have depreciated after 3 years?

3. A barn is expected to be functional for 50 years. What is the anticipated depreciation after 8 years?

Answers: *1. 100% ÷ 40 = 2.5% annual rate of depreciation*
2. 100% ÷ 15 = 6.667% annual rate of depreciation
6.667% x 3 = 20% after 3 years
3. 100% ÷ 50 = 2% annual rate of depreciation
2% x 8 = 16% depreciation after 8 years

Appreciation problems work the same way, except value is added to, rather than subtracted from, the property value.

Example: If a property has appreciated 4% a year for the past six years, how much appreciation has occurred?

4% x 6 (years) = 24%

Handle Like a Profit & Loss Problem

If a property has depreciated a total of 22%, it is worth 78% of its original value (100% - 22% = 78%). Conversely, if the property has appreciated in value by a total of 19%, it is worth 119% of its original value. Use the same formula as you used for profit and loss problems:

value before x gain or loss = value after

Example: Jones bought a home that had an estimated useful life of 40 years. After 8 years of straight line depreciation, the depreciated value was estimated at $94,500. What did Jones originally pay for the property?

Answer: This is a two-part problem. First, determine the amount of depreciation.

1. *100% ÷ 40 = 2.5% annual rate of depreciation*
2. *2.5% x 8 = 20% total accrued depreciation*

Next, treat the problem like any other profit or loss problem. In this case, the depreciated value was 80% of the original value (100% - 20% = 80%).

3. *? x .80 = $94,500*
4. *$94,500 ÷ .80 =$118,125 original purchase price*

Lot Appreciates/Building Depreciates

Sometimes the building will lose value while the lot is actually gaining in value.

Example: It cost $74,000 to build a house six years ago. The lot at that time was worth $21,000. If the house has been depreciating at 2.5% a year and the lot has been appreciating at 5% a year, what is the value of the property today?

Answer: Depreciate the house and appreciate the lot separately, then add your conclusions together.

1. *2.5% x 6 = 15% total house depreciation*
2. *$74,000 x .85 = $62,900 present house value*
3. *5% x 6 = 30% total lot appreciation*
4. *$21,000 x 1.30 = $27,300 present lot value*
5. *$62,900 + 27,300 = $90,200 present property value*

Quiz
Depreciation/Appreciation Problems

1. Carlson bought a property for $200,000, paid $150,000 cash down and executed a $50,000 first trust deed and note for the balance. The land was valued at $50,000 and the building had a salvage value of $15,000. The basis for computing straight line depreciation for the life of the property would be:

   a. $200,000
   b. $165,000
   c. $150,000
   d. $135,000

2. A property supporting a six-plex was purchased at a total cost of $173,000. The land was valued at $23,500. At the time of purchase, the purchaser estimated 3% of the building cost for salvage value. Based on a 50-year economic life, what would the property's book value be at the end of the seventh year?

   a. $148,780.00
   b. $148,212.90
   c. $144,310.00
   d. $152,697.90

3. A small factory was constructed on a lot which cost $25,000. The cost of the land and improvements was $160,000. The estimated economic life of the improvements was 30 years. Using straight line depreciation, the book value of this property at the end of the twelfth year is:

   a. $106,000
   b. $81,000
   c. $85,000
   d. $119,000

4. A property was purchased for $122,500, which included a land value of $24,500. The economic life of the improvements was set at 40 years. Using the straight line method of depreciation, what was the book value of the property after 14 years?

   a. $79,625
   b. $63,700
   c. $88,200
   d. $42,875

5. Smith paid $24,200 for a freezer for a grocery store. For depreciation purposes, the economic life is 15 years and the salvage value is $4,500. Based upon the straight-line schedule, what would the book value be at the conclusion of the sixth year?

   a. $16,320
   b. $14,250
   c. $9,680
   d. $7,880

6. A commercial property cost $190,000. The land was valued at $30,000, and the salvage value of the building was estimated at $10,000. Which of the following figures would the owner use when establishing a depreciation schedule?

   a. $180,000
   b. $150,000
   c. $190,000
   d. $160,000

7. An investment property is purchased for a total price of $200,000, including $27,500 attributable to the land. The economic life of the property is set at 40 years. What would be the book value of the improvements at the end of the fourth year if the straight-line method of depreciation is used?

   a. $180,000
   b. $172,000
   c. $155,250
   d. $182,750

8. The cost of an improved property is $200,000. The land is valued at $50,000. There is an existing first lien of $50,000 and it is anticipated there will be a salvage value of $10,000. What would the property's book value be at the end of the first year, presuming an economic life of 40 years?

   a. $186,500
   b. $196,500
   c. $136,500
   d. $146,500

9. An investor bought a property valued at $160,000 which depreciated over a 30-year period. The land was valued at $30,000 and after 11 years of depreciation on a straight line basis, the depreciated value of the property is most nearly:

   a. $131,000
   b. $101,000
   c. $82,000
   d. $112,000

10. The replacement cost of a home is $114,500, less 14 years of accrued depreciation at the rate of 1½% per year. The lot is currently valued at $20,000. What is the current value of the property?

    a. $94,500
    b. $110,455
    c. $90,455
    d. $101,270

11. The following information was presented to you by the buyer for analysis. The price of a building was $160,000, excluding the lot. Fifteen years remain to be depreciated and the building is 37½% depreciated.

    a. The building has depreciated for 10 years
    b. The book value is now $120,000
    c. The depreciation exceeds 4% per year
    d. None of the above

Answers to Depreciation/Appreciation Problems

1. d) The downpayment and trust deed amounts are irrelevant to the problem. To determine the amount and rate of depreciation, deduct the land value and the salvage value from the price. Then divide by the anticipated economic life (e.g., 30, 40, 50 years).

   200,000
   – 50,000
   – 15,000
   135,000

2. d) $173,000 - $23,500 (land value) = $149,500 value of improvements
   $149,500 x .97 (improvement value minus 3% salvage value) = $145,015 amount to be depreciated
   $145,015 ÷ 50 (years) = $2,900.30 annual depreciation
   $2,900.30 x 7 = $20,302.10 depreciation after 7 years
   $173,000 - $20,302.10 = $152,697.90 depreciated property value

3. a) $160,000 - $25,000 = $135,000 improvement value
   $135,000 ÷ 30 = $4,500 annual depreciation
   $4,500 x 12 = $54,000 total depreciation
   $160,000 - $54,000 = $106,000 depreciated value of property

4. c) $122,500 - $24,500 = $98,000 improvement value
   $98,000 ÷ 40 = $2,450 annual depreciation
   $2,450 x 14 = $34,300 annual depreciation
   $122,500 less $34,300 = $88,200 depreciated value of property

5. a) $24,200 - $4,500 = $19,700 amount to be depreciated
   $19,700 ÷ 15 = $1,313.33 annual depreciation
   $1,313.33 x 6 = $7,880 total depreciation
   $24,200 - $7,880 = $16,320 book value

6. b) $190,000 - $30,000 = $160,000 improvement value
   $160,000 - $10,000 = $150,000 depreciable portion of property

7. c) $200,000 - $27,500 =$172,500 value of improvements
   $172,500 ÷ 40 = $4,312.50 annual depreciation
   $4,312.50 x 4 = $17,250 total depreciation
   $172,500 - $17,250 = $155,250 depreciated value of improvements

8. b) The existing first lien of $50,000 is irrelevant to the problem.
   $200,000 - $50,000 = $150,000 improvement value
   $150,000 - $10,000 = $140,000 to be depreciated
   $140,000 ÷ 40 =$3,500 annual depreciation
   $200,000 - $3,500 = $196,500 property value after one year

9. d) $160,000 - $30,000 = $130,000 improvement value
   $130,000 ÷ 30 = $4,333.33 annual depreciation
   $4,333.33 x 11 = $47,666.67 total depreciation
   $160,000 - $47,666.67 = $112,333.33

10. b) $114,500 x .015 - $1,717.50 annual depreciation
    $1,717.50 x 14 = $24,045 total depreciation
    $114,500 - $24,045 = $90,455 depreciated value of improvements
    $90,455 + $20,000 = $110,455 depreciated value of property

11. c) The unknown is the building's economic life. If 15 years of economic life remain, they represent 62½% of the total economic life (100% - 37½%). Arrange your equation as follows:
    ? x .625 = 15 years
    15 ÷ .625 = 24 years
    100% of the building value ÷ 24 = .0415 or 4.16% annual rate of depreciation

11. Proration Problems

To prorate is to divide and allocate an expense equally or proportionately according to time or use. When a transaction is ready to close, certain settlement expenses must be charged to the buyer, to the seller or proportionately to both. Included among these expenses are hazard insurance premiums, property taxes, interest on mortgages and installment payments on special assessments.

The process of accurately allocating these charges between the buyer and seller involves three steps:

1. Determine the annual charge. What are the annual taxes? Annual interest? Annual insurance premium?

2. Divide annual charge by 360 (days). Prorations are based on 360 day years, 30 day months. By dividing the annual charge by 360, you determine the per day cost — called the **per diem.**

3. Count the days for which the buyer or seller is responsible and multiply by the per diem. For instance, if a buyer owes 14 days taxes and the per diem is $3.14, multiply $3.15 x 14 = $44.10.

Example: Jones has paid the year's property taxes of $1,052. He sells his home and the deal closes on March 20th. What is the amount of Jones' credit for property taxes at closing?

Answer: Jones is responsible for the property taxes through March 19. The buyer assumes responsibility for the taxes from the date of closing forward. As such, the buyer must be charged, and Jones credited, for the property taxes from March 20 through December 30.

Step 1. *Determine the annual charge. Already established at $1,052.*

Step 2. *Divide by 360 days.*
$1,052 ÷ 360 = $2.92 per diem.

Step 3. *Count the days and multiply by per diem.*

March	*11*
April	*30*
May	*30*
June	*30*
July	*30*
August	*30*
September	*30*
October	*30*
November	*30*
December	*30*
	281 days
	x 2.92 per diem
	$820.52 charge to buyer and credit to seller

Quiz
Proration Problems

1. Mr. Johnson paid his taxes of $390.60 for the year. On May 1st, he sells his home. What is the amount of the remaining pre-paid protion?

   a. $118.82
   b. $246.41
   c. $300.72
   d. $260.40

2. A 3-year fire insurance policy was purchased on January 1, 1987, for $470. If the house was sold on July 16, 1988, what was the unused portion?

   a. $181.45
   b. $121.25
   c. $141.25
   d. $228.55

3. A house is sold on July 16. The taxes of $846 for the year have been paid. The fire insurance premium of $122 for the calendar year has also been paid. How much will the buyer pay the seller at closing?

   a. $401.12
   b. $411.18
   c. $443.67
   d. $431.08

4. Jones sold her apartment building to Brown on the 13th of the month. She had already collected $8,450 in rent, plus $1,250 in back rent for the previous month. How much does she owe Brown at closing for prorated rental payments?

   a. $5,070
   b. $7,620
   c. $6,140
   d. $3,751

5. A seller has prepaid her homeowners insurance for the first half of the calendar year. The six month premium is $180. If the sale closes on June 10, and the buyer assumes the seller's policy, how much will the buyer owe the seller for insurance?

   a) $19
   b) $20
   c) $21
   d) $22

6. Adele is buying a triplex from Byron. Byron has already collected rents from the tenants for the month of September. If the monthly rents are $2,700, and the sale closes on September 18, how much will Byron owe Adele for prepaid rents?

   a) $1,140
   b) $1,170
   c) $1,200
   d) $1,300

7. A seller of real estate has paid money into a reserve account with a lender to cover property tax payments of $11,600 per year. There is currently enough in the account to cover all taxes accruing through August. If the property is sold on April 8, what will be the seller's refund of tax reserves?

   a) $4.080
   b) $4,226
   c) $4,422
   d) $4,608

Answers to Proration Problems

1. d) Taxes have been paid for the year in the amount of $390.60. The period in question is from May 1st to December 30 (eight months). Bear in mind that in this context, the date of sale means the date the deed is given and accepted. The buyer assumes the responsibility for the taxes of the day the deed is accepted, in this case, May 1st.

   $390.60 ÷ 12 = $32.55 per month
   $32.55 x 8 (months) = $260.40

2. d) The policy is paid for, so the period in question is from the selling date to the end of the policy. January 1, 1987 to July 16, 1988 = 18½ months the policy is in force
   $470 ÷ 36 months = $13.06 monthly premium
   36 (mos.) - 18½ (mos.) = 17½ months of unused policy
   $13.06 x 17.5 = $228.55 unused portion of premium

3. c) Taxes and insurance have been prepaid, so period in question is from sale date to end of the calendar year (July 16 to December 30 — 5½ months).

   Both amounts are for same period, so they can be combined, $846 + $122 = $968.

   $968 ÷ 12 (months) = $80.67
   $80.67 x 5.5 (months) = $443.67

4. a) The back rent belongs to the seller; it is only the current rent that needs to be prorated.

   $8,450 ÷ 30 (days) = $281.67
   $381.67 x 18 (days) = $5,070

5. c) June 10 through June 30 = 21 days
   $180 ÷ 180 = $1 per diem
   21 x $1 = $21

6. b) Sept 18 through Sept 30 = 13 days
   $2,700 ÷ 30 = $90 per diem
   13 x $90 = $1,170

7. d) April 8 through August = 143 days
   $11,600 ÷ 360 = $32.22 per diem
   143 x $32.22 = $4,608 (rounded)

Section Three
Review Questions

1. Nature of Real Property

1. A complete definition of real property includes:

   a) land
   b) land and buildings
   c) land, fixtures and appurtenances
   d) land, fixtures and chattels

2. Any right that goes with the land and cannot be separated from it is classified as:

   a) an appurtenance
   b) a leasehold estate
   c) an estate for years
   d) a life estate

3. Which of the following normally run with the land?

   a) Covenants
   b) Easements
   c) Air rights
   d) All of the above

4. Light and air is a right that can be an:

   a) alienable right
   b) appurtenance
   c) easement
   d) All of the above

5. Which one of the following is considered to be real property?

   a) Chattel
   b) Chattel real
   c) Fixture
   d) Trade fixture

6. An underground pipeline for irrigation of a farm is:

   a) personalty
   b) realty
   c) a riparian right
   d) an emblement

7. Which of the following are clearly a part of the real property?

   a) Fences
   b) Shrubs
   c) Trees
   d) All of these

8. All of the following would be considered chattels, except:

   a) velvet drapes
   b) a refrigerator
   c) a kitchen sink
   d) cut trees

9. The air rights are:

   a) limited to area directly over structure only
   b) limited to space taken up by the buildings
   c) the use of air over an airport
   d) None of these

10. How can an owner divide his land?

    a) Horizontally and vertically
    b) Vertically only
    c) Horizontally only
    d) None of these

11. The law guarantees a property owner his right to:

    a) subjacent support
    b) lateral support
    c) Both
    d) Neither

12. When the contract for the sale of real property includes the sale of certain removable fixtures, such as refrigerators and radiator covers, upon delivery of the deed the seller should also deliver a:

a) bill of sale
b) estoppel certificate
c) chattel mortgage
d) satisfaction piece

13. Broker Green sold a home and the buyers moved in. After two months the seller came back with a list of items he said he forgot to take with him. None were mentioned specifically in the sales agreement. Which of the following items would the seller normally be entitled to as being personal property?

a) A chair left in the garage
b) The thermostat on the water heater
c) Venetian blinds affixed with screws
d) Oranges on the trees

14. Which of the following is considered personal property?

a) House
b) Garage
c) Fences
d) Trade fixtures

15. A tenant abandoned the premises used for manufacturing purposed before the term expired, but he continued to pay rent. The tenant left a water cooling system and certain electric systems, which he had installed and used in his manufacturing processes. The landlord contended that the items of equipment were fixtures, which became a part of the leased premises. Under these circumstances:

I. the fixtures belong to the tenant.
II. there was no abandonment of the lease.

a) I only
b) II only
c) Both I and II
d) Neither I nor II

16. Emblements legally belong to the:

a) landlord
b) state
c) tenant
d) decedent's estate

17. Which of the following tests would be used to determine if an item of personal property has become a fixture?

a) The adaptability of the item to the premises
b) The intention of the parties
c) An agreement between the parties involved
d) All of the above

18. All of the following are true, except:

a) Fixtures installed after the mortgage is recorded become subject to that mortgage lien
b) A person tears down a fence with the intention that it remain permanently down and stacks the fencing — it becomes real property
c) Trade fixtures installed in a building can be removed by the tenant
d) A gas furnace installed in a house becomes real property

19. The doctrine of constructive severance would apply to:

a) wrecking or the removal of buildings
b) removal of trade fixtures
c) the sale of growing crops
d) All of the foregoing

20. A man sold timber rights on his rural property to a lumber company; later he sold the entire property before any actual lumbering had been done. Who holds title to the lumber?

a) Seller, as timber has not actually been cut yet, but his sale severed the timber in the eyes of the law
b) Buyer, as the timber is not yet cut, and lumber company would be entering on his land
c) Lumber company
d) Governed by terms of buyer's and seller's contract

21. A farmer is in need of additional working capital and wishes to encumber his crops. In order to complete a loan, he would probably be required to sign a:

a) release of crops
b) financing statement
c) assignment of crops
d) trust deed

22. The document used to secure the financing when personal property is sold is the:

a) financing statement
b) agreement of sale
c) bill of sale
d) security agreement

23. A riparian owner is one who owns land bordering on:

a) a wild orchard
b) sub-marginal land
c) existing subdivision
d) a river or lake

24. The term "riparian rights":

a) gives a landowner absolute ownership of the adjacent waters
b) is set forth and protected in a standard title insurance policy
c) may be determined by examining public records
d) None of these

25. Jones obtains the right from Smith to take water from his property. He obtained this right by:

a) doctrine of correlative user
b) accretion
c) riparian rights
d) appropriation

26. Jones owns acreage through which runs a natural drainage ditch, but it is too small to handle the flow during excessively heavy rains. So, he dug a bypass ditch which diverted part of the water onto adjacent land which was currently unused for any purpose. Jones was:

a) within his right, as it is any man for himself as far as natural flood waters are concerned
b) guilty of an illegal act as he did not get permission from the county engineer
c) within his rights as adjoining land was unused and there was no danger created to life, limb and property
d) In violation as one cannot divert natural flow onto the property of another

27. Underground water not confined to a well-defined channel is known as percolating water and:

a) is owned by the state
b) is owned absolutely by the landowner
c) may be used judiciously by neighboring landowners
d) is not available to others

28. Oil and gas are:

a) considered to be personal property before being mined
b) owned by the surface owner
c) not subject to ownership as such until reduced to possession
d) considered to be real property before being mined

1. c) Real property may be defined as the land, fixtures, (that which is permanently attached), and appurtenances.

2. a) An appurtenance is defined as something that goes with or pertains to the land.

3. d) All are interests that would bind or be of benefit to all future owners. Each is appurtenant to the land.

4. d) The right to light and air may be transferred; it is considered to be something that goes with the land; and may be acquired by someone other than the owner, if the latter is willing to give it up. An alienable right is one that may be sold or given away.

5. c) A fixture is anything permanently affixed to the land and is considered real property. A chattel, chattel real, and trade fixture are all personal property.

6. b) Real property (realty) includes that which is affixed to the land, here, the pipeline.

7. d) Real property includes land, fixtures, and the things that grow on land.

8. c) Chattels are personal property, including removable fixtures. Here, a kitchen sink would not be considered a removable fixture.

9. d) Theoretically, land includes that which extends from the center of the earth to the upper limits of the sky. Landowners have the right to reasonable use of the air above their properties.

10. a) An owner may sell his surface and subsurface separately or together.

11. c) A property owner has the right to have his land undisturbed and supported in its natural state.

12. a) Title to personal property, here the removable fixture, is transferred by a bill of sale.

13. a) The chair, because it is not permanently attached to the land.

14. d) Trade fixtures are property used by a tenant to carry on his business which can be removed by him.

15. c) They were trade fixtures and removable by the tenant. Since he continued to pay rent, there was no legal abandonment.

16. c) Emblements are crops planted by the lessee while leasing the land and are legally his, even after his lease expires.

17. d) All are methods employed by the courts to distinguish real from personal property.

18. b) Once the fence is no longer permanently attached to real property, it is considered personal property.

19. c) Growing crops which are agreed to be severed before the sale of the land are treated as goods and in most states are governed by the Uniform Commercial Code.

20. c) When the timber was sold, it was constructively severed from the real property and became the personal property of the lumber company.

21. b) The financing statement is the instrument filed of record to perfect the creditor's security interest in personal property used as collateral for a loan.

22. d) As provided by the Uniform Commercial Code, to secure personal property financing, the security agreement is used and the financing statement filed of record to perfect (serve constructive notice) of the creditor's interest.

23. d) A riparian owner is defined as one who owns land and has the right to reasonable use of the water from the river or lake that borders his property. If a body of water is in movement, an adjoining owner is a riparian owner; if the water is not flowing, as with a pond, small lake or ocean, the abutting owner is a littoral owner.

24. d) Riparian rights are those of the property owner which allow him reasonable use of surface waters on his property. They are not of public record. Furthermore, the property owner does not own the water, only the right to use it reasonably. He may not dam or divert it from its natural flow.

25. d) If Jones has taken the water for his own use for a certain period of time from Smith's property, he may have acquired the right by appropriation.

26. d) If you divert a natural drainage channel and the water damages the property of another, he may collect damages.

27. c) Underground water is transitory, since it is constantly moving, and is not owned by anyone. Landowners above are entitled to reasonable use of the water, providing there is no trespass in reaching the water.

28. c) While in the ground, oil and gas percolate (move without a definite channel) and as such, are not subject to ownership. Once extracted they become personal property.

2. Estates In Land

1. The right to possess property and have exclusive use of that property is best defined as:

   a) equity
   b) an estate in real property
   c) sole proprietorship
   d) joint ownership

2. An estate of inheritance, or for life is known as:

   a) freehold
   b) less than a freehold
   c) greater than a freehold
   d) None of the above

3. Which of these is a freehold estate?

   a) Estate at will
   b) Life estate
   c) Estate for years
   d) Leasehold

4. Which of the following is not a characteristic of a fee simple estate?

   a) Freely transferable
   b) Freely inheritable
   c) Definite duration
   d) Unlimited duration

5. Which of the following is true?

   a) A fee simple estate is a freehold estate
   b) An estate for years is not considered real property; instead it is chattel real
   c) A life estate is a freehold estate
   d) All of the foregoing are true

6. A base or qualified fee is:

   a) a sale of land with a number of easements
   b) a sale for a particular use or purpose (school or church) and where such use is ended, the property reverts to grantor
   c) tenure by adverse use until real owner brings court action to reclaim title
   d) a term in description of land acquired by patent

7. A conveyance of title with the condition that the land shall not be used for the sale of intoxicating beverages creates:

   a) a less than freehold estate
   b) a defeasible estate
   c) an estate on covenant precedent
   d) reservation

8. Bates conveys a fee simple title to the Avon Baptist Church, by deed, to be used for church purposes, in 1950. In 1974, the church abandons the property, due to environmental changes. Title to the property will:

   a) remain in the church
   b) escheat to the state
   c) revert to Bates
   d) be owned by the church and Bates, as joint tenants

9. "C" grants an estate to "B" for the life of "X". "B" dies. The estate:

   a) ceases to exist
   b) reverts to the original owner
   c) vests in "X" in trust until "C's" death
   d) reverts to heirs of "B"

10. By will, Calhoun devises his property to his daughter, Mary Calhoun, for life, and at her death to "her children." At Calhoun's death, Mary, 30 years of age and unmarried, deeds a fee simple estate to Davis. The title is:

a) valid
b) invalid
c) Davis obtains a fee simple estate
d) Davis is a tenant

11. Mrs. Black inherited a life estate in the family home from her mother, with provision that it go to the grandson in fee simple after her death. Which of the following is false?

a) Mrs. Black can rent the home from month to month
b) She can convey fee simple title to the lot but not the house
c) She can mortgage her interest
d) She can sell an interest in the title she holds

12 Mr. Ackerman leased a property for five years to Mr. Bones. During this term, Mr. Ackerman died and then Mr. Bones discovered that Mr. Ackerman's interest was a life estate. The owner of the property was correct in advocating which of the following?

a) Mr. Bones' leasehold estate is valid for the length of the lease
b) Mr. Bones' interest was terminated upon Mr. Ackerman's demise
c) Mr. Ackerman's heir would receive the fee title
d) The owner has an estate in remainder

13. Jones grants a life estate to Smith for the life of Mrs. Jacobs.

a) Jones has a reversionary interest and Smith has a life estate
b) Jones has a remainder interest and Smith has a life estate
c) Jones has a life estate and Mrs. Jacobs has a remainder interest
d) It would be illegal for Jones to do this

14. Mary gives Jane a life estate with the provision that, after Jane's death, the property should go to Robert if Robert is still alive. Robert has:

a) a life estate
b) a reversionary interest
c) no interest
d) a contingent remainder

15. Which of the following is a less-than-freehold estate?

a) Fee simple defeasible
b) Fee simple absolute
c) Leasehold estate
d) Life estate

16. If an individual owns an estate in fee and desires to change his interest to a less-than-freehold estate, he must:

a) sell and lease back
b) lease the property out
c) demise the property
d) sell the property

17. Which one of the following applies to a landlord-tenant relationship?

a) Tenancy in common
b) Tenancy at sufferance
c) Joint tenancy
d) Tenancy by the entireties

18. A couple's five year lease had expired, but they continued living on the premises. If they now pay rent on a quarterly basis, this type of tenancy is:

a) month to month
b) periodic
c) at will
d) sufferance

19. A lease for a definite period of time is:

a) a lease at will
b) a fee simple
c) an estate for years
d) a tenancy at sufferance

20. An estate at will is a:

a) form of concurrent ownership
b) tenancy of uncertain duration
c) inheritance of property by will
d) life estate

21. Mr. Rob leases an apartment to Ms. Hall. Mr. Rob is called the:

a) lessee
b) lessor
c) vendor
d) vendee

22. Rent may be defined as:

a) a month to month tenancy
b) the lessee's interest in real property
c) consideration for the use and possession of real property
d) a contract between a landlord and a lessee

23. A lease to be binding must be signed by the:

a) broker
b) beneficiary
c) lessor only
d) lessor and lessee

24. Leases cannot be recorded unless they are acknowledged by:

a) lessor
b) lessee
c) Both lessor and lessee
d) Neither lessor nor lessee

25. Mr. Brown owned a drug store on property under a twenty year lease with ten years to go. Mr. Brown died. The lease was:

a) valid for ten remaining years
b) voidable at option of new property owner
c) void from the beginning as business property leases are limited to fifteen years by law
d) void as Mr. Brown was not a registered pharmacist

26. When real estate under lease is sold, the lease:

a) expires
b) is broken
c) must be renewed
d) remains binding upon new owner

27. Assume that Mr. and Mrs. Davis did not sign the lease agreement, but upon taking possession of the apartment on August 1st were handed a signed copy by landlord Smith. On August 20th Mr. and Mrs. Davis move out claiming that, since they had not signed the agreement, it was a mere tenancy at will. Smith could:

a) do nothing
b) sue Davis immediately for the unpaid portion of the lease
c) sue Davis for the inconvenience of leasing the premises to another
d) keep only the security deposit

28. Sole ownership by an individual is ownership:

a) in common interest
b) in gross
c) in severalty
d) in joint tenancy

29. Real property owned by a city or county, such as parks, school buildings, city hall, etc.,is owned in:

a) joint tenancy
b) community property
c) severalty
d) tenants in common

30. Joint tenancy ownership to be effective must have:

a) ownership of community interest
b) unity of severalty, possession occupancy and estate
c) mutual interest as tenants in common
d) unities of interest, possession, time and title

31. One of the following is wrong or doesn't make sense. Joint tenants always have:

a) equal right to use of the property
b) the right to bequeath good title to heirs
c) their interests during the same period of time
d) exactly the same title to the property

32. William Alberts and his daughter Jane Alberts buy a tract of land for all cash, and the property is deeded to them with right of survivorship. William and Jane are:

a) joint tenants
b) tenants by the entireties
c) tenants in common
d) any of these

33. Andrew Erbel, a single man, and William Rush, a single man, wish to take the title to real property so that each will own a one half interest, and if either of them dies, the other will own the entire property. The granting clause should read:

a) Andrew Erbel, a single man, and William Rush, a single man, each an undivided one half interest as tenants in common
b) Andrew Erbel, and William Rush, single men as joint tenants
c) Andrew Erbel, a single man, and William Rush, a single man, jointly and severally
d) Andrew Erbel and William Rush, single men, as co-owners

34. A joint tenant cannot dispose of his interest in real property by:

a) lease
b) sale
c) gift
d) will

35. Two brothers, John and Bill owned valuable property left to them by their father, as joint tenants. Both married later, and then Bill died intestate. His widow would acquire:

a) no interest in the property
b) half interest as joint tenant with John
c) half interest as tenant in common
d) one quarter interest in the property

36. Mary and Tom Smith were joint tenants. Mary deeded her interest to Jack Jones. Jack Jones and Tom Smith are now:

a) tenants in severalty
b) partners
c) survivorship tenants
d) tenants in common

37. Which of the following would create a tenancy in common?

a) One of three joint tenants dies
b) A joint tenant wills property to a third person
c) A joint tenant gives his interest to a third person
d) None of the above

38. An undivided interest, without the right of survivorship is:

a) joint tenancy
b) tenancy in common
c) tenancy in severalty
d) tenancy by the entirety

39. You own property as a tenant in common. You always have the unity of:

a) time
b) title
c) interest
d) possession

40. Alberts devises his property, one-half to his son, Bert, one-sixth to a nephew, Harold, and two-sixths to a niece, Mabel, as tenants in common. The Acme Motor Co., the holder of a judgment lien against Bert, causes Bert's interest in the property to be sold at a sheriff's sale. Acme, itself is the successful bidder. Which is true?

I. The sheriff's sale is void.
II. The Acme Motor Co. becomes an owner in common with Harold and Mabel.

a) I only
b) II only
c) Both I and II
d) Neither I nor II

41. One of the features of taking title to real estate, as tenants in common, is that:

a) ownership interest must be equal
b) each co-owner's interest may be conveyed separately
c) a co-owner cannot will his interest in a property
d) the last survivor always owns property in severalty

42. Concerning tenancy in common, which of the following is correct?

a) Each party's interest must be equal
b) Each tenant must acquire a title at the same time
c) Any party may sell without the consent of the others
d) All of the above

43. A type of co-ownership where the parties must be husband and wife is:

a) tenancy in common
b) tenancy by the entireties
c) joint tenancy
d) periodic tenancy

1. b) An estate in real property is defined as the right to possess property and have exclusive use.

2. a) A freehold estate is either an estate of inheritance or life estate. If an estate is not freehold, it is less than freehold.

3. b) There are two classifications of estates: freehold and leasehold. An estate at will and estate for years are leasehold estates, not of indeterminable duration like a freehold estate.

4. c) An estate that has a definite or limited duration cannot be a fee simple estate. For an estate to be a fee, it must be freely transferable, freely inheritable and of unlimited duration.

5. d) All of the foregoing are true. Chattel real is personal property. An estate for years is a lease which is generally an interest in personal property.

6. b) A base fee, also called a qualified or defeasible fee is a fee simple estate that will revert to the grantor when a condition is breached.

7. b) A defeasible estate is one that will be defeated upon the happening of a certain event.

8. c) As a conditional, defeasible estate, it will terminate when the condition is broken, here, no longer using the property for church purposes.

9. d) Since the life estate is based upon the life of "X" it is not terminated by the death of "B." "B's" interest still exists and it would be transferred to his heirs.

10. b) Mary can only convey a life estate measured by the duration of her life. A fee simple estate is of indeterminable duration.

11. b) She holds no fee simple in the property to convey. She could sell the property to another for her lifetime. She holds a life estate and could only convey the same.

12. b) This question illustrates the rare situation where a lease may be terminated by death. The lessor can only lease the property for the term of his life. Upon the lessor's death, he no longer has an interest in the property and the lessee's interest also ceases.

13. a) Upon Mrs. Jacob's death, Jones will regain his full "bundle of rights" to the property. Smith's estate is measured by the life of Mrs. Jacobs.

14. d) The estate is contingent upon Jane outliving Robert. Therefore, it is a contingent remainder estate.

15. c) Under a less-than-freehold estate, the holder does not have title to the property. A less-than freehold estate is a leasehold estate. A leasehold merely gives possession of the property and not title.

16. a) There are two classifications of estates: freehold and leasehold. A property owner might sell his land and lease it back if he wants to get his equity (cash) out of the property while retaining the right to possess and make use of it.

17. b) Tenancy at sufference is where the tenant holds over after the expiration of the lease period without landlord permission.

18. b) Since the lessees are paying rent, they are not tenants at sufference. With the payment of rent on a quarterly basis, they are entitled to possess the property for the next three months. This cannot be considered month to month and would be classified as a periodic tenancy.

19. c) Any lease that is negotiated for a set period of time is known as an estate for years. This would include a lease for one week, two months, one year or ten years, etc.

20. b) An estate at will is one created with consent of the owner for an indefinite period.

21. b) One who rents the property is called the lessor.

22. c) One leases property and pays rent.

23. c) Though it is a good practice to have both the lessor and lessee sign a lease, only the lessor needs to sign it. If the lessee takes possession of the property and pays rent, he implies his acceptance of the terms of the agreement and is bound by it.

24. a) The person who is giving up an interest must acknowledge this by his signature. The lessor gives up his right to possession in a leasehold estate. A lessor acknowledges the lease; a notary public accepts the acknowledgment.

25. a) Death of the lessor or lessee does not ordinarily cancel the lease. If the tenant dies, the lessor should make his claim for rent against the tenant's estate, as most written leases bind the heirs and administrators of the estate.

26. d) The buyer takes title "subject to" the existing lease; he must recognize it.

27. b) By taking possession, the Davises impliedly accepted the agreement and would be liable for the unpaid portion. Only the lessor needs to sign the lease.

28. c) The legal term "severalty" means sole, seperate, and exclusive possession, dominion or ownership." An estate in severalty indicates sole ownership — by one person only.

29. c) Severalty is ownership by a single person or legal entity, including a city, county or state.

30. d) We have mixed these up a little to confuse you, but the essentials are "time, title, interest and possession."

31. b) As the surviving joint tenant receives the interest of the deceased joint tenant, there is nothing for the latter to leave by will.

32. a) A characteristic of joint tenancy is the right of survivorship, the survivor obtaining automatic title by surviving the other tenant.

33. b) A characteristic of joint tenancy is the right of survivorship.

34. d) A joint tenant cannot dispose of his interest in real property by will.

35. a) John would acquire the property as he was joint tenant and Bill's interest was his separate property.

36. d) Because the unities of time and title are no longer present, Tom and Jack are tenants in common with an equal right to possession.

37. c) If a joint tenant transfers his interest to a third party, the unity of time and possibly the unity of interest will be broken. Unless otherwise provided, the new interest held would be tenants in common. A joint tenant cannot will his interest as it goes to the surviving joint tenant(s) on his death.

38. b) Tenants in common have no right of survivorship; they may will their interest.

39. d) Tenancy in common is ownership by two or more persons who hold an undivided interest without the right of survivorship. Their interests need not be equal nor need they take title at the same time.

40. b) An ownership in the form of tenancy in common allows creditors to attach a tenant's interest. Upon obtaining such an interest, the creditors become tenants in common with the other tenants.

41. b) Each co-owner may convey or devise his interest separately. Interests do not have to be equal.

42. c) In a tenancy in common, any party may sell without the consent of the others. He may also will his share without consent.

43. b) Tenancy by the entireties is a form of ownership between husband and wife.

3. *Acquisition and Transfer of Land*

1. Involuntary alienation of an estate means:

   a) no person can be compelled to transfer title without his consent
   b) aliens are forbidden to own estates in fee simple
   c) ownership of estates may be transferred by operation of law
   d) None of the foregoing

2. An example of involuntary alienation is where title to real estate passes by:

   a) quit claim deed
   b) trust deed
   c) grant deed
   d) sheriff's deed

3. What is the maximum number of grantees that can be named in a deed?

   a) Two
   b) Any number
   c) Four
   d) Ten

4. Which of the following is not capable of receiving title by means of a deed?

   a) Incompetent
   b) 17 year old
   c) Infant
   d) None of these

5. Which of the following is essential to a valid deed?

   a) Must be in writing
   b) Parties must be competent to convey and capable of receiving grant of property
   c) There must be a granting clause
   d) All of these

6. A valid deed must contain:

   a) an adequate consideration
   b) a verification
   c) grantee's signature
   d) a granting clause

7. Which of these is not essential to the validity of a deed?

   a) Consideration
   b) Competent grantor
   c) Description
   d) Capable grantee

8. In order to be valid, a deed must:

   a) be in writing
   b) be recorded
   c) be signed by all parties
   d) All of the above

9. A deed must:

   a) contain the street address identification
   b) state nature of the improvements on the land (dwellings)
   c) contain adequate description to identify the property being conveyed
   d) state total area in the tract

10. Of the following, which would cause a deed to be void?

    a) Grantee is fictitious person
    b) It was signed by a mark
    c) Grantee used an assumed name
    d) None of these

11. When a valid grant or warranty deed is prepared, title passes when it is:

a) acknowledged
b) delivered
c) signed
d) recorded

12. To be valid, a grant deed must:

a) be delivered by grantor to grantee personally
b) recite every warranty it carries
c) state some consideration
d) be delivered personally or by agent of grantor

13. After Carson dies, a will and deed are found in his safe; the deed is made out to his church; the will does not mention his house. Therefore, the church should be concerned with:

a) acknowledgement
b) delivery
c) statute of frauds
d) statute of limitation

14. Mr. Brown and Mrs. Brown held title as tenants in common to a piece of property. Mrs. Brown wanted a niece to inherit her share of the property when she died, but did not want to tell her husband. So she made out a proper grant deed conveying her interest to her niece, with her signature duly acknowledged, and gave it to a close friend who agreed to hand it over to the niece after Mrs. Brown's death. Mrs. Brown died and the friend carried out the instructions. The deed was:

a) invalid for lack of proper delivery
b) invalid as she could not deed her interest in the property
c) valid because the friend could testify to Mrs. Brown's intent
d) valid as deed was delivered to a close relative after grantor's demise

15. Which of the following forms of deeds have one or more warranties of title?

a) Quitclaim deed
b) Warranty deed
c) Executor's deed
d) All of these

16. A deed that promises grantor will defend against all adverse claims is known as:

a) a warranty deed
b) a special warranty deed
c) a grant deed
d) All of these

17. Which type of deed limits the covenants of the grantor when he conveys real estate?

a) Quitclaim deed
b) Special warranty
c) General warranty
d) None of these

18. A quitclaim deed is most commonly used to:

a) cure title defects
b) give notice to the world
c) give after-acquired title
d) None of the above

19. A quitclaim deed:

a) warrants that there are no encumbrances on the property
b) warrants that there are no encumbrances of record
c) does not insure against encumbrances and guarantees nothing
d) conveys any after-acquired title

20. A woman bought property under her maiden name, Mary Wilson, and later sold it after her marriage under her married name, Mary Howard. This would:

a) create a cloud on the title
b) become valid one year after recording under her married name
c) create a joint tenancy
d) permit her husband to claim title in a suit as it is now community property

21. Which of the following would most likely constitute a cloud on the title of real property?

a) An easement for utility wires
b) A zoning restriction that is adverse to the highest and best use of the land
c) A recorded installment sales contract or real estate contract
d) A lock-in clause in a mortgage

22. There are implied warranties by the grantor in a grant deed. One of the following is not among them.

a) Property has not been encumbered by grantor except as disclosed
b) The interest being conveyed has not previously been conveyed to others
c) The interest held by grantor is being transferred to the grantee
d) The grantor holds a certificate of title

23. The person who acquires real property under the terms of a will is known as a/an:

a) devisee
b) administrator
c) testator
d) executor

24. Bequeath is to personal property as devise is to:

a) bill of sale
b) real property
c) transfer of title
d) deed

25. A will entirely written, dated and signed in the testator's own handwriting is called a:

a) holographic will
b) nuncupative will
c) intestate will
d) witnessed will

26. Probate means an action to:

a) cure a defect by a quit claim deed
b) prove title by adverse possession
c) process a will to establish its validity
d) obtain access to a safe deposit box

27. When real property is being sold as part of the estate of a deceased person:

a) the sale must be at public auction
b) the executor must accept highest bid resulting from newspaper
c) any offer accepted by executor must be approved by court
d) the person who buys property must pay all cash

28. Broker Green sold real property belonging to an estate being probated. The amount of his commission was determined by:

a) his exclusive listing
b) the court
c) the executor
d) the probate code

29. The Probate Court appoints a person to handle the estate of one who has died intestate. This person would be called:

a) a trustee
b) an executor
c) an administrator
d) a vendor

30. If Mathews dies intestate, his property would:

a) be distributed according to his will
b) be distributed to his heirs
c) escheat to the county where the property is located
d) go to his church

31. When a person dies intestate and no heirs can be found for intestate succession, his real property will revert to the state through a process known as:

a) reconveyance
b) reversion
c) escheat
d) succession

32. Possession under a claim of adverse possession must be:

a) open and notorious
b) hostile
c) continuous
d) All of these

33. Title acquired by adverse possession may be perfected by:

a) court action
b) quitclaim deed
c) grant deed only
d) Either A or B

34. George Crow, owner of a tract of land, occupied ten feet over on Delbert's land upon the erroneous belief as to the true boundary. During this adverse occupation, Delbert notified Crow that he was a trespasser. The period for adverse possession passed, and Delbert now sues Crow.

a) Crow now owns the subject ten feet
b) Delbert continues to own the land since he gave effective notice to Crow
c) Crow must pay Delbert the reasonable value of the ten feet
d) Crow can occupy only one-half of the ten feet, or five feet

35. First grant or patent in chain of title is issued by:

a) a sovereign power
b) U. S. Government Patent Office
c) the recorder of deeds
d) the grantee of a fee simple deed

36. Which of these describes a partition action?

a) Action of water eroding the soil
b) Request for a building code variance
c) Court action where co-owners seek to sever their joint ownership
d) Court action to dissolve a partnership

37. The process in which natural causes gradually deposit soil on the land increasing the amount of land is known as:

a) appreciation
b) accretion
c) avulsion
d) ademption

38. Accretion, the gradual accumulation of land due to natural causes, is most nearly the opposite of:

a) alluvium
b) reliction
c) avulsion
d) None of the above

39. Recording of instruments which transfer or encumber real property does not:

a) give constructive notice of instrument's contents
b) create a presumption of delivery
c) give actual notice of instrument's contents
d) give priority over subsequently re-recorded instruments

40. The purpose of recording a real estate contract is to:

a) establish responsibility for payment of property tax
b) assure payment of excise tax
c) serve notice to the world of buyer's interest
d) establish priorities of subsequent liens

41. The county auditor's office is required by law to maintain:

a) phonetic filing system
b) microfilm equipment for making copies of records
c) index filing system
d) records of sales tax paid by all businesses

42. For a conditional sales contract to be recorded, it must:

a) be signed and acknowledged by the seller
b) contain a granting clause
c) be signed and acknowledged by the seller and buyer
d) be signed and acknowledged by the buyer

43. In order for a title insurance company to examine rapidly and economically, and to insure title to real property, it is essential that they have a:

a) data processing plant
b) notary public
c) title plant
d) large accounting staff

44. Which Title Insurance guarantees against every threat?

a) Standard Policy
b) Extended Coverage
c) A.L.T.A.
d) None of these

45. Chain of title means:

a) a measurement used by a surveyor
b) a listing of all recorded instruments affecting the subject title
c) certificate of title
d) heirs named in a will to inherit property after a death of testator

46. A document setting forth a brief synopsis of all matters of record affecting the title to the real estate in question is referred to as:

a) a title insurance policy
b) a certificate of title
c) an abstract of title
d) None of the above

47. A purchaser should obtain which of the following to be sure there is no encroachment?

a) Title insurance policy
b) Survey
c) Declaration of no set off certificate
d) Each of the above

48. The Title Company is least likely to make an on site inspection if the policy is:

a) an A.L.T.A. policy on a residence
b) an extended coverage policy on a residence
c) an extended coverage policy on rural property
d) a Standard policy on a residence

49. The standard title insurance covers all of the following except:

a) transferability of title
b) risks of deed
c) rights of others in possession
d) conveyance by incompetents

50. A title insurance policy, standard form, insures:

a) that there are no judgment liens against the property
b) that the property is free and clear of all encumbrances
c) the title only as it appears of record, subject to stated exceptions
d) All of these

51. A.L.T.A. policy covers all except:

a) unrecorded easements
b) unrecorded liens
c) rights of parties in possession
d) losses resulting from government restrictions

52. The A.L.T.A. title policy is available to:

a) owners of real property
b) owners and lenders
c) lenders
d) county recorders

1. c) Involuntary alienation of an estate means the transfer of ownership by operation of law. Examples include eminent domain and foreclosure procedures.

2. d) A sheriff's deed is given by court order in connection with a sale of property to satisfy a judgment or on completion of the one year redemption period following a mortgage foreclosure.

3. b) There is no limit to the number of buyers of real property that can be specified in a deed.

4. d) Grantors must be sane and at least 18 years old to give up their title, but a person need only be alive in order to be capable of receiving title.

5. d) A valid deed must have: written form, granting clause, capable grantee, adequate description, competent grantor, and acknowledgement.

6. d) A valid deed must have: written form, granting clause, capable grantee, adequate description, competent grantor, and acknowledgement.

7. a) There must be a competent grantor, description, and a capable (alive) grantee. No consideration need be stated in the deed.

8. a) Of course, a deed must be in writing. Recording is recommended, but not necessary. The grantee protects his interest in the property by recording it — making it a matter of public record. Grantors sign deeds, but not grantees.

9. c) A legal description is not necessary. All that is required is sufficient description of the property being transferred.

10. a) The grantee in a deed must be a living person; a fictitious person is not living.

11. b) To pass title, a valid grant or warranty deed (which is acknowledged) must be delivered. This manifests an intent of the grantor to pass title. Recording protects one's interest after title has passed.

12. d) Delivery of the deed is important; usually the escrow agent is authorized to do this. It need not be delivered by the grantor personally. Regardless of whether it's a grant deed (used in California) or a warranty deed (Washington), the warranties are implied by law and need not be spelled out in the deed. The consideration paid by the grantee is usually not stated in the deed.

13. b) Since the deed was not delivered during Carson's lifetime, no valid delivery was made.

14. a) A deed cannot be delivered after the death of the grantor. There was no proper delivery.

15. b) A warranty deed warrants that the grantor has good title and will defend the title against adverse claims.

16. a) A warranty deed warrants that the grantor has good title and will defend against all adverse claims. The special warranty deed limits the claims that the grantor will defend.

17. b) The special warranty limits the covenants. A general warranty deed does not limit the covenants of the grantor; the quitclaim deed warrants nothing.

18. a) While a quiclaim deed may convey title, should the person conveying the land have title, these deeds are generally used to cure title defects, such as to correct a faulty legal description.

19. c) The quitclaim deed is generally used to remove clouds on title and warrants nothing.

20. a) Clouds on title affect or impair the owner's title. Here, there will be some doubt as to the name and identity of the grantor.

21. c) Clouds on title can affect or impair one's title, if valid. Here, a recorded installment sales contract could impair good title and the seller's right to ownership in the event of buyer's default.

22. d) These "implied warranties" or guarantees are considered by law to be a part of the deed, even though they are not stated.

23. a) A devise is a transfer of real property under the terms of a will. The person receiving the real property is known as the devisee.

24. b) Personal property is bequeathed and real property is devised by will.

25. a) A holographic will is one that is entirely in the handwriting of the testator. No printed material may appear on the will, such as a printed letterhead or typed date.

26. c) Probate is an action by the superior court to establish the validity of a will.

27. c) The sale of a deceased person's property is controlled by the probate court. Any negotiation by the executor must be approved by this court. It is not necessary to auction the property nor for the buyer to purchase it for all cash.

28. b) The court determines the compensation but usually will allow the customary rate. The executor or administrator cannot bind the estate, or give an exclusive listing.

29. c) An administrator is appointed by the court, and the executor is appointed by the testator when he makes a will. Both perform the same functions. To die intestate means to die without a will.

30. b) When one dies intestate, his property is distributed to the heirs; if there are no known heirs, the property escheats to the state.

31. c) The transfer to the state of real property of a person who dies intestate and had no heirs is known as escheat.

32. d) The requirements for title by adverse possession are open and notorious use for the statutory period; hostile to the will of the owner; the adverse possessor must pay the taxes during this period and be in possession of the property under claim of right or color of title.

33. d) A party acquiring title to real property by adverse possession may call upon the court to perfect the title or could obtain a quitclaim deed from the previous owner.

34. a) Crow owns the land because his possession was open, notorious and hostile to the will of the owner. Delbert should have taken legal action to have Crow removed before statute of limitations expired.

35. a) A patent is the document used by the state or federal government to convey title to government owned land to a private individual.

36. c) A partition action is court action to sever a joint tenancy relationship.

37. b) Accretion is the addition to land through natural causes, usually by water.

38. c) Avulsion is the sudden tearing away of land, usually by the action of water.

39. c) Actual notice is notice that has really (actually) come to the awareness of someone else.

40. c) One of the effects of recording may be the establishment of priority over subsequent liens, but the purpose of recording is to give notice to the world (constructive notice) of the buyer's interest.

41. c) The index is usually alphabetized according to the names of grantors and grantees or trustors and trustees.

42. a) Only the giver of an interest acknowledges the document used to convey that interest. The recipient (buyer) signs the agreement but does not acknowledge it.

43. c) A title plant is a collection of records retained by the title company.

44. d) No policy of title insurance will insure against governmental regulations such as zoning changes, etc.

45. b) Chain of title is a history of conveyances and encumbrances affecting the title.

46. c) An abstract is a condensed history of conveyances and encumbrances affecting one's title to real property.

47. b) Encroachments would only be revealed by a physical inspection, a survey.

48. d) A Standard Policy insures items disclosed by the record; it has no coverage against defects not disclosed.

49. c) Rights of others in possession would require a physical inspection. The standard title insurance covers only those defects of record.

50. c) A standard title insurance insures against those defects of record.

51. d) An A.L.T.A. policy covers everything the standard policy covers and more, including matters that will not be disclosed by search of the public records. Nothing, however, protects against government actions.

52. b) The A.L.T.A. policy is designed for lenders but is available to property owners who desire the extended coverage.

4. *Methods of Land Description*

1. A section of a township contains the following number of acres:

   a) 360
   b) 580
   c) 640
   d) 560

2. How many square, one-acre lots could be subdivided aiong one side of a quarter section?

   a) 20
   b) 13
   c) 12
   d) 24

3. What percent of a section would equal 1/60 of a township?

   a) 60%
   b) 70%
   c) 80%
   d) 90%

4. What part of a section measures 1/4 of a mile by 1/4 of a mile?

   a) 1/4 of a section
   b) 1/8 of a section
   c) 1/16 of a section
   d) 1/36 of a section

5. Choose the correct legal description.

   a) Section 6, T. 6S, R. 6N
   b) Section 10, T. 8S, R. 4W
   c) Section 16, T. 6S, R. 2N, W. B & M
   d) Section 20, T. 18 N, R. 8E, W. B & M

6. How far is it between the boundary lines of a township?

   a) 6 miles
   b) 60 miles
   c) 1 mile
   d) 2 miles

7. Sections in a township are numbered consecutively 1 through 36. The first section in the township would be located in the:

   a) southeast corner
   b) southwest corner
   c) northeast corner
   d) northwest corner

8. Which of the following is the largest area:

   a) 10% of a township
   b) three sections
   c) two miles square
   d) 5,280 x 5,280

9. How many 50' by 110' lots could be obtained from an acre of land?

   a) 6
   b) 10
   c) 9
   d) 7

10. How wide is a four acre easement that runs along the western edge of a section?

    a) 33 feet
    b) 55 feet
    c) 66 feet
    d) 88 feet

11. If you combined the E½ of the W½ of the NE¼ of Section 8 and the S½ of the N½ of the NW¼ of Section 10, how many acres would you have?

a) 20
b) 40
c) 60
d) 80

12. Section 6 in a township is:

a) next to Section 22 in the adjacent township
b) due south of Section 23 in the same township
c) an inside section of the same township
d) part of the west boundary of the same township

13. How many acres in an area of land which measures 330 by 660 feet?

a) 2
b) 25
c) 16
d) 5

14. What is the distance around the boundaries of a section?

a) 21,220
b) 10,560
c) 21,120
d) None of the above

15. An area of one square mile would be equal to a:

a) township
b) tract
c) section
d) quarter section

16. Lot 17 of Benton Addition, City of Topanga would be part of what type of legal description?

a) Township survey
b) Metes and bounds
c) Platted subdivision
d) Condominium

17. The government survey system utilizes a grid of:

I. north and south lines called meridians.
II. east and west lines called parallels.

a) I only
b) II only
c) Both I and II
d) Neither I nor II

18. When describing a compass direction in a metes and bounds description, it is customary to:

a) measure the number of degrees the angle deviates from north and south
b) measure the deviation of the angle from east or west
c) use magnetic north as a basis for measurement
d) describe degrees as a bearing from 0 degrees through 180 degrees

19. How many miles separate Section 2 from Section 34 in Township 6 South, Range 2 East, Humboldt Meridian?

a) 2
b) 4
c) 7
d) 3

20. In a recorded plat, the lots are described by:

a) distances and courses
b) reference to townships
c) lot and block number
d) None of the above

21. A column of townships running north and south is called:

a) a tier
b) a range
c) a section
d) None of the above

22. Land description by measurement and direction is called description by:

a) metes and bounds
b) recorded plat
c) government survey
d) None of the above

1. c) A section of a township contains 640 acres.

2. c) A quarter section measures ½ mile on each side, which is equal to 2,640 feet. A square acre measures 208.71 feet on each side for a total area of 43,560 sq. ft. 208.71 divided into 2,640 goes slightly more than 12 times.

3. a) There are 36 sections in a township, so one section equals 1/36 of a township.
% x 1/36 = 1/60
% = 36/60
% = 60%

4. c) A section is one mile on each side. A quarter section is ½ mile on each side. A quarter quarter section measures ¼ mile on each side and is equal to 1/16 of the area of the section.
(¼ x ¼ = 1/16)

5. d) A government survey description must refer to the principal meridian that is being used. Townships are counted to the north and south of the baseline; ranges are counted to the east and west of the principal meridian.

6. a) A township measures six miles on each side.

7. c) Township sections are numbered across and down in snake-like fashion, starting from the northeast corner of the township.

8. c) 10% of a township is 3.6 sq. mi. Three sections is 3 sq. mi. Two miles square is 4 sq. miles. 5,280 ft. x 5,280 ft. is 1 sq. mi.

9. d) A 50' x 110' lot contains 5,500 sq. ft. An acre contains 43,560 sq. ft. 5,500 divided into 43,560 goes more than 7 but not quite 8 times.

10. a) Four acres equals 4 x 43,560 square feet, a total of 174,240 square feet. A section is one mile (5,280 feet) on each side. Area equals length times width, so 174,240 = 5,280 X width. Dividing 174,240 by 5,280 gives the answer, 33 feet.

11. d) A section is 640 acres; a quarter section is 160 acres. Half of half of a quarter section is ½ x ½ x 160 = 40 acres. Twice that amount is 80 acres.

12. d) Section six is in the northwest corner of the township.

13. d) 330 x 660 = 217,800 square feet. An acre is 43,560 square feet. 217,800 divided by 43,560 equals 5.

14. c) A section is one mile (5,280 feet) on each side.
4 x 5,280 = 21,120.

15. c) A section is one mile square.

16. c) Subdivision descriptions refer to lot numbers on a recorded plat.

17. c) In the government survey, land is described by reference to north/south meridians (also called range lines) and east/west parallels (also called township lines).

18. a) Compass bearings in metes and bounds descriptions are given relative to north or south, whichever is closer.

19. b) Section two is on the north boundary of the township. Section 34 is below it on the south boundary. Four one-mile wide sections lie in between.

20. c) Lot and block numbers are used to identify lots on a subdivision plat.

21. b) A range is a north/south column of townships that is between two consecutive range lines.

22. a) Metes and bounds descriptions describe boundaries by course (direction) and distance.

5. Encumbrances on Land

1. Any interest in or right to land held by third persons, adversely affecting the title, and possibly the value of property is an:

   a) encumbrance
   b) encroachment
   c) appurtenance
   d) escrow

2. One of the following encumbrances affects the physical use of property.

   a) An easement
   b) A trust deed
   c) A money judgment
   d) Delinquent taxes

3. Encumbrances can:

   a) affect or relate to the title
   b) affect or relate to the actual physical conditions upon realty
   c) Both A and B
   d) Neither A nor B

4. As to encumbrances, which of the following is true?

   a) All easements are liens
   b) Encumbrances must be recorded to be effective
   c) Restrictions beneficial to the grantee are encumbrances
   d) Encumbrances never lower real property values

5. Which of the following is not classified as a lien against real property?

   a) Unpaid real property taxes
   b) An easement appurtenant
   c) Installment payment on an assessment bond
   d) Recorded abstract of judgment

6. In real estate, we speak of general and specific liens. Examples of specific liens would be:

   a) mortgages
   b) real property taxes
   c) mechanic's liens or laborer's liens
   d) all of the foregoing

7. A lien covering all property of a debtor would most likely be a:

   a) blanket lien
   b) property tax lien
   c) mechanic's or laborer's lien
   d) general lien

8. Which of the following would be a voluntary lien?

   a) Mortgage
   b) Mechanic's or laborer's lien
   c) Real property tax lien
   d) All of the foregoing

9. An option is a contract by which the owner of property gives another person the right to purchase his property for a stated sum within a given period of time. An option of this type is a(n):

   a) voluntary lien
   b) involuntary encumbrance
   c) voluntary encumbrance
   d) none of these

10. A property owner uses a piece of land as security against a loan, but retains effective possession of it. He is said to have:

    a) pledged it
    b) hypothecated it
    c) apothecated it
    d) used it

11. A charge levied against real estate for municipal functions is:

a) an assessment
b) a tax
c) a lien
d) a judgment

12. Real estate property taxes are:

a) general — involuntary liens
b) general — voluntary liens
c) specific — voluntary liens
d) specific — involuntary liens

13. The tax on a given piece of real property is always determined by multiplying the tax rate by the:

a) selling price
b) assessed valuation of the property
c) mortgage loan value
d) book value

14. When calculating the amount of real property taxes to be assessed on property, the rate is applied to the property:

a) ad valorem
b) ad hoc
c) Lis Pendens
d) ad valendum

15. A government official who evaluates property for tax purposes is a/an:

a) assayer
b) assessor
c) administrator
d) surveyor

16. A charge levied by a local government to finance street paving is:

a) an ad valorem tax
b) a zoning charge
c) an equalizer
d) an assessment

17. If the title company discovers a delinquent sewer assessment, the party that would normally be required to pay for the portion that is in arrears is:

a) the buyer
b) the seller
c) both the buyer and the seller
d) to be settled by mutual agreement

18. An instrument which requires recordation to be legally effective is a/an:

a) mechanic's lien
b) agreement to sell real estate
c) will
d) deed

19. When an owner pays a contractor in full and a notice of completion has been filed:

a) he can be sure that no mechanics' liens will be filed against him
b) he can avoid a mechanic's lien by filing a notice of completion
c) he may be held responsible if the contractor failed to pay sucontractors or material suppliers
d) None of the above

20. The final payment of a new construction loan is made to the contractor:

a) when the notice of completion is recorded
b) when the lien period expires
c) when the owner acknowledges and accepts the work
d) 60 days after the notice of completion is recorded

21. After selling on a conditional sales contract, a builder discovered that the buyer was having the home painted another color. In order to protect himself against possible liens, the builder could:

a) warn the painters he would not be responsible
b) file a Lis Pendens
c) file a notice of completion
d) post a notice of non-responsibility and record it

22. Mr. and Mrs. Davis, tenants, decide to have their apartment redecorated on June 15th. Contractor Jones says he will do the job for $4,000 and informs Smith (property owner) by registered letter the job will be completed by June 30th. Upon completion, Davis tells Jones to see Smith for payment.

a) Smith is not liable since he did not contract with Jones.
b) Smith may be liable since he had notice and did nothing.
c) Smith is not liable since his wife signed for the registered letter.
d) Mr. and Mrs. Davis only are liable.

23. Smith owned a home subject to a bank loan, secured by a trust deed and note. After living there a year, his cesspool caved in and he contracted to have a new one dug and connected. About that time, he lost his job and couldn't pay the bill. The contractor filed a mechanic's lien. Then the bank foreclosed and sold the property for the amount the borrower owed them. Which of the following is true?

a) The bank secured title subject to the mechanic's lien
b) The contractor loses out, as his lien although valid, cannot be satisfied and Smith is insolvent
c) The machanic's lien has first priority from the proceeds of the sale
d) Holders of mechanic's liens can never recover from a foreclosure sale

24. Johnson helped dig a sewage ditch for property owner Smith on February 21 and 22. On March 9, a mortgage was recorded against the property. On March 11, still unpaid, Johnson filed a mechanic's lien of record. Which of the following is true?

a) The bank's mortgage lien was recorded first and has priority over the mechanic's lien
b) The mechanic's lien could have priority over the mortgage lien if the owner had failed to record a notice of non-responsibility
c) The mechanic's second lien status precludes a foreclosure action by Johnson
d) The mechanic's lien has priority over the mortgage lien

25. If debtor owns three pieces of real estate and a judgment is entered against him, it will be a lien against:

a) the property first acquired
b) the property last acquired
c) all three properties
d) homestead property only

26. A judgment takes effect from the time the:

a) materials were first delivered
b) verdict is rendered
c) judgment is recorded
d) writ of execution is obtained

27. Lewis entered a judgment of $12,800 January seventh against Brown, who owns a tract of land. Brown gave a mortgage for $22,500 to Carlson on January twenty-third. The mortgage is in default by August second, and Brown agrees to deed the property to Carlson in satisfaction of the mortgage debt.

I. The deed is void
II. Carlson will take the property subject to the judgment of Lewis

a) I only
b) II only
c) Both I and II
d) Neither I nor II

28. Judgments are enforced by a process known as:

a) execution
b) enforcement
c) attachment
d) any of these

29. Which of the following is a recorded notice of a pending lawsuit?

a) Ad valorem
b) Nolo contendre
c) Lis pendens
d) Prima facie

30. When at the commencement of a legal action, a plaintiff asks the court to confiscate certain property belonging to the defendant, to act as security for the satisfaction of the judgment he's seeking, the plaintiff is asking the court to issue a:

a) garnishment
b) writ of possession
c) writ of attachment
d) none of these

31. In distinguishing between an attachment and a judgment lien, the:

a) first must cover all property held by an owner
b) first is recorded after a court decision
c) second is recorded prior to a court decision
d) latter is recorded after a court decision

32. The law, in all states, that bars legal claims beyond a certain time is known as the:

a) Doctrine of Limited Use
b) Statute of Frauds
c) Statute of Limitations
d) Uniform Commercial Code

33. Certain documents must be acknowledged before they can be recorded. To acknowledge means:

a) to admit or declare that you signed a document
b) to make an affidavit
c) to authenticate the contents of a document
d) None of the above

34. Who's signature must be acknowledged for the document to be recorded?

a) Lessor
b) Grantee
c) Lessee
d) Lessor and lessee

35. A sold his home to B; B did not record his deed but moved in. A then sold to C who examined the county auditor's records, but did not inspect the property. C recorded his deed. Therefore:

a) title vests in C
b) B will maintain title
c) B and C have equal rights of ownership
d) priority of recordation prevails

36. Among purchasers for value and without notice, the first to record is the first in right. Of the following, which would not be classified as a bona fide purchaser without notice?

a) A person buying unoccupied land from the last recorded owner
b) A person buying a residence occupied by the grantor who is also the present owner of record
c) A person buying a residence without inspection of the premises
d) A person buying a vacant store building from the recorded owner

37. Which of the following has priority of claim over an already recorded trust deed?

a) Divorce decree
b) Judgment lien
c) Unpaid property taxes
d) None of the above

38. A property tax lien has priority against other interest in property:

a) according to date lien was recorded
b) regardless when it becomes lien of record
c) on the basis of when the tax law passes
d) only if owner agrees to assume the debt

39. If two trust deeds were in existence on the same property and you wished to find out which one was the first trust deed and which was the second trust deed, you could secure this information at the county auditor's office. The priority is usually established by:

a) the printed trust deed forms which have the words "first trust deed" or "second trust deed" on the face
b) the date and time of recordation
c) the county auditor's stamp "first trust deed" or "second trust deed"
d) the execution date of each trust deed

40. A lot owner started building a home and ran out of money. To complete it, he borrowed $2,000 from a friend, giving him a first trust deed which was at once recorded. Later he got into a dispute with the contractor who paved the driveway, and the latter filed a mechanic's lien, which:

a) had priority over the trust deed note as work on the house had started when note was given and recorded
b) lacked priority over the trust deed as it was subsequently recorded
c) had priority as this is always true of a mechanic's lien
d) lacked priority because paving was not a part of the house

41. Creating an easement means:

a) restricting the style or cost of a house which can be built in a subdivision of lots
b) placing a dwelling over your property line onto another's property
c) giving someone the right, advantage or privilege to use your land
d) None of these

42. The acquired legal interest, short of an estate, for use of or enjoyment of the property owned by another is known as:

a) easement
b) lease
c) deed
d) riparian rights

43. Which of these is not a characteristic of an easement?

a) It is an interest that can be protected against interference by third persons
b) It is capable of being created by conveyance
c) It is considered a non-possessory interest
d) It is an interest that can be terminated at will by the possessor of the land

44. An easement lies outside of and adjacent to a parcel of land. The land benefitted is:

a) the dominant tenement
b) the servient tenement
c) a fee simple estate
d) the land on which the easement lies

45. Jones and Smith owned adjoining tracts of land. There was a 30-foot access easement running the full length of Smith's property on the contiguous side. Smith allowed Jones to use it any time he wished. The burdened owner was:

a) Smith, servient tenant
b) Jones, the dominant tenant
c) Smith, the dominant tenant
d) Jones, the servient tenant

46. Which one of the following is true?

a) An easement is an encumbrance to the dominant tenement
b) An easement is appurtenant to the servient tenement
c) An easement is appurtenant to the dominant tenement
d) All of the foregoing are true statements

47. An easement in gross may be defined as:

a) an easement that Smith has over Williams' property
b) a public easement that all persons have over your land
c) an easement that a public utility company has over your land
d) All of the foregoing

48. A gross easement benefits:

a) the dominant tenant
b) the dominant tenement
c) Both of the above
d) Neither of the above

49. One of the following is an example of a gross easement.

a) In selling some of his land near the highway, an owner retains the right of access to the road for the remainder of his property
b) An owner sells lake-front property, but retains right to fish in the lake
c) A community driveway serving more than four properties
d) None of the above

50. All of the following statements pertaining to easements are correct except:

a) a lessee may create an easement across the leased property for the benefit of a third party for the duration of the lease
b) an easement can be created by dedication
c) a deed to an unlocated easement is invalid
d) an easement may be created by prescription in the state of Washington if the property is used openly for a period of ten years

51. One morning at breakfast, the family saw a telephone pole being placed in the rear of their yard. On calling the telephone company, they were informed that the original subdivider had recorded an easement for their benefit along the rear of all lots. On checking the deed, Father found no reference to the telephone company, but it recited, 'subject to easements and rights of way of record'. The easement was:

a) ineffective as it was over ten years old
b) valid because the area needed telephones
c) invalid because the deed did not specifically mention it
d) valid because an easement of record is sufficient notice to purchasers

52. Mr. Jones, by deed, held an appurtenant easement over Mr. Smith's property giving him the right to run a sewer line across Smith's land. Mr. Jones sells his lot to Mr. Jacobs but does not mention the easement in his deed. The easement:

a) is lost by prescription
b) reverts to Mr. Smith
c) goes with the property to Mr. Jacobs
d) is reatined by Mr. Jones

53. An easement can be created by all of the following except:

a) deed
b) implication of law
c) orally
d) prescription

54. Which of the following is not a method of acquiring an easement?

a) Prescription
b) Grant deed
c) Statutory dedication
d) Trust deed

55. Prescription most nearly means gaining an easement by:

a) agreement
b) succession
c) deed
d) open and notorious use for a statutory period of time

56. If one obtained an easement through prescription, the least likely requirement would be:

a) hostile to the true owner
b) open and notorious use
c) exclusive use
d) pay assessments and property taxes for period of time

57. The creation of an easement by prescription is analogous to acquiring ownership of property by:

a) adverse possession
b) assessed value
c) alluvium
d) succession

58. Mr. Brown owned two pieces of property and sold the property on the road to Mr. Jones, reserving in the deed an easement for access to the rear property for himself. Brown did not use the easement for more than ten years, and Mr. Jones claims Mr. Brown no longer has an easement because of non-use.

a) The easement was invalid because any easement not used for ten years is lost
b) The easement was still valid because non-use can never terminate an easement
c) Mr. Jones could sue for quiet title action on the easement and would probably be successful
d) The easement was still valid

59. Which of the following is generally true of easements?

a) Created by verbal agreement
b) Cannot be revoked
c) Are of temporary duration
d) Are purely personal rights and do not run with the land

60. An easement that has been acquired by prescription may be terminated or extinguished by:

a) merger
b) written agreement
c) non-use
d) All of these

61. Jones has an easement appurtenant over Smith's property. Jones buys Smith's property. Which of the following is correct:

a) The easement goes with the land
b) The easement is unaffected
c) The easement is dissolved
d) All of the foregoing

62. A right to use another's land, which may be revoked and does not run with the land, is considered to be:

a) an easement
b) an easement in gross
c) a license
d) None of the above

63. A man bought a house in a hurry and, after escrow closed, discovered that two years before, a neighbor had built a fence that was three feet over the property line on his side. The broker was unaware of this. If the two neighbors were unable to reach an amicable settlement, the:

a) sale would be invalid
b) buyer could sue the neighbor for encroachment based on trespass
c) neighbor had acquired title by adverse possession
d) buyer could sue the broker

64. Bill Miser builds a bridge across a stream. Although the entire stream is contained within the property, the anchorings of the bridge extended onto his neighbor's land. This is known as:

a) a party wall
b) an encroachment
c) an easement
d) adverse possession

65. Brown recorded a subdivision map in 1936 and also recorded a declaration of restrictions to run for fifty years for the benefit of lot owners. In 1974, Black bought one of the lots and violated the twenty-foot set-back provision. The other owners in the tract were upset about it. Relief through court action may be sought with reasonable possibility of success by:

a) only the owners of lots contiguous to Black's
b) any present lot owner in the tract
c) any lot owner who bought direct from Brown
d) no owner, as restrictions outlaw after twenty years

66. The penalty regarding violations of covenants and conditions would be:

a) the same of covenants as conditions under most circumstances
b) more severe regarding the condition
c) more severe regarding the covenant
d) the same under all conditions

67. Conditions and covenants differ in that:

a) conditions can only be imposed by deed
b) covenants can only be imposed by deed
c) conditions are created by the government
d) conditions run with the land

68. A parcel of land (ten lots) is plotted and sold with the deed restriction that the property "may only be used for residential development." Later a buyer wishes to purchase a house on one of the lots as a residence, with one of the rooms to become a barber shop. This is probably permissible if:

a) eight of the ten lots are now used for commercial purposes
b) eight out of ten of the property owners are willing to agree to such use
c) the area has just been rezoned
d) None of the above

69. A deed restriction in a subdivision is normally put into effect by the:

a) FHA
b) developer
c) local building inspector
d) planning commission

70. By experience, which restrictions in a subdivision have been found least effective and hardest to enforce?

a) Maximum height of improvements
b) Minimum lot size
c) Minimum square footage of improvements
d) Minimum cost of improvements on each lot

71. "CC&R's" as used in the real estate industry refer to:

a) the Federal Housing Commissioner
b) Department of Public Works Construction Certificate
c) a certificate of value
d) private restrictions

72. As contained in a deed, a covenant:

a) binds all subsequent grantees
b) can be classified as subsequent or precedent to vesting of the estate
c) is the same as an easement
d) can require title reversion to grantor on grantee's violation of the covenant

73. The best way to impose restrictions on a large subdivision is to:

a) publish them in a newspaper of general circulation
b) include them as covenants in each deed
c) record them as specified by law – refer to them in the deed
d) post them on the property

74. Which of the following can run with the land?

a) Covenants
b) Easements
c) Mutual Water Co. stock
d) All of the above

75. Bates developed a subdivision in 1940. Each deed to the purchaser contained a restriction "no building except a private dwelling house shall be erected on said lot". Curtis, a purchaser of two lots, sold them to Bacon in 1977. On February 21, 1978, Bacon started to excavate for the erection of a four-story garden type apartment building. Since 1960, the street had been widened to a four lane artery, a pony league baseball park has been built across the street, flanked by several business establishments. Under these circumstances:

I the apartment building will be permitted
II the apartment building will be permitted upon damages in favor of the protesting property owners

a) I only
b) II only
c) Both I and II
d) Neither I nor II

76. An order of a court prohibiting or compelling an act of a real property owner is called a(n):

a) judgment lien
b) restriction
c) attachment
d) injunction

1. a) This is a good definition of an encumbrance.

2. a) Encumbrances affect either the owner's title or the manner in which he may use his property. Non-financial encumbrances, such as easements, zoning ordinances or private restrictions, affect his use of the property. Financial encumbrances (liens) affect the title — meaning an owner cannot sell his property free and clear of the debt(s).

3. c) All encumbrances can affect or relate to the title of an owner's property in the sense that, although the owner is able to sell his property when encumbered, the purchaser takes the property subject to each and every encumbrance. Encumbrances such as easements or zoning regulations affect the physical use of the property.

4. c) Any restriction, regardless of who it benefits, is an encumbrance as it restricts the rights of the owners and any future owners.

5. b) A lien is a financial encumbrance. Since an easement is a right to use the real property of another, it does not constitute a financial interest in real property.

6. d) A specific lien affects one parcel of property only. A general lien can affect all property owned by a debtor. This means that in the event the owner fails to meet his financial obligations (as evidenced by the lien), a forced sale of his property can be provoked in order to satisfy his debt. If the lien was specific, such as mortgages, mechanics' liens, special assessments and property taxes, only the specific property acting as security for the debt may be sold; any other property he owns remains unaffected. If the lien was general, like I.R.S. and judgment liens, any or all of his property is subject to a forced sale.

7. d) Even a blanket lien only affects certain parcels of land and not necessarily all the property the debtor owns. A general lien can encumber all the property a debtor owns (and subsequently acquires) in every county of every state.

8. a) Mortgages and deeds of trust are voluntary liens. At the same time the property owner receives the loan, he voluntarily gives the bank a lien on his property to act as security for the loan. Mechanics' liens and property tax liens are involuntary, specific liens.

9. c) The property owner voluntarily contracts with a prospective purchaser and receives consideration for the option contract. An option contract is an encumbrance since any transaction involving the property is "burdened" by the right of the holder of the option to purchase the property within the time and price specifications of the option contract.

10. b) Hypothecate is defined as to give something as security without the necessity of giving up possession of it. There is no such word as apothecate. To pledge is to use something as security and also give up possession. In Washington, as well as most states, real property is always hypothecated.

11. b) Municipal functions are paid out of general property taxes and include schools, police, fire departments, etc. An assessment is a "one-time" tax for a specific public service such as sewer installation.

12. d) If a property tax is unpaid, the tax can be satisfied only from the sale of the specific property upon which the tax was levied. The only voluntary liens are mortgages and deeds of trust.

13. b) The assessed value of property is the County Assessor's determination of one hundred percent of the true and fair market value of the property.

14. a) Ad valorem means according to value - the higher the value the higher the amount of tax.

15. b) By state law, the county assessor is required to assess all taxable property within the county at one hundred percent of its true and fair market value.

16. d) Because it's for a particular property's or properties' benefit only, it's called a special assessment. Only the property benefitted by the street paving is billed for the cost of the work. An assessment is commonly charged according to the property's front footage, and not its value (ad valorem).

17. b) Generally, it is the seller's responsibility to discharge all encumbrances against the property and deliver clear title to the purchaser, but either party could pay the assessment (the government doesn't care who pays it). If the owner of the property refuses to pay, the county could force a sale of the property to satisfy its specific involuntary lien.

18. a) A mechanic's lien does not exist unless it is recorded within the time specified by law. The mechanic's lien is one of the few documents that must be recorded to be legally effective. Some others include a limited partnership agreement, satisfaction of mortgage and deed of reconveyance.

19. c) The general contractor is the property owner's agent and principals are responsible for the acts of their agents. If the general contractor failed to pay the subcontractors, laborers or suppliers, the owner is vulnerable to the mechanic's liens that are filed within the statutory period (ninety days). The owner could, of course, sue the contractor for damages.

20. b) The final payment is frequently withheld until after the lien period has expired so as to cover the cost of any valid mechanic's liens filed during the lien period.

21. d) The notice can be posted on the site (actual notice) or recorded (constructive notice).

22. b) Smith must pay the contractor. He may, however, take legal action against Davis. Smith should have filed a notice of nonresponsibility as soon as he learned the work was being done.

23. b) The trust deed and note held by the bank has priority over the mechanic's lien because it was recorded first and there were no excess funds after foreclosing.

24. d) The labor was provided before the mortgage lien was filed of record. It is the date of the labor, not the date the mechanic's lien was recorded, that determines priority.

25. c) A judgment lien is a general, involuntary lien, affecting all properties owned by a debtor in the county where the judgment was rendered, as well as any he acquires subsequent to the judgment.

26. c) From the moment the judgment is recorded in the clerk's office, it constitutes a lien on all real property of the judgment debtor in that county.

27. b) There is no law against transferring an interest in property encumbered by a judgment. However, the new owner, Carlson, takes the property subject to Lewis' judgment lien.

28. a) When a judgment is rendered, a lien is created on the debtor's property. If payment of the debt is not forthcoming, the creditor can ask the court to order the sale of the property to satisfy the debt. The court's order is called a writ of execution.

29. c) A lis pendens is a written notice filed in the public records for the purpose of preventing any sale of the property which would otherwise thwart the purpose of a pending lawsuit. A lis pendens and a writ of attachment have the same effect; the difference is in who files them. A writ of attachment is an order from the court ordering the county sheriff to file, and a lis pendens is filed by the plaintiff or the plaintiff's attorney.

30. c) The writ of attachment is sought so as to lien the property of the defendant pending the outcome of the lawsuit. A writ of attachment is a lien.

31. d) Attachment is when property is seized and held as security for satisfaction of a judgment yet to be secured. A judgment lien is created by recording the final order of a court as the result of a lawsuit.

32. c) The policy of the law (Statute of Limitations) is against those who "sleep upon their rights". The law specifies the period of time in which an action must be brought in a court of law. If a creditor fails to act within this period, he is barred by the Statute of Limitations.

33. a) An acknowledgment is a declaration, witnessed by a notary public, that the declarant did sign a document.

34. a) The party giving the interest has a name which always ends in "or". Examples: grantor, mortgagor, vendor, optionor, lessor, etc.

35. b) By being in possession of the property, B has imparted constructive notice to the world of his interest in the property. The law assumes a buyer will inquire of anyone in possession as to what that party's claim to the land is.

36. c) The purchaser is not "bona fide" when he has not inspected the premises; after all, a party in possession imparts constructive notice to the world of some claim to the possession or ownership of the premises.

37. c) Property taxes and assessments have priority, always. That is why most lenders require them to be paid promptly when due.

38. b) Property taxes and special assessments have priority over other liens of record.

39. b) The priority of trust deeds is set by the date of recording. The trust deed recorded first will be the first trust deed, and any subsequent recorded trust deeds would be junior trust deeds.

40. a) This is a good thing to remember if you lend money on a property where construction has already started. Work that has been done or materials that have been supplied have priority for payment over a subsequently recorded mortgage or trust deed – even though the laborer or supplier doesn't file the mechanic's lien of record until after the mortgage/trust deed is recorded.

41. c) However, title to the land is not granted when an easement is created, only use rights regarding the land.

42. a) This is a common definition of the term. An estate is the right to possess and have exclusive use of land. An easement interest is not as great an interest in the land as is an estate interest because the easement right is limited to some specific use, such as ingress and egress, while an estate brings with it the right to exclusive possession and use. The key words in the question are, "short of an estate". A leasehold interest is an estate.

43. d) The possessor or owner of the land is the servient tenant, and this party cannot simply terminate the easement rights of the dominant tenant.

44. a) The dominant tenement benefits from the easement. The servient tenement is burdened (encumbered) by it.

45. a) Jones was benefited by the easement, Smith burdened by Jones' use of it.

46. c) If the dominant tenant sells his land, the easement appurtenant (a right incidental to owning the land) transfers with it. The easement is an encumbrance to the servient tenement.

47. c) Easements in gross are personal rights not attached to any specific piece of land, yet they encumber the land. Easements in gross have no dominant tenements and the most common form is the public utility easement. It should be noted, there is a dominant tenant – in this case, the public utility company – but no dominant tenement.

48. a) A dominant tenant has the right to use the servient tenant's land. It doesn't matter whether it is an easement appurtenant or easement in gross. Remember, there is no dominant tenement with an easement in gross.

49. b) Alternatives a) and c) refer to easements that serve dominant tenements. This is not the case with b). When the former owner (dominant tenant) dies, the easement in gross is extinguished. Also the former owner cannot assign his easement rights to anyone else.

50. c) The mere fact that the deed refers to an easement in an area that cannot be located does not necessarily invalidate the deed. The easement could be in an area that has not been properly mapped or finalized. The easement would still exist and would become effective when the exact location has been spotted.

51. d) The family was put on notice by the reference in the deed, and the easement was good. It is customary not to specifically recite all of the easements in the deed. It is up to the family to check the records if they are interested.

52. c) An easement appurtenant, created by deed, is said to run with the land. Once created, no mention need be made of it in future conveyances.

53. c) Any interest in real estate in the state of Washington, other than a leasehold of less than one year in duration, must be in writing to be enforceable.

54. d) A deed of trust, like a mortgage, is a financial lien and does not create an easement.

55. d) An easement acquired by prescription is gained without the knowledge of the landowner, or with the owner's knowledge but not his approval.

56. d) Under an easement acquired through prescription, it is not necessary to pay the taxes and assessments for the prescriptive period. This payment is only necessary when you are acquiring title by adverse possession.

57. a) Analogous means resembling or comparable in certain respects. An easement gained by prescription resembles adverse possession except that, under adverse possession, one may gain title to real property and not an easement. All of the essential requisites are present in both cases, except the adverse possessor must also pay the taxes for the statutory period and, in most cases, have "color of title".

58. d) Easements are normally created by deed or agreement by implication of law, or by virtue of long use. Those created by deed or agreement "run with the land" and are not lost by non-use unless it specifically states so in the agreement.

59. b) Easements cannot be revoked. Most easements are appurtenant and run with the land, the dominant tenement. The owner of the servient tenement cannot revoke the easement right.

60. d) Any easement can be terminated by merger or written agreement. Any prescriptive easement can be terminated in the same way it was created: by prescription. "Merger" means the dominant tenements fall under one ownership.

61. c) The easement is dissolved by merger of ownership. One may not have an easement in his own property.

62. c) The key phrase here is, "may be revoked". Easements are not revocable; licenses are.

63. b) The fence is an encroachment. The encroachment could ripen into an easement, or even title, if the requisites for a prescriptive easement or adverse possession are met by the party guilty of encroachment.

64. b) Any improvement that intrudes on the land of another is an encroachment.

65. b) Any present lot owner can sue to enforce the restrictions, whether or not he was an original buyer. Such restrictions are enforceable for the period of time specified, or until public policy prohibits their enforcement, or until conditions have changed so drastically that to enforce the restriction would not serve the purpose originally intended.

66. b) A covenant is a promise within an agreement and, if broken, the remedy is for money damages. A condition, in the strict legal sense, usually means a loss of title when violated.

67. a) Conditions and covenants are private restrictions that run with the land. The only way a condition can be created is by the grantor in a deed, whereas covenants can be created by private deed or in a declaration of restrictions filed by a developer.

68. a) If the original purpose of the restriction can no longer be achieved, courts generally won't enforce them. Note that with choice (b), the original purpose may still be obtainable, in which case all of the property owners must agree to the new use.

69. b) The developer is the seller—the grantor. He will invariably draft a set of restrictions—called a declaration of restrictions—to assure uniformity of property use in his subdivision. He does this to satisfy prospective purchasers that there will be ongoing homogeneity and continuity of land use in the development throughout their period of ownership.

70. d) Courts are reluctant to force property owners to spend a certain amount of money. Consider, too, the problem of enforcement when a person desires to improve their home by their own effort, or the effect that inflation would have on "minimum cost" restrictions.

71. d) "CC&R's" refer to covenants, conditions and restrictions of record. Covenants and conditions are private restrictions—imposed on grantees by grantors—while zoning ordinances, building codes and fire regulations are public restrictions.

72. a) But note: only the grantor or other grantees can enforce the covenant. Choices (b) and (d) refer to conditions, not a covenant.

73. c) Most often, each individual's deed will only refer back to any conditions, covenants or restrictions of record. The developer will initially record his declaration of restrictions and then refer to them in each deed given.

74. d) The term run with the land means "to go with the land". If title passes, existing covenants, easements and stock in a mutual water company will be part of the transfer and will go with the title.

75. a) In situations like these, the court will exercise some judicial discretion. Where the purpose of the original restriction is no longer achieveable, the courts will not enforce the restrictions. In this instance, the residential character of the neighborhood has been destroyed and the restriction no longer serves a useful purpose.

76. d) This is the definition of an injunction. If the injunction is not complied with, the person may be found in contempt of court and punished by a fine, imprisonment, or both.

6. Public Restrictions on Land

1. Although a property owner is said to have a "bundle of rights" in his property, these rights are limited by three powers of government. Which of the following is not one of the three powers?

   a) Eminent domain
   b) Condemnation
   c) Police power
   d) Taxation

2. Smith wants to turn his garage into a small furniture factory. He applies to the City Planning Commission, and his request for a variance is denied. He may:

   a) start his furniture factory
   b) sue in Federal District Court
   c) appeal to the City Council
   d) sue the chairman of the planning commission

3. The type of structure that an owner can build can be controlled by:

   a) zoning
   b) deed restrictions
   c) Both A and B
   d) Neither A nor B

4. A zoning regulation permits a specific use of the property, but the deed contains a restriction limiting the use of the property. In such a case, which prevails?

   a) Deed restrictions
   b) Zoning variance
   c) Master zoning law
   d) Building code

5. Owners of a home decided to build a six foot fence around their lot since they own a dog and want him to have run of the property. Before building this fence, the owners should carefully check applicable:

   a) restrictions
   b) zoning regulations
   c) esthetic requirements of non-coterminus landowners
   d) Both A and B

6. An area of land set off by municipal authorities for a specific use is called a:

   a) cul de sac
   b) subdivision
   c) zone
   d) territory

7. The primary reason for zoning is to:

   a) control the physical conditions of buildings
   b) control the number of similar businesses
   c) contribute to the public's health, safety and welfare
   d) insure the conformity of like structures in the area

8. Zoning would most likely cover:

   a) methods of financing
   b) size of buildings and architectural styles
   c) use and setbacks
   d) racial restrictions

9. In zoning, a use established after passage of a zoning ordinance, and in violation of it, is called:

   a) a non-conforming use
   b) a variance
   c) illegal
   d) spot zoning

10. Application for a change in zoning so as to permit intended use by buyer should be made by:

    a) broker
    b) seller
    c) purchaser
    d) broker and purchaser

11. Where zoning precludes the intended use of the premises under contract of sale, the objection might be overcome by obtaining a/an:

    a) order of court
    b) variance
    c) non-conforming use
    d) hardship permit

12. You list an old home on a corner in an older residential area. The home has an addition on the front which has been used as a small neighborhood grocery store but which has been vacant for some time. Your prospect wants to re-establish the grocery business and wants to know if there is anything to prohibit it.

    a) You can assure him it is permitted as it has recently been used as a grocery store
    b) It is permissible as there is a similar store two blocks away
    c) You should check with the zoning authorities as the business may have been a hold-over when the area was re-zoned
    d) You can assure buyer it is O.K. as the seller would know if a business could not be started

13. An officially-appointed group that studies city growth and recommends zoning policies is called a:

    a) city growth board
    b) master zoning board
    c) city policy commission
    d) planning commission

14. Members of the City and County Planning Commissions:

    a) are elective officers
    b) are appointed in cities, elected in counties
    c) are required by law to have experience in real estate subdivision
    d) are authorized to make recommendations to city council or board of supervisors regarding subdivisions

15. Some communities, rather than strictly prescribing the height, setback and side yard requirements for buildings, have enacted ordinances allowing for an alternate method, which is known as the:

    a) modified zoning plan
    b) variance system
    c) restricted ordinance method
    d) floor area ratio method

16. A land use in existence at the time a zoning ordinance is adopted or amended that does not conform to the new or amended ordinance is called a/an:

    a) non-conforming use
    b) ipso facto compliance
    c) variance
    d) None of these

17. Where zoning applies to a particular piece of property in such a way as to virtually preclude its use, thus causing the owner undue hardship, the owner can seek which of the following in pursuit of relief?

    a) Special exception permit
    b) Conditional use exception
    c) Non-conforming use exemption
    d) Variance

18. There are situations when a special use is necessary for the community welfare but is not permitted within the applicable zone, as with some churches or schools. To put property to use in such a way, the owner must first obtain a:

    a) conditional use permit
    b) variance
    c) non-conforming use
    d) zoning modification

19. A property owner wants to build a duplex on his vacant lot. The applicable zoning permits such a building. However, the private restrictions which affect the property prohibit any structures other than single family dwellings. Which of the following is true?

a) Government ordinances prevail over private restrictions; the duplex may be built
b) Private restrictions are superior to government ordinances in most instances, and for this reason the duplex may not be built
c) Whether or not the duplex can be built depends on whether the zoning ordinance predates the private restrictions
d) The duplex cannot be built because the more prohibitive of the two restrictions (public or private) will rule

20. Jones owns some property which the city desires for the purpose of widening the street. Jones refuses to sell, so the city takes the land anyway and compensates Jones. This process is called:

a) eminent domain
b) adverse possession
c) condemnation
d) police power

21. Against his will, farmer Malden was forced to sell his land in order that a municipal dam could be built. The principle which justifies this is known as:

a) lis pendens
b) caveat emptor
c) eminent domain
d) adverse possession

22. Mr. Marshall buys a home on the outskirts of a residential area. The city administrators approach Mr. Marshall and his neighbors to take some of their frontage for the purpose of widening the streets. Mr. Marshall refuses. The city administrators initiate condemnation proceedings. They take the property and compensate Mr. Marshall pursuant to court order. This would most properly be described as an exercise of:

a) forfeiture
b) severance
c) eminent domain
d) police power

23. Which of these is associated with the right of eminent domain?

a) Subdivision regulations
b) Severance damages
c) Building codes
d) None of these

24. If a railroad company needs to extend its property ownership beyond its present lines, it may get the needed land by:

a) eminent domain
b) injunction
c) writ of attachment
d) writ of execution

25. The authority to enact zoning ordinances comes from:

a) state legislature
b) eminent domain
c) state's rights
d) police power

26. The difference between police power and eminent domain can best be determined by:

a) whether or not the action was by sovereign power or by statute
b) whether or not any compensation was paid to the owner
c) whether or not the improvements are to be razed
d) whether or not the owner's use was affected

27. An example of police power would be:

a) enforcement of health ordinances
b) zoning
c) building code enforcement
d) All of the foregoing

28. The power of the state to license brokers and salesmen is an exercise of:

a) police power
b) eminent domain
c) state's rights
d) executive power

29. An action which results from the physical invasion of property by a governmental agency which damages the property, or the government regulation of property, such as planning or zoning, which restricts development of the property to the point where the owner can make no reasonable use of the property is referred to as a:

a) partition suit
b) specific performance action
c) interpleader proceeding
d) inverse condemnation action

30. Police and fire protection are examples of services paid for by:

a) special assessments
b) general property taxes
c) improvement taxes
d) Both A and B

31. Once levied, general real estate taxes become:

a) specific, voluntary liens
b) general, involuntary liens
c) specific, involuntary liens
d) general, voluntary liens

32. General property taxes are sometimes called ad valorem taxes because:

a) the amount of the tax is proportionate to the value of the property
b) the rate of taxation varies from one taxing district to the next
c) property taxes are used to pay for public services and "valorem" is latin for public benefit
d) they benefit specific landowners and are not uniformly assessed

33. An owner's share of a special assessment is determined by:

a) the value of his property in relation to surrounding properties
b) the cost of the special improvement
c) the assessment rate as set by the legislature
d) the area of land or the number of front feet contained in the parcel

1. b) The three powers are eminent domain, police power and taxation.

2. c) The City Planning Commission is an appointed body that recommends to the City Council, the elected body of city officials. You may appeal to the City Council when denied by the Planning Commission the right to do something.

3. c) Both public (zoning) and private (deed) restrictions may affect the use to which a property owner may put his land.

4. a) A deed restriction in this situation will prevail over a zoning regulation. Any reasonable deed restriction may be enforced by the original grantor or heirs, regardless if the city zoning laws permit a broader use of the property. Whichever (of the zoning or deed restriction) is more restrictive, is the applicable restriction which must be complied with.

5. d) Both private deed restrictions and public zoning regulations will apply, and the more restrictive of the two will be controlling over any uses to which the property owner may wish to put his land.

6. c) This is a definition of zoning.

7. c) This is the reason the government becomes involved in such matters.

8. c) It is difficult for the local government to try to impose a certain architectural style; racial restrictions are against the discrimination laws; the method of financing is not a concern of the government, since the public "health, safety and welfare" is not at stake.

9. c) Unless a 'variance' is granted by the local government, the use would be illegal and could be prevented by the government, but not by private citizens.

10. b) Only the seller has the existing legal interest (namely, ownership of the land) necessary to request a zoning change. Also, the buyer doesn't want to purchase the land, apply for the zoning change, and find his petition turned down.

11. b) A variance will be granted where the owner can show a reasonable need for the change, balancing his "hardship" against the needs of the local community.

12. c) Sometimes when an area is rezoned, they permit a non-conforming use to continue, but will not allow it to be revived after discontinuance.

13. d) This is the definition. Such a group will adopt a "master plan" for the locality.

14. d) This is a statement of fact.

15. d) F.A.R. (floor area ratio) is a regulation of the ratio between the area of building floor space and the area of the lot it occupies.

16. a) This is a nonconforming use and is permitted to remain.

17. d) An owner can seek a variance from the local zoning authority if he feels it is unjust and that his private injury far outweighs the benefit of strict enforcement of the zoning.

18. a) Schools and churches are common examples of conditional uses.

19. d) The most restrictive of the two prevails. If the private restrictions had allowed the building but the zoning prohibited it, it could not be built.

20. c) The process is condemnation. The right of the government to condemn is known as eminent domain.

21. c) Eminent domain refers to the government's right to take private property for public use. Eminent domain is the right, condemnation is the process.

22. c) Eminent domain is the right of the government to take private land, but unlike the exercised government's police power, the government must compensate the property owner when they take the property.

23. b) Severance damages refer to any loss in value to property retained by a landowner after the government has taken what it needs. For example, Smith owned ten acres of industrial land worth about $50,000 an acre. The city takes seven acres. The remaining acres are now valued at $35,000 an acre because the smaller area of land is not as useful. Smith is entitled not only to compensation for the land taken, but for the loss in value to the land left him.

24. a) The right of eminent domain can be extended to private corporations whose functions serve the public good. Railroads, airports, seaports, and public utility companies are often granted the right of eminent domain for some specific purpose.

25. d) The government's right to regulate the use of private property stems from the police power of the government. Eminent domain refers to the government's right to take private property for the public good. Police power is the government's right to regulate private property to insure the health, safety and welfare of the public.

26. b) The use of property is affected by both government powers, but only when the right of eminent domain is exercised is compensation to the property owner involved.

27. d) Police power is the right of the state to enact laws and enforce them for the order, safety, health, morals, and general welfare of the public. Another classic example of the state exercising its police power is in the area of licensing individuals who sell real estate.

28. a) The theory and purpose behind licensing brokers and salesmen is that such regulation serves the general welfare of the public.

29. d) An inverse condemnation action is an option available to a property owner who believes a government action has exceeded the police power and that his property has been taken without just compensation.

30. b) General property taxes support the general operation and services of government, such as police and fire protection. Schools are also funded by general property taxes.

31. c) General property taxes are specific in that they lien only the property being taxed, and they are involuntary in that they are levied without the owner's consent.

32. a) Ad valorem is a latin term meaning according to value. General property taxes are based on the value of the property; the greater the value, the higher the tax.

33. d) The theory is the parcel which benefits from a special improvement, like street lighting, increases in value proportionate to its size. So assessments are usually levied according to the number of square feet or front feet contained in the parcel. The larger the parcel, the greater its share of the total special assessment.

7. Contract Law

1. An agreement between two persons to do or not to do certain things is called a:

   a) declaration
   b) contract
   c) affidavit
   d) testament

2. Consideration is an essential element of valid contracts. Consideration may be:

   a) a promise
   b) the giving up of some legal right
   c) labor
   d) All of the above

3. In a listing agreement, the seller of real estate agrees to pay the broker a commission if the broker procures a buyer "ready, willing and able" to buy. In the agreement, the broker agrees to use due diligence in procuring a buyer. This agreement is a(n):

   a) bilateral contract
   b) unilateral contract
   c) agreement of sale
   d) deposit receipt

4. An executory contract is one which:

   a) is made by executor of an estate for the sale of probate property
   b) is yet to be performed
   c) has been completely performed
   d) has been proposed but not accepted by either party

5. A valid contract is best described by which of the following statements?

   a) A deliberate agreement between two or more parties, on legal consideration, to do or abstain from doing some act
   b) A deliberate agreement between competent parties to do or abstain from doing a legal act
   c) A deliberate agreement between competent parties, on legal consideration, to do or abstain from doing some legal act
   d) A deliberate agreement between two or more parties on legal consideration, to do or abstain from doing some legal act

6. Persons who lack capacity may:

   a) appoint a guardian to contract on their behalf
   b) appoint a guardian who cannot contract on their behalf but is limited only to supervising their activities
   c) contract, providing any agreement they enter into is ratified by the appointed guardian
   d) None of the above

7. Authority of a corporation to enter into real estate agreements lies with the:

   a) board of directors
   b) corporate attorney
   c) president and secretary
   d) duly appointed general manager

8. A salesman is sent to a local church, which is moving to a new location, to secure a listing. He is not sure who must sign the listing agreement. What must he do?

   a) Call the real estate office and ask his broker
   b) Have the church minister sign
   c) Consult the church by-laws
   d) Have the church minister and his wife sign

9. In order for a contract to be valid and binding, there must be:

a) mutuality
b) mutual assent
c) oofer and acceptance
d) All of the above

10. Once a definite offer is made, it:

a) cannot be withdrawn until acted upon by the other party
b) can be withdrawn at any time prior to notification of acceptance by offeree
c) can be withdrawn only after the forty-eight hour statute has expired
d) can't be withdrawn

11. A counteroffer:

a) terminates the original offer
b) will result in a valid contract if accepted by the other party
c) both of the above
d) neither of the above

12. Taylor signs an offer to purchase real property, but suddenly dies before the listing agent notifies him of the unqualified acceptance of his offer by the seller.

a) Taylor's death constitutes a revocation of the offer
b) The contract is binding on the heirs providing they are to be found financially capable
c) The contract is binding if the administrator is notified of the seller's acceptance prior to revoking the offer
d) both A and C

13. On October 2, a buyer made an offer, which he agreed to keep open for three days. The seller made a counter offer, which the buyer rejected. The seller then accepted the original offer. The contract is:

a) unenforceable
b) enforceable
c) void
d) invalid

14. Acceptance of an offer must be which of the following?

a) Absolute and unqualified
b) Expressed or communicated
c) Within time limits
d) All of the above

15. Which of the following is the definition of actual fraud?

a) Failure to disclose information which you have a duty to disclose
b) Entering a promise with no intent to fulfill
c) Devious practices in business
d) All of the above

16. Where there is a confidential or fiduciary relationship or one party has some special knowledge which the other cannot gain, false statements which are innocently made without an intent to deceive the other party may constitute:

a) actual fraud
b) constructive fraud
c) mistake of fact
d) none of the above

17. A contract signed under duress is:

a) voidable
b) void
c) illegal
d) invalid

18. Where one party to a contract was induced to sign under physical threat to his person, the contract is:

a) void
b) voidable
c) illegal
d) any of these

19. In order to be enforceable, a contract must:

a) be in writing
b) have a possible objective
c) both A and B
d) neither A nor B

20. A bilateral contract is one in which:

a) an offer is considered open until revoked
b) one party agrees to do several acts at different times
c) one party's promise is exchanged for the promise of another
d) one party's promise is exchanged for the action of another

21. A void contract is one that is:

a) not in writing
b) not enforceable by law
c) rescindable by agreement
d) amortized

22. After an earnest money has been signed by the purchaser, an alteration made by the broker is:

a) valid if initialed by broker
b) valid if intitaled by broker and seller
c) voidable by buyer
d) void

23. Voidable most nearly means:

a) unenforceable
b) fully performed by both parties
c) void
d) valid until rejected

24. A voidable contract becomes enforceable by:

a) ratification
b) novation
c) estoppel
d) None of the above

25. Taking unfair advantage of another's distress or weakness of mind is:

a) duress
b) fraud
c) undue influence
d) collusion

26. Which one of the following would be required for a valid contract of sale for real estate?

a) An acknowledgement
b) An insured title
c) A recorded instrument
d) An instrument in writing

27. An oral contract for the exchange of real estate is:

a) enforceable
b) unlawful
c) unenforceable
d) enforceable under specific provisions of the real estate law

28. One can execute a promise by:

a) novation
b) performance
c) accord and satisfaction
d) All of the above

29. When the parties to a contract put themselves in the same position they were in before they entered into a contract, the contract has been:

a) cancelled
b) rescinded
c) revoked
d) None of the above

30. The term "rescind" in real estate most nearly means:

a) rewritten
b) rejected
c) reworded
d) terminated

31. When the parties to a contract cease to take any further steps to carry out the contract, but past acts are not affected, the contract has been:

a) sold
b) rescinded
c) cancelled
d) None of the above

32. Which one of the following statements would be true with respect to the assignment of a lease?

a) The original lessee would still retain a right to use the property for a limited time
b) The original lessee is the sole party liable for the payment of the rent
c) It is the same as a sublease
d) The entire leasehold is transferred but the original lessee remains secondarily liable on the lease

33. The mutual agreement to substitute a new obligation for an old one is:

a) a mutual rescission
b) a novation
c) accord and satisfaction
d) an assignment

34. Failure to perform or fulfill a contract is termed a:

a) defect
b) novation
c) breach
d) delinquency

35. Failure to perform or fulfill a contract is termed:

a) delinquency
b) default
c) demise
d) liquidated damages

36 A sum agreed to be full damages if a certain event occurs is called:

a) just compensation
b) deficiency judgment
c) consideration
d) liquidated damages

37. If the buyer defaults and no provision is made in the contract for liquidated damages, the seller may sue:

a) for damages
b) for specific performance
c) Either
d) Neither

38. Jones agrees to buy Smith's property and they sign a valid contract. Smith refuses to perform one week later. Since Jones wants the property, his best course of action would most likely be:

a) rescission
b) money damages
c) specific performance
d) novation

39. An offer by one of the parties to the contract to carry out his part of the agreement is called:

a) estoppel
b) performance
c) tender
d) all of these

40. Tender of deed to the buyer is not necessary where:

I. time is of the essence of the agreement
II. there has been an anticipatory repudiation

a) I only
b) II only
c) Both I and II
d) Neither I nor II

41. Mr. Rees and Mrs. Best make an oral agreement concerning the sale of Mrs. Best's apple orchard. Such a contract would be unenforceable in a court of law because of the:

a) Statute of Frauds
b) Statute of Limitations
c) laws of agency
d) state licensing laws

42. An oral agreement of sale may be enforced where:

a) the consideration price is less than $2,500
b) there is a downpayment of twenty percent of the consideration
c) the purchaser has gone into possession, paid part of the purchase price, and made improvements
d) the broker guarantees performance

43. A valid earnest money agreement is:

a) an express, written, bilateral, executed contract
b) an implied, written, bilateral, executory contract
c) express, written, bilateral, executory contract
d) None of these

44. A properly drawn deposit receipt,which is signed by the prospective buyer of real property and is to be submitted to the seller, constitutes a/an:

a) offer
b) binding, enforceable contract
c) valid contract
d) all of these

45. The description of land sold under an agreement of sale should:

a) give the house number and street
b) give a full legal description
c) describe the improvements
d) be handwritten and signed

46. A contract of purchase or sale of real property should be signed by the:

a) broker
b) agent and seller
c) seller only
d) buyer and seller

47. A real estate listing is:

a) a list of all property held by one owner
b) employment of a broker by owner to sell or lease real property
c) a written list of improvements on the land
d) a rendition of property for taxation

48. An owner signed a listing with a broker where it was understood that if the property was sold through the efforts of any other broker, or the owner, the listing broker would not be entitled to a commission. This kind of contract is called:

a) a net listing
b) an exclusive agency listing
c) an exclusive right to sell listing
d) an open listing

49. Seller signs a non-exclusive listing agreement with a broker. Seller then sells the property himself and so notifies the broker. The listing agreement is:

a) voidable
b) enforceable
c) terminated
d) illegal

50. The type of listing affording a broker the least amount of protection is:

a) exclusive agency
b) net listing
c) open listing
d) exclusive right to sell

51. A broker is authorized to show property under terms of an open listing agreement. According to the terms of most open listing agreements, he should:

a) write a memo to the seller giving the names of the prospects to whom he has shown the property
b) phone the seller and notify him of the prospects' names
c) introduce the parties
d) write a memo to his office

52. A listing agreement in which the owner promises to pay a commission under all circumstances, except where he sells the property himself, is known as:

a) exclusive right to sell
b) exclusive open
c) exclusive agency
d) net listing

53. An exclusive right to sell listing provides a:

a) full commission to seller if principal sells the property
b) commission to the agency
c) commission to the agent only if principal sells the property
d) commission to the agent no matter who sells the property

54. Mary Pearl listed her home with broker Smith. She subsequently sold her home without any assistance from broker Smith. Nonetheless, a court rules that Mary owed broker Smith a full commission on the sale of her home. The logical explanation for the court's action must be that:

a) Smith had an option on the house
b) Smith had an exclusive agency listing
c) Smith had an open listing
d) Smith had a contract with an exclusive right to sell clause

55. Which type of contract affords the broker the greatest protection?

a) An open listing
b) An exclusive agency listing
c) A written listing
d) An exclusive right to sell listing

56. When the amount of commission is the excess amount of selling price over listing price, the listing is called:

a) an open listing
b) an exclusive agency
c) an exclusive right to sell
d) a net listing

57. When a seller gives equitable ownership to a buyer, the instrument used is:

a) land contract
b) conditional sales contract
c) installment sales contract
d) All of the above

58. The seller of real estate in a land contract is sometimes called the:

a) vendor
b) contractor
c) grantor
d) lessor

59. If title to real property remains in the seller's name after it is sold on a monthly payment plan, the buyer would have purchased it under a(n):

a) FHA mortgage
b) conventional mortgage
c) land contract
d) VA approved mortgage

60. An installment purchase contract does not give the buyer:

a) possession
b) right to lease the property
c) title to the property
d) right to devise the property

61. A provision preventing a purchaser from recording his land sales contract is:

a) enforceable
b) unenforceable
c) illegal
d) valid

62. Upon the signing of a land contract:

a) the legal title passes to purchaser
b) the equitable title passes to purchaser
c) no title to the real estate passes
d) the seller keeps his rights of possession

63. On the resale of a land contract, which of the following pertains?

a) Vendor may sell title but must assign contract
b) Vendee may assign or sell unless contract prohibits
c) Both (a) and (b)
d) Neither (a) nor (b)

64. Under a land contract, the seller may:

a) occupy the property
b) not encumber the property
c) sell the title
d) None of these

65. A contract supported by a consideration in which one party promises to keep an offer open for a stated period of time is:

a) a listing contract
b) an exchange agreement
c) a counter offer
d) an option agreement

66. Preston gives Pearson an option to purchase Preston's ranch.

a) Pearson has a lien on Preston's ranch
b) Pearson has an offer to enter into a contract
c) Pearson has a contract to enter into a contract
d) None of the above

67. An option differs from an offer because:

a) the option can be revoked at any time upon written notification to optionee
b) offer can be revoked at any time prior to notification of acceptance
c) an offer needs consideration, an option does not
d) offer and option are the same

68. Which of the following statements usually applies to an option?

a) It may be assigned by the person holding it
b) It may be recorded
c) The optionor may not revoke it before its term expires
d) All of the above are correct

69. An option:

a) may always be assigned by the optionee
b) may be exercised within 30 days of expiration date
c) without actual consideration is enforceable
d) should recite in detail the terms of the purchase in event it is exercised

70. When compared to a conditional sales or installment contract for sale of real estate, the principal distinguishing characteristic of a real estate option is:

a) irrevocability
b) contract mutuality
c) lack of mutuality in obligations
d) Both (a) and (b)

71. In order to secure an enforceable option to buy, the optionee should:

a) actually pay a valuable consideration which is agreed to by the optionor
b) always pay optionor at least $10 in cash
c) never give jewelry or other valuables as a consideration
d) never give a note as the consideration

1. b) An agreement between two persons to do or not to do certain things is the definition of a contract.

2. d) Virtually anything of value may be consideration.

3. a) Broker and seller have exchanged promises. This creates a bilateral contract.

4. b) A contract is considered to be executory until it is fully performed by both parties.

5. c) This answer includes all four of the elements of a contract: capacity of the parties, mutual consent, consideration and lawful object.

6. d) Guardians are appointed by the court and supervised by the court. They can contract on behalf of the individual they reprsent but must answer to the court. Persons lacking capacity cannot contract under any circumstances.

7. a) Normally, the board of directors passes a resolution authorizing the transaction and appointing an officer to execute the agreement.

8. c) The by-laws of the organization will indicate who has authority to act on behalf of that group.

9. d) All three of the choices represent different ways of saying the same thing.

10. b) Any offer can be withdrawn prior to notification of acceptance by the offeree (receiver of offer).

11. c) A counteroffer operates as a rejection of the original offer. If it is accepted by the original offeror, a contract will be formed.

12. a) Death of the offeror revokes the offer. His heirs will not be forced to enter into the contract.

13. c) The seller's counteroffer had the effect of rejecting the original offer. The seller can not later change his mind and accept it.

14. d) All of the above apply to a valid acceptance.

15. d) Actual fraud requires a knowing misrepresentation or suppression of a material fact with the intent that the other party rely upon that deceit.

16. b) There is no intent to deceive; nevertheless, deception occurs.

17. a) Duress is the use of threat or force. The person who signed the contract under duress could enforce it against the other person. It is voidable at his option.

18. b) This would be a contract signed under duress, which would be voidable.

19. b) The courts will not enforce a contract that is impossible to perform — that is, impossible for anyone to perform, not just impossible for the parties to the contract to perform.

20. c) A bilateral contract is always an exchange of a promise for a promise. Under a bilateral contract both parties are obligated.

21. b) If a contract is void, it cannot be enforced by the courts.

22. d) Only the parties to the contract may change the terms of the contract. The broker is not a party to the contract.

23. d) The contract is valid until the party who has the power to void the contract does so.

24. a) If the party who has the right to void a contract ratifies it instead, the contract becomes valid and enforceable.

25. c) Undue influence is taking advantage of another's weakness of mind, distress or necessity.

26. d) The Statute of Frauds requires all real estate contracts to be in writing.

27. c) The Statute of Frauds requires all contracts for the sale or exchange of real property to be in writing.

28. b) Performance is the only way to execute an agreement (contract).

29. b) A 'rescission' can be by agreement between the parties, or by order of the court. In either event, they must be put in the same positions (or as nearly as possible) as they were in before starting to carry out the agreement.

30. d) To rescind a contract means to terminate the contract and place both parties in their original positions.

31. c) Cancellation is unlike rescission in that the cancellation doesn't involve placing the parties in their initial positions; rescission does.

32. d) To assign a contract is to assign all rights and interests that the assignor has, but the legal burdens remain. The assignor remains secondarily liable on the lease agreement unless specifically released by the lessor.

33. b) Novation is the substitution of a new contract for an existing one; it must contain all four essentials of any contract.

34. c) When either party fails to perform his or her obligations under a contract, that failure is called a breach of contract.

35. b) Default is another name for breach.

36. d) The sum agreed upon in advance as payment for a breach of contract is liquidated damages.

37. c) A seller may sue a buyer for either 'specific performance' or damages, but not both. If there has been a provision in the contract calling for the buyer to forfeit his 'good faith' (earnest money) deposit in the event of default, the seller could not sue for 'damages' but could sue for 'specific performance'.

38. c) Specific performance is an action to compel performance of a contract, in this case, sale of the property to Jones.

39. c) A party to a contract will 'tender' (make good) his offer, usually when he or she anticipates the other pary to the agreement does not intend to perform.

40. b) Anticipatory repudiation by the buyer would relieve the seller of the necessity of making a tender.

41. a) The Statute of Frauds requires contracts for the sale of land to be in writing.

42. c) When one has partially performed by taking possession and making improvements, the oral agreement becomes enforceable against the non-performing party. This part performance removes the contract from the requirements of the Statute of Frauds.

43. c) A valid earnest money agreement is express (terms spelled out, written), bilateral (exchange of promises), executory contract (in the process of being performed).

44. a) A deposit receipt or earnest money agreement is only an offer until accepted by the seller.

45. b) A requirement for a land sale contract is that the property be properly described.

46. d) The agreement must be signed by seller and buyer.

47. b) The listing agreement is the contract that establishes the broker's agency. Without a valid listing, the broker has no authority to act for the seller.

48. d) An open listing permits the seller to list with any number of brokers and be obligated to pay a commission only to the first broker to produce an offer from a ready, willing and able buyer at the listing price or price acceptable to the seller.

49. c) Sale of the property listed under an open listing by the owner would terminate the agency relationship between seller and broker.

50. c) Under an open listing, the broker must be the "procuring cause" in order to be entitled to a commission. If any other broker or the seller sells the property, the broker has no claim to a commission.

51. a) This would be the best way for the broker to prove that he was the procuring cause of a subsequent sale to one of the prospects.

52. c) An exclusive agency protects a broker, except where seller sells the property himself.

53. d) Under an exclusive right to sell listing, the broker is entitled to a commission if the property is sold during the term of the listing, regardless of who sells it.

54. d) Under an exclusive right to sell, the owner is obligated to pay a commission to the broker, regardless of who sells the property.

55. d) Under this arrangement, no one, not even the seller, can sell the property during the life of the listing without the broker being entitled to his commission.

56. d) Under a net listing, the owner requires a certain sum from the sale. Anything over that amount goes to the broker as his or her commission.

57. d) Equitable ownership, equitable interest, are synonymous. The same holds true for land contract, contract of sale and conditional sales contract.

58. a) The terms seller and vendor are the same.

59. c) Under this type of financing arrangement, title does not pass until the full purchase price has been paid.

60. c) Title remains with seller until the contract is fully performed. The buyer receives possession and the right to use the property, which is an equitable interest.

61. b) Such a provision would not make the land contract void, but it (the provision) could not be enforced in a court of law. The buyer can and should record his interests.

62. b) When the contract is entered into, equitable title passes to the buyer. This gives the buyer right to possession, but not legal title.

63. c) Both vendor and vendee can assign their interests in the contract unless the contract prohibits such assignment.

64. c) The seller can encumber the property, providing the encumbrances don't monetarily exceed the contract balance. He can also sell the title (assignment of deed and real estate contract).

65. d) An option is a contract to keep an offer open.

66. c) The option is a unilateral contract, which gives Pearson the right for a specified length of time, to accept or not accept an offer to sell the property.

67. b) An offer can be revoked, whereas an option is a contract to keep an offer open, that is, the offer is irrevocable.

68. d) All of the foregoing are correct statements.

69. d) Unless details of the purchase are set forth in the option, the optionor could demand all cash and disputes might arise over payment of title charges, etc.

70. c) Under an option, only the optionor is obligated. The optionee can choose whether or not to exercise the option.

71. a) One of the requirements of a good option is that the optionee (person securing the option) give a valuable consideration for it.

8. Agency Law and Ethical Conduct

1. In real estate, the term principal is another name for the:

   a) customer
   b) client
   c) both
   d) neither

2. On a listing contract, whose name should appear?

   a) Listing salesman's
   b) The branch office's
   c) The broker's
   d) The selling salesman's

3. Most real estate brokerage agency agreements are created by:

   a) express written agreement
   b) implied agreement
   c) ratification
   d) estoppel

4. An agency relationship can be created by each of the following except:

   a) express agreement
   b) ratification
   c) estoppel
   d) none of the above

5. Hanson owns a five-acre tract of commercial property that Allison wants to purchase. During negotiations, Hanson allows Allison to assume that broker Timmons is his agent. Allison discusses it with broker and can rely on representations the broker makes because:

   a) an express agency has been created
   b) Timmons is Hanson's general agent
   c) Timmons is an ostensible agent of Hanson
   d) any information obtained from a licensed broker may be relied on by prospective buyers

6. An agency relationship can be terminated by which of the following?

   a) Mutual rescission
   b) Incapacity of either party
   c) Expiration of the subject matter
   d) All of the above

7. A general power of attorney is terminated upon:

   a) the death of the agent
   b) the death of the principal
   c) the agent's express renunciation
   d) all of the above

8. The disability of the principal, requiring a wheelchair:

   a) will terminate the agency
   b) will not terminate the agency
   c) will require a new power of attorney from the principal
   d) will be voidable at principal's election

9. A broker had forty-two listings when she died, her daughter, a licensed broker, took the business over. The daughter must:

   a) notify sellers of her take-over
   b) renegotiate the listings with sellers
   c) continue the business with the listings
   d) get listings from mother's estate executor

10. A broker's listing contract may not be terminated by the owner before its expiration date, where:

    a) the broker negotiated the sale to the owner
    b) the broker has advertised the property
    c) the agency is coupled with an interest
    d) the owner desires to list the property with a more active real estate firm

11. An apartment owner appointed a broker to collect rents on the apartments. All rents were due on the first of the month. On July 1, the broker had collected all of the rents except from one tenant. On July 2, the owner died. The broker called the remaining tenant on July 3, but the tenant refused to pay the rent to the broker, saying that the death of the owner had revoked the broker's right to collect. The tenant:

a) was right
b) could not refuse, as the broker's authority continued until the appointment of an executor or administrator
c) could not refuse, because the rent was due on July 1
d) has to pay the rent until notified by the owner or his representative not to

12. A real estate broker is liable to the buyer if he:

a) executes a contract in seller's name after proper power of attorney authorization
b) acts in excess of the authority given him by his principal
c) makes statements based on misrepresentations by the seller
d) gives buyer's earnest money to seller and sale later fails through no fault of agent

13. The relationship of a licensed real estate broker to his principal is that of a:

a) trustee
b) salesman
c) fiduciary
d) beneficiary

14. A broker owes a fiduciary obligation to the seller. To the purhcaser he owes:

a) a duty of fairness and good faith
b) nothing, as the seller is the principal and the one paying the commission
c) an obligation to honestly answer only those questions asked by the purchaser
d) an obligation to provide only answers to questions directly relevant to the sales price and the physical condition of the property

15. A broker should never do which of the following?

a) Accept a commission from two parties on the same transaction
b) Employ sub-agents
c) Misrepresent facts to clients
d) All of the above

16. A broker has a written promise of a $5,000 commission if he can secure certain acreage. The owner agress to sell if he can keep one-fourth of the mineral rights and will pay the broker $5,000 commission. The transaction was closed. The seller knew of the broker's dual commission arrangement; the buyer did not. Which of the following is true?

a) Broker made a clever deal and was entitled to the extra earnings
b) Broker is subject to disciplinary action
c) Since the seller knew of the fee paid by the broker, it was ethical
d) Broker violated the statute of frauds

17. Seller listed his home with a broker at $90,000; he asked for a quick sale. Broker showed it to buyer saying that the seller was financially insolvent and would take $78,000. Buyer offered $78,000 and seller accepted. Regarding broker's action, which of these is true?

a) He did not violate his fiduciary obligation to seller because seller did accept the offer
b) He did not violate his fiduciary obligation because seller hired him to sell the property which he did
c) He violated his fiduciary obligation to seller because he acted in excess of his authority by offering the property for sale at less than the listed price
d) He was unethical and violated his obligation to seller, but as seller accepted offer, no harm was done

18. Two salesmen without the knowledge of their broker, who had lots listed for sale, bought the lots in name of a "dummy" and resold them at a good profit. They provided in escrow for regular commission to go to their broker, who paid them their share. Seller later learned the details of the transaction.

a) Broker could lose his license
b) Broker may have to reimburse seller with amount of profit made by salesmen
c) Salesmen were in the clear as they acted as principals
d) Seller had no recourse as deal was closed and funds distributed

19. Where a broker negotiates a deal of $48,000 and the agreement recites a $1,500 deposit, but the buyer has only $500 in cash, the broker should:

a) obtain a "hold" check from the buyer for $1,000 dated one day before the closing date
b) obtain a note for $1,000 due ten days before the closing date
c) disclose to the seller the true amount of the deposit
d) do nothing and require the buyer to pay the full balance due at the closing

20. Michael Martin negotiates a sale of a dwelling for Allen, a builder, at $85,000 and receives an earnest money deposit of $2,000. At the closing, the buyer Phelps claims that the builder has used second grade facing brick contrary to specifications, and refuses to close the deal. Under these circumstances, the broker should:

I. Refund the money to Phelps
II. Report the matter to the real estate commission

a) I only
b) II only
c) Both I and II
d) Neither I nor II

21. Jones, broker, negotiates the sale of a house of $47,000. The agreement recites a deposit of $1,000; Jones receives $300 cash and a $700 note. The buyer seeks FHA financing. Jones certifies to the lending institution that he has received a $1,000 deposit from the buyer. Under these circumstances:

I. Jones is guilty of a criminal act
II. Jones' license can be revoked

a) I only
b) II only
c) Both I and II
d) Neither I nor II

22. A salesman made an offer to purchase real property listed in his broker's office. The seller accepted the offer and the transaction closed and all parties seemed satisfied at the time. Later the seller wrote a letter to the director complaining that the salesman had neglected to inform him that he was a licensed real estate agent.

a) The seller should have known better
b) The salesman was not ethical but did not violate the real estate law
c) Both the broker and salesman are subject to disciplinary action
d) The salesman only is subject to disciplinary action

23. Where a buyer, after signing a valid agreement of sale, asks the broker for permission to move into the property before the closing, the broker should:

a) deny permission
b) grant oral permission
c) refer him to the owner
d) have the buyer execute a temporary lease

24. A property is listed with a broker at $48,500. He finds a prospect who is willing to sign an offer at $47,000 but will pay $48,500 if the owner declines the offer. The broker should:

a) buy the property himself at $48,500
b) submit the $47,000 offer
c) persuade the buyer to make his $48,500 offer now
d) refuse to submit the $47,000 offer

25. A broker is engaged by a client to buy property for a specified sum. The broker locates a suitable property and purchases it for himself at the lower price. The broker then offers it to his client for the higher price without revealing the price he had paid for it. This is an example of:

a) secret profit
b) divided agency
c) fiduciary
d) false promise

26. A broker took a deposit and a check made out to the broker's trust account. The exclusive agency agreement stated that the owner would accept only a cashier's check made payable to the seller. The broker should:

a) refuse to deposit the check in escrow
b) hold the check for one day before returning it to the prospective purchaser
c) endorse the check to the seller's attorney
d) advise the seller that he has the check before he accepts the offer

27. A property was listed at $68,500. A prospect told the broker that he wanted the property and would pay that price but asked the broker to submit a signed offer of $56,600 and see if the owner would accept that price. The owner accepted but later learned what had happened and refused to pay the commission. Later, the broker sued him for commission

a) He can recover
b) He cannot recover
c) He can recover from the buyer
d) He can file a suit for "unjust enrichment" against the buyer

28. Broker McCormick agrees to cooperate with broker Davey in the sale of the principal's home. McCormick writes up an offer on the exact terms and conditions of the listing agreement as shown, and on the same day, broker Davey writes up a lower offer, all cash with a closing in thirty days. Broker McCormick should:

a) insist that the principals accept her offer since she is the listing broker
b) present both offers to the principals for their decisions
c) refuse to present broker Davey's offer
d) not present either offer to the principals

29. A broker has several salespeople working for him. One of his salespeople receives a written offer accompanied by a deposit on property listed by the broker. Later the same day, one of the other salespeople in the office obtains an offer, also with a deposit, on the same property. Pursuant to the salesmen's agreement, it is decided to submit only the first offer until it is accepted or rejected. The broker's action is:

a) permissible because only the first offer must be submitted, if the second offeror is notified in writing that there already is a full-price offer
b) permissible only if the first offer is substantially higher than the second offer
c) not permissible because all offers must be submitted to the seller
d) not permissible because the broker has a fiduciary responsibility to both buyer and seller

30. An earnest money receipt recites a deposit of $1,000. The buyer gives the broker a post-dated check in that amount. A commission auditor checks the broker's escrow account in the interim. The broker:

a) should have placed the check in his escrow account
b) should have opened a special account in his accounting procedure
c) deposit the check in his personal account
d) should have notified the owner when he received the check

31. If a broker holds an option as well as the listing and decides to exercise his option, he must:

a) reveal in writing to the owner the amount of his expected profit
b) obtain the written consent of the owner
c) disclose to his buyer that he is dealing as a principal, not as an agent
d) All of the above are correct

32. A broker obtained an exclusive listing on a property for thirty days at $120,000. On the last day of the listing the broker brought an offer to purchase the property signed by E. Gilligan. When asked who E. Gilligan was, the broker replied, "A client of our firm". The deal was closed. Actually, the buyer was the mother-in-law of the broker and was a member of his household. Later the seller brought action to rescind the transaction.

a) The transaction will be rescinded
b) It will not be rescinded since the property was sold at the listing price
c) The transaction will not be rescinded, but the broker will have to forfeit his commission
d) The buyer will own the property as trustee for the seller

33. Broker secures a signed open listing in which owner asserted that sewers were in and connected. Broker thought there were no sewers in this block, checked it out, and found he was right. Broker showed house to buyer who did not ask about sewers and broker did not volunteer information. Buyer discovers absence and files a complaint. Which is true?

a) Broker had a right to rely on the listing even though he knew it was incorrect
b) Broker owed a duty to tell buyer, even if not asked
c) Buyer was at fault. He could have checked with the city
d) No provision at law covers this situation

34. Jenkins inspects a piece of realty and agrees to purchase it "as is". Shortly after closing, he discovers that the electrical wiring is defective. What recourse does he have?

a) Jenkins can recover from the seller because the doctrine of "caveat emptor" only covers those conditions open to observation
b) Jenkins has no recourse unless the broker knew about it and failed to make disclosure
c) Jenkins has no recourse because he purchased "as is"
d) Jenkins has no recourse against the seller, but can hold the broker responsible, as it is his responsibility to inspect the wiring

35. A seller listed house with broker and advised him that the roof was old, leaked, and needed repair. Broker showed to prospective buyer and gave assurance that roof was in excellent condition. After purchase, a rain storm caused loss by water damage. If the buyer takes legal action, he would probably sue:

a) broker for breach of authority
b) seller alone; broker was his agent
c) broker and seller for fraud
d) multiple listing service for false advertising

36. In July, Jones bought Adams' home through a broker; in November the tile roof leaked badly. Jones sued Adams and the broker for repair. Court testimony showed that Adams had mentioned the new roof need to the broker, but the latter didn't report it because Jones "didn't ask about it." The most likely result was:

a) Jones was successful in his suit against Adams, who could recover damages, in turn, from the broker
b) Jones recovered from Adams, but the broker was not liable to Adams
c) the broker was liable to Jones, but Adams was not
d) Jones is not entitled to recover from either

37. Seller told broker Green that floors, carpeted wall-to-wall, were oak. The information was repeated in the signed listing. After sale, buyer found they were pine. Green had quoted the owner. The responsibility for the misrepresentation or mistake was that of:

a) the broker
b) broker and seller
c) the buyer, as he is charged with making reasonable examination of the property
d) the seller

38. A seller did not disclose a hidden material defect he knew of when listing it; the broker, with no knowledge of the defect, procured a buyer. When the buyer discovered the defect after the sale closing, he could:

a) sue both seller and broker
b) do nothing since he should have inspected the structure
c) sue the broker who failed to inform him of the defect
d) sue the seller since he concealed the defect from the broker, thus relieving the broker of liability

39. A listing is taken on a multiple listing service standard form. Other members of that multiple listing service, in attempting to sell the property, are:

a) agents for the seller
b) subagents working through the listing broker
c) other brokers are agents but their salesmen are subagents to the listing broker
d) None of these

40. An attorney-in-fact, in executing the powers given him under the provisions of a power of attorney, has the right to do all of the following except:

a) sign his principal's name
b) collect money for his principal
c) encumber the principal's property with the attorney-in-fact as beneficiary
d) No exceptions

41. Broker Green sold a home and buyer gave him a $500 check as a deposit. Green did the improper thing when he:

a) endorsed it over to seller upon financial acceptance of the offer
b) held check until all financing was completed in escrow
c) cashed check and put the money in his trust account
d) cashed check and gave money to seller when his acceptance was communicated to the buyer

42. If a listing held by a broker does not authorize him to accept a deposit and, if he finds a purchaser and accepts a deposit, he then holds the deposit:

a) as agent of the bank
b) as agent of the purchaser
c) as agent of the seller
d) in his personal bank account

43. Broker is given authority to collect a deposit according to the listing agreement with the seller. Purchaser gives broker a deposit at the time purchase agreement is signed. Broker misappropriates the funds. Who has liability for the loss?

a) Buyer, because he should have delivered the deposit directly to the seller himself
b) Buyer, because he should have put the money in escrow until the transaction was closed
c) Seller, because broker was authorized to accept deposit
d) Seller is liable, because he should not have appointed the broker to accept deposits for him

44. A buyer puts down a deposit on February eleventh with an offer to purchase. In the deposit receipt, the offer is described as 'irrevocable for five days'. The next day, before the seller has been told of the offer, the buyer calls the broker and demands return of the deposit.

a) The broker must return the deposit upon buyer's demand
b) The broker should hold the deposit in neutral escrow for five days
c) The broker has until February fifteenth to secure acceptance
d) The broker has until Feburary sixteenth to secure acceptance

45. Broker Green was happy when he got buyer and seller to execute a sales agreement and then sign escrow instructions. He also had in his pocket $500 cash deposit by buyer paid outside escrow. The buyer and seller mutually agreed to rescind the transaction and seller instructed Green to return deposit in his possession to the buyer. The proper action by Green is to:

a) tell seller he had earned his commission and was retaining the $500 as part payment
b) agree to refund any part in excess of his commission in accordance with the forfeiture clause in the standard sales agreement
c) put the $500 in his trust account and let the parties sue if they wanted to
d) return the $500 to buyer as per instructions and make demand upon seller for his full commission

46. An earnest money agreement is negotiated by broker Blanchett. Before closing, buyer Baker decides not to continue with the transaction. The $1,000 earnest money:

a) must be returned to Baker as the transaction was not yet fully consummated
b) belongs to the seller as Baker failed to perform as agreed
c) belongs to broker Blanchett as he is the one who produced a ready, willing and able purchaser
d) stays in trust until broker determines whether or not Baker acted in good faith

47. Buyer Jones makes a full price offer to purchase to seller Smith who rejects offer outright. What recourse does Jones have?

a) Sue Smith for damages
b) Sue Smith for specific performance
c) Both of these
d) None of these

48. A broker had an open listing on a house. To collect a commission, he would have to prove which of the following?

a) He had a license
b) He had a ready, willing and able buyer
c) He was the procuring cause of the sale
d) All of the above

49. Wilson made a deposit on the purchase price to broker Henry. Before the transaction was completed, Wilson requested permission from Henry to enter the house to make minor repairs. Which of the following is true?

a) Henry can give permission to Wilson provided he signs a rental agreement
b) Wilson is an equity owner and doesn't need permission from anybody
c) Henry must obtain written permission from the owner to let Wilson do the work
d) Buyer and seller must sign a written agreement stating the nature and extent of the work

50. An authorization to a person to act for and in behalf of another in his absence is called:

a) an option
b) an easement
c) a power of attorney
d) a release

51. The attorney-in-fact under a general power of attorney, may do all of the following except:

a) encumber the principal's property with a mortgage naming another person as mortgagee
b) perform acts which are authorized by the power of attorney
c) in the absence of the principal, sign the principal's name
d) sell real property without recording the power of attorney

52. Which of the following is true?

a) Any person may be given a power of attorney
b) Any person may be an attorney-in-fact
c) Both A and B
d) Neither A nor B

1. b) The principal is normally referred to as the agent's client. Third parties are called customers.

2. c) The listing is an employment contract employing the broker to act as agent for the seller (client) in procuring a buyer (customer) for the property.

3. a) Real estate brokerage agency agreements are created by express, written contract.

4. d) Express agreement is the most common method of creating an agency. Ratification is an express authorization of an agent's prior contracts. Estoppel occurs when the authorization is not full ratification but the principal, because of his or her prior acts, is prohibited from denying the agent's authority. All are methods of creating an agency.

5. c) Hanson's allowing Allison to assume that Timmons was his agent resulted in the creation of an ostensible agency. Ostensible agencies are created by estoppel.

6. d) An agency relationship may be terminated by mutual agreement, revocation by principal, renunciation by agent, expiration of its term, extinction of its subject matter, death or incapacity of either principal or agent.

7. d) A general power of attorney creates an agency relationship which can be terminated in the same ways as other agency relationships.

8. b) It is mental incapacity that terminates the agency, not a physical disability.

9. b) The listings with mother terminated with her death and would have to be renegotiated.

10. c) The contract may not be terminated where the agency is coupled with an interest.

11. a) The death of either the agent or the principal cancels any agency agreement. Since the owner died on July 2, the agency between the owner and the broker ceased, and the broker is no longer permitted to act on behalf of the deceased. This does not mean that the rent is not due to the heirs of the deceased, it means the broker cannot collect it on behalf of the estate.

12. b) A broker may be held liable for acting in excess of his authority, but not normally for making misrepresentations based on statements from the owner.

13. c) A licensee is normally acting as an agent, which is a fiduciary position. Fiduciary means confidence and trust.

14. a) To the purchaser, a broker owes a duty of fairness and good faith, an obligation to answer questions honestly and to disclose hidden defects known to the broker.

15. c) In some circumstances, a broker may be permitted to accept a commission from both sides in a transaction (when full disclosure is made to both sides) or to employ subagents (if authorized by the principal to do so), but should never misrepresent facts to the principal/client or anyone else.

16. b) Since broker was being paid by both sides, there was a duty of full disclosure to both sides, not just the seller.

17. c) It is a breach of the broker's fiduciary obligations to the principal to disclose that the principal is in financial need and/or would accept less than the listing price.

18. b) While the broker will not lose his license if he has no knowledge of the dishonest acts of the salesmen, he may be held civilly liable and a court might order him to refund the secret profit gained by the salesmen and refund the commission.

19. c) The broker must inform the seller of the exact amount of the deposit received as well as its form, cash, check, etc.

20. d) This is apparently a contractual dispute concerning performance by the seller/builder and therefore the right of the buyer to recover the earnest money. Such disputes would have to be resolved by the parties themselves or a court of law. The broker should hold the funds in trust until the matter is resolved.

21. c) Under these circumstances, both I and II could apply.

22. c) Real estate law requires that a broker exercise reasonable supervision over the activities of his salesmen. The broker knew, or should have known, that his salesman was buying the property. Both the salesman and the broker are subject to disciplinary action and may be sued for any secret profit. Regardless of circumstances, any licensed person must make his licensed status known to anyone he is involved with in a real estate transaction.

23. c) The broker does not have the authority to give the buyer permission to move on to the property before closing and should refer all such requests to the owner.

24. c) The broker should persuade the buyer to make his $48,500 offer now. He must work to serve the best interests of his client, the seller.

25. a) The real estate law forbids a licensee from taking any secret profit or compensation.

26. d) The law requires that the broker deposit the check in his trust account immediately, unless restricted otherwise. Immediately is interpreted by the courts to mean the next business day. The fact that the earnest money was not in the form required by the listing agreement would have to be disclosed to the seller.

27. b) The broker's duty of loyalty to the seller would require disclosure of the fact that the buyer was willing to pay the full price.

28. b) All offers must be presented to the principals for their decision. A refusal to do so is not only a violation of the real estate law, but a violation of the Realtor Code of Ethics, Article 20.

29. c) It is not permissible because all offers must be submitted to the seller. The broker's fiduciary obligation is to the seller only.

30. d) The form of the earnest money deposit, in this case a post-dated check, should be disclosed to the seller.

31. d) All of the above are correct.

32. a) The failure to disclose the true relationship between buyer and broker was a breach of the broker's fiduciary obligation to seller and could result in the seller's being able to rescind the transaction.

33. b) Silence about a known defect is a form of misrepresentation. The broker's obligation requires that he disclose all facts detrimental to the property, known to him, which would not be revealed by a physical inspection.

34. a) "As is" or "caveat emptor" means the purchaser takes subject to those defects that could be discovered by a visual inspection of the premises.

35. c) Both knew roof was in need of repair and the broker, as the agent of the seller, made a misrepresentation. The seller is responsible for the acts of his agent; of course, the agent is accountable for his own acts.

36. a) In this case, both Adams and broker would be liable to the seller for damages caused to the seller by the broker's breach of his obligation to inform the buyer of hidden defects after being informed of such defects by the seller.

37. d) While the seller was probably responsible in this case, the broker should use reasonable precaution not to misrepresent.

38. d) In this case, he could sue the seller since he concealed the defect from the broker, thus relieving the broker of liability.

39. b) The multiple listing form normally allows the broker to appoint other brokers as subagents.

40. c) Such action would constitute a breach of the fiduciary relationship between principal and attorney-in-fact.

41. b) If made out to him, he should cash it and put the money in his trust account.

42. b) If the listing agreement does not authorize the broker to collect a deposit and if he collects one, he does so as agent of the buyer and not the seller.

43. c) Since the broker was authorized to accept the money for the seller, he or she was acting as agent for the seller in holding the funds and loss would be borne by the seller.

44. a) An offer can be withdrawn at any time. Even though a buyer makes an offer on one date and agrees that the offer will stand for a period of five days, he may cancel this at any time prior to acceptance and notification of acceptance.

45. d) When the parties rescind a purchase and sale contract and the principal instructs the broker to return the deposit, he does not have the right to hold it as a guarantee that his commission will be paid. If he believes he has earned a commission, he can sue the principal for it.

46. b) As the buyer apparently defaulted without legal excuse, the seller would be entitled to the earnest money. Answer (d) would be incorrect because it would be up to a court of law, not a broker, to determine whether or not a party to a contract acted in good faith.

47. d) Since Smith refused the offer, there was no contract created, and Jones has no legal complaint. At this point, Smith is not obligated to sell his property. However, if the property was listed with a broker, the latter could successfully sue for his full commission.

48. d) If the listing was an exclusive right of sale, the broker would not have to prove he was the procuring cause — the person responsible for making the deal. However, with the more limited protection provided by the open listing, he must do all of these.

49. c) Until the transaction is complete, the home belongs to the seller.

50. c) The power of attorney is a document used to give someone else the power to represent you. The person conferring such authority is the principal, the person receiving it is the agent, called the attorney-in-fact.

51. d) If an attorney-in-fact is authorized to sell his principal's real property, the power of attorney conferring such authority must be recorded in the county where the real property is situated.

52. d) Minors and incompetents lack the capacity to act as agent for another.

9. Real Estate Finance

1. Rates on mortgages are influenced by:

   a) the interest paid on corporate bonds
   b) supply and demand for money
   c) Both
   d) Neither

2. The type of interest usually charged on home loans is:

   a) annuity
   b) simple
   c) compound
   d) accrued

3. The interest paid on principal and the resulting interest is referred to as:

   a) simple interest
   b) compound interest
   c) usurious interest
   d) All of the above

4. Mr. Smith purchased a duplex for $200,000, paying $40,000 down. Two years later he sold it for $280,000 and realized a 200% profit on his original investment. This is an example of:

   a) escalation
   b) leverage
   c) plottage
   d) highest and best use

5. The lender that specializes in real estate home loans, allows a higher loan-to-value ratio, deals in non-government loans, services its own loans, makes many medium to long-term loans, and usually charges a higher interest rate than other institutional lenders is a/an:

   a) savings and loan association
   b) commercial bank
   c) insurance company
   d) mutual savings bank

6. The largest source of single-family home financing on a conventional basis is:

   I. commercial banks
   II. savings and loan associations

   a) I only
   b) II only
   c) Both I and II
   d) Neither I nor II

7. The first institutions to develop amortization of home loans were:

   a) commercial banks
   b) holding companies
   c) insurance companies
   d) savings and loan associations

8. The lender that invests a major portion of its assets in long-term real estate loans, does not like to service its own loans, does not prefer construction loans, and likes large loans on commercial properties is a/an:

   a) commercial bank
   b) savings and loan association
   c) insurance company
   d) mutual mortgage company

9. Jones bought a farm for $9,000 twenty-five years ago. It is now free and clear and valued at $130,000. He asks a real estate broker to get him a $100,000 loan against the property. The broker would least likely apply to which of the following for the loan?

   a) Commercial bank
   b) Mutual savings bank
   c) Savings and loan association
   d) Insurance company

10. Which lending institution prefers to make local loans, considers the previous relationship with the customer to be of great importance, and prefers short-term interim loans?

a) Savings and loan association
b) Commercial bank
c) Mortgage company
d) Life insurance company

11. An authorized agent appointed by a secondary market mortgage lender to process and serve its mortgage loan investments is described as a:

I. loan processor
II. mortgage loan correspondent

a) I only
b) II only
c) Both I and II
d) Neither I nor II

12. A real estate syndicate can operate as a:

a) partnership
b) real estate investment trust
c) corporation
d) Any of the above

13. Loan amounts are usually based on:

a) sales price
b) appraised amount
c) appraised amount or sales price, whichever is less
d) appraised amount or sales price, whichever is greater

14. Before issuing a loan, a prudent lender will take into consideration which of the following?

a) The borrower's ability to repay the debt
b) The market value of the property used as security
c) Matters affecting title
d) All of the above

15. From the real estate lender's point of view, which of the following is generally true?

a) Their margin of safety is based on the assumption that all properties increase in value in time
b) Most lenders will lend on all types of property
c) General appearance of the property seldom has a bearing on the loan terms
d) The underlying security for the loan is the property itself

16. The Federal Housing Administration made major contributions to mortgage lending in providing:

I. underwriting standards
II. a secondary mortgage market so that funds available in capital surplus areas could be invested in areas of capital shortage

a) I only
b) II only
c) Both I and II
d) Neither I nor II

17. A prospective homebuyer desiring an FHA-insured loan would apply to:

I. FHA
II. approved mortgagee

a) I only
b) II only
c) Both I and II
d) Neither I nor II

18. If a borrower defaults on an FHA-insured loan, any losses sustained by the lender as a result of the foreclosure are made up through:

a) an attachment lien against the borrower
b) an assessment against the lender
c) mutual mortgage insurance plan
d) U. S. Treasury

19. According to FHA and VA regulations, what is the maximum number of points a borrower can pay for obtaining an FHA or VA loan?

a) one point
b) two points
c) seven points
d) No maximum

20. The purchase price of a home is $68,000. Broker Smith has a customer who wants to buy the home with an FHA loan. The maximum FHA loan for the property is $65,100. The buyer does not have enough cash to make up the difference, but the seller is willing to finance $1,500 of the purchase price. The buyer agrees. Broker Smith should:

a) arrange for private financing to cover the additional money
b) go ahead with the transaction as agreed
c) show the sale to be at $66,600 and treat the $1,500 as a separate transaction
d) not go ahead with the transaction

21. A requirement of a borrower under an FHA insured loan is that he:

I. pay the MIP required
II. certify he will occupy the premises if that is a condition of the FHA's approval

a) I only
b) II only
c) Both I and II
d) Neither I nor II

22. One of the advantages of buying a home with FHA insured financing, as opposed to a conventional type loan, is that:

a) FHA provides life insurance
b) FHA insured loans are quicker to close and easier to obtain
c) an FHA insured loan is always tailored to your needs
d) payments are likely to be lower with an FHA insured loan

23. The penalty for prepaying an FHA insured loan is:

a) 2% of the loan balance at the time of prepayment
b) 1% of the loan balance at the time of prepayment
c) 1% of the original loan amount
d) None of the above

24. Which of the following may be financed by an FHA insured loan, but may not be financed by a VA guaranteed loan?

a) Farm home
b) Farm equipment
c) Duplex
d) Non-owner occupied rental home

25. In the case of a VA guaranty or insured loan, the borrower may:

I. sell the property "subject to" the loan
II. not repay the loan ahead of schedule

a) I only
b) II only
c) Both I and II
d) Neither I nor II

26. The Veterans Administration will guarantee loans wherein the purchase price exceeds the appraised value if:

I. the veteran pays in cash from his own resources the difference between the purchase price and the appraised value, and the loan amount does not exceed the appraised value
II. the veteran signs the required certification

a) I only
b) II only
c) Both I and II
d) Neither I nor II

27. VA guaranteed loans:

a) are limited by the VA to $100,000
b) are insured loans
c) require a ten percent down payment if the sales price is above $100,000
d) None of the above

28. A Certificate of Reasonable Value is commonly used in the real estate business. It is issued by:

a) Federal National Mortgage Association
b) Veterans Administration
c) Federal Housing Administration
d) All of the above

29. Under the VA guaranty program, upon foreclosure the Veterans Administration may:

I. keep the property and reimburse the lender in full
II. give the lender the house and the guaranty amount

a) I only
b) II only
c) Both I and II
d) Neither I nor II

30. The amount a qualified lending institution may loan to a qualified veteran on a VA guaranteed loan is limited by the VA to:

a) the assessed value of the property
b) $100,000
c) the amount of the veteran's entitlement
d) the amount shown on the Certificate of Reasonable Value

31. If a non-veteran purchases a property encumbered by a VA guaranteed loan, the debt:

I. must be repaid immediately
II. can be assumed by the new purchaser

a) I only
b) II only
c) Both I and II
d) Neither I nor II

32. Most conventional loan funds are derived from:

a) individual savings deposits
b) mutual funds
c) FNMA
d) insurance companies

33. With respect to conventional, FHA-insured and VA-guaranteed loans, which of the following is correct?

a) All three are insured or guaranteed, but VA-guaranteed loans have lower interest rates than either FHA or conventional loans
b) FHA-insured loans are at a higher loan-to-value ratio than VA-guaranteed loans, but lower loan-to-value than most conventional loans
c) Conventional loan interest rates are lower, but these loans are not insured or guaranteed
d) Conventional loans are usually at a lower loan-to-value ratio, and the interest charged on FHA-insured or VA-guaranteed is lower

34. The Federal Reserve System is one of the most powerful entities controlling the economy and the real estate market. If a member bank falls below the reserve requirements, additional cash may be raised by:

a) selling bonds from the bank's portfolio
b) borrowing from other member banks
c) borrowing from the Federal Reserve
d) All of the above

35. Which of the following is not a true statement regarding the Federal Reserve System?

a) The United States is divided into 12 districts with a reserve bank in each district
b) The system is administered by state governors
c) All federally chartered banks must be members
d) The Federal Reserve Bank regulates the flow of money and credit

36. Funds for conventional, single-family loans are supplied by:

I. the Federal National Mortgage Association
II. savings and loan associations

a) I only
b) II only
c) Both I and II
d) Neither I nor II

37. What was the original purpose behind the formation of the Federal National Mortgage Association?

a) To buy existing FHA-insured loans
b) To provide a stimulus to the housing construction market, as well as to the mortgage market
c) To make more funds available to purchasers buying homes
d) All of the above

38. A real estate investor, in discussing a specific loan in his portfolio, mentioned the loan was "seasoned." He was referring to:

a) the time of the year the loan was due
b) the fact that the loan had reached maturity
c) the loan being paid in a timely manner
d) the loan being delinquent

39. A promissory note calling for payment of interest only during its term is called a/an:

a) amortized note
b) installment note
c) negotiable note
d) straight note

40. In real estate financing, lenders refer to a "nominal" rate of interest. This means the rate:

a) is minimal
b) would exceed the legal rate
c) is the maximum rate allowed by law
d) is specified in he promissory note

41. Installment notes often include an "or more" provision. These important words:

a) allow for an accelerated pay-off
b) make it possible to borrow additional funds on the same note
c) provide for a loan moratorium in the event of a disaster
d) indicate the note has several makers

42. When a buyer assumes an existing loan, the:

a) seller is released from obligation by the lender
b) seller becomes secondarily liable for the loan
c) seller remains primarily liable for the loan
d) buyer is liable only to the seller for the loan

43. A note in which the principal amount is systematically reduced through regular payments of both principal and interest is known as a/an:

a) junior loan
b) straight note
c) amortized note
d) None of the above

44. Interest charged for real property loans:

a) is normally paid in advance
b) is adversely affected by the supply of loan funds
c) declines in ratio directly proportionate to the declining loan balance
d) may be augmented by mortgage discount to increase the mortgagor's yield

45. The clause in a deed of trust or mortgage or promissory note which permits the lender to declare the entire unpaid balance due and payable at once, upon default of the borrower, is a/an:

a) acceleration clause
b) escalator clause
c) forfeiture clause
d) default clause

46. A clause in a deed of trust, mortgage or promissory note which permits the lender to call the outstanding balance due and payable should the property be sold by the borrower, is a/an:

a) acceleration clause
b) balloon payment clause
c) exculpatory clause
d) alienation clause

47. A real estate contract or land contract is described as a method of financing often substituted for mortgage or trust deed financing. Consequently, a land contract can be:

a) the same as a mortgage
b) a security device
c) similar to a lease
d) a lease with an option to buy

48. Washington is a lien theory state. This means:

a) the first to record is the first in right
b) liens recorded against a property can be foreclosed through the courts
c) mortgages and trust deeds are liens and do not give the lender title to the property
d) All of the above

49. The trustor in connection with a trust deed is the party who:

a) lends the money
b) receives the payments
c) signs the note
d) holds the deed of trust

50. Under a mortgage, the mortgagor is the party who:

a) lends the money
b) receives the payments on the note
c) holds the mortgage
d) signs the note and gives the mortgage

51. Which of the following documents accompanies the deed of trust?

a) A deed
b) An abstract of title
c) A contract of sale
d) A promissory note

52. To be a valid and enforceable instrument, a deed of trust must contain a clause requiring the trustor to:

a) keep the property insured against fire
b) keep the property in good condition
c) pay taxes and assessments before delinquent
d) None of these

53. In order to foreclose a mortgage, a mortgagee would:

a) notify the trustee of default
b) file an attachment in the amount of the debt
c) notify the mortgagor of default, wait 90 days, and publish a notice of default in a local paper
d) file a court action

54. Money realized in excess of the indebtedness and the foreclosure costs at a mortgage foreclosure belong to the:

a) sheriff conducting the sale
b) court
c) mortgagee
d) mortgagor

55. At a trustee's sale, a property was sold for $160,800. The fees and costs amounted to $1,600. The property was encumbered with a first deed of trust in the amount of $156,500, and a second deed of trust in the amount of $2,000. Which of the following is correct?

a) There would be a surplus which would go to the beneficiary
b) There is a surplus which would go to the trustor
c) There is a surplus which would go to the trustee
d) The beneficiary of the second trust deed could initiate court action for a deficiency against the trustor

56. A recorded deed of trust is removed from the county records:

a) by recording a new deed of trust
b) when final payment is made by the trustor
c) by posting a surety bond
d) when the deed of reconveyance is recorded

57. Who would sign a deed of reconveyance?

a) Trustor
b) Trustee
c) Beneficiary
d) Lender

58. An agent sold a piece of property, obtaining a new first and second loan for the purchaser. A bank made the first loan; the seller carried the second. The agent is to record a request for notice of default. This would be done to protect the:

a) first mortgagor
b) first mortgagee
c) second mortgagor
d) second mortgagee

59. A note which may be increased by advancing additional funds to the borrower under the same document is a/an:

a) hypothecated note
b) package note
c) open-end note
d) amortized note

60. A budget mortgage is best defined as one that:

a) includes principal and interest payments
b) is made to people with lower incomes
c) includes personal as well as real property
d) includes payments for principal, interest, taxes and insurance

61. A mortgage on real estate that includes such personal property items as refrigerators, ranges and dishwashers, is referred to as a:

a) blanket mortgage
b) package mortgage
c) participation mortgage
d) all-inclusive mortgage

62. A purchase money mortgage is:

I. one taken back by the seller from the buyer to finance part of the purchase price
II. used to refinance real property

a) I only
b) II only
c) Both I and II
d) Neither I nor II

63. The owner of five parcels of land desires to obtain a loan and use all five parcels as security for the debt. The mortgage he will be required to execute will be a/an:

a) purchase money mortgage
b) amortized mortgage
c) blanket mortgage
d) package mortgage

64. A tract of land is encumbered by a blanket trust deed. The trust deed should contain a release clause which would permit:

a) the release of the developer from future liability
b) the developer to turn over the sale of the tract to real estate agents
c) the developer to obtain partial reconveyance deeds as individual lots are sold and a proportionate amount of the debt satisfied
d) the release of the beneficiary from all liability

65. If a property owner wishes to secure a second mortgage and realizes he may later want to refinance his first mortgage, the presence of which of the following will be necessary?

a) A lien waiver
b) A subordination clause
c) An acceleration clause
d) An alienation provision

66. The greatest risk to a lender is found in:

I. construction loans
II. take-out loans

a) I only
b) II only
c) Both I and II
d) Neither I nor II

67. A builder finances an apartment building through a local bank. If money is released to him at various stages of construction, these payments are called:

a) release payments
b) acceleration advances
c) obligatory advances
d) sight drafts

68. Construction loans are normally paid off:

I. through amortization
II. by means of permanent financing at the end of the construction period

a) I only
b) II only
c) Both I and II
d) Neither I nor II

69. With respect to financing, the term "take-out" loan refers to:

a) truth-in-lending requirements
b) junior loans
c) loans against the land
d) construction loans

70. Which of the following two terms are synonymous?

a) Take-out loans/secondary financing
b) Construction loan/take-out loan
c) Interim loan/construction loan
d) Obligatory advances/installment loan

71. The entity that has responsibility for this country's fiscal management is the:

a) Federal Reserve System
b) Federal Home Loan Bank
c) FNMA
d) U. S. Treasury

72. The most significant FHA loans fall under:

a) Title VIII of the Fair Housing Act
b) Title II of the National Housing Act
c) The Readjustment Act of 1944
d) All of these

73. The Federal agency that makes and insures loans to ranchers and farmers who are unable to obtain financing elsewhere is the:

a) FmHA
b) Federal Land Bank
c) Federal Housing Administration
d) Cooperative Farm System

74. Which of the following is a division of the Department of Housing and Urban Development?

a) Veterans Administration
b) F.D.I.C.
c) GNMA
d) All of these

75. A power of sale clause is found in which of the following financing instruments?

a) Promissory Note
b) Notice of Default
c) Mortgage Note
d) Deed of Trust

76. A statement in a mortgage or trust deed to the effect that when a debt has been paid the lien will be canceled is a/an:

a) defeasance clause
b) alienation clause
c) liquidation provision
d) habendum clause

77. A clause which requires a lender to release certain parcels from a blanket lien when agreed upon segments of a debt have been paid is known as a:

a) partial reconveyance provision
b) quiet title clause
c) quitclaim clause
d) None of these

78. A trust deed given by a buyer to a seller to secure a portion of a purchase price is called a:

a) hard money trust deed
b) budget deed of trust
c) purchase money deed of trust
d) package trust deed

79. The initials P.M.I. in financing circles refer to:

a) high loan-to-value conventional loans
b) construction loans
c) VA loans
d) FHA loans

80. Which of the following is not an accepted disbursement plan for construction loans?

a) Fixed disbursement system
b) Voucher system
c) Warrant system
d) Insured lien system

81. At the lowest point in the real estate market cycle:

a) vacancy rates are high
b) rents are beginning to increase
c) Both of the above
d) None of the above

82. Industry in the United States is currently shifting to:

a) suburban locations
b) urban locations
c) Both of the above
d) None of the above

83. Supply and demand in a particular market area are most reliably predicted by:

a) prevailing rental rates
b) occupancy rates
c) new construction
d) population data

1. c) Interest rates are determined by the availability of money and the demand for it.

2. b) All real estate loans involve simple interest.

3. b) Compound interest is interest which is computed not only on the principal but any interest the principal has accrued in the past.

4. b) Using borrowed funds to turn a profit is called "leverage."

5. a) These are the characteristics of a savings and loan.

6. b) Savings and loan associations.

7. d) Savings and loans first introduced the amortized loan, as opposed to interest-only loans, in about 1936.

8. c) These are the characteristics of insurance companies.

9. d) Insurance companies prefer to invest their money through loan correspondents and do not usually make loans at the primary market level.

10. b) These are the characteristics of a commercial bank.

11. b) Mortgage loan correspondents help institutional investors place their money in various regions in the country. They will usually service the loans as well.

12. d) A syndicate is a pooling of funds by a group of individuals. The syndicate may take the form of a partnership, a real estate investment or a corporate structure.

13. c) The term "loan-to-value" means the maximum loan in relation to the appraised value; however, the lender will always base the maximum loan on sales price or appraised value, whichever is less.

14. d) The lender would consider all three aspects in considering an application for a loan.

15. d) The property is the real security for the loan.

16. a) FHA's underwriting system has proven its effectiveness and is copied by lending institutions everywhere. However, the FHA does not provide mortgage money for any purpose.

17. b) FHA insures loans made by approved mortgagees, that is, lenders who have met FHA's requirements for approval to make FHA loans. FHA does not make loans.

18. c) Under the Mutual Mortgage Insurance Plan, private lenders are protected against losses when they foreclose properties acting as security for FHA-insured loans.

19. d) The FHA no longer places restrictions on who must pay the points for an FHA loan.

20. d) Second mortgages or trust deeds in excess of maximum FHA loan amount are not permitted in connection with FHA financing.

21. c) FHA requires MIP for all loans and if the buyer is applying for an owner-occupied loan, he must certify he intends to occupy the property.

22. d) Historically FHA and VA loans have interest rates below conventional rates.

23. d) Neither FHA nor VA permit lenders to assess a prepayment penalty.

24. d) FHA has a non-owner occupancy program; the VA does not.

25. a) The VA holds the original veteran responsible unless the new buyer is a veteran and arranges for a "substitution of entitlement". Any VA loan can be prepaid, and VA does not allow a prepayment charge.

26. c) The VA will allow the veteran to pay over the appraised value, provided he does not borrow the money to do so. He must sign a statement acknowledging he realizes he is paying over value.

27. d) VA guaranteed. This is no maximum loan amount, but the guaranty amount is limited.

28. b) The CRV is a Certificate of Reasonable Value and is a VA appraisal.

29. c) The VA has the option of either.

30. d) While there is no maximum VA loan amount the loan cannot exceed the appraised value.

31. b) All VA loans can be assumed.

32. a) Savings of individuals make up the greatest amount of funds available to banks for loan purposes.

33. d) Conventional loan-to-value ratios are lower than those set by FHA or VA, and the conventional interest rates are usually higher.

34. d) The FED requires a certain percentage of a member bank's total deposits be deposited in the FED. If the bank's deposits increase, its reserves must also increase. If the bank is short of its reserve requirements, it can solve the problem by any of the methods described in the questions.

35. b) The FED is governed by the twelve member Federal Reserve Bank Board.

36. c) Savings and Loans are the primary source; FNMA is a secondary source.

37. d) This is what the federal government had in mind when it created FNMA.

38. c) This is the defintion of a seasoned loan.

39. d) A straight note calls for interest payments only during the term of the loan, with a balloon payment in the end.

40. d) The nominal rate is the rate shown in the note.

41. a) The words "or more" allow a prepayment. Without them the borrower could be forced to pay the loan over its entire term, with no prepayment privilege.

42. b) The seller would become secondarily liable if the note were assumed by the buyer.

43. c) This is a definition of an amortized loan. Amortization is sometimes referred to as "liquidation" of a debt.

44. c) The interest is computed on the declining loan balance. As the debt goes down, so does the interest.

45. a) An acceleration clause gives the lender the right to "accelerate" the loan's due date to the present, usually for nonpayment or some other form of default.

46. d) This is a definition of an "alienation clause."

47. b) The real estate land contract secures the debt for the seller (vendor).

48. c) In Washington mortgages and trust deeds act as liens; they do not give a lender any form of title. This is the meaning of "lien theory."

49. c) The trustor is the borrower under a deed of trust.

50. d) The borrower is the mortgagor; the lender is the mortgagee.

51. d) The promissory note is secured by a deed to trust or mortgage.

52. d) The deed of trust doesn't have to have provisions regarding these matters, but they should, and they usually do.

53. d) Mortgages are foreclosed by suing the borrower for default in a court of law.

54. d) The borrower (mortgagor) is entitled to any excess funds received at the foreclosure sale.

55. b) The total of the liens and foreclosure costs was $160,100. The property sold for $160,800, with a surplus of $700. It belongs to the trustor — the borrower.

56. d) The deed of reconveyance must be recorded before a trust deed is released as a lien.

57. b) The party holding the trust deed—the trustee—signs the deed of reconveyance and delivers it to the trustor, who records it to serve public notice the debt has been retired.

58. d) The holder of the second would want to be notified if the borrower were to default on the first lien.

59. c) An open-end note is the type which allows additional funds to be advanced to the borrower without the necessity of writing a new note for each advance.

60. d) A budget mortgage is one that calls for installments which include principal, interest, taxes and insurance.

61. b) A package mortgage is one used to finance real and personal property with one security instrument.

62. a) Though it is any mortgage (or trust deed) given as security for a loan to finance a purchase, it is generally used to define the mortgage given by a buyer to a seller.

63. c) The blanket mortgage would encumber all five parcels, and in the event of default, all five would be foreclosed.

64. c) The developer would need this to deliver title clear of the blanket liens.

65. b) His first lien holder will not refinance unless there is a subordination clause in the second. A refinance is a new loan, and without the subordination provision, the refinance would place the first lien holder in a second lien position.

66. a) There are many pitfalls to construction lending; a lender must be cautious.

67. c) Advances called for in a construction loan agreement are referred to as obligatory advances.

68. b) A permanent loan is also called a "take out" loan. It takes the construction loan out of the picture.

69. d) The take out loan is the permanent loan used to finance the acquisition of property and take the construction loan out of the picture.

70. c) An interim loan is a temporary loan used to finance the construction. It is paid off with a permanent loan.

71. d) The Treasury Department is fiscal manager for the United States.

72. b) FHA-insured residential loans fall under Title II of the National Housing Act.

73. a) The FmHA is the federal agency that makes loans to ranchers and farmers who are unable to obtain loans from private sources, such as the Federal Land Bank.

74. c) The GNMA, the FHA and the OILSR are divisions of HUD.

75. d) The power of sale clause, found in a trust deed, authorizes a trustee to sell the secured property at public auction in the event of default by the borrower (trustor).

76. a) The defeasance clause states that, when paid in full, a mortgage or deed of trust lien will be canceled.

77. a) It is known as a partial reconveyance provision if the security instrument is a trust deed and a partial satisfaction piece if the debt is secured by a mortgage.

78. c) When a seller extends credit to a purchaser, the debt is secured by a mortgage or deed of trust, and under these circumstances the security instrument is referred to as a purchase money mortgage or purchase money deed of trust.

79. a) P.M.I. refers to Private Mortgage Insurance, which is used in connection with 90% and 95% conventional loans.

80. d) There is no such thing as an insured lien system.

81. c) At the lowest point in the cycle, the rental market is poor and vacancy rates are high; as the cycle passes the low point, rents will begin to increase.

82. a) The shift to the suburbs is due, in part, to the fact that the labor force can use automobiles to commute to work in outlying areas.

83. b) A high occupancy rate indicates a shortage of space and the possibility of rental increases, while a low occupancy rate will result in tenant demands for lower rents and/or other concessions by the landlord.

10. Real Estate Appraisal

1. The function of an appraiser is to:

   I. set value
   II. estimate value

   a) I only
   b) II only
   c) Both I and II
   d) Neither I nor II

2. The real estate appraisal is an estimate of value:

   a) based on replacement costs
   b) based on analysis of fact as of a specific date
   c) derived from data covering the preceding six months
   d) derived from tax assessments covering the past five years

3. The conditions of sale will affect the:

   a) price of the subject property
   b) cost of the subject property
   c) value of the subject property
   d) utility of the subject property

4. The sum of money at which a property is offered for sale is the:

   a) value
   b) book value
   c) price
   d) market value

5. The prime requisites of value are:

   a) demand, transferability, cost, scarcity
   b) demand, scarcity, utility, transferability
   c) demand, cost, transferability, age
   d) demand, cost, transferability, utility

6. What is the relationship between desire of property and the prospective purchaser?

   a) Utility
   b) Value
   c) Need
   d) Purchasing power

7. What would you say is the real basis for value of the average property; i.e., the economic characteristics of value?

   a) Opportunity for a profit if purchased
   b) Its relative scarcity and the demand for it
   c) How it is zoned
   d) Replacement costs

8. The accumulation of several contiguous properties under one ownership, thus creating a large parcel of proportionately greater value, involves:

   a) depreciation
   b) plottage
   c) corner influence
   d) zoning value

9. In directional growth, which center is involved?

   a) Manufacturing
   b) Residential
   c) Industrial
   d) Commercial

10. The value of all vacant land is influenced by its best potential use. One of the leading factors or influences in the valuation of urban industrial land is:

    a) front footage
    b) size or acreage
    c) corner influence
    d) unearned increment

11. In an appraiser's viewpoint, on which side of the street would be best to locate a retail business?

a) East
b) North
c) South
d) West

12. Corner influence can add most to the value of:

a) industrial property
b) apartment property
c) agricultural property
d) retail business property

13. 4-3-2-1 is a familiar approach to one facet of real estate practice. It normally refers to which of the following?

a) Lot, house, garage and furniture
b) Tract, parcel, quadrant in county
c) House, lot, furnishing and garage
d) Method used in appraising vacant land of different depths

14. As a lot increases in depth:

a) its value decreases, but front foot value increases
b) its value increases, and front foot value increases
c) its value decreases, and front foot value decreases
d) its value increases, and front foot value decreases

15. Frontage is of most concern when appraising:

a) commercial property
b) raw land
c) income producing property
d) residential property

16. Pedestrian traffic counts are usually taken to determine:

a) urban population
b) size of shopping area
c) rental value of a location
d) average age group

17. How the improvement is located in relation to the lot is best described as:

a) orientation
b) topography
c) placement
d) plottage

18. An increase in the appraised value of property which is considered an unearned increment is most likely to be caused by:

a) increase in population
b) capital improvements
c) management expense
d) increase in amenities

19. As a concept of value, the highest and best use is the use that:

a) contributes to the best interest of the community
b) complies with zoning and deed restrictions
c) produces the highest gross income
d) produces the greatest net return on the investment

20. The highest and best use to which a lot could be put is determined by:

a) what use would presently produce the largest net income
b) what use would produce the greatest net income in future years
c) how tall a building the neighborhood would warrant
d) what similar vacant lots are being leased for

21. The concept holding that it's the future, not the past, which is of prime importance in estimating value is called the:

a) principle of substitution
b) principle of change
c) principle of supply and demand
d) principle of competition

22. Plans have been announced for a multimillion dollar shopping center to be built next door to a vacant lot you own. Property values in the area of the proposed site will tend to increase as a result of this announcement. This is an example of the principle of:

a) anticipation
b) highest and best use
c) supply and demand
d) substitution

23. An appraiser wants to determine if it is economically feasible for the owner of an apartment building to put in a swimming pool for his tenants' use. The appraiser would be most concerned with the principle of:

a) regression
b) substitution
c) conformity
d) contribution

24. One of the most important factors in upholding the value of residential property is:

a) that a majority of homes were purchased with low down payments
b) that the ratio of rentals to owner-occupied homes is equal
c) that the owners' incomes are substantially equal and the homes have approximately the same value
d) that the owners have substantially the same income

25. The stability of the value of single-family homes is least protected in a neighborhood where there is:

a) a similarity of homeowners' income
b) an increase in the mixture of average quality homes with good quality homes
c) a minimum of violations to existing restrictions
d) a predominance of individuals from one ethnic group or religious affiliation

26. In the event a person integrated a high quality home costing $80,000 into a neighborhood where other homes were valued at $35,000, he would suffer a loss in value by economic obsolescence due to:

a) regression
b) supply and demand
c) progression
d) aversion

27. There are three approaches to valuation and all three should be used. Depending on the type of property being appraised, however, one approach will have more weight and should afford greater authority. The comparison approach is given greater weight in the appraisal of:

a) apartment property
b) service property
c) single-family dwellings
d) industrial property

28. One of the chief advantages of the market data approach in the appraisal of real property is that:

a) it is the easiest method for a beginner to learn and use
b) it is more economical and timely
c) there are always a great number of comparable properties in the neighborhood
d) None of the above

29. If you are asked to appraise a vacant lot for the purpose of building a single-family residence, which approach would you most likely use?

a) Construction cost approach
b) Capitalization approach
c) Market data approach
d) Correlation of A and B

30. Whenever possible, all three approaches to value are used. Comparison approach is given greater weight than the others when appraising:

a) apartment property
b) service property
c) one family dwellings
d) industrial property

31. In which of the following situations would the comparative method of appraisal be least reliable?

a) When all comparables are in the same price range
b) In a real estate market that is inactive
c) When the comparables are located in another neighborhood
d) In all of the above

32. A property with amenities is best appraised by:

a) capitalization
b) observed condition
c) replacement cost
d) comparative analysis

33. An unimportant factor influencing the value o a home would be:

a) potential rental income
b) demand of a financially qualified buye
c) quality of construction
d) functional plan of the home

34. An appraiser, in the appraisal of a single family residential home, would use:

a) recent sales prices
b) exchange prices
c) offering prices
d) listing prices

35. An appraiser who is using the comparison method to appraise a single family residence would never use the selling price of which of the following?

a) A similar home that sold over six months ago
b) A similar home that sold recently but is located in another neighborhood
c) A similar home that was sold by owners who were forced to sell at any price because of financial difficulties
d) A home of similar size but situated on a corner lot

36. Which of the following is not relevant in appraising a home?

a) Circumstances of sale
b) Original cost to build twelve months previously
c) Square footage of improvements
d) Recent selling price of comparables

37. The conditions of sale will affect the:

a) price of the subject property
b) cost of the subject property
c) value of the subject property
d) utility of the subject property

38. In appraising a property, the square footage for replacement cost purposes would be determined by:

a) measuring the inside of the various rooms and adding together
b) measuring the outside of the house and garage
c) measuring the inside of the house as a whole
d) measuring the outside of the house, excluding the garage

39. When appraising property, which of the following would be least important when using the replacement cost approach?

a) Current construction cost per square foot
b) Rental cost per square foot
c) Depreciated expense
d) Estimated land value

40. It cost forty-five dollars per square foot to build a home of 2,500 square feet. The cost per square foot to build a home of the same quality that has 1,500 square feet should be:

a) less
b) more
c) the same
d) None of the above

41. All other factors being equal, comparable areas of living space in a two story house usually:

a) cost more than in a one story house
b) cost less than in a one story house
c) cost the same as in a one story house
d) have no correlation as to construction cost when compared to a one story house.

42. The most expensive and time consuming method of estimating the cost of construction is:

a) unit-in-place
b) quantity survey
c) comparison method
d) income approach

43. You would use the comparative method in the appraisal of property by the cost approach method:

a) to evaluate worn-out or otherwise non-repairable fixtures
b) to compute the land value
c) to determine the value of amenities
d) All of the above

44. Which of the following would be the most expensive method of appraisal of large income-producing properties?

a) Market data approach
b) Comparative approach
c) Replacement cost approach
d) Captitalization approach

45. The replacement cost method of appraising real property:

a) tends to set the upper limits of value
b) would be the method used in appraising special purpose properties
c) is good as to new improvements
d) would be satisfactory for any of the foregoing

46. The market value of an improved property may:

a) exceed or be less than replacement cost of the improvements added to the market value of the land
b) be greater than the cost of land and improvements but never less than their cost
c) never be greater nor less than the cost of the land and improvements
d) equal but at no time exceed the value of the land and current reproduction costs of the improvements

47. On a service property, which approach to value is most reliable?

a) Capitalization approach
b) Comparison approach
c) Reproduction cost
d) Gross multiplier

48. An appraiser was hired to estimate the value of city hall, a very beautiful and unique structure with Roman architecture. Which appraoch to value did he use?

a) Capitalization
b) Reproduction
c) Comparison
d) Any of the above

49. The replacement cost method of appraising is most applicable to:

a) older homes converted to apartments
b) apartment houses
c) single-family dwellings
d) service type buildings

50. In the appraisal of real property, accrued depreciation is best described as:

a) difference between cost of replacement new as of appraisal date and the present appraised value
b) the amount of depreciation that may take place in the future
c) an entry made in accounting records to reflect depreciation accrued over the economic life of an improvement
d) None of these

51. Physical deterioration results from:

a) tax liens
b) overcrowded occupancy
c) deferred maintenance
c) management cost

52. The decrease in value because of outmoded function is known as:

I. functional obsolesence
II. deterioration

a) I only
b) II only
c) Both I and II
d) Neither I nor II

53. Functional obsolescence may be caused by:

a) physical deterioration
b) deferred maintenance
c) change in zoning
d) design

54. Functional utility in a dwelling is dependent upon:

a) desires of its occupants
b) floor plan and equipment
c) zoning in area
d) condition of heating system

55. Hathaway, a builder, has just completed a four-bedroom, one bath, 2,500 square foot home. It has already depreciated due to:

a) functional obsolescence
b) economic obsolescence
c) over-improvement
d) It has not depreciated

56. In real estate, the greatest loss occurs from:

a) deterioration
b) obsolescence
c) lack of maintenance
d) passage of time

57. Which of the following types of depreciation would be most difficult to eliminate?

a) Physical deterioration
b) Functional obsolescence
c) Physical depreciation
d) Economic obsolescence

58. Capitalization is a process to:

I. determine potential future value
II. convert income into value

a) I only
b) II only
c) Both I and II
d) Neither I nor II

59. The capitalization approach to value would be widely used:

I. on residential property in a new subdivision
II. on lease property in a shopping center

a) I only
b) II only
c) Both I and II
d) Neither I nor II

60. In analyzing gross income of a property, the characteristic of the income that the appraiser is concerned with is:

a) quantity
b) quality
c) durability
d) All of the above

61. In determining the value of a twenty unit apartment property, the appraiser has established the gross income from rents. After deducting the loss for vacancies and collection losses from this gross income, he would have established the:

a) effective gross income
b) gross income
c) net income
d) spendable income

62. In the income approach to value the net income is determined by deducting the expenses from the:

a) operating profit
b) gross income
c) effective gross income
d) None of the above

63. Which of the following is not acceptable in figuring the capitalized value of a five-plex?

a) Maintenance cost
b) Managerial fees
c) Principal payments
d) Vacancy factor

64. A newly appraised apartment house is valued by the income approach. Under which of the following circumstances would you deduct a management cost from the effective gross income?

a) The owner manages the apartments and occupies one of them
b) A tenant manages the complex in exchange for free rent
c) Where an occupant/manager of an adjacent apartment house also manages this apartment complex at no additional cost to the investor
d) All of the above

65. A common way to establish a capitalization rate is to:

a) analyze market prices
b) analyze stability of building's occupants
c) refer to tables prepared by the American Institute of Real Estate Appraisers
d) select the rate based only on your desired return

66. The capitalization rate has considerable effect upon the appraisal value of property. Which of the following statements is true?

a) The capitalization rate consists only of the component related to return on investment
b) An increase in the capitalization rate produces an increase in the appraisal value
c) A decrease in the capitalization rate produces an increase in the appraisal value
d) The capitalization rate will be higher for property where a long term tenant has shown a good record of payment, than for one with a relatively new tenant with a poor record of payment.

67. The reasonable rent expectancy if the property were available for rent at the time of its valuation would be termed:

a) developed rent
b) economic rent
c) contract rent
d) None of the above

68. The gross multiplier method is used primarily for:

a) commercial properties
b) residential rentals
c) industrial sites
d) None of the above

69. To obtain a gross rent multiplier, the appraiser must obtain from comparable properties:

a) the cost and annual income
b) the monthly rent and selling price
c) the net income and selling price
d) the net income and rate of capitalization

70. An appraiser has been requested to place a value on a residential home. He finds that the home, when originally built, had an estimated total economic life of forty years. At this time the home is ten years old. In viewing the home, he finds that it has been exceptionally well cared for and maintained in such a lovely manner that he plans to consider its age as only six years. This age is known as the:

a) actual age
b) effective age
c) undepreciated age
d) remaining life

71. When improvements on land reach that age when the income from the total property does not pay reasonable return on the land value, the buildings are said to have reached the end of their:

a) amortization
b) highest and best use
c) economic life
d) lease value

72. To establish the value of an income property you would capitalize the net income. In itemizing the expenses, provision can be made to allow for the return of the investment. This expense would be:

a) interest
b) depreciation
c) principal payments
d) income taxes

73. If you set aside $5,000 each year in a bank so that in five years you will have $30,000 to replace equipment, it would be called:

a) fiscal mismanagement
b) a sinking fund
c) straight-line method
d) a declining balance method

1. b) An appraiser does not set value; he or she estimates what the value is.

2. b) An appraiser's estimate of value is considered to be valid only for that point in time for which the estimate was made.

3. a) The conditions of a sale, such as forced sale, may affect the market price of the property (the amount paid) but would have no affect on its cost, value or utility.

4. c) According to the American Institute of Real Estate Appraisers, price is "the amount of money paid, asked or offered where a sale is contemplated." Market price, specifically, is the amount paid for the property.

5. b) The four essentials of value are scarcity, transferability, utility and demand.

6. a) Utility is the ability to arouse the desire for possession and the ability to satisfy that desire.

7. b) This is an example of supply and demand. All other matters affecting the property's value revolve around its usefulness and scarcity.

8. b) Contiguous means adjoining. The question represents the definition of plottage.

9. b) Directional growth refers to the general direction a city's residences are growing.

10. b) The vital factor for an industrial site is the size of the parcel. Industrial complexes usually require considerable space and are not concerned with exposure to the retail public.

11. c) The south side of the street is generally considered to be the shadiest during the entire period of the day. The west side would be the next choice because it receives the morning sun but is in the cooler area later in the day.

12. d) A corner location provides greater accessibility, increased pedestrian count, prominence, and display area.

13. d) This is one of several depth tables. Under this rule a lot is divided into quarters, with the front quarter carrying forty percent of the value of the land, the next quarter, thirty percent, the third, twenty percent, and the last, ten percent.

14. b) The deeper the lot the greater its value. Since the front footage remains the same and the value increases, the front foot value must also increase.

15. a) Retail properties are usually sold on a per front foot basis, meaning at a certain amount of dollars per front foot. Commercial land with 100 feet fronting on the street might sell for $200.00 per front foot, or $20,000.00. Residential land is usually sold according to square footage (frontage times depth) and industrial land by the square foot, or more often, by the acre.

16. c) Major shopping centers can promise potential tenants a large number of patrons (pedestrian traffic) and, accordingly, can command higher rents for their facilities.

17. a) This is the definition of orientation.

18. a) Unearned increment is an increase in value of real estate due to no effort on the part of the owner, often due to an increase in population. Amenities may or may not be due to the owner's effort.

19. d) Emphasis is on net return or net income, as opposed to gross income.

20. a) The highest and best use is the use which at the time of the appraisal would produce the greatest net return.

21. b) This is the definition of the principle of change.

22. a) This would be an example of the principle of anticipation, which holds that value is created by the expectation of benefits to be derived in the future.

23. d) Will the proposed improvement — the swimming pool — contribute enough value in the form of higher rents from tenants and, ultimately, net income to the owner, to justify the expense of installing it?

24. c) The maximum value of residential property will be found where there is a high degree of conformity. A person who builds an $80,000 home in an area of $30,000 homes will probably see his property lose value (regress).

25. b) A mixture of average and good quality homes in the same neighborhood would violate the principle of conformity.

26. a) A loss in value caused by association with many lesser valued houses in close proximity.

27. c) The comparison approach would be the most reliable method regardless of the type property being appraised, because recent sales prices of similar type properties reflect the attitudes of buyers and sellers on the open market—an invaluable guide for any appraiser. However, when appraising something other than a residence, the appraiser very often is not able to find enough sales of similar properties to serve as reliable value indicaters and he must then apply other techniques.

28. a) The market data method is the easiest method to learn and use but cannot be used if there are few or no comparable properties. The expense in time to gather the data may prove to be quite high.

29. c) Market data is the applicable method for residential land. For that matter, it is the best method when appraising virtually any kind of land.

30. c) The comparison of market data approach is most often used in appraising residential property because of the widespread availability of acceptable comparables. The comparison approach loses its reliability when there are few comparable sales.

31. b) There is no available data in an inactive market. If however, the appraiser has had some recent sales and can determine the rate of appreciation, he can update sales that occurred six months ago or more.

32. d) Amenities are benefits incidental to property ownership, such as views, close proximity to shopping and public transportation or even the prestige that goes with living in a certain area. The only way to estimate what buyers will pay for these benefits is to compare the subject property's amenities against similarly endowed properties that have sold in the recent past.

33. a) A home's amenity value—benefits derived from residing therein— will invariably serve as a more reliable indication of value than any rental income it has the potential of producing. Compared to other types of real estate, residences are poor investments, and the capitalization approach to value under these circumstances is impractical. Alternative b) refers to demand implemented by purchasing power—one of the four essential ingredients to value.

34. a) The market data or comparison approach is based upon the willing buyer in terms of money which a property will bring if exposed for sale in the open market, allowing a reasonable time to find a purchaser with knowledge of the property's use and capabilities for use. It is the price at which a willing seller would sell and a willing buyer would buy, neither being under abnormal pressure.

35. c) The price of a forced sale is never used in making comparisons of selling prices for appraisal purposes. The selling price of a home that was sold one year ago can be adjusted to reflect any inflationary trend, and selling prices of homes in other neighborhoods can also be used by allowing for differences in the neighborhood.

36. a) Circumstances of the sale do not affect the value of the property, though they may very well affect the sales price. The original cost to build just a year ago will have some relevance since very little depreciation would have taken place in the ensuing 12 months.

37. a) Conditions of the sale, such as a forced sale, may affect the price paid for a property but would have no effect on its cost, value, or utility.

38. b) When calculating square footage for replacement cost purposes, you measure the outside of all the improvements. This should not be confused with the process of determining the number of square feet in the improved living area, which is the outside measurements of the house, excluding garage.

39. b) The cost method involves estimating the current cost of construction, less the amount of accrued depreciation, then adding back in the value of the land.

40. b) The larger the home, the less it should cost per square foot. There are certain fixed costs, such as kitchens and bathrooms, which must be included in every home, regardless of size. Furthermore, the cost of grading the lot and installing plumbing and sewage systems exists no matter how small the home.

41. b) The construction costs for a 2,000 square foot two story house will be less than those of a 2,000 square foot one story house because the two story structure will have only half the foundation and roof area of the one story home. These are not the only savings but are indicative of the economy of two story construction.

42. b) The quantity survey is the most time consuming of the methods employed in the cost approach to estimate replacement cost.

43. b) Land cannot be manufactured, therefore the comparative method (market data approach) must be used to arrive at a value of land.

44. c) The replacement cost method is normally the most time consuming and expensive method.

45. d) The cost approach method is frequently used to set a ceiling upon the value established by the other two approach methods. It is particularly appropriate for appraising newly built improvements where the construction represents the highest and best use of the land. It is also the most appropriate method for appraising service type properties such as public schools, city halls, libraries, etc.

46. a) While the replacement cost normally sets the upper limit of value, in times of unusual demand, market value may exceed replacement cost. Examples of such occasions would be the World War II years when there was a moratorium on building and, more recently, the Alaskan boom when demand far outstripped the ability of builders to create the supply.

47. c) Since they do not produce income and are not frequently sold the only method of appraisal is by the replacement or reproduction cost approach. A library or public swimming pool would fall into this category.

48. b) Reproduction is the only approach available. There is no income for capitalization and there are no comparable sales.

49. d) Replacement cost means the cost to replace the structure with one having utility equivalent to that being appraised, but constructed with modern materials and according to current standards, design, and layout. It is the only way service buildings, which do not earn money and have no market, can be appraised.

50. a) Accrued depreciation is that which has already taken place. The key words in the question are, "in the appraisal of real property." Appraisers are concerned with actual depreciation, not hypothetical losses in value for accounting purposes.

51. c) Physical deterioration is a type of depreciation resulting from wear and tear, deferred maintenance, etc.

52. a) Outmoded function or out of date design or material are examples of functional obsolescence, such as a one car garage.

53. d) Functional obsolescence is a form of depreciation that can result from unappealing design.

54. b) Good planning and design result in functional utility.

55. a) Functional obsolescence is a loss of value resulting from such things as poor design, or outmoded design according to modern tastes. Residential styles today would dictate that a home of this size with four bedrooms have more than one bathroom.

56. b) Functional and economic obsolescence cause the greatest losses in value.

57. d) Economic obsolescence is considered incurable. No amount of investment can correct an adverse zoning change or blighting influences.

58. b) The capitalization process is a means of determining present value.

59. b) The income (capitalization) approach is normally used for income property, and is impractical when appraising residential property.

60. d) Quantity means adequacy of income. Quality refers to financial stability and creditworthiness of tenants. Durability concerns itself with terms of the building's leases.

61. a) Effective gross income is the term used to designate the income remaining after deducting the bad debt/vacancy factor from the potential gross income. From effective gross income you subtract the building's operating expenses to arrive at net earnings.

62. c) Gross income less bad debt/vacancy factor equals effective gross income; less operating expenses equals net income.

63. c) Principal and interest payments are not deducted to reach net income for capitalization.

64. d) A prudent investor will consider all expenses to arrive at a net income. Free rent is certainly an expense. Also, that the apartment is presently managed by the owner or by someone else at no cost does not alter the fact that management is necessary and a potential operating expense for anyone contemplating a purchase of the property.

65. a) The most often used method for selecting a capitalization rate is to research the market to determine what other informed investors are demanding in the way of a return on their real estate investments.

66. c) A decrease in capitalization rate would indicate less risk and, therefore, greater value of the investment.

67. b) Economic rent is what a landlord presently could get from tenants on the open market, as opposed to contract rent, which is what he is actually getting as a result of lease agreements.

68. b) It can be applied with respect to any rental income-producing property. It is most applicable to residential rentals because of their abundance and desirability for market analysis purposes.

69. b) The gross rent multiplier is obtained by dividing the sales price by the monthly gross rental income, or annual gross income.

70. b) The effective age is the age established by the appraiser through his judgment. Even though a building is ten years old, it enjoys the condition of a six-year-old property with a remaining economic life (useful life) of 34 years.

71. c) Economic life is the period over which buildings may be profitably utilized.

72. b) The improvements (buildings) on an income property will eventually wear out and will no longer earn income. Therefore, the investment in the improvements diminishes to zero. To allow for this gradual wearing out, depreciation is allowed as an expense in the annual calculation for income. By setting aside a sum each year (depreciation), enough money is eventually accumulated to replace or return the investment.

73. b) A sinking fund is one in which money is set aside from income-producing properties which, with accrued interest, will eventually pay for replacement of the improvements.

11. Federal Regulation of Real Estate Transactions

1. A land developer plans to subdivide a parcel into 150 lots. He plans to sell lots in other states through direct mail and ads. Which of these statements is correct under the Interstate Land Sales Full Disclosure Act provisions?

   a) Purchasers have 48 hours to cancel a purchase agreement from time of execution
   b) Purchasers lose cancellation rights if they inspect property before signing a contract
   c) Purchasers are not entitled to cancel contract as the offering is a house-and-lot package and such offering is exempt from the law
   d) Purchasers are not entitled to cancel as there are less than 300 lots in the subdivision

2. Who administers the Interstate Land Sales Full Disclosure Act of 1968?

   a) HUD
   b) FTC
   c) Real Estate Division
   d) Bureau of Land Management

3. ILSFDA does not apply to developments where each lot is:

   a) one acre or more
   b) two acres or more
   c) three acres or more
   d) five acres or more

4. With respect to the Interstate Land Sales Full Disclosure Act of 1968, the purchaser may not rescind if:

   a) he has personally inspected the property, and all lots are free and clear
   b) the subdivision contains fewer than 50 lots
   c) each of the lots is five acres or larger
   d) Any of the above

5. The sale of subdivided lands is regulated by:

   a) state
   b) cities and counties
   c) federal law
   d) All of these

6. Title VIII of the Civil Rights Act of 1968 is also called the:

   a) Open Housing Act
   b) Federal Fair Housing Act
   c) Equal Opportunity in Housing Act
   d) Washington Discrimination Law

7. The Federal Fair Housing Law declares a U.S. policy of:

   a) building housing for minority groups throughout the U.S.
   b) guaranteeing separate but equal housing in all of the states
   c) providing fair housing throughout the U.S.
   d) eliminating prejudice throughout the U.S.

8. Title VIII of the Civil Rights Act of 1968 precludes:

   I. discrimination in housing
   II. discrimination in lending

   a) I only
   b) II only
   c) Both I and II
   d) Neither I nor II

9. The Federal Open Housing Act has a direct impact on:

   a) federal housing
   b) federally-insured loans
   c) non-federal housing
   d) All of the above

10. Which of the following is exempt from the Federal Fair Housing Law of 1968?

    a) A broker selling vacant lots in a subdivision
    b) A salesman selling a multi-family dwelling
    c) An owner selling his unoccupied single family dwelling
    d) None of the above

11. Seller Colwell employs Salesman Mathews who brings a full price offer from a qualified black purchaser. Broker then produces a low offer from a white purchaser. Seller Colwell rejects both offers. Salesman Mathews then submits an offer from Colwell's neighbor who makes the offer because he opposes blacks moving into the neighborhood, and Colwell accepts this offer. According to the 1968 Federal Fair Housing Act, who would not be liable?

    a) Seller
    b) Neighbor
    c) Mathews
    d) First offeror

12. According to the 1968 Civil Rights Act, a person who feels he has been discriminated against can:

    a) seek injunctive relief and sue for damages in a state or federal court
    b) file criminal charges in a federal court
    c) file criminal charges in a superior court
    d) sue for specific performance in a federal or state court

13. The U.S. Attorney General would be most likely to take action to enforce the Federal Open Housing Law when:

    a) state laws are not enforced by state officials, or there are no state anti-discrimination laws
    b) a complaint is filed with H.U.D.
    c) a conspiracy to violate this law is suspected
    d) an owner of more than four units is charged with violation of this law

14. Who does not have to display an Equal Opportunity Housing sign?

    a) An owner selling his own business
    b) A broker selling a single family dwelling
    c) A real estate office in a subdivision
    d) A manager of an apartment house

15. What does the following symbol stand for?

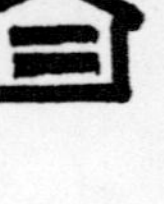

    a) H.U.D.
    b) N.A.R.
    c) Equal Opportunity Housing
    d) United States Fair Housing Act

16. Assume that Susan Jones, licensee, finds a buyer ready, willing, and able to buy property. She prepares a real estate purchase and sale agreement. When she telephones the principals on the offer, they request information on the national origin of the buyers.

    a) Susan, under the law of agency, must convey this information
    b) Susan should tell the principals to withdraw their property from the market quickly
    c) If Susan gives this information, she has violated the fair housing laws
    d) Susan may volunteer this information without liability

17. Blockbusting is an acceptable practice:

    a) only under the supervision of real estate licensees
    b) only when approved by either H.U.D. or the Justice Department
    c) under no circumstances
    d) only if the seller and buyer mutually agree

18. "Racial steering" means to:

    a) steer brokers to minority prospects
    b) steer minority prospects toward a limited number of choices
    c) steer minority prospects toward affordable property
    d) prejudicial behavior among cows

19. The 42nd U.S. Code, Section 1982, bans all racial discrimination as a result of the outcome of the Jones vs. Mayer case. Constitutionality for this rests on the:

    a) 5th Amendment
    b) 12th Amendment
    c) 13th Amendment
    d) 24th Amendment

20. A deed restriction created in 1920 that prohibits the sale of property to a non-Caucasian until after 1995 is:

    a) valid until all the property owners agree to eliminate the restriction
    b) enforceable
    c) unenforceable
    d) covered by title insurance

21. Where property is subject to deed restrictions prohibiting it from being conveyed to a black person, a deed naming a black person as grantee of said property would be:

a) void
b) valid
c) the restriction would prevail and the property could not be conveyed
d) the restriction is unenforceable and deed consequently void

22. RESPA applies to:

a) all mortgages and deeds of trust
b) first mortgages and deeds of trust
c) installment contracts
d) discriminatory conduct

23. Violation of RESPA is punishable by:

a) a fine of up to $10,000
b) up to one year in prison
c) Both of the above
d) None of the above

24. Under RESPA, within how many days of a loan application must the lender give the borrower a good faith estimate of settlement costs?

a) 1
b) 3
c) 7
d) 10

25. RESPA requires use of a form document called a:

a) disclosure statement
b) Uniform Settlement Statement
c) Uniform Disclosure Statement
d) None of the above

26. The Home Mortgage Disclosure Act helps to enforce the prohibition against:

a) redlining
b) steering
c) blockbusting
d) None of the above

27. The Truth-in-Lending Act:

a) sets a maximum interest rate which lenders can charge borrowers
b) requires the disclosure of certain information
c) Both of the above
d) None of the above

28. Regulation Z applies to:

a) personal credit transactions under $25,000
b) personal credit transactions over $25,000
c) agricultural credit transactions over $25,000
d) All of the above

29. Regulation Z covers credit offered which is payable in how many installments?

a) More than one installment
b) More than four installments
c) More than ten installments
d) None of the above

30. Under the Truth-in-Lending Act, the annual percentage rate:

a) is the total annual cost of the loan including loan fees, finder's fees, service charges, points and interest
b) includes attorney's fees, title fees and closing costs
c) Both of the above
d) None of the above

31. Under Regulation Z, a borrower has how long to rescind a credit transaction without penalty?

a) Until midnight of the third business day
b) Until midnight of the seventh business day
c) A borrower can always rescind without penalty
d) A borrower can never rescind without penalty

32. Regulation Z applies to:

a) all creditors
b) all creditors who regularly arrange for or extend credit
c) all mortgagors
d) None of the above

33. If an advertisement subject to the Truth-in-Lending Law mentions the amount of the payments on the loan, it must also mention:

a) all the cash price of the loan
b) the amount of the down payment
c) the due dates of the payments
d) All of the above

1. b) If buyers have personally inspected the property, they have not cancellation rights under the Interstate Land Sales Full Disclosure Act.

2. a) It is administered by the Office of Interstate Land Sales Registration (OILSR), a division of H.U.D.

3. d) If the subdivision is 50 or more lots, any one of which is less than five acres, it must be registered with the Office of Interstate Land Sales Registration.

4. d) There are four exemptions from the Federal Land Disclosure Act: the three noted above and where the land being sold is improved by a building or in which there is a contract obligating the seller to erect one within two years of the sale. Where there is an exemption, there is no right to rescind.

5. d) The state regulates through the Washington Land Development Act, the federal government under the Interstate Land Sales Full Disclosure Act, while cities and counties exercise regulatory control by approving or denying proposed subdivisions, zoning ordinances, etc.

6. b) Title VIII of the 1968 Civil Rights Act is that portion of the Civil Rights Act which addresses discrimination in housing. It is called the Federal Fair Housing Law.

7. c) Title VIII of the Civil Rights Act of 1968, also called the Federal Fair Housing Law, declares a national policy of providing housing free from discrimination (fair housing).

8. c) The Civil Rights Act prohibits discriminatory practices when selling, renting, advertising, or financing housing.

9. d) The act prohibits certain discriminatory acts which concern federal and non-federal housing and both federally-insured and private loans.

10. c) One exemption would be if no broker were involved, the owner owned no more than three such dwellings, and the owner did not sell more than one such dwelling in any two year period in which he or she was not the most recent occupant. However, there are other federal, state, and local laws prohibiting discrimination which do not provide for such an exemption.

11. d) Salesman Mathews should have refused to continue to represent Seller Colwell when it became clear the latter was selling on a discriminatory basis. The seller and his neighbor were working together to keep blacks from coming into the neighborhood.

12. a) Criminal charges are filed by a prosecuting attorney or U.S. attorney general, not by private individuals. Specific performance is a remedy for breach of contract, not violation of civil rights laws.

13. a) If a state has equivalent anti-discrimination legislation, the complainant is first required to bring an action in state court.

14. a) As of May 1, 1972, the Equal Opportunity poster must be displayed by brokerage offices, model homes, mortgage lenders and so on. The equal opportunity in housing laws do not apply to the sale of businesses.

15. c) The Equal Opportunity poster, displaying the symbol above, must be shown conspicuously in the offices of brokers, lenders, and others.

16. c) The giving of such information constitutes discrimination and is in violation of the real estate law and the fair housing laws.

17. c) Blockbusting is an illegal and discriminatory practice whereby some person induces a property owner to enter into a real estate transaction from which the first person may benefit financially, by claiming that an inevitable influx of minority families into the neighborhood will cause property values to decline.

18. b) "Steering" refers to showing minority buyers only areas receptive to minority groups. It is illegal.

19. c) Constitutionality for this statute rests on the 13th Amendment to the U.S. Constitution, which bars slavery.

20. c) A deed containing such a provision is valid, but the restriction is unenforceable.

21. b) The deed would be valid and title would be conveyed. The restriction in the deed relating to discrimination would be unenforceable.

22. b) RESPA, the Real Estate Settlement and Procedures Act, applies to new first mortgages or deeds of trust on residential property which are given to federally-regulated mortgage lenders.

23. c) Violation of RESPA is punishable by a fine of up to $10,000 and up to one year in prison.

24. b) A lender must give a borrower an estimate within three days of the loan application.

25. b) RESPA requires use of the Uniform Settlement Statement.

26. a) The Home Mortgage Disclosure Act helps to enforce the prohibition against redlining by requiring institutional lenders with assets in excess of $10 million to file an annual report of all loans made during that year. Loans are categorized according to locations of various properties so redlining can be more easily discovered.

27. b) The Truth-in-Lending Act requires the disclosure of certain information that allows those in need of consumer credit to readily compare the various credit terms available to them.

28. a) Regulation Z applies to credit when it is applied for other than business purposes (unless the business purpose is agriculture). Personal and agricultural credit transactions over $25,000 are exempt from Regulation Z.

29. b) Regulation Z covers credit offered which is payable in more than four installments.

30. a) The annual percentage rate is the total annual cost of the loan including loan fees, finder's fees, service charges, points and interest.

31. a) A borrower has until midnight of the third business day.

32. b) Regulation Z applies to all creditors who regularly arrange for or extend credit. Thus, an owner of a single-family home does not ordinarily have to adhere to Regulation Z disclosure requirements, even if he sells under a real estate contract payable in more than four installments.

33. d) If an advertisement mentions the amount of payments, it must also mention the cash price of the loan, the amount of the down payment and the due dates of the payments.

12. Real Estate Math

1. An owner sold a lot with a front footage of 90 feet and a depth of 250 feet for $2.25 per square foot. What was the selling price?

   a) $347.50
   b) $607.50
   c) $24,300
   d) $50,625

2. A building used for storage measures 100 feet by 220 feet. It rents for $.32 per square foot per year. What is the rent over a year's time?

   a) $7,040
   b) $7,400
   c) $50,880
   d) $58,080

3. Which of the following is smaller than an acre?

   a) 4,860 square yards
   b) 180 square rods
   c) 180 feet by 240 feet
   d) 0.16% square mile

4. A rectangular property with 8,690 square yards has 318 front feet. What is the depth of the property?

   a) 245.94 feet
   b) 27.32 feet
   c) 27.32 yards
   d) 81.98 feet

5. The third quarter interest on a $7,600 loan at 8% interest is:

   a) $608
   b) $76
   c) $152
   d) None of the above

6. A client wants $63,000 for his property after he pays a 7% commission and 4½% other sales and closing costs. The sales price will have to be:

   a) $71,186
   b) $70,245
   c) $65,968.59
   d) $67,742

7. In order to earn $60 per month on a 9.5% investment, how much do you need to invest?

   a) $632
   b) $7,200
   c) $7,579
   d) $758

8. Mr. Smith sold three lots for a total of $39,000. He sold Lot A for $1,000 more than for Lot C, and Lot B for $4,000 more than Lot A. Mr. Smith sold Lot C for:

   a) $10,000
   b) $11,000
   c) $12,000
   d) $13,000

9. The assessed value is $48,700. The tax rate is $1.02 per $100 of assessed valuation. The tax is:

   a) $496.74
   b) $489.60
   c) $584.40
   d) $594.14

10. The outside dimensions of a two-story house measures 32.5 feet by 45.8 feet. The cost of construction of the first story was $31 per square foot and of the second story was $22 per square foot. A detached garage measuring 21.6 feet by 20.8 feet cost $16 per square foot. What was the total cost of construction?

a) $86,079
b) $78,890
c) $53,332
d) $99,475

11. Mr. Jones borrows $6,000 for two years at 8% interest per year. If the interest is prepaid, he will receive:

a) $6,000
b) $5,520
c) $5,040
d) $6,960

12. A property earns a net income of $210 per month. The capitalization rate is 7%. The value of the property is:

a) $17,640
b) $3,000
c) $30,000
d) $36,000

1. d) The area of the lot is 90 x 250 = 22,500 square feet. The sales price is 22,500 x 2.25 = $50,625.

2. a) The area of the building is 100 x 220 = 22,000 square feet. The annual rent is .32 x 22,000 = $7,040.00.

3. c) An acre is 43,560 square feet, which is equal to 4,840 square yards, 160 square rods, or 1/640 (.156%) of a square mile. 180 x 240 = 43,200 square feet.

4. a) 8,690 square yards equals 78,210 square feet (9 x 8,690 = 78,210). The area of a rectangle divided by its length gives the depth, so 78,210 divided by 318 = 245.94 feet, the depth of the lot.

5. c) 8% of $7,600 is $608.00 (.08 x 7,600 = 608). One quarter of $608.00 is $152.00 (.25 x 608 = 152).

6. a) 63,000 = 100% of sales price — 11½% of sales price
63,000 = (100% — 11½%) of sales price
63,000 = .885 x sales price

Rearrange the equation to isolate the unknown:

63,000 divided by .885 = sales price or $71,186.44.

7. c) I = P x R x T
60 = P x 9.5% x 1/12
60 = P x .095 x 1/12
P = 60 divided by (.095 x 1/12) = $7,578.95

8. b) A = 1,000 + C; B = 4,000 + A; A + B + C = 39,000.

Rearrange the first equations: C = A — 1,000 and then substitute into the third equation:

A + (4,000 + A) + (A — 1,000) = 39,000
3A + 4,000 — 1,000 = 39,000
3A = 39,000 — 3,000 = 36,000
A = 12,000

Since A = 1,000 + C, C must equal $11,000

9. a) (48,700 divided by 100) x 1.02 = 487 x 1.02 = $496.74

10. a) Each floor of the house has an area equal to 32.5 x 45.8 or 1,488.5 square feet. The cost of the first floor is 1,488.5 x 31 = $46,143.50. The cost of the second floor is 1,488.5 x 22 = $32,747.00. The area of the garage is 21.6 x 20.8 = 449.28 square feet, so its cost is 449.28 x 16 = $7,188.48. The total cost is, therefore, 46,143.50 + 32,747.00 + 7,188.48 = $86,078.98.

11. c) 8% of $6,000 is .08 x 6,000 = $480.00. Interest for two years is 2 x 480 = $960.00. Mr. Jones receives $6,000 minus $960.00, or $5,040.00.

12. d) First convert monthly to annual income: $210/month times 12 equals $2,520/year. Then use the capitalization formula: net income equals value times rate, or 2,520 = V x 7%.

Rearrange the equation to isolate the unknown and convert the percent to a decimal:

2,520 divided by .07 = V. The value is, therefore, $36,000.

13. Real Estate Escrow and Closing Statements

1. When a real estate deal is put in escrow, which of these is a true statement?

   a) Escrow need not be in writing for enforcing under Statute of Frauds
   b) Delivery or execution of a deed into escrow is sufficient to pass title
   c) Title insurance charges are uniform throughout the nation as to buyer and seller
   d) Recording of documents after escrow is completed, may or may not evidence title passing

2. When handling an escrow for both parties, the escrow holder is acting as:

   a) agent
   b) employee
   c) independent contractor
   d) beneficiary

3. Escrows are opened for protection of the:

   a) broker's commission
   b) public
   c) buyer and seller
   d) mortgagee

4. An escrow account is:

   a) always under the jurisdiction of the broker
   b) beyond the control of either party to it
   c) voidable after three years
   d) voidable by either buyer or seller

5. Smith purchases land and puts the deal in a 30-day escrow. He resells the land before the escrow closes with the contingency that the sale depends upon the closing of the first escrow. In this case, we have:

   a) an illegal escrow
   b) a perfect escrow
   c) a complete escrow
   d) a double escrow

6. It is the general practice of escrow companies to base their prorations on a year consisting of:

   a) 365 days
   b) 360 days
   c) 365½ days
   d) 365¼ days

7. Jones sells real property to Smith and each has fully performed his duties and obligations to the escrow. Jones dies prior to the recordation of the deed and transfer of title. The escrow is:

   a) null and void
   b) void as death always terminates an escrow
   c) valid and Smith is entitled to demand that the transaction close and the deed be recorded as provided for in the escrow instructions
   d) invalid and the heirs of Jones may ask the court to set aside the contract

8. Prior to the performance of conditions set forth in the escrow instructions, the escrow agent is trustee for:

   a) the seller only
   b) the buyer only
   c) all parties
   d) the lender only

9. The party responsible for the payment of the title closing is determined by:

a) agreement of the parties
b) law
c) broker
d) title officer

10. By state law, does a seller have to furnish a title insurance policy?

a) Yes
b) No
c) Only if no recent survey exists
d) Only if a mortgage is held on the property

11. Which is normally paid by the grantee?

a) Commission
b) Revenue stamps
c) Excise tax
d) None of the above

12. In closing a real estate transaction, the costs of standard title insurance will usually fall to:

a) the seller
b) the buyer
c) the broker
d) the seller and the buyer

13. Who usually pays the cost of recording a deed in a cash sale of property?

a) Buyer
b) Seller
c) Broker
d) None of these

14. Whose duty is it to affix the revenue stamps to the deed?

a) Seller
b) Broker
c) Both A and B
d) Neither A nor B

15. At the closing of a deal, which item is generally charged to the seller?

a) Recording deed
b) A.L.T.A. policy
c) Revenue stamps
d) Survey

16. The maximum real estate commission that may be charged is:

a) 7%
b) 12%
c) the usury limit
d) No maximum

17. Loan discounts in VA loans are generally paid by:

a) the lender
b) the purchaser
c) the seller
d) None of these

18. One discount point is equal to:

a) one percent of the sales price
b) ten percent of the down payment
c) one percent of the loan amount
d) None of these

19. The cost of examination of title for mortgagee and preparation of mortgage papers, at the closing, should be charged to:

a) the broker
b) the mortgagee
c) the seller
d) the buyer

20. Which of the following is usually paid by the buyer?

a) Recording the deed
b) Acknowledgment to the deed
c) Cost for preparing deed
d) All of these

21. The amount of transfer taxes to be attached to a warranty deed, at the rate of fifty cents for each $500 or fraction thereof, is always determined by the:

a) total selling price
b) cash payment made by the buyer
c) value of the seller's equity conveyed
d) cash payment and amount of any second trust deed not given by buyer

22. When must the excise tax be paid on a real estate sale on a real estate contract (land contract)?

a) When the deed is recorded
b) After contract is recorded
c) Before contract is recorded
d) None of these

1. b) Once a seller delivers a deed to the escrow holder, a valid conveyance of title will likely occur. Only a refusal to accept the deed or breach of contract by the grantee will prevent title from passing.

2. a) Specifically, a dual agent.

3. c) The buyer and seller employ a neutral third party to act as stakeholder.

4. b) When a valid escrow has been established, neither party can unilaterally alter or terminate the agreement on which it is based.

5. d) A double escrow exists when two escrows on the same piece of property are in existence at the same time, the second escrow dependent upon the closing of the first.

6. b) All prorations are computed as though there were 360 days in a year and 30 days in each of the 12 months.

7. c) When a valid escrow exists, death of either party does not terminate it.

8. c) From the time escrow is opened, until terminated or performed, the escrow agent is a trustee for all principal parties.

9. a) Though local custom usually dictates who shall be responsible for the various closing costs, there is no law requiring the costs be paid by the buyer or seller.

10. b) A title insurance policy is not required by law, and who pays for it is a matter of custom.

11. d) The grantee is the buyer, and each of the items listed is customarily paid by the seller.

12. a) The seller usually pays for the standard policy of title insurance, and when there is new financing involved, the buyer will pay for the lender's extended coverage policy—the A.L.T.A. policy.

13. a) If the buyer wants to make his deed a matter of public record—and he should—he assumes the cost of recording it. The cost is minimal.

14. a) It is the seller's responsibility. A deed is the only document to which revenue stamps are attached.

15. c) The buyer will record his deed and bear the cost of doing so. He also is generally responsible for the A.L.T.A. title insurance policy. If the purchaser wants a survey to confirm the property's actual boundaries, he must pay for it. Revenue stamps, however, are customarily a charge to the seller.

16. d) There is no maximum by law. The amount is determined by agreement between seller and broker.

17. c) The purchaser can't pay them according to VA regulations.

18. c) Discounts are computed as a percentage of the loan amount—not the sales price.

19. d) The mortgagee's (lender's) title policy is the A.L.T.A. policy and is customarily charged to the buyer who, in this instance, is also a borrower (mortgagor).

20. a) The grantor (seller) acknowledges the deed and usually assumes any charge related to its preparation. The buyer will want to record his deed—though he is not required to by law—and will bear the costs of making it a matter of public record.

21. c) Revenue stamps—a form of taxation—are computed on the amount of "new money" introduced at the new sale. If the sales price is $60,000, with the buyer to pay $20,000 cash down payment and assume the existing 9% loan of $40,000, the only new money presented at the time of purchase would be the $20,000 down payment. The charge is 50 cents per $500 of the new money or $20 and is customarily paid by the seller.

22. c) The excise tax must be paid before a real estate contract will be accepted for recording.

14. Real Estate License Law

1. An applicant for a real estate license can solicit buyers and sellers after (or upon):

a) applying for a license
b) taking license examination
c) notification of passing examination
d) receipt by broker of individual's license

2. Those exempted from the real estate examination are, in part:

a) any person who purchases property or business opportunity for his own account or in any way disposes of the same
b) any authorized attorney in fact or attorney at law while acting in that capacity
c) any escrow agent, receiver, trustee in bankruptcy, executor, administrator, guardian or any person acting under a court order
d) All of the above

3. The current fee for the real estate salesman's license is:

a) $65
b) $75
c) $35
d) $10

4. When a salesman or associate broker ceases to represent a broker:

a) license ceases to be in force
b) notice must be given in writing to director by person leaving broker's employ
c) licensee becomes a free agent
d) None of these

5. Which of the following is required to have a real estate license?

I Resident manager of an apartment building
II Property manager specializing in handling store buildings in business districts

a) I only
b) II only
c) Both I and II
d) Neither I nor II

6. Which group is exempt from the licensing law?

a) Referee in bankruptcy
b) Person handling leases only
c) Salesman employed by builder
d) All of the above

7. Which one is not required to have a real estate license to practice?

a) Trustee in bankruptcy
b) One who sells for a builder on a subdivision
c) Person who lists properties but is not involved in selling
d) A property manager who just leases

8. The first step necessary for a licensed broker to recover a commission is to:

a) find a buyer
b) find a seller
c) have a contract of employment
d) advertise the property for sale

9. No suit or action regarding commissions can be brought by a salesman against a seller without:

a) informing his broker
b) proving he was a licensed salesman at the date of the sale
c) filing a lis pendens
d) None of the above

10. A broker is assured a commission in a non-exclusive agency only if he:

a) was duly licensed at the time the deposit receipt was entered into
b) produced a ready, willing and able purchaser
c) can prove he was the procuring cause
d) All of the above

11. If an owner refuses to pay the broker an earned commission, the broker may properly seek relief by:

a) filing a mechanic's lien
b) bringing a formal complaint with the division of real estate
c) bringing a court action
d) bringing a quiet title action against the seller

12. A broker is required to maintain certain records for at least three years. Those records include copies of:

a) offer to purchase agreements
b) pay records of employed salesmen
c) Both A and B
d) Neither A nor B

13. Deposit money received by a salesman is turned over to the:

a) seller of the property
b) Real Estate Commission
c) broker to deposit in his trust fund
d) seller's attorney

14. A salesman may operate from:

a) the broker's principal office
b) any branch office of his broker
c) the address on his license
d) any office the broker designates

15. A salesperson should usually advise a husband and wife who are buying a home to take title as:

a) joint tenants
b) tenants in common
c) community property
d) None of the foregoing as he should give no advice on this subject

16. Which of the following documents can legally be prepared by a real estate broker?

a) Deed
b) Purchase and Sale Agreement
c) Title insurance policy
d) None of these

17. Which of these acts could result in license suspension or revocation?

a) Conviction of a forgery crime
b) Accepting compensation from more than one party in a transaction without full disclosure
c) Advertising in the name of an associate
d) All of these listed

18. Which of the following would normally be a reason for suspension or revocation of a real estate license?

I. Charging more than a regular commission
II. Offering property for sale on terms or at a price other than stipulated by the owner

a) I only
b) II only
c) Neither I nor II
d) Both I and II

19. Which of the following actions on the part of a real estate broker or salesman could result in revocation of his license?

I. Failing to submit to an owner, before his acceptance of an offer, all formal, written offers received for property listed for sale
II. Quoting to prospective buyers of a property a sale price other than the one stipulated by the owner

a) I only
b) II only
c) Either I or II
d) Neither I nor II

20. A license may be revoked upon proof of:

a) charging more than the usual rate of commission
b) dispute between broker and salesman as to a commission
c) violation of Federal Fair Housing law
d) refusal to accept a listing

21. A salesman who is guilty of any act which is grounds for disciplinary action may:

a) be subject to a criminal prosecution
b) have his license suspended or revoked
c) be subject to A and B
d) be subject to a civil action by his broker

22. When a licensee misrepresents facts in property sales, he is subject to which action?

a) Action in civil court
b) Action in criminal court
c) Action by state's licensing entities
d) All of these

23. A real estate broker sold property on Friday morning and received a $2,000 deposit in cash. Afraid to carry the money, he quickly deposited it in his own account in a nearby branch of his bank. This is clearly an example of:

a) judicious caution
b) conversion
c) commingling
d) cohabitation

24. A broker is sued for conversion. It is alleged he:

a) committed destructive fraud
b) mixed principal's money with his own
c) misappropriated principal's funds
d) Any of these

25. An ad in the newspaper must appear under the name of:

a) the branch office
b) the broker of record
c) the listing salesman
d) None of the above

26. If a licensee places a blind ad in the paper, he has not disclosed:

a) the licensee's address
b) the licensee's name
c) the sale price of the property
d) the address of the property

27. Persons found guilty of operating in the real estate business without a license may be fined by:

a) the district attorney
b) a court of law
c) the real estate director
d) the attorney general

28. Which of the following acts is in violation of the law?

a) Discrimination
b) Blockbusting
c) Both A and B
d) Neither A nor B

29. Where the license law requires a broker to give owner a copy of listing contract, which broker fails to do, broker:

a) cannot collect a commission
b) is subject to disciplinary action
c) is deemed untrustworthy
d) is subject to criminal action

30. Which of these statements concerning a salesman's legal status as a licensee is (are) correct?

I He's an agent of his broker
II A salesperson can be held liable for any misstatement made during a real estate deal, even though not a party to the sales agreement

a) I only
b) II only
c) Both I and II
d) Neither I nor II

31. Commingling is the opposite of:

a) segregation
b) neutral depository
c) mingling
d) trust account

32. A broker, who has earnest money in his escrow account, may, after the deal is closed:

a) retain the commission money in his escrow account indefinitely, without interest
b) retain the commission money in his escrow account, indefinitely, so as to earn interest
c) may immediately withdraw his commission, even though the deed and mortgage have not yet been recorded
d) withdraw one-half of the commission money, and leave one-half in the escrow account

33. A broker must keep which of these funds in his trust account?

I Rental monies received
II Fire insurance premium monies not part of a real estate transaction

a) I only
b) II only
c) Both I and II
d) Neither I nor II

34. Funds received by a broker in a real estate transaction must be deposited in a trust account not later than:

a) first banking day after funds received
b) within first week after funds received
c) within 24 hours after funds received
d) within first banking day after deal closes

35. According to the Real Estate License Law, a transaction and trust account record must be kept for a minimum of how many years?

a) Two
b) Three
c) Six
d) Seven

36. A broker's license may be suspended or revoked for which of the following causes?

a) Over-charge of a sales commission in a real estate transaction
b) Conviction of a motor vehicle violation
c) Failure to pay a moeny judgment entered by a clerk of the court
d) Failure to account for or remit funds belonging to others

37. Which one of the following funds should not be placed in the real estate trustee account?

a) Earnest monies
b) Rental collections
c) Installment land contract collections
d) Insurance premiums

38. An exception to the requirement that a real estate broker maintain a valid record of trust of all funds handled by him would be:

a) when a check is received payable to an escrow company and delivered immediately
b) when a check is received payable to seller and delivered immediately
c) when there is a deposit and offer to purchase with a contingency
d) None of the above

39. A trust fund account maintained by a licensed broker need not:

a) provide for withdrawal of funds without previous notice
b) have a regular specified minimum balance
c) designate the broker as trustee
d) be the subject of a record showing deposits and withdrawals

1. d) It is unlawful for anyone to solicit buyers and sellers without first being licensed under a broker.

2. d) Also exempt are appraisers and certain people handling real property securities transactions.

3. c) The current fee is $35.

4. a) The license ceases to be in force.

5. b) The manager of an apartment complex in which the manager resides is not required to be licensed.

6. a) A referee in bankruptcy is exempt from the licensing law while acting in the capacity.

7. a) A trustee in bankruptcy is exempt from the licensing requirements.

8. c) Without a written contract of employment, a broker cannot successfully maintain a suit for commission.

9. d) It is the broker, not the salesman, who must maintain a suit for commission against the seller.

10. d) All of the above apply.

11. c) In this case, the broker may seek relief by bringing a court action. He sues to enforce the terms of the listing contract.

12. a) A broker is required to maintain a transaction folder containing all agreements for each transaction.

13. c) This money goes to the broker to deposit in his trust fund.

14. c) The salesman may operate from the address on his license. If he wants to transfer to another branch, the license must be returned to the Department of Real Estate and another issued showing the new location.

15. d) If they ask, he should tell them to consult an attorney.

16. b) Although a legal document, a broker may prepare a purchase and sale agreement without being guilty of practicing law.

17. d) All three are grounds for suspension or revocation.

18. b) The commission is a matter of private contract between the principal and broker. Answer II would be a demonstration of bad faith, untrustworthiness, or incompetency and therefore grounds for suspension or revocation.

19. c) A licensee is required to present all written offers to the seller for acceptance or refusal. Answer II would indicate dishonesty, bad faith, untrustworthiness or incompetence.

20. c) This is the best of the four answers. The others concern matters and conditions of private contract.

21. c) The license may of course be suspended or revoked and, depending upon the violation involved, the licensee may also be subject to criminal prosecution.

22. d) Misrepresentation can lead to loss of a license and both criminal and civil liability.

23. c) Depositing trust funds in the broker's personal account would be commingling.

24. c) Conversion is converting someone else's property (in this case, trust funds) to your own use.

25. b) Ads must be placed under the name of the broker as licensed.

26. b) He has not disclosed the licensee's name.

27. b) The director may suspend or revoke licenses, but a fine would have to be imposed by a court.

28. c) Blockbusting (inducing owners to list their property for sale by spreading rumors that minorities are moving into the neighborhood and depressing property values) is a discriminatory practice, and discriminatory acts are prohibited by real estate licensing statutes.

29. b) This would be a violation of the real estate law which could result in disciplinary action.

30. c) A salesman is his broker's agent and he can be held personally responsible for misstatements made by him in the course of real estate transactions.

31. a) To commingle in real estate means to mix personal funds with those held in trust. To keep them separate is to segregate them.

32. c) Once the deal has closed, the broker must withdraw the money held in trust. From this money, he may subtract his commission.

33. a) Rental income collected on behalf of another must be held in trust.

34. a) Trust money collected on a Friday, or on the day preceding a holiday, must be deposited in the broker's trust account no later than the first banking day thereafter.

35. b) The Division of Real Estate requires that brokers keep these records for three years; however, the broker's civil liability continues for another three years – a total of six years.

36. d) The broker is always accountable for money held in his trust account.

37. d) The first three alternatives refer to money collected on behalf of a client. Insurance premiums would be paid to an insurance company.

38. d) A broker must keep a record of all monies handled by him.

39. b) Since only monies of others are to be placed in the trust account, it is not necessary that the broker maintain a minimum balance.

15. Washington Real Estate Taxes

1. Unpaid real property taxes constitute a lien:

   a) prior to a mortgage
   b) concurrent with a mortgage
   c) after a mortgage
   d) None of the above

2. Real estate property taxes are:

   a) general – involuntary liens
   b) general – voluntary liens
   c) specific – voluntary liens
   d) specific – involuntary liens

3. Farmer Jones is unable to pay the county taxes on his farm. The delinquent taxes would be:

   a) liens
   b) attachments
   c) easements
   d) appurtenances

4. A charge levied by a local government to finance street paving is:

   a) an ad valorem tax
   b) a zoning charge
   c) an equalizer
   d) an assessment

5. Real estate taxes become a lien on property on:

   a) January 1st
   b) February 1st
   c) April 30th
   d) October 31st

6. Which of the following liens would be given higher priority?

   a) the current real estate tax
   b) a mortgage dated last year
   c) a judgment rendered today
   d) a mechanic's lien for work started before the mortgage was made

7. Which of the following taxes are used to distribute the cost of civic services among real estate owners?

   I. General real estate taxes
   II. Special assessments

   a) I only
   b) II only
   c) Both I and II
   d) Neither I nor II

8. Which of the following municipalities or agencies usually make levies for general real estate taxes?

   I. School districts
   II. Counties

   a) I only
   b) II only
   c) Both I and II
   d) Neither I nor II

9. Real property is assessed at what percentage of its fair market value in Washington?

   a) 25%
   b) 50%
   c) 100%
   d) None of the above

10. A LID:

   a) is a local improvement district
   b) can finance special assessments
   c) Both of the above
   d) None of the above

11. The holder of a certificate of delinquency:

a) receives title to the property subject to the certificate
b) receives a lien for payment of the certificate
c) Both of the above
d) None of the above

12. An excise tax on transfers of realty is levied:

a) by the state
b) by counties
c) for the provision of police and fire protection services
d) None of the above

13. A conveyance of real property valued at $30,000 is subject to how much state tax on the conveyance?

a) $30.00
b) $60.00
c) $3.00
d) None of the above

14. Which of the following properties is/are exempt from real estate taxes?

a) Publicly owned property
b) Nonprofit museum property
c) Both of the above
d) None of the above

15. By what date are the first half of general real estate taxes due?

a) January 1st
b) April 30th
c) June 1st
d) October 31st

16. Ad valorem means:

a) fair market value
b) base value
c) according to value
d) book value

17. The tax on a given piece of property is always determined by multiplying the tax rate by the:

a) sales price
b) book value
c) mortgage loan value
d) assessed valuation

18. A charge levied by a local government to finance street paving is:

a) an ad valorem tax
b) a zoning charge
c) an appurtenance
d) an assessment

19. The County Assessor must assess property at:

a) market value
b) book value
c) sales price
d) mortgage loan value

1. a) Regardless of the date of the recording of a mortgage, general property taxes are always the first liens to be satisfied from the forced sale of property.

2. d) If a property tax is unpaid, the tax can be satisfied only from the sale of the specific property upon which the tax was levied. The only voluntary liens are mortgages and deeds of trust.

3. a) County taxes, if unpaid, become a financial claim or lien upon the specific property in question. If not paid, eventually the county will sell the property at a public auction and satisfy the tax liens from the proceeds of the sale.

4. d) A charge for the benefit of particular properties only is called a special assessment.

5. a) Real property taxes become a lien on January 1st of the year in which they are levied.

6. a) Real estate tax liens always have the highest priority, even though other liens were previously recorded or created.

7. a) General real estate taxes are levied to support general governmental functions while special assessments are levied to pay for benefits to particular parcels of property.

8. c) Both counties and school districts may levy general real estate taxes.

9. c) Real property is assessed at 100% of its fair market value in Washington.

10. c) A LID is a local improvement district and is often used to finance special assessments.

11. b) The holder of a certificate receives a lien for payment of the certificate price plus interest; he does not receive title.

12. b) State law allows counties to collect a 1.07% excise tax on real estate transfers for the benefit of the state's common schools.

13. a) The state levies and collects 50 cents for each $500 of value. Thus the conveyance tax on real property valued at $30,000 is $30.

14. c) Both publicly-owned property and non-profit museum property are exempt from taxation.

15. b) The first half of general real estate taxes are payable on April 30th.

16. c) Ad valorem means according to value. The general real estate tax is also called the ad valorem tax because the greater a property's value, the higher the general real estate tax that is levied against it will be.

17. d) The assessed value is the County Assessor's determination of 100% of the true and fair market value of the property.

18. d) A charge to finance street paving is a special assessment. Only the property benefited by the street paving is billed for the cost of the work.

19. a) By law, the County Assessor must assess property at 100% of its true and fair market value.

16. Washington Land Use Controls

1. A long-range guide for the development of a community is called a:

   a) comprehensive plan
   b) zoning map
   c) environmental impact statement
   d) None of the above

2. Comprehensive plans are adopted by the:

   a) city or county council
   b) planning commission
   c) board of adjustment
   d) hearing examiner system

3. Zoning laws:

   a) implement comprehensive plans
   b) must conform to the directives of comprehensive plans
   c) Both of the above
   d) None of the above

4. Zoning laws are adopted by the:

   a) city or county council
   b) planning commission
   c) board of adjustment
   d) hearing examiner system

5. Zoning changes are made by:

   a) the city or county council
   b) the planning commission or a hearing examiner
   c) the board of adjustment
   d) initiative

6. A variance may be obtained from:

   a) the city or county council
   b) the planning commission
   c) the board of adjustment or a hearing examiner
   d) Any of the above

7. SEPA applies to:

   a) state developments
   b) local developments
   c) private developments which require the approval of the state, city or county
   d) All of the above

8. An EIS is:

   a) an environmental impact statement
   b) required by SEPA for acts of state and local agencies which may have a significant effect on the quality of the environment
   c) Both of the above
   d) None of the above

9. The Shoreline Management Act regulates development within how many feet of various bodies of water?

   a) 100 feet
   b) 200 feet
   c) 250 feet
   d) None of the above

10. Under the Shoreline Management Act, developers of shoreline property must obtain:

a) a Shoreline Substantial Development Permit
b) an EIS
c) a declaration of non-significance
d) a variance

11. Vertical subdivision is:

a) the division of land into two or more smaller tracts
b) the separation of surface and sub-surface interests in a particular tract
c) Both of the above
d) None of the above

12. A short plat is:

a) 2 lots
b) 4 or fewer lots
c) 10 or fewer lots
d) None of the above

13. A subdivision plat must contain:

a) a legal description of the land to be subdivided
b) a statement of the landowner's consent to the subdivision
c) provisions for any dedications which may be required
d) All of the above

14. Subdivided lots cannot be sold before approval of:

a) the preliminary plat
b) the short plat
c) the final plat
d) B or C

15. The Washington Land Development Act applies to subdivisions with:

a) four or more lots
b) five or more lots
c) ten or more lots
d) None of the above

16. A Property Report is required by:

a) SEPA
b) the Land Development Act
c) the Shoreline Management Act
d) None of the above

17. If a Property Report is not given a purchaser before a sale, how many days does he have to rescind?

a) Three days
b) Seven days
c) He may rescind at any time in the future
d) None of the above

18. Under the Land Development Act, short-form registration is available for subdivisions:

a) registered with the Office of Interstate Land Sales
b) of four or fewer lots
c) registered with H.U.D.
d) None of the above

19. The Land Development Act does not apply to subdivisions with:

a) less than ten lots
b) lots all in excess of five acres
c) buildings on all lots
d) All of the above

20. Washington recognizes:

a) riparian rights
b) appropriative rights
c) Both of the above
d) None of the above

1. a) A long-range guide for development of a community is called a comprehensive plan.

2. a) Comprehensive plans are adopted by the local city or county council, upon recommendation of the planning commission.

3. c) Zoning laws implement comprehensive plans and must conform to the directives of comprehensive plans.

4. a) As with comprehensive plans, zoning laws are adopted by the local city or county council, upon recommendation of the planning commission.

5. a) Zoning changes are made by the city or county council after fact-finding hearings are conducted by the planning commission or a hearing examiner.

6. c) A special exception to the zoning laws, such as a variance or conditional use permit, may be obtained upon approval of the local board of adjustment or a hearing examiner.

7. d) SEPA applies to state, local and private developments which require the approval of the state, a city or a county.

8. c) An EIS, (environmental impact statement), is required by SEPA for acts of state and local agencies which may have a significant effect on the quality of the environment.

9. b) The Act regulates development within 200 feet of the high water mark of various bodies of water.

10. a) A developer must obtain a Shoreline Substantial Development Permit.

11. a) Vertical subdivision is the division of land into two or more smaller tracts.

12. b) A short plat is comprised of four or fewer lots.

13. d) A subdivision plat must contain a legal description, statement of consent and provisions for any dedications.

14. d) Approval of a final plat or short plat is a prerequisite to the sale of any lot in a subdivision.

15. c) The Act applies to subdivisions with ten or more lots.

16. b) A Property Report is required by the Land Development Act.

17. c) The purchaser may rescind at any time in the future.

18. a) Short form registration is available for subdivisions registered with the Office of Interstate Land Sales.

19. d) The Act does not apply to subdivisions with less than ten lots, lots all in excess of five acres or with buildings on all lots.

20. c) Washington recognizes both riparian and appropriative rights.

17. Aspects of Washington Real Estate Finance

1. A declaration of homestead is an instrument recorded in the auditor's office for the purpose of:

   a) acquiring title to property
   b) conveying property to another
   c) exempting property from execution
   d) satisfying a debt

2. A valid declaration of homestead may be filed on a home by:

   a) the lessee
   b) trustee
   c) mortgagee
   d) head of family

3. Which of the following may be homesteaded?

   a) A triplex, one-third of which is owner-occupied
   b) A family dwelling that includes 500 acres of land
   c) A family dwelling with a fair market value of $150,000
   d) Any of the foregoing may be homesteaded

4. A valid declaration of homestead will always terminate when the declarant:

   a) leases the property
   b) sells the property
   c) separates from his wife
   d) makes more than $50,000 per year income

5. All of the following would cause a homestead to be invalid except:

   a) selling of the property
   b) renting the property
   c) filing an abandonment of homestead
   d) making untrue statements in the declaration

6. Which of the following claims will not be defeated by a homestead?

   a) Mortgages and trust deeds executed and acknolwedged by husband and wife or by an unmarried claimant
   b) Mechanic's liens for work or materials furnished upon the premises
   c) Debts secured by a deed of trust on the premises
   d) All of the above are correct

7. Which of the following statements is true?

   I. A first mortgage is always larger than a second mortgage
   II. A second mortgage cannot be foreclosed without the consent of the first mortgagee

   a) I only
   b) II only
   c) Both I and II
   d) Neither I nor II

8. Who furnishes the funds when a loan is evidenced by a note secured by a deed of trust?

   a) grantor
   b) beneficiary
   c) grantee
   d) trustee

9. The trustor in connection with a trust deed is the party who:

   a) lends the money
   b) receives the payments on the note
   c) signs the note
   d) holds the property in trust

10. Which is an example of an involuntary lien?

    a) Attachment lien
    b) Deed of trust
    c) Mortgage
    d) None of the above

11. Where is a notice of mechanic's lien filed?

a) Recorder's Office
b) Office of the County Auditor
c) Either of the above
d) None of the above

12. A mechanic's lien expires:

a) 3 months after it is recorded
b) 6 months after it is recorded
c) 8 months after it is recorded
d) 9 months after it is recorded

13. State tax liens have priority:

a) according to the time they were recorded
b) according to the time they were created
c) over all other liens, always
d) None of the above

14. Charging interest in excess of the rate allowed by law is:

a) reversion
b) usury
c) acceleration
d) forfeiture

15. How many days does a subcontractor have to file a mechanic's lien if a notice of completion is filed?

a) 10
b) 30
c) 60
d) 90

16. Property is sold by a trustee because of:

a) default
b) attachment
c) usury
d) All of the above

17. In Washington, the usury rate is:

a) 12%
b) 4% over the rate of interest on 26-week Treasury Bills in the preceding month
c) Either of the above, whichever is greater
d) None of the above

18. Which of the following is a voluntary lien?

a) Deed of trust
b) Mortgage
c) Real estate contract
d) All of the above

19. The trustor in connection with a trust deed is the party who:

a) lends the money
b) receives the payments on the note
c) signs the note
d) holds the property in trust

20. Washington is a:

a) lien theory state
b) title theory state
c) Both of the above
d) None of the above

21. A deed of trust may be foreclosed:

a) judicially
b) non-judicially
c) Either of the above
d) None of the above

22. A deficiency judgment:

a) must be provided for in a mortgage to be allowed
b) is not allowed if non-judicial foreclosure is used
c) Both of the above
d) None of the above

23. Under a mortgage, the mortgagor is the person who:

a) lends the money
b) receives a note as holder in due course
c) holds the property in trust
d) signs the note as the maker

24. A successful bidder at a mortgage foreclosure sale receives a:

a) certificate of sale
b) sheriff's sale
c) certification in lieu of foreclosure
d) quitclaim deed

25. Money realized in excess of indebtedness and foreclosure expenses at a mortgage foreclosure belong to the:

a) bank
b) county auditor
c) mortgagee
d) mortgagor

26. How long do redemption rights extend in Washington?

a) 6 months
b) 8 months
c) One year
d) Either B or C

1. c) A declaration of homestead exempts the debtor's home from execution and forced sale, except as provided by the statute, if the exemption amount does not exceed the amount of the debt.

2. d) Married persons, widows or widowers, and single persons with relatives living with them may file homesteads.

3. d) Any of the foregoing may be homesteaded. A homestead may be declared on the declarant's dwelling house together with land and improvements, or on unimproved land on which the declarant intends to build a dwelling and live.

4. b) The homestead may be terminated by conveying the property or filing a declaration of abandonment.

5. b) Renting the property will not affect the homestead if the declarant was residing on the property at the time it was filed.

6. d) All of these are exceptions to the general protection provided by the homestead declaration.

7. d) Whether a mortgage is a first, second or third, etc., depends on when it is recorded (first to record, first in right) and not on its size. A second mortgage holder does not need the consent of the first lien holder to foreclose.

8. b) When a deed of trust is used as a security instrument, the lender is known as the beneficiary.

9. c) The trustor is the borrower. The lender is the beneficiary and the trustee is the neutral third party who ultimately releases the deed of trust as a lien or conducts the foreclosure sale, if necessary.

10. a) An attachment lien is involuntary because it occurs without the consent of the property owner.

11. b) A notice of mechanic's lien is filed at the Office of the County Auditor.

12. c) A mechanic's lien expires eight months after it is filed.

13. c) State tax liens have priority over all other liens, regardless of the times the state tax liens were created or recorded.

14. b) Usury is the charging of interest in excess of the rate allowed by law.

15. d) A subcontractor has 90 days to file a mechanic's lien if a notice of completion is filed.

16. a) Property is sold by a trustee under a deed of trust because of default.

17. c) In Washington, the usury rate is either 12% or 4% over the rate of interest on 26-week Treasury Bills in the preceding month, whichever is greater.

18. d) The deed of trust, mortgage and real estate contract are all voluntary liens.

19. c) The trustor, in connection with a deed of trust, is the party who borrows money and signs the note.

20. a) Washington is a lien theory state. This means when title to a piece of property is used as security for the repayment of an obligation, the borrower retains title and the lender merely holds a lien for security of his debt.

21. c) A deed of trust is usually foreclosed non-judicially; however, it may also be foreclosed judicially, as if a mortgage.

22. c) A deficiency judgment is not allowed with a mortgage unless provided for in the mortgage and is never allowed if non-judicial foreclosure is used with a deed of trust.

23. d) Under a mortgage, the mortgagor is the person who signs the note as the maker and gives a lien on the property to the mortgagee/lender.

24. a) The high bidder receives a sheriff's certificate of sale.

25. d) Money in excess of indebtedness and expenses belongs to the mortgagor.

26. d) The basic time limit on redemption rights is one year after the sheriff's sale, but an eight-month limit applies if the lender expressly waives all rights to seek a deficiency judgment.

18. Joint Ownership of Property

1. Which one of the following statements best describes a condominium?

   a) It is an undivided interest in the whole
   b) It is a separate interest in the whole
   c) It is a separate interest in unit space and an undivided interest in the common area
   d) It is an undivided interest in unit space and a divided interest in common areas

2. A person who owns an undivided interest in common in a parcel of real property, together with a separate interest in space in a residential, industrial or commercial building on such real property, is said to have an interest in a:

   a) community apartment project
   b) planned development project
   c) condominium project
   d) stock cooperative

3. A condominium is an estate in real property consisting of an undivided interest in common in a portion of the project together with separate complete ownership of space. It may be a/an:

   a) fee simple only
   b) estate for life only
   c) estate for years only
   d) Any of the above

4. All of the following statements concerning condominium law are true, except:

   a) the law does not provide for individual assessements and liens for real estate tax purposes
   b) the unit ownership can be deeded for indefinite duration
   c) the interest can be held in residential, industrial or commercial property
   d) there is non-severability of common and separate interests

5. Condominium projects are expected to grow in demand in the future primarily due to which of the following factors?

   a) Increased real property taxes
   b) Land value
   c) Comfort of unit owners
   d) Demand for sociability

6. An individual owns five acres of land and wishes to subdivide a portion of it for a community apartment project. Under the present real estate law, this would not be considered a subdivision until he has at least:

   a) two apartments
   b) four apartments
   c) five apartments
   d) six apartments

7. A group of investors seeking additional investors who want to limit their liability should form a:

   a) limited partnership
   b) corporation
   c) REIT
   d) Any of the above

8. Personal assets of each principal in which of the following organizations can be looked to by creditors?

   a) Corporation
   b) Partnership
   c) Limited partnership
   d) None of the above

9. A basic difference between a general partner and a limited partner is:

   a) determined by the amount of capital each contributes
   b) that the general partner manages the enterprise and the limited partner contributes capital and does not participate in the management of the partnership
   c) that the general partner is liable for the debts of the partnership only if the limited partner fails to discharge the partnership debts
   d) None of these are correct

10. Under the federal income tax laws, limited partnerships:

   a) are taxed like corporations
   b) are taxed like associations
   c) are not taxed as an entity
   d) None of these

11. The law recognizes a corporation as a:

   a) legal person
   b) artifical person
   c) Both
   d) Neither

12. The law considers a corporation as:

   a) an artificial person
   b) one person selected as a broker
   c) brokerage
   d) licensed broker

13. Real estate syndications are usually organized as:

   a) business corporations
   b) limited partnerships
   c) non-profit corporations
   d) trusts

14. A five-year lease which provides for specified increases in rent from year to year is a/an:

   a) percentage lease
   b) escalation lease
   c) graduated lease
   d) net lease

15. A lease for more than one year must be in writing because:

   a) it is the customary procedure to protect the tenant
   b) the lease can then be assigned to another person
   c) the tenant must sign the agreement to pay rent
   d) the Statute of Frauds requires it

16. A percentage lease is a lease which provides for:

   a) a rental of a percentage of the value of a building
   b) a definite periodic rent not exceeding a stated percentage
   c) a definite monthly rent plus a percentage of the tenant's gross receipts in excess of a certain amount
   d) a graduated amount due monthly not exceeding a stated percentage

17. Gross leases are most often used with:

   a) apartments
   b) retail space
   c) office space
   d) industrial property

18. If a lease is assigned, the assignee becomes:

   a) primarily responsible for the rent
   b) secondarily responsible for the rent
   c) the lessor
   d) the subtenant

19. Probate is handled in:

   a) federal court
   b) superior court
   c) court of appeals
   d) supreme court

20. A nuncupative will is:

   a) formally witnessed
   b) oral
   c) in the testator's handwriting
   d) None of the above

21. Codicil and devise pertain to which of the following?

   a) Wills
   b) Contracts
   c) Deeds
   d) All of the above

22. At least how many people are required to form a real estate investment trust?

   a) 10
   b) 75
   c) 100
   d) There is no minimum requirement

23. A limited partner:

- **a) is limited to a $10,000 investment in the business**
- **b) is personally liable for partnership debts caused by actions of a general partner**
- **c) has limited liability for debts of a partnership**
- **d) None of the above**

24. A contract conveying community real property:

- **a) is valid if signed by the husband only**
- **b) must be signed by both husband and wife**
- **c) must be prepared by a real estate broker**
- **d) is invalid unless recorded**

1. c) Sometimes called a vertical subdivision, a condominium consists of separate ownership of a unit and a shared (undivided) interest in the common areas.

2. c) This is a good definition of a condominium.

3. d) A condominium is a form of cooperative ownership; an estate in a condominium can be held in any of these forms.

4. a) The individual units are assessed and taxed separatedly. Alternative d) means an owner cannot sell his space and interest in the common areas separately.

5. b) All of the above may contribute to the increasing popularity of condominiums, but scarcity of land will be the primary factor.

6. a) Cooperative ownership, such as a condominium or stock cooperative, is classified as a subdivision when two or more parcels or units are involved.

7. d) Certain investors enjoy limited liability. In a limited partnership, these are the limited partners; in a corporation, it is the stockholders; and in a R.E.I.T. (Real Estate Investment Trust), it is the certificate of ownership holders.

8. b) Unless referred to specifically as a limited partnership, the term "partnership" means general partnership, where all partners have unlimited liability with respect to the debts of their firm.

9. b) A limited partner does not actively participate in management of the firm. If he does, he loses his limited liability status and is treated as a general partner.

10. c) Limited and general partnerships distribute their earnings to the various partners, who are taxed individually.

11. c) A legal person is either a natural person (human being) or an artifical person (corporation). A corporation is a legal, artificial person.

12. a) The corporation is an artificial person with perpetual existence.

13. b) Limited partnerships are the most common form of real estate investment syndicates.

14. c) A graduated lease is one in which the payments begin at one rate, but increase at agreed intervals over the time of the lease.

15. d) The Statute of Frauds requires leases for more than one year to be in writing.

16. c) The typical percentage lease provides for a minimum rental amount plus a percentage of the tenant's business income above a stated minimum.

17. a) A gross lease (sometimes called a "fixed," "flat" or "straight" lease) is most commonly used for residential apartment rentals.

18. a) In an assignment, the assignee becomes primarily liable to pay rent to the landlord and the tenant, or assignor, becomes secondarily liable to pay the rent.

19. b) Probate is handled in superior court.

20. b) A nuncupative will is a spoken will made under threat of impending death.

21. a) A codicil is an addition to or deletion from a will. To devise is to transfer real property by will.

22. c) A minimum of 100 persons are required to form a real estate investment trust.

23. c) A limited partner is only liable for partnership debts up to the amount of his capital contribution.

24. b) A contract conveying community real property must be signed by both husband and wife.

19. Miscellaneous Topics

1. The term Realtor is a copyrighted word and can be used only by:

   a) a licensed broker
   b) brokers who are full time
   c) members of the National Association of Real Estate Boards
   d) None of the foregoing

2. An organization of brokers was formed in 1947. They are known as:

   a) S.R.A.
   b) Realtors
   c) Realtist
   d) M.A.I.

3. Escrow agents in Washington must be registered with the:

   a) Real Estate Division
   b) Insurance Commissioner
   c) Escrow Division
   d) None of the above

4. An escrow agent must place trust funds in a bank no later than:

   a) the next banking day after receiving them
   b) three banking days after receiving them
   c) seven banking days after receiving them
   d) None of the above

5. WLTA title insurance:

   a) is a standard policy
   b) is an extended coverage policy
   c) protects against all unrecorded matters
   d) None of the above

6. In Washington, who usually pays for the buyer's standard title insurance coverage?

   a) The buyer
   b) The seller
   c) The lender
   d) The title insurance company

7. What is the statute of limitations for an action based upon a written contract?

   a) Three years
   b) Four years
   c) Five years
   d) Six years

8. If your neighbor has just built a fence which encroaches onto your property, how long do you have to take legal action?

   a) One year
   b) Two years
   c) Three years
   d) Four years

1. d) Members of the National Association of Realtors — not Real Estate Boards — may call themselves Realtors.

2. c) In 1947 the National Association of Real Estate Brokers was formed in Miami, Florida and, in turn, adopted the name Realtist. It is an organization of predominantly black real estate brokers. A Realtist must be a member of the local board as well as of the national organization.

3. a) Escrow agents must be registered with the Real Estate Division (except in certain cases).

4. a) An escrow agent must place trust funds in a bank no later than the next banking day after receiving them.

5. a) The WLTA title insurance policy is a standard policy that insures against defects in title, including hidden risks such as forgery.

6. b) By custom, the seller usually pays for the buyer's standard coverage.

7. d) An action on a written contract must be brought within six years.

8. c) The Statute of Limitations on a trespass is three years.

Section Four
Sample Examinations

Sample Examination 1

1. To "assume" a mortgage is to do all of the following, except:

   a) agree to make its payments
   b) become legally liable for its provisions
   c) relieve the liability of the original mortgagor
   d) be responsible for maintaining the property

2. A property owner orally listed a parcel of land with a broker at a price of $20,000. The broker later found a prospective purchaser who was willing to pay $22,000. The broker then requested and received from the owner an option on the property at $20,000. When the broker attempted to exercise the option, the owner found out about the purchaser's offer and refused to honor the option.

   a) Since the listing was only oral, it was not enforceable and no agency relationship was created. Therefore, the broker had no fiduciary obligation to the owner, and there was nothing improper about his conduct in this case. He would be able to enforce the option contract against the owner.
   b) An agency relationship was created by the oral listing, but the owner is still liable under the option contract with the broker and would have to honor the option or pay damages.
   c) Since an agency relationship was created, even though the listing was oral, the broker had an obligation to tell the owner about the $22,000 offer. His failure to do so was a breach of a fiduciary obligation, and the owner would have the right to void the option contract.
   d) An agency was created. The broker breached his fiduciary obligation to the owner by failing to disclose the offer to purchase for $22,000, but he can still hold the owner to the option because the owner would get his full $20,000 asking price and would, therefore, not be damaged in any way by the option contract.

3. 4-3-2-1 is a familiar approach in one facet of real estate practice. It normally refers to which of the following?

   a) Lot, house, garage and furniture
   b) Tract, parcel quadrant, and county
   c) House lot, furnishings and garage
   d) Method used in appraising vacant land of different depths

4. In distinguishing between an attachment and a judgment lien, the:

   a) first must cover all property held by an owner
   b) first is recorded after a court decision
   c) second is recorded prior to court decision
   d) latter is recorded after a court decision

5. Ashton has a special Power of Attorney for the purpose of selling Elton's house. All of the following are true, except:

   a) Ashton may sell the property to himself if he pays the fair market value or better
   b) the Power of Attorney must be recorded in order for Ashton to sell the property
   c) the Power of Attorney is terminated in the event Elton is declared incompetent
   d) Ashton is not allowed to give the property away

6. Mary sold property A for 42% more than she paid for it. She reinvested the profit from property A by buying property B. She made a 17% profit when she sold property B. Her profit on property B was $1,740. What she paid for property A is closest to:

   a) $5,000
   b) $24,370
   c) $17,162
   d) $34,605

7. Unearned income would be:

a) past due rents
b) increased value due to selection of tenants
c) increased rents due to remodeling
d) an increase in income and value due to increased demand

8. Aaron purchased a recreational home in a large recreational development three days ago. He first became aware of the availability of the cabins and surrounding lands through promotional literature received in the mail and a series of unsolicited phone calls urging him to buy. Although no misrepresentations about the property were ever made by the developer, Aaron has changed his mind and wishes to rescind the contract.

a) He cannot rescind because he knew what he was signing and no misrepresentation was ever made to him
b) He cannot rescind because the ILSFDA applies only to undeveloped property
c) He has until midnight of the third business day to cancel the purchase agreement
d) He can sue the developer in a civil court for not complying with the ILSFDA

9. A placement fee of two points and an interest rate of three points above prime on a construction mortgage of $1 million when the prime rate is 7% results in which of the following as placement fee and interest rate?

a) $20,000, 9%
b) $20,000, 10%
c) $50,000, 7%
d) $50,000, 10%

10. The SE¼ of the NW¼ of the NE¼ of Section 24 of a specified township includes:

a) 160 acres
b) 10 acres
c) 40 acres
d) 80 acres

11. In a sale and leaseback:

I. the seller/vendor retains title to the real estate
II. the buyer/vendee gets possession of the property

a) I only
b) II only
c) Both I and II
d) Neither I nor II

12. The final estimate of value of any single-family residence is:

a) influenced mostly by the net income return
b) an average of the three values obtained using the three various appraisal approaches
c) usually limited by the replacement cost of the building
d) never affected by the zoning

13. Which one of the following does not finance residential loans?

a) Federally chartered commercial banks
b) The Federal Housing Administration
c) Federally chartered savings associations
d) Federally-regulated pension funds

14. Discount points are determined by:

I. the American Bankers Association
II. conditions in the money market

a) I only
b) II only
c) Both I and II
d) Neither I nor II

15. Which of the following is not a security instrument?

a) Mortgage
b) Deed of Trust
c) Option
d) Agreement of Sale

16. A house was listed and sold "as is". The seller went on a vacation prior to the close of escrow. During this period the buyer said he would cancel his purchase unless a new screen was installed. In order to save the deal and his commission, the broker paid for a new screen out of his personal funds. Under these circumstances:

a) seller would have to pay for the screen
b) buyer had to pay because he agreed to purchase "as is"
c) broker will have to bear the cost unless the seller agreed to pay for the screen
d) None of the above

17. A commercial acre is most nearly:

a) any property used for commercial purposes which is 43,560 square feet or larger
b) the portion of a farm that is actually used for agricultural purposes
c) what's left of a developed acre after dedication of streets, alleys, etc.
d) a parcel of undeveloped land zoned for commercial purposes

18. A deed of reconveyance would be signed by the:

    a) grantee
    b) beneficiary
    c) trustor
    d) trustee

19. A broker has several salespeople working for him. One of his salespeople receives a written offer accompanied by a deposit on property listed by the broker. Later the same day, one of the other salespeople in the office obtains an offer, also with a deposit, on the same property. Pursuant to the salesmen's agreement, it is decided to submit only the first offer until it is accepted or rejected. The broker's action is:

    a) permissible because only the first offer must be submitted, if the second offeror is notified in writing that there is a full price offer
    b) permissible only if the first offer is substantially higher than the second offer
    c) not permissible because all offers must be submitted to the seller
    d) not permissible because the broker has a fiduciary responsibility to both buyer and seller

20. The best definition of a voidable contract is:

    a) one that is no contract at all
    b) one that appears valid on its face but can be voided by either party
    c) one that appears valid on its face but can be voided by damaged party
    d) one missing just one of the elements of a contract

21. When a person buys a piece of property on a real estate contract, the title is held by the:

    a) title company
    b) trustee
    c) bank of the buyer's choice
    d) seller

22. A provision in a real estate loan preventing any prepayment for a specified time is called a:

    a) prepayment privilege
    b) prepayment penalty
    c) lock-in clause
    d) due-on-sale clause

23. A broker negotiates a sale of a dwelling for a builder at $95,000 and receives an earnest money deposit of $2,000. At the closing, the buyer claims that the builder has used second grade facing brick contrary to specifications, and refuses to close the deal. Under these circumstances, the broker should:

    I. refund the money to the buyer
    II. report the matter to the real estate division

    a) I only
    b) II only
    c) Both I and II
    d) Neither I nor II

24. The Consumer Credit Protection Act, the Truth-in-Lending Act, and Regulation Z all refer to which of the following?

    a) The interest rate must be disclosed to the borrower and cannot exceed 12 percent per year
    b) The true cost of consumer credit must be disclosed to the borrower
    c) A uniform settlement statement, information booklet, and estimated settlement costs must be provided to the borrower by the lender
    d) None of the above

25. A subdivider recorded a declaration of restrictions for the benefit of all lot owners in the tract and made special reference to the recording in each deed delivered. They provided that no two-story dwellings could be built as they would block the ocean view. It was specified that restrictions would run 50 years. Twenty-one years later, a two-story house was started. Other lot owners in the tract brought suit to prohibit the construction, claiming the restrictions were still valid.

    a) They were wrong as such restrictions cannot run over 20 years
    b) They were wrong because the subdivider had died in the meantime
    c) They were right as the restrictions are good for the term specified in the declarations
    d) They were wrong as you cannot prohibit building of two-story houses

26. Which of the following in an old store building would most likely be a cause of incurable functional obsolescence?

    a) Deficient lighting
    b) Closely spaced internal columns
    c) Unattractive store front
    d) Lack of air conditioning

27. Mr. Snead, who is leasing a dwelling, notifies Mr. Barton, the lessor, that there is a broken pipe and demands that the leak be repaired as he has no water pressure inside his house. If Mr. Barton fails to repair the broken water pipe, Mr. Snead:

a) has no remedy against Mr. Barton since he holds an estate for years
b) has no remedy against Mr. Barton since maintenance of the property is the responsibility of Mr. Snead
c) may make the repairs but must pay for them himself
d) may move without further liability under the lease

28. Covenants and conditions differ in that:

a) conditions can never be created by deed
b) covenant is always granted in a deed
c) covenant runs with the land
d) violation of a condition may result in forfeiture of the title to the grantor

29. A salesperson prepares an offer from a buyer; there is a large earnest money deposit, but it is in the form of a non-interest bearing note. The salesman should:

a) tell the buyer he can't present the offer unless there is a cash deposit
b) tell the seller before he signs anything that the deposit is a note
c) not mention it to the seller as he may not accept the offer
d) send the seller a letter following acceptance informing the seller that the deposit is a note

30. Which of the following are essentials to a deed of real estate?

a) Covenant of seisen
b) Legal description
c) "Habendum" clause
d) Signature of seller

31. Which of the following is not a characteristic of a fee simple estate?

a) Freely transferable
b) Freely inheritable
c) Definite duration
d) Unlimited duration

32. When an owner pays a contractor in full and a notice of completion has been filed:

a) he can be absolutely sure that no mechanic's liens will be filed against him
b) he can avoid a mechanic's lien by filing a notice of non-responsibility with a notice of completion
c) he may be held responsible if the contractor failed to pay subcontractors or material suppliers
d) None of the above

33. Which of the following statements regarding the Real Estate Settlement Procedures Act is not true?

a) Persons obtaining a new mortgage loan to purchase a residence must receive a copy of HUD's "Settlement Costs and You"
b) Brokers may not split a commission with cooperating members of their multiple listing services
c) RESPA covers all sales of one to four-family residences when the buyer is obtaining a federally related mortgage loan to purchase the property
d) A lender may not collect a referral fee for steering a seller to a specific title company

34. By experience, which restrictions in a subdivision have been found least effective and hardest to enforce?

a) Maximum height of improvements
b) Maximum lot size
c) Minimum square footage of improvements
d) Minimum cost of improvements on each lot

35. Fannie Mae:

I. is an agency of the federal government
II. sells bonds guaranteed by the federal government

a) I only
b) II only
c) Both I and II
d) Neither I nor II

36. Which of the following is NOT a physical characteristic of land?

I. indestructibility
II. Homogeneity

a) I only
b) II only
c) Both I and II
d) Neither I nor II

37. When completing a budget forecast, the property manager should:

I. study past budgets and income and expense reports
II. be optimistic about future rental income

a) I only
b) II only
c) Both I and II
d) Neither I nor II

38. An estate in real property:

a) must run forever
b) must be created by a written instrument
c) must allow possession now
d) can be an estate within an estate

39. All of the following could be the result of recording a subordination clause, except:

a) it allows for construction loans to take priority
b) it increases seller's risk which may cause increased cost to the buyer as well as a more stringent release clause
c) it allows the first trust deed to be refinanced and extended without the loss of priority
d) it causes hardship on the buyer by placing the lender of a larger sum of money in a favored position

40. If a seller wanted a minimum return of $50,000 and the broker was to receive a 7% commission, what would the minimum gross selling price have to be?

I. $50,000 plus 7% of $50,000
II. $53,000

a) I only
b) II only
c) Both I and II
d) Neither I nor II

41. Condominium conditions, covenants, and restriction declarations:

I. are more stringent than rules and regulations for most cooperatives
II. establish owners' associations under most state laws

a) I only
b) II only
c) Both I and II
d) Neither I nor II

42. Which of the following is the basic principal of value which supports the comparative analysis approach?

a) Substitution
b) Integration and disintegration
c) Highest and best use
d) Change

43. Margaret's magnolia has several branches overhanging your property. You can:

I. cut the tree down
II. remove overhanging branches

a) I only
b) II only
c) Both I and II
d) Neither I nor II

44. In his or her business relations, a broker should:

I. utilize the services of other brokers when it is in the best interest of his or her clients
II. not publicly criticize the business practices of a competitor

a) I only
b) II only
c) Both I and II
d) Neither I nor II

45. At the lowest point in the real estate rental market cycle:

I. vacancy rates are high
II. rents are beginning to increase

a) I only
b) II only
c) Both I and II
d) Neither I nor II

46. Timber on land becomes personal property by:

a) sale of the land
b) written declaration of owner
c) severance
d) eminent domain

47. After Ronald Donaldson had purchased his house and moved in, he discovered that his neighbor uses Donaldson's driveway to reach a garage located on the neighbor's property. Donaldson's attorney explained that ownership of the neighbor's real estate includes an easement appurtenant that gives him the driveway right. Donaldson's property is properly called:

a) the dominant tenement
b) a leasehold
c) the servient tenement
d) None of the above

48. Which of these is not a characteristic of an easement?

a) It is an interest that can be protected against interference by third persons
b) It is capable of being created by conveyance
c) It is considered a non-possessory interest
d) It is an interest that can be terminated at will by the possessor of the land

49. The lower the loan-to-value ratio the higher the:

a) interest rate
b) equity interest
c) degree of risk
d) loan amount

50. A valid contract is best described by which of the following statements?

a) A deliberate agreement between two or more parties, on legal consideration to do or abstain from doing some act
b) A deliberate agreement between competent parties to do or abstain from doing a legal act
c) A deliberate agreement between competent parties, on legal consideration to do or abstain from doing some act
d) A deliberate agreement between two or more parties on legal consideration

51. A cautious buyer paid consideration in the amount of $500 for an option, good for four months, to purchase a $75,000 property. In this regard, all of the following are true, except:

a) the $500 option money paid by the optionee is adequate consideration
b) the optionee acquires a legal interest in the property
c) the optionee does not have to purchase the property
d) the optionor, in temporarily relinquishing his right to sell the property to anyone other than the optionee, has given valuable consideration

52. Normally a listing agreement authorizes a broker to:

a) guarantee the seller will accept an offer
b) convey title to the property
c) locate a buyer, obtain an offer which will bind the principal
d) locate a buyer, fill out an earnest money, obtain an offer and present it to the owner

53. If an agent shows an open listing to his purchaser, what should the agent do to protect his interest?

a) Write an office memo
b) Write a letter informing the buyer
c) Give the purchaser's name to the seller
d) Inform all other brokers who have open listings

54. A purchaser who will be financing with a VA loan would be least likely to finance through:

a) national bank
b) insurance company
c) mortgage company
d) mutual savings bank

55. A property owner listed a parcel of undeveloped land with a broker at a price of $10,000 with a stipulation that at least one-half the price be in cash. The agreed-upon commission was 10%. The broker subsequently found a buyer, Brown, who was willing to pay $12,000 but could only pay $3,000 in cash. Shortly afterward, the broker located another buyer, Johnson, who agreed to purchase for $10,000, all cash, and then sell immediately to Brown for $12,000. The broker reported Johnson's $10,000 cash offer to the seller who accepted it and paid the broker a $1,000 commission. Johnson then sold to Brown and also paid the broker a 10% commission. The seller, upon learning about the second sale, sued the broker to recover the commission.

a) The seller would be entitled to recover the commission because the broker breached a fiduciary obligation by failing to tell the seller about the offer to purchase for $12,000 even though the offer did not meet the terms stipulated in the listing
b) The seller will not be able to recover the commission because the broker complied exactly with his instructions and, in fact, was able to get for the seller a better deal than requested, full cash rather than half cash
c) The seller would not be able to recover the commission because the Johnson to Brown sales transaction did not occur until after the seller's sale to Johnson, which ended the agency relationship between broker and seller. There was, therefore, no breach of that agency relationship and no grounds for the seller to recover
d) The seller could recover the amount of the commission and the loss of profit from either the broker or Johnson

56. Adams listed his property for sale with Wilkins, a broker, at $42,000. Wilkins obtained several offers below the listed price and one bona fide offer at $43,000 from Gordon. Adams, himself, obtained an offer of $40,000 from Bryant, a member of his country club, which he accepted. Gordon has:

   a) an action for specific performance against Adams
   b) no action against Adams
   c) a cause of action against Wilkins
   d) a cause of action against Bryant

57. Which of the following affects mortgage money the most?

   a) The national money market
   b) Length of the loans
   c) Balance between conservative investors and optimistic investors
   d) Cost of the property

58. If an owner refused to pay a broker a commission which he has earned, the broker may seek relief by filing:

   a) a complaint with the Division of Real Estate
   b) a lawsuit in a civil court
   c) a mechanic's lien
   d) an unlawful detainer action against the buyer

59. The difference between police power and eminent domain can best be determined by:

   a) whether or not the action was by sovereign power or by the statute
   b) whether or not any compensation was paid to the owner
   c) whether or not the improvements are to be razed
   d) whether or not the owner's use was affected

60. Which of the following is usually appurtenant to land?

   a) Easements in gross
   b) Written reservation of growing crops
   c) A license to enter another's land for a particular purpose
   d) Stock in a mutual water company

61. A developer is going to finance the purchase of some vacant land. It would be in his best interest to include in the mortgage a:

   a) subordination clause
   b) subjacent clause
   c) subrogation clause
   d) severalty clause

62. The maximum number of parcels that may be used to secure a loan before the loan becomes a blanket encumbrance is:

   a) one
   b) two
   c) three
   d) four

63. Which is true in regard to an option?

   I. Option holder has no interest or title in the property
   II. An option agreement is binding upon a subsequent owner of the property.

   a) I only
   b) II only
   c) Both I and II
   d) Neither I nor II

64. The local government ruined Fisher's property by mistakenly removing the topsoil as part of a nearby road project. The action which Fisher might bring is:

   a) escheat proceedings
   b) adverse possession action
   c) inverse condemnation action
   d) All of the above

65. Regulation Z requires lender to:

   I. properly inform buyers and sellers of commercial property of settlement costs in a real estate transaction
   II. inform prospective home mortgage or trust deed borrowers of all charges, fees, and interest involved in making a home mortgage or trust deed loan

   a) I only
   b) II only
   c) Both I and II
   d) Neither I nor II

66. The capitalization rate has considerable effect upon the appraisal value of property. Which of the following statements is true?

   a) The capitalization rate consists only of the component related to return on investment
   b) An increase in the capitalization rate produces an increase in the appraised value
   c) A decrease in the capitalization rate produces an increase in the appraised value
   d) The capitalization rate will be higher for property where a long-term tenant has shown a good payment record than for one with a relatively new tenant with a poor record of payment

67. Mortgage bankers do all of the following except:

a) accept savings deposits
b) collect payments
c) arrange discounts
d) lend their own money

68. Industrial property would most likely be sold by the:

a) gross acre
b) cubic foot
c) square foot
d) front foot

69. Byrd executes a contract for the sale of his dwelling to Stephanson. One month before closing, Byrd dies. The result is:

a) the deal is automatically terminated
b) Stephanson can compel the executor or administrator of Byrd's estate to complete the sale
c) the deal is subject to judiciary review
d) the deal is voidable at the option of the deceased's heirs

70. Zoning powers are conferred on municipal governments:

I. by state enabling acts
II. through police power

a) I only
b) II only
c) Both I and II
d) Neither I nor II

71. In a real estate transaction, the potential buyer is usually called a/an:

a) exclusive agency
b) client
c) customer
d) principal

72. If a broker secures an open listing and promises to try to procure a ready, willing and able purchaser, he has what type of contract?

a) Express, bilateral, executed
b) Express, unilateral, executory
c) Implied, unilateral, executed
d) Express, bilateral, executory

73. In the income approach to value:

I. the reproduction or replacement cost of the building must be computed
II. the capitalization rate must be estimated

a) I only
b) II only
c) Both I and II
d) Neither I nor II

74. A counter offer:

I. terminates the original offer
II. will result in a valid contract if accepted by the original offeror

a) I only
b) II only
c) Both I and II
d) Neither I nor II

75. In determining value of a site, a chain store firm is most concerned with:

a) spot zoning
b) pedestrian count
c) traffic count during store hour
d) latest census figures

76. Thadwick makes an offer to purchase a piece of property, inserting the statement, "this offer will remain open for 72 hours and will not be revoked before that time." Under these circumstances, Thadwick could:

a) revoke the offer at any time prior to being notified of the seller's acceptance
b) not revoke before 72 hours
c) revoke the offer, but would have to forfeit the earnest money deposit
d) None of the above

77. Encumbrances can:

I. affect or relate to the title
II. affect or relate to the actual physical conditions upon realty

a) I only
b) II only
c) Both I and II
d) Neither I nor II

78. Which one of the following statements best explains why instruments affecting real estate are recorded with the recorder of deeds of the county where the property is located?

a) Recording gives constructive notice to the world of the rights and interests in a particular parcel of real estate
b) The law requires that they be recorded
c) They must be recorded to comply with the Statute of Frauds
d) Recording proves the execution of the instrument

79. In the same neighborhood there were two different properties located side by side which were not only built at the same time at the same cost but contained the same amount of square footage and were equally maintained. If one of the two properties is worth less than the other, it would be the result of:

a) economic obsolescence
b) wear and tear
c) functional obsolescence
d) deterioration

80. A property owner lists a home and lot for sale with a broker. Among other things, the owner tells the broker that she has had some problems lately with the plumbing backing up. She also tells the broker that she wants to move because she has read in the paper that the city council is contemplating changing the zoning in the neighborhood to permit apartment houses and other multi-family residences and that she does not wish to live in a neighborhood with a mixture of single and multi-family dwellings. Even if not asked, the broker would be obligated to tell prospective purchasers about:

I. the defective plumbing
II. the contemplated zoning change

a) I only
b) II only
c) Both I and II
d) Neither I nor II

81. Which factor would have little effect in determining the value of commercial property?

a) Purpose of appraisal
b) Income of property
c) Original cost of property
d) Zoning

82. The most logical first step for a subdivider who wants to develop unimproved land is to:

a) acquire the land
b) obtain proper financing for the property's development
c) determine the best location
d) analyze the market

83. A parcel of land (ten lots) is platted and sold with the deed restriction that the property "may only be used for residential development." Later, a buyer wishes to purchase a house on one of the lots as a residence, with one of the rooms to become a barber shop. This is probably permissible if:

I. eight of the ten lots are now used for commercial purposes
II. eight out of ten of the property owners are willing to agree to such use

a) I only
b) II only
c) Both I and II
d) Neither I nor II

84. A property was listed with a broker for sale by the owner at $80,000, commission to be 7%. During the exclusive period, the property was condemned by the state which paid the owner $80,000 for the property. Under these circumstances:

I. the broker is entitled to a commission from the state
II. the broker is entitled to the commission from the owner

a) I only
b) II only
c) Both I and II
d) Neither I nor II

85. "The N¼ of the SW½ of Sec. 6 T24N R4E WM" is an example of:

a) government survey description
b) metes and bounds description
c) Torrens system description
d) None of these

86. When appraising a property that is not often sold and on which the net income is difficult to determine, the most likely used approach would be:

a) cost
b) income
c) comparison
d) property residual

87. Local municipal building codes are concerned with:

I. the cost of construction material
II. the structural strength of a building

a) I only
b) II only
c) Both I and II
d) Neither I nor II

88. Value can be measured in conjunction with depth tables by using which of the following?

a) lineal foot
b) square foot
c) cubic foot
d) front foot

89. Upon the sale of a home, the seller agreed to pay $2,750 to a lender for "discount points." The buyer obtained a maximum FHA loan. All details of the sale were processed through escrow. The payment of the points would be provided for by:

a) a deduction from the principal amount of the loan to the buyer
b) a deduction from the amount due the seller
c) an addition to the principal amount of the buyer's loan
d) a deduction from the buyer's down payment

90. A real estate broker included the following clause in his exclusive listing forms, "In consideration of execution of the foregoing, the undersigned broker agrees to procure a purchaser in a diligent and timely manner." This clause:

a) is superfluous
b) is important in creating a unilateral contract
c) is important in creating a bilateral contract
d) requires the broker to advertise

91. The Federal Equal Credit Opportunity Act prohibits lenders from discriminating against potential borrowers on the basis of all but which of the following?

a) Race
b) National origin
c) Dependence on public assistance
d) All of the above reasons for discrimination are prohibited by the law

92. A deed:

a) does not have to be recorded to transfer title
b) cannot be recorded in more than one county
c) that is recorded does not give the grantor protection of recording by law if a quitclaim deed is used
d) that is recorded imparts actual notice of its contents

93. A man bought a house and, after escrow closed, discovered that two years before, his neighbor had built a fence that was three feet over the property line on his side. The broker was unaware of this. If the two neighbors were unable to reach an amicable settlement, the:

a) sale would be invalid
b) buyer could sue the neighbor for trespass
c) neighbor had acquired title by adverse possession
d) buyer could sue the broker

94. Stewart owned a home subject to a bank loan, secured by a trust deed and note. After living there a year, his septic tank caved in and he contracted to have a new one installed. About that time, he lost his job and couldn't pay the bill or the payments on the home. The contractor filed a mechanic's lien. Then the bank foreclosed and sold the property for the amount Stewart owed the bank. Which of the following is true?

a) The bank secured title subject to the mechanic's lien
b) The contractor loses out as his lien, although valid, cannot be satisfied and Stewart is insolvent
c) The mechanic's lien has first priority as to the proceeds of the sale
d) Holders of mechanic's liens can never recover from a trust deed

95. Which of the following must be specifically stated in an option?

a) A statement that the offer will remain open for a specified time
b) A statement to the effect that the agreement is irrevocable
c) The time during which the optionee must purchase
d) A statement to the effect that the optionor may retain the option money if the option is not exercised

96. To protect the interests of his or her clients, a broker should:

I. keep informed of proposed legislation relating to real estate
II. conceal pertinent facts about a client's real estate that might discourage buyers

a) I only
b) II only
c) Both I and II
d) Neither I nor II

97. The person who prepares an abstract of title for a parcel of real estate:

I. writes a brief history of the title after inspecting the county records for documents affecting the title of the property
II. insures the condition of the title

a) I only
b) II only
c) Both I and II
d) Neither I nor II

98. The four essential elements of market value are:

a) location, demand, financing, and qualifications of the borrower
b) possession, encumber, will, and sell
c) time, title, interest, and possession
d) utility, scarcity, demand, and transferability

99. The conditions of sale will affect the:

a) price of the subject property
b) cost of the subject property
c) value of the subject property
d) utility of the subject property

100. The most expensive and difficult type of appraisal is which of the following?

a) quantity survey
b) square foot method
c) unit-in-place method
d) development method

101. A nonresident broker's trust account for transactions in Washington must be in a:

I. bank in the state of domicile
II. bank in Washington state

a) I only
b) II only
c) Both I and II
d) Neither I nor II

102. Which of the following represents a proper disbursement of funds from a broker's trust account?

a) Advertising bills of the broker's office
b) Gas bills for the broker's office
c) A bonding company to bond a fiduciary agent who will be authorized to withdraw money from the trust account
d) Plumbing repair bills of a property on which the broker has a management contract

103. How many days does a subcontractor have to file a mechanic's lien if a notice of completion is filed?

a) 10
b) 30
c) 60
d) 90

104. A salesman may operate from:

a) broker's principal office
b) any branch office of his broker
c) the address on his license
d) wherever his broker designates

105. The trustor in connection with a trust deed is the party who:

a) lends the money
b) receives the payments on the note
c) signs the note
d) holds the property in trust

106. Legal proceedings referred to as a possessory action to recover personal belongings that have been unlawfully taken for nonpayment of rent culminate in a court order for recovery called a:

a) writ of possession
b) writ of attachment
c) writ of replevin
d) writ of garnishment

107. A licensed broker, associate broker or salesman may operate and/or advertise under a name other than the one under which the license is issued:

a) under no conditions
b) by written consent of the director
c) Both A and B
d) Neither A nor B

108. A real estate broker hired a woman to work in a subdivision on weekends. Which of the following could she do without violating the real estate law?

a) Type real estate documents for the salesmen
b) Quote prices over the phone
c) Show the houses
d) Discuss terms with prospects

109. A fee broker is:

a) the owner of a brokerage business who pays himself a salary
b) a non-owner, manager who is paid an override of commissions
c) a designated broker of a corporation who is a vice-president and is paid a salary plus a bonus
d) a non-owner, non-manager who rents his license

110. Each branch office is required:

a) to have at least one licensed broker authorized by designated broker to perform the duties of a broker
b) to have at least one licensed salesman authorized by designated broker to perform the duties of a broker
c) to have an associate broker as office manager
d) to have more than one salesman

111. By state law, does a seller have to furnish a title insurance policy?

a) Yes
b) No
c) Only if no recent survey exists
d) Only if a mortgage is held on the property

112. Which items would appear on a subdivision plat?

I. Storm sewer easement
II. Powerline easements

a) I only
b) II only
c) Both I and II
d) Neither I nor II

113. Funds received by a broker as earnest money must be deposited in trust account:

a) first banking day after funds received
b) one banking day after closing
c) never; they are given to seller
d) within seven days

114. A lease which provides for a step-by-step increase in rentals at regular intervals is called:

a) an installment
b) a percentage lease
c) an open lease
d) a graduated lease

115. Real estate taxes become a lien on property on:

a) January first
b) February first
c) April thirtieth
d) October thirty-first

116. Broker Brown often buys and sells property herself, customarily selling shortly after buying the property. She sells generally by real estate sales installment contract, naming herself as vendor and the buyer as vendee. In order to make maximum use of her money, she usually prearranges with a bank to discount the real estate sales installment contract and buy out her interest. Brown must:

a) comply with all of the requirements of RESPA except when she sells the home she occupies
b) comply with all of the requirements of Regulation Z except when she sells the home she occupies
c) disclose her licensed status to all buyers and sellers except when she sells the home she occupies
d) All of the above

117. Under a construction mortgage, which of the following patterns of loan disbursements is not correct?

a) A lender pays the builder in a series of equal draws
b) A lender pays the builder in a series of unequal draws
c) A lender pays the builder the total amount of the loan in advance
d) A lender pays the contractors as their work is completed

118. A township is:

a) unincorporated city
b) municipality of less than 5,000
c) 640 square acres
d) six miles square

119. Real property is assessed at what percentage of its fair market value in Washington?

a) 25%
b) 50%
c) 100%
d) None of the above

120. A title insurance company holding papers for an escrow is:

a) a subagent
b) an agent
c) a real estate broker
d) all of the foregoing

121. If your neighbor has just built a fence which encroaches onto your property, how long do you have to take legal action?

a) one year
b) two years
c) three years
d) four years

122. Which of the following is a voluntary lien?

a) Deed of trust
b) Mortgage
c) Real estate contract
d) All of the above

123. Real estate syndications are usually organized as:

a) business corporations
b) limited partnerships
c) non-profit corporations
d) trusts

124. An "exculpatory" clause in a lease releases which one of the following from certain liability under a leasehold agreement?

a) Lessor
b) Sub-tenant
c) Lessee
d) Assignee of lease

125. A broker has a customer interested in buying a property which is owned by an incorporated group. The broker wants to get a listing before he makes any negotiations, but does not know who legally can sign the listing. The broker should:

a) secure the signatures of all members of the board of directors
b) inspect the charter and by-laws of the organization
c) secure the signatures of a majority of the members of the group
d) have the secretary of the corporation furnish a certified copy of the resolution of the board of directors designating the authorized officer

126. Which of the following municipalities or agencies usually make levies for general real estate taxes?
I. School districts
II. Counties

a) I only
b) II only
c) Both I and II
d) Neither I nor II

127. A basic difference between a general partner and a limited partner is:

a) determined by the amount of capital each contributes
b) that the general partner manages the enterprise and the limited partner contributes capital and does not participate in the management of the partnership
c) that the general partner is liable for the debts of the partnership only if the limited partner fails to discharge the partnership debts
d) None of these are correct

128. Pursuant to a court order, a foreclosure sale of the property is held on which a homestead has been recorded. The proceeds of the sale must be used first to:

a) satisfy the execution
b) discharge all prior liens and encumbrances on the property
c) pay the homestead claimant
d) satisfy the judgment creditor

129. A condominium owner would own the following fee simple:

a) the common hallways
b) the individual unit occupied by him
c) the common laundry area
d) All of the foregoing

130. The successful bidder at a Sheriff's Sale receives:

a) a certificate of sale
b) sheriff's deed
c) bill of sale
d) equitable redemption

131. Assume that Lillian, a real estate licensee, finds a buyer ready, willing and able to buy property. She prepares a real estate purchase and sale agreement. When she telephones the principals on the offer, they request information on the national origin of the buyers.

a) Lillian, under the law of agency, must convey this information
b) Lillian should tell the principals to withdraw their property from the market quickly
c) if Lillian gives this information, she has violated the fair housing laws
d) Lillian may volunteer this information without liability

132. Where must a non-resident broker maintain a place of business if licensed in Washington?

I. Washington State
II. Resident state

a) I only
b) II only
c) Both I and II
d) Neither I nor II

133. The state of Washington requires listings to be in writing. Doe obtains a listing from Smith, but no mention is made of the commissions to be charged. Later Doe tells Smith his commission will be 7%. Doe obtains a buyer, whom Smith accepts. Under these circumstances:

I. Doe is entitled to 7 percent commission
II. Doe can recover on a quantum merit basis

a) I only
b) II only
c) Both I and II
d) Neither I nor II

134. Lawton entered a judgment of $12,500 January seventh against Newton who owns a tract of land. Newton gave a mortgage for $11,500 to Carter on January twenty-third. The mortgage is in default by August second, and Newton agrees to deed the property to Carter in satisfaction of the mortgage debt.

I. The deed is void
II. Carter will take the property subject to the judgment of Lawton

a) I only
b) II only
c) Both I and II
d) Neither I nor II

135. Provided that he or she is licensed, a salesperson may:

I. leave the employment of one broker and become associated with another without reporting the change
II. act as an agent for a seller in his or her own right

a) I only
b) II only
c) Both I and II
d) Neither I nor II

136. A broker is prohibited from purchasing real estate on his own behalf:

a) by the real estate division
b) state law
c) the law of agency
d) None of the above

137. The Real Estate Commission is responsible to:

I. prepare and administer the real estate exam
II. set licensing fees

a) I only
b) II only
c) Both I and II
d) Neither I nor II

138. Who administers the Washington Land Development Act?

a) Bureau of Land Management
b) Department of Natural Resources
c) Land Use Association
d) Real Estate Division

139. According to Washington state statutes, a deed must be:

a) recorded
b) acknowledged
c) Both A and B
d) Neither A nor B

140. A Washington state developer purchases a large parcel of land which he divides into 22 lots; each being less than ten acres in size. The State will want to:

a) approve sales material
b) approve sales price of each lot
c) approve prospective purchasers of lots
d) the State would not be involved

1. c) The original mortgagor retains a secondary liability unless the new owner applies for a substitution of mortgagor which, if approved by the lender, would release the original mortgagor.

2. c) A verbal agreement is sufficient to create a fiduciary obligation, which the broker obviously breached.

3. d) The 4-3-2-1 rule is a depth table used occasionally by appraisers.

4. d) An attachment is recorded prior to the court's decision; a judgment is recorded after the court's decision. A judgment replaces an attachment.

5. a) Ashton is representing, as an attorney-in-fact, the interests of the property owner. It would be a violation of the fiduciary relationship if Ashton were to sell the property to himself.

6. b) $1,740 profit on B divided by .17 = $10,235.29
$10,235.29 (price paid for B) divided by .42 = $24,369.75, which is price paid for A.

7. d) Earned (property) income is something caused by the owner. An increase in demand that drives rents up is an external force beyond the owner's control.

8. b) Washington and federal requirements for land development disclosures relate to vacant land. Aaron bought a home.

9. b) A 2% placement fee on $1,000,000 is $20,000; prime (7%) + 3% = 10% interest.

10. b) Section 24 = 640 acres; the NE¼ of Section 24 = 160 acres; the NW¼ of the NE¼ of Section 24 = 40 acres, and the SE¼ of the NW¼ of the NE¼ = 10 acres.

11. d) In a sale/leaseback, the seller/vendor sells the property and leases it back from the buyer. The buyer receives the title and the seller retains possession under a lease.

12. c) The replacement cost of the building tends to set the upper limits of value because no one will pay more for the property than it would cost to build a suitable replacement.

13. b) The FHA insures loans; it does not make or service loans.

14. b) Discount points are sometimes called prepaid interest. How many points the lender will charge are determined by the state of the money market.

15. c) Mortgages, trust deeds and real estate (land) contracts secure debts; options do not.

16. c) The broker was not authorized to replace the screen so his principal, the seller, would not be responsible. Nor could the broker make the buyer reimburse him.

17. c) This is a good definition of a commercial acre.

18. d) The trustee, upon notification from the beneficiary that the debt has been fully paid, releases the lien of the trust deed by signing and delivering to the trustor a deed of reconveyance.

19. c) All offers must be submitted to the seller at once. In most real estate agencies, the fiduciary responsibility is owed to the seller, not to the buyer.

20. c) Most voidable contracts can be voided only by the damaged party.

21. d) The seller/vendor keeps the title; the buyer/vendee acquires an equitable interest.

22. c) This is the definition of a lock-in clause.

23. d) The broker should try to achieve a resolution through negotiation. If neither seller nor buyer will budge, the broker should interplead the money, which means turn the matter over to the court.

24. b) The most important disclosures are the total finance charges and the annual percentage rate.

25. c) They were right. They would seek an injunction preventing the completion of the house.

26. b) Incurable functional obsolescence is a problem within the property, other than physical deterioration, that causes a loss in value that is either impossible or too expensive to correct.

27. d) Barton's refusal to fix the water pipe makes the dwelling uninhabitable and constitutes constructive eviction.

28. d) Violation of a condition could result in a forfeiture of title; violation of a covenant could result in an injunction and, possibly, money damages.

29. b) The seller's decision to accept or reject the offer could be influenced by the fact that the buyer's deposit is a note and not cash.

30. d) The essentials to a deed in Washington are granting clause, capable grantee (alive), adequate description, signature of grantor and acknowledgment by grantor.

31. c) A fee simple estate is of indefinite or unlimited duration. It is also freely transferable and freely inheritable.

32. c) The owner is the principal, and he is responsible for his contractor/agent's actions. The mechanic's liens would have to be filed within the appropriate period of time to be effective.

33. b) RESPA has nothing to do with commission agreements.

34. d) A declaration of restrictions can control building heights, lot sizes and the square footing in subdivision buildings. Courts, however, have been very reluctant to enforce restrictions which insist upon minimum improvement costs.

35. b) FNMA is a private corporation and raises cash for its purchase of mortgages by selling its own government guaranteed debentures at market interest rates.

36. b) Land is held to be indestructible; also, each parcel is considered unique, unlike any other. It is NOT homogeneous.

37. a) Past income and expense reports can provide valuable information about the cost of operating and maintaining a property. The property manager, however, should be very careful (conservative) when projecting future income.

38. d) For instance, a lease is a less-than-freehold estate within a freehold estate.

39. d) A lender's position as a first or second lienholder is of little issue to a buyer/borrower, and it creates no hardship for him. Alternative (b) refers to a purchase money mortgage or trust deed carried by a seller who, before agreeing to a subordination provision in the security agreement, insists on a higher price and some very strict requirements relating to the subordination.

40. d) The sales price would have to be at a minimum $53,763.44 if the seller is to net $50,000 after 7% commission. $50,000 divided by .93 = $53,763.44.

41. b) If anything, CC&R's for a condominium are less restrictive than a cooperative because the actions of individual coop owners more directly affects other coop owners. The Horizontal Property Regimes Act is the law that pertains to condominiums in Washington.

42. a) The principle of substitution holds that nobody will pay more for a property than they would have to pay for an equally desirable substitute (comparative) property.

43. b) The branches encroaching on your land can be trimmed. The tree, which is placed on Margaret's land, cannot be cut down by anyone other than Margaret.

44. c) The first alternative is in fulfillment of the fiduciary obligation owed to the seller; the second is a matter of ethics, specifically referred to in the NAR code of ethics.

45. c) This is what happens at the lowest point in the rental cycle.

46. c) The severance can be "actual," which means the trees were actually cut down, or "constructive," meaning sold to someone while they remain rooted in the ground.

47. c) Donaldson's property is the servient tenement; Donaldson is the servient tenant.

48. d) The possessor of the land is the servient tenant, and he cannot terminate the dominant tenant's use right at will.

49. b) Equity is the difference between the property's value and the total of the charges against it. The lower the loan-to-value, the larger the equity.

50. c) This definition includes all the essentials to a valid contract: capacity, mutual consent, lawful object, consideration. If it had said, "a real estate contract," you would add a fifth essential: in writing.

51. b) The optionee (potential purchaser) has no right or interest in the property until he exercises the option (purchases the property).

52. d) The broker cannot commit the seller to sell the property. He has been hired only to find a ready, willing and able purchaser.

53. c) The agent should inform the seller of the names of all prospective purchasers to whom the agent shows the property.

54. b) Insurance companies seldom make loans direct to residential borrowers.

55. a) The broker failed to present all offers; furthermore, he made an undisclosed profit, the second commission.

56. b) The seller can accept or reject any offer, provided his motives are not discriminatory.

57. a) Specifically, supply and demand.

58. b) This is the only way he can enforce the payment of a commission.

59. b) When land is taken under the right of eminent domain, the owner is entitled to just compensation. Police power is the sovereignty's right to regulate without compensation.

60. d) In certain areas property owners mutually own the water company that serves their lands. The stock that evidences ownership is legally tied to the land and transfers with it when sold. It is appurtenant to the land.

61. a) The subordination clause will enable the developer to obtain first lien construction financing in the future when he begins to build on the land.

62. a) A mortgage securing two or more parcels is a blanket lien.

63. c) The option holder (optionee) has no interest in the land, but he can exercise the right even if the optionor has sold the property to someone else in the meantime.

64. c) This is a court action by a landowner against the government seeking compensation for damage to his property caused by the government's action.

65. b) Commercial transactions are exempt from Regulation Z (truth-in-lending).

66. c) Conversely, if the cap rate increases, the value decreases.

67. a) Mortgage companies service loans; they do not accept deposits as would a bank or savings and loan association.

68. c) The value measure for industrial property is a certain price per "square foot" or per "commercial acre," not per gross acre.

69. b) Death of a seller does not affect the sale.

70. c) Zoning is a valid exercise of police power, which is derived from the state constitution.

71. c) The buyer is generally the customer; the seller is the client/principal.

72. d) "Express" means the agreement is stated in words, rather than implied; "bilateral" means an exchange of promises (seller will pay a commission, broker will try to find a buyer); "executory" means the contract is in the process of being performed.

73. b) Reproduction or replacement cost has nothing to do with the income approach to value.

74. c) A counteroffer is actually a new offer, usually made by a seller back to the buyer.

75. b) Pedestrian counts provide reliable indications of what the store can expect in the way of foot traffic.

76. a) An offer can be revoked at any time prior to notification of acceptance. No exceptions.

77. c) A lien affects title; easements and private restrictions affect physical use.

78. a) Recorded instruments give constructive notice "to the world" of their contents.

79. c) It could only be functional obsolescence, because they were equally maintained (comparable wear and tear) and were situated in the same neighborhood (equivalent economic obsolescence).

80. c) This is simply honesty and good faith, which is required in any business relationship.

81. c) The original cost of a property is not relevant to its present value.

82. d) The first step is to determine that an adequate market exists for the proposed subdivision.

83. a) If the majority of landowners are already in violation of the restriction, a court will not require compliance of the remaining owners. On the other hand, 100% of the owners would have to agree to the violation if owners' consent is to be the reason one believes the violation will be permitted.

84. d) The broker is not entitled to a commission.

85. a) This is a government survey description.

86. a) In an inactive market, the only way to appraise a non-income producing property is by the (replacement) cost approach.

87. b) Building codes address minimum construction standards—not costs.

88. d) A depth table is a table of depth factors containing the estimated percentage relationship between the front foot value of a lot of any given depth and the front foot value of a lot of standard depth.

89. b) The cost of discount points was charged to the seller.

90. a) Exclusive listings are impliedly bilateral. The broker need not incorporate such language into the exclusive listing agreement to make it bilateral. Such language is necessary before an open (non-exclusive) listing is considered bilateral.

91. d) Lenders may not refuse credit for any one of these reasons.

92. a) A deed does not have to be recorded to transfer title, but it should be recorded to protect the grantee's interest.

93. b) The sale would be valid, but the buyer could sue for removal of the fence.

94. b) The mechanic's lien would not have priority over the bank's lien because the latter was recorded before the contractor did the work. The contractor is still owed the money, but the property no longer serves as security for the debt.

95. c) The option period must be clearly spelled out in the option. The other three alternatives are implied by law and need not be expressly stated in the option agreement.

96. a) Alternative (b) would be dishonest.

97. a) This is a concise description of an abstract of title.

98. d) Demand, Utility, Scarcity and Transferability (D.U.S.T.)

99. a) Conditions of sale, such as a seller acting under extreme pressure, will influence the price paid and accepted, NOT THE VALUE.

100. a) The quantity survey method of estimating replacement cost is very detailed, time-consuming and accurate.

101. b) The nonresident broker must maintain an office in his own state (state of domicile), but the trust account must be in a Washington bank.

102. d) Money held in trust by a property manager can be used to pay the property's bills.

103. d) Ninety days from the date the notice of completion or cessation is recorded.

104. c) The salesman must work out of the office (address) shown on his license.

105. c) The trustor, which is the borrower, signs the promissory note.

106. c) This is the definition of a writ of replevin.

107. b) With written consent of the Director of the department of licenses.

108. a) Mechanical skills, such as typing, etc., can be utilized without a license being required.

109. d) This is illegal in Washington.

110. c) The branch manager must be an associate broker.

111. b) No, but it is the custom in Washington.

112. c) A plat is a map of a town, section or subdivision indicating the location and boundaries of individual properties. On the face of the map will be shown lot numbers, area, block numbers, section, streets, public easements, etc.

113. a) By the close of the next banking day.

114. d) This describes a graduated lease, which is common to long-term business leases.

115. a) January 1st.

116. c) She must disclose her licensed status, but RESPA and Regulation Z do not apply to the sale of personal residences, even though she extends credit and plans to sell the contract.

117. c) The lender can disburse in equal or unequal amounts as the construction proceeds. It can also pay bills submitted by the builder as they are incurred. The lender will not, however, release all of the construction loan proceeds in advance of construction.

118. d) A township is six miles by six miles (six miles square); it contains 36 sections which have 640 acres each.

119. c) 100% of fair market value.

120. b) Specifically, a dual agent.

121. c) The statute of limitations is three years.

122. d) All are voluntary.

123. b) The limited partnership is the most popular kind of syndicate.

124. a) An exculpatory clause is sometimes called a "hold harmless" clause. Frequently found in leases, it is designed to relieve a landlord of liability for damage caused by things within the leased premises such as faulty construction or structural deterioration. Courts often ignore exculpatory clauses.

125.d) Authority to act on behalf of a corporation is created by a resolution from the board of directors.

126. c) Schools and counties.

127. b) Limited partners cannot allow the partnership to use their names, nor can they participate in the management of the partnership.

128. b) Before the owner can expect protection from the homestead, all liens, voluntary or otherwise, prior to the homestead must be satisfied.

129. d) The individual unit is owned separately while the hallways and laundry are owned in common; but all is owned in fee simple, as opposed to a life or leasehold estate.

130. a) The successful bidder receives a certificate of sale; one year later, after the redemption period, the bidder receives a sheriff's deed.

131. c) To reveal this information is to violate fair housing laws.

132. b) In his resident state (state of domicile).

133. b) Since the amount of the commission was not agreed upon, in the absence of an amicable resolution, the court would award a commission on a "quantum meruit" basis, which is Latin for "that which is earned" or "the worth of a thing."

134. b) The deed is valid, but Carter will take title subject to the judgment.

135. d) Any change of employer must be reported to the real estate division, and a salesperson cannot act directly for a seller; he must act through the employing broker.

136. d) There is no such restriction imposed on real estate agents.

137. a) The real estate commission prepares and administers license exams; the state legislature sets fees.

138. d) The real estate division.

139. b) The deed must be acknowledged; it SHOULD be recorded.

140. d) The Washington Land Development Act applies when, among other things, ten or more lots are sold or advertised for sale in a twelve-month period, with at least one of the lots being smaller than five acres. The question indicates the lots are smaller than ten acres but not five acres.

Sample Examination 2

1. How much must be invested at 7% in order to provide the investor with $640.00 monthly income?

   a) $9,143
   b) $91,429
   c) $109,714.28
   d) $53,760

2. Buying property with the lowest possible down payment is called:

   a) amortizing
   b) puffing
   c) cashing out
   d) leverage

3. A property sold for $35,200 and the owner realized a 10% profit in addition to what he paid for it. His profit amounts to:

   a) $3,200
   b) $3,560
   c) $3,810
   d) $3,970

4. Subdivider Smith wishes to create several lots from a parcel of land which he owns in the NW¼ of standard Section No. 6. The parcel is contiguous to a paved county road that parellels the northern boundary of the section. He plans to sell square one-acre lots each fronting on the paved road. How many lots can he create from the parcel?

   a) 6
   b) 8
   c) 10
   d) 12

5. Most loan defaults occur when a borrower does not:

   a) pay the property taxes when due
   b) make the principal and interest payments on time
   c) pay the hazard insurance premium when it is due
   d) maintain the collateral

6. "The price a willing buyer would pay and a willing seller would accept, both being fully informed and under no abnormal pressure, with the property being exposed for a reasonable period of time." This is the definition of:

   a) market price
   b) market value
   c) cost
   d) book

7. Which of the following is covered by the Civil Rights Act, Title VIII?

   a) Refusal to sell or lease on the basis of race, sex, religion, color or national origin where a broker's services are utilized
   b) A lender quoting different rates to different people based on their credit rating
   c) A private club refusing to rent to other than club members
   d) All of the above

8. When you turn a check over and sign, "Pay to the order of (named transferee)" along with your signature, you have given the check a __________ endorsement.

   a) blank
   b) special
   c) restrictive
   d) qualified

9. The cost approach to appraising is most appropriate for:

   a) commercial properties
   b) industrial properties
   c) older homes
   d) new improvements

10. Mortgages differ in certain areas from trust deeds; the widest degree of time difference occurs in the area of:

    a) possession
    b) title
    c) period of redemption
    d) recording

11. You are a builder and you buy ten lots ready for immediate development, paying 10% down. You will want your agreement to contain:

    a) subrogation agreement
    b) subordination clause
    c) take out loan
    d) lock-in clause

12. A budget mortgage is best defined as one that:

    a) includes just principal and interest
    b) is made to people with low incomes
    c) includes personal property as well as real property
    d) includes principal, interest, taxes and insurance

13. Quitclaim deeds:

    a) convey an after acquired title
    b) contain no implied or express warranties and guarantee nothing
    c) warranty previously conveyed title by the grantor
    d) warranty against encumbrances unknown to the grantor

14. An executory contract is one which:

    a) is made by executor of an estate for the sale of probate property
    b) is yet to be performed
    c) has been completely performed
    d) has been proposed but not accepted by either party

15. An easement is a/an:

    a) general lien on real property
    b) specific lien on real property
    c) encumbrance on real property
    d) equitable restriction on real property

16. The doctrine of constructive severance would apply to:

    a) wrecking or the removal of buildings
    b) removal of trade fixtures
    c) the sale of growing crops
    d) All of the foregoing

17. Which of the following is the definition of actual fraud?

    a) Failure to disclose information which you have a duty to disclose
    b) Entering a promise with no intent to fulfill
    c) Devious practices in business
    d) All of the above

18. The determination of the type of deed used in conveying title can be made by examining:

    a) the grantor's name
    b) the grantee's name
    c) the granting clause
    d) the consideration

19. A broker obtained an exclusive listing on a property for 30 days at $20,000. On the last day of the listing the broker brought an offer to purchase the property signed by E. Gilligan. When asked who E. Gilligan was, the broker replied, "A client of our firm." The deal was closed. Actually, the buyer was the mother-in-law of the broker and was a member of his household. Later the seller brought action to rescind the transaction.

    a) The transaction will be rescinded
    b) It will not be rescinded since the property was sold at the listing price
    c) The transaction will not be rescinded, but the broker will have to forfeit his commission
    d) The buyer will own the property as trustee for the seller

20. Joint tenants have unity of:

    a) title
    b) time
    c) possession
    d) All of these are correct

21. To determine whether or not a location can be used for a retail store, one would examine:

    I. the city building code
    II. the city's list of permitted nonconforming uses

    a) I only
    b) II only
    c) Both I and II
    d) Neither I nor II

22. Assume that Susan Jones assured the principals the exclusive authorization and right to sell that they signed was an exclusive agency agreement. The principals thereafter sold their own home and agent Jones sued for a commission. Upon proof in court that she had given this assurance:

a) a full commission plus two percent of the sales price would be awarded to Jones
b) Jones' claim to a commission would be denied
c) a full commission would be awarded to Jones
d) the principals would be obliged to pay one-half the agreed-upon commission

23. The northwest corner of Section 23 adjoins:

a) southeast corner of Section 16
b) northwest corner of Section 24
c) southwest corner of Section 13
d) northeast corner of Section 22

24. Recording a deed or other instrument gives:

a) actual notice
b) constructive notice
c) acknowledged notice
d) occupying right

25. If you have an estate in severalty, you have title as:

a) community property
b) a syndicate
c) a sole owner
d) in any form that involves others as co-title owners

26. A broker would become liable to a buyer in the event that:

a) he unknowingly misrepresents a property based upon information furnished to him by the seller
b) he gave the buyer's deposit to the seller and, through no fault of the agent, a default occurs
c) the broker acts in excess of the authority given him by the seller
d) the broker signs a contract for the seller under a Power of Attorney given to him

27. G.N.M.A. is involved with:

a) title insurance
b) secondary mortgage market
c) junior trust deeds
d) None of the above

28. A person who does nothing but appraisals is required to have:

a) a real estate broker's license
b) a real estate appraiser's license
c) membership in the Appraisal Institute
d) None of the above

29. FHLMC's major area of activity is:

a) buying and selling FHA-VA loans
b) buying and selling conventional loans
c) insuring member associations' savings deposits
d) refinancing long-term Treasury debt instruments

30. The broker must obey all instructions given to him by his principal. Should the principal instruct the broker to violate the law, the broker should:

a) do as instructed
b) not do as instructed
c) withdraw from the transaction
d) sue the principal

31. How the improvement is located in relation to the lot is best described as:

a) orientation
b) topography
c) assemblage
d) plottage

32. The person most likely to record a Request for Notice of Default would be:

a) junior lien holder
b) junior lien trustor
c) beneficiary of first trust deed
d) first trust deed trustee

33. An investor deducted $27,000 as operating expenses from his gross annual income. If this figure amounted to 30% of the gross income, what would be the value of his property using a capitalizaion rate of 12½%?

a) $90,000
b) $196,000
c) $504,000
d) $720,000

34. Good real estate advertising practice includes:

I. never revealing the selling price of the property in an ad
II. playing upon the reader's imagination

a) I only
b) II only
c) Both I and II
d) Neither I nor II

35. Under a legal contract for a deed, the buyer receives:

a) legal title
b) equitable title
c) possession
d) security for the property

36. A lot owner started building a home and ran out of money. To complete it, he borrowed $2,000 from a friend, giving him a first trust deed which was at once recorded. Later he got into a dispute with the contractor who paved the driveway, and the latter filed a mechanic's lien, which:

a) had priority over the trust deed note as work on the house had started when note was given and recorded
b) lacked priority over the trust deed as it was subsequently recorded
c) had priority as this is always true of a mechanic's lien
d) lacked priority because paving was not a part of the house

37. The rights of a borrower to redeem his property after a foreclosure are described as:

a) foreclosure rights
b) equitable rights of redemption
c) statutory rights of redemption
d) statute of frauds

38. If property is held by two or more owners as tenants in common, upon the death of one owner, ownership of his or her interest would pass:

a) to the remaining owner or owners
b) to the heirs or whoever is designated under the deceased owner's will
c) to the surviving owner and/or his or her heirs
d) to the owner's surviving spouse

39. The type of loan where principal and interest are spread out into equal monthly payments over a long period of time is:

a) straight loan
b) balloon payment loan
c) amortized loan
d) None of the above

40. The sale of subdivided lands is regulated by:

a) state
b) cities and counties
c) federal law
d) All of these

41. In the appraisal of real property, accrued depreciation is best described as:

a) difference between cost of replacement new as of appraisal date and the present appraised value
b) the amount of depreciation that may take place in the future
c) an entry made in accounting records to reflect depreciation accrued over the economic life of an improvement
d) None of these

42. To obtain a gross rent multiplier, an appraiser must obtain from comparable properties the:

I. monthly rent and selling price
II. net income and selling price

a) I only
b) II only
c) Both I and II
d) Neither I nor II

43. You would consider which of the following in determining net income for the capitalization method of appraising?

a) Payments on loan principal
b) Management costs
c) Interest payments
d) All of the foregoing

44. Under Regulation Z, a borrower has how long to rescind a credit transaction without penalty?

a) Until midnight of the third business day
b) Until midnight of the seventh business day
c) A borrower can always rescind without penalty
d) A borrower can never rescind without penalty

45. An oriental man requests to see a property listed with a broker. When does a broker not have to show this property?

a) Never
b) When the seller has asked the broker not to show the property to orientals
c) The broker must show the property only if the oriental demanded to see it
d) When the owner is out of town and has given strict instructions that his home not be shown when he is not present

46. In appraising, which approach to value tends to set the uppermost limit of value?

a) Market data
b) Summation
c) Income
d) None of the above

47. Annual gross income of a fourplex is $7,680. Cost of the fourplex is $72,900. Gross multiplier is most nearly:

a) 9.5
b) .105
c) 95
d) 105

48. The amenities of a property are most easily appraised with a ____________ approach.

a) market data
b) cost (replacement)
c) capitalization
d) All of the above are correct

49. Which of the following would be a voluntary lien?

a) Mortgage
b) Mechanic's or laborer's lien
c) Real property tax lien
d) All of the foregoing

50. The matters usually covered by zoning ordinances include:

a) base lines
b) setback lines
c) deed restrictions
d) prescription

51. As an employee of a real estate broker, a real estate salesperson has the authority to:

I. act as an agent for another person
II. assume responsibility assigned by his or her employer

a) I only
b) II only
c) Both I and II
d) Neither I nor II

52. The most lengthy and awkward type of land description is:

a) metes and bounds
b) U. S. Government section and township system
c) recorded map
d) All are equally lengthy and awkward

53. A real estate broker discovers the words "government patent" contained in a preliminary title report. This refers to:

a) the power of eminent domain
b) a conveyance
c) judgment concerning an invention
d) an easement

54. Which of the following statements is true?

I. A first mortgage is always larger than a second mortgage
II. A second mortgage cannot be foreclosed without the consent of the first mortgagee

a) I only
b) II only
c) Both I and II
d) Neither I nor II

55. The person who is obligated to pay money month after month under a deed of trust is the:

a) trustor
b) trustee
c) beneficiary
d) creditor

56. A salesman employed by another broker wishes to join your firm. What ethical procedure should you follow?

a) Employ him immediately
b) Write to the real estate commission
c) Notify the other broker in writing
d) Call the other broker and have an understanding with him

57. Capitalization is a process to:

I. determine potential future value
II. convert income into value

a) I only
b) II only
c) Both I and II
d) Neither I nor II

58. The Airport Commission changed the path of flight so that it passed directly over a new subdivision. This would be an example of:

a) physical obsolescence
b) functional obsolescence
c) economic obsolescence
d) progressive obsolescence

59. Depth tables are prepared and used by:

a) mutual water companies to show the depth where water is found in desert areas
b) appraisers to determine the value of retail business property where lots vary in depth
c) accountants to facilitate the figuring of interest payments on declining balances
d) the Department of Recreation in connection with beach properties in relation to high tides

60. The maintenance program for each specific property must be based on:

I. the owner's objectives
II. the size of the building

a) I only
b) II only
c) Both I and II
d) Neither I nor II

61. An appraiser recognizes four agents in the production of income. Which of the following is not one of those agents?

a) Depreciation
b) Coordination
c) Capital
d) Land

62. A conditional commitment by FHA is good for:

a) 30 days
b) 60 days
c) 90 days
d) six months

63. You would be least likely to use the following for the market data approach in appraising:

a) a similar home sold across town
b) a similar home sold in the same neighborhood
c) a similar home sold last year
d) a home sold under distress conditions

64. In a contract for a deed, which of the following relationships is not correct?

a) Buyer/vendor
b) Seller/lender
c) Buyer/borrower
d) Borrower/vendee

65. If the owner of real estate does not take action to evict an encroacher before the prescriptive period has passed, then the encroacher may acquire:

I. an easement by necessity
II. license

a) I only
b) II only
c) Both I and II
d) Neither I nor II

66. Jones, broker, negotiates the sale of a house of $47,000. The agreement recites a deposit of $1,000; Jones receives $300 cash and a $700 note. The buyer seeks FHA financing. Jones certifies to the lending institution that he has received a $1,000 deposit from the buyer. Under these circumstances:

I. Jones is guilty of a criminal act
II. Jones' license can be revoked

a) I only
b) II only
c) Both I and II
d) Neither I nor II

67. For a broker to act for more than one party in a real estate transaction without the knowledge and consent of all parties is:

a) ethical
b) grounds for disciplinary action
c) contrary to the administrative code
d) all right if no party suffers monetary damage

68. Which of the following could be effective against a mechanic's lien?

a) Notice of completion
b) Notice of non-responsibility
c) Notice of cessation
d) All of these

69. Smith wants to turn his garage into a small furniture factory. He applies to the City Planning Commission, and his request for a variance is denied. He may:

a) start his furniture factory
b) sue in Federal District Court
c) appeal to the City Council
d) sue the chairman of the planning commission

70. Any right that goes with the land and cannot be separated from it is classified as:

a) an appurtenance
b) a leasehold estate
c) an estate for years
d) a life estate

71. All of the following statements pertaining to easements are correct, except:

a) a lessee may create an easement across the leased property for the benefit of a third party for the duration of the lease
b) an easement can be created by dedication
c) a deed to an unlocated easement is invalid
d) an easement may be created by prescription in the State of Washington if the property is used openly for a period of ten years

72. Under the law of agency, a real estate broker owes his or her principal the duty of:

I. care
II. obedience

a) I only
b) II only
c) Both I and II
d) Neither I nor II

73. In a purchase agreement wherein a buyer's performance is conditioned upon his obtaining satisfactory leases, the agreement is:

a) illusory
b) an enforceable contract
c) a combination of a unilateral and a bilateral contract
d) unenforceable because of the Statute of Limitations

74. In most circumstances, which is correct?

a) Seller is client, buyer is customer
b) Seller is customer, buyer is client
c) Seller is client, buyer is client
d) Seller is customer, buyer is customer

75. In seeking listings, which of the following advantages can a broker offer to those selling their real estate?

I. Multiple listing service participation
II. Knowledge of financing

a) I only
b) II only
c) Both I and II
d) Neither I nor II

76. Which of the following types of title insurance policy will cover every claim that is made against the title?

a) Standard
b) Extended
c) ALTA
d) None of these

77. An offer by one of the parties to a real estate transaction to carry out that party's part of the contract is called a:

a) gratuity
b) satisfaction
c) recourse
d) tender

78. C, C, & R's would usually be found in:

a) judgments
b) deeds
c) tax liens
d) listings

79. A listing may be terminated by:

I. the broker's failure to spend time on it
II. expiration of the time period stated in the listing

a) I only
b) II only
c) Both I and II
d) Neither I nor II

80. There is a presumption of delivery of a deed if that deed is:

a) acknowledged
b) recorded
c) signed by grantor
d) There is never presumption; proof always is required

81. Sally enters into a contract with Bob under duress and in fear for her safety if she does not sign. The contract is:

a) valid
b) void
c) voidable
d) unenforceable

82. Tucker leases his property to Rothwell for a five year period. The lease contains a convenant which prohibits assignment unless written permission is first obtained from Tucker. If Rothwell assigns the lease without Tucker's permission, the lease is considered to be:

a) voidable
b) void
c) invalid
d) terminated

83. Matilda Fairbanks bought acreage in a distant county, never went to see the acreage, and did not use the ground. Harold Sampson moved his mobile home onto the land, had a water well drilled, and lived there for many years. Sampson may become the owner of the land if he has complied with the state law regarding:

I. requirements for a valid conveyance
II. adverse possession

a) I only
b) II only
c) Both I and II
d) Neither I nor II

84. In a listing agreement, the seller of real estate agrees to pay the broker a commission if the broker procures a buyer "ready, willing and able" to buy. In the agreement, the broker agrees to use due diligence in procuring a buyer. This agreement is a/an:

a) bilateral contract
b) unilateral contract
c) agreement of sale
d) deposit receipt

85. An officially appointed group that studies city growth and recommends zoning policies is called a:

a) city growth board
b) master zoning board
c) city policy commission
d) planning commission

86. The primary reason for zoning is to:

a) control the physical conditions of buildings
b) control the number of similar businesses
c) contribute to the public's health, safety and welfare
d) insure the conformity of like structures in the area

87. If after the sales contract is signed, the seller decides not to sell:

I. the seller may cancel the contract and retain the buyer's earnest money deposit
II. the buyer may institute a suit for specific performance of the contract or for money damages

a) I only
b) II only
c) Both I and II
d) Neither I nor II

88. All of the following are true, except:

a) some consideration must pass from optionee to optionor
b) in lease option, the provisions of the lease are sufficient consideration to support the option
c) an optionee has a legal interest in the property
d) the duration of the option must be specifically stated

89. The essentials for a real estate contract are:

a) in writing
b) capacity of both parties
c) consideration
d) All of the above

90. The term "tender" as used in contract law means:

a) a promise to perform, such as to buy or sell
b) actual payment of money or delivery of a deed
c) an offer of money or deed or other performance
d) a fully executed contract

91. To be enforceable, a listing agreement must be signed by:

a) broker
b) seller
c) buyer
d) tenant

92. Which one of the following statements would be true with respect to the assignment of a lease?

a) The original lessee would still retain a right to use the property for a limited time
b) The original lessee is the sole party liable for the payment of the rent
c) It is the same as a sublease
d) The entire leasehold is transferred but the original lessee remains secondarily liable on the lease

93. The law, in all states, that bars legal claims beyond a certain time is known as the:

a) Doctrine of Limited Use
b) Statute of Frauds
c) Statute of Limitations
d) Uniform Commercial Code

94. If a debtor owns three pieces of real estate and a judgment is entered against him, it will be a lien against:

a) the property first acquired
b) the property last acquired
c) all three properties
d) homestead property only

95. Restrictions can be eliminated from a deed by:

a) quiet title action
b) zoning commission appeal
c) agreement between owners of property affected
d) the grantee's discretion

96. Which is not a less than freehold estate?

a) Life estate
b) Tenancy at sufferance
c) Estate for years
d) Month to month tenancy

97. The capitalization rate will:

a) go up when the risk decreases
b) go up when the risk increases
c) go down when the risk increases
d) remain steady in all cases

98. Hugh Frank and Mary Frank, his wife, are the owners of a property. On May 1, 1987, they list the property for sale at $55,000, six percent commission, with Stone, realtor, for 90 days. The listing is signed by Hugh Frank, but Mary Frank, who is present, does not sign the listing. On June 24, 1987, Jim Sales procures a buyer at $55,000 cash. The Franks refuse to pay a commission.

I. Stone can recover from Hugh Frank
II. Stone can recover from Mary Frank

a) I only
b) II only
c) Either I and II
d) Neither I nor II

99. A valuable factor affording a display area and entrances on two streets is called:

a) pedestrian count
b) corner influence
c) accessibility
d) side location

100. The forfeiture remedy is available in transactions using:

a) a mortgage
b) a land contract
c) a deed of trust
d) None of the above

101. Ad valorem means:

a) fair market value
b) base value
c) according to value
d) book value

102. Under the terms of a net lease:

I. the tenant is usually responsible for paying the real estate taxes for the leased property
II. the tenant has an option to buy the leased property within a specified length of time

a) I only
b) II only
c) Both I and II
d) Neither I nor II

103. A valid declaration of homestead may be filed on a home by:

a) the lessee
b) trustee
c) mortgagee
d) head of family

104. Before the director may suspend or revoke a real estate license in a discrimination case, which of the following must have occurred? The licensee must have been:

I. found guilty by a Human Relations Commission of the state
II. afforded a hearing before the director

a) I only
b) II only
c) Both I and II
d) Neither I nor II

105. After you pass your licensing exam, you have ____________ from the date of the exam to obtain your real estate license.

a) four years
b) two years
c) one year
d) six months

106. State tax liens have priority:

a) according to the time they were recorded
b) according to the time they were created
c) over all other liens, always
d) None of the above

107. A C.P.A. would be a/an:

a) appraiser
b) accountant
c) contractor
d) real estate broker

108. A condominium can be:

a) industrial units
c) residential units
c) commercial units
d) Any of the foregoing

109. Community property is property owned by:

a) the city
b) husband and wife
c) parks and recreation department
d) State of Washington

110. Leasehold estates that continue for a specified period of time include:

I. estate from period to period
II. tenancy at sufferance

a) I only
b) II only
c) Both I and II
d) Neither I nor II

111. A deficiency judgment:

a) must be provided for in a mortgage to be allowed
b) is not allowed if non-judicial foreclosure is used
c) Both of the above
d) None of the above

112. Where must a salesman have his license displayed?

a) On his wall
b) In his wallet
c) Both A and B
d) Neither A nor B

113. A quarter section of land is:

a) 240 acres
b) 40 acres
c) 80 acres
d) 160 acres

114. A tax paid upon sale of property and based on the sales price is the:

a) excise tax
b) special assessment
c) business and occupation tax
d) income tax

115. When a business fails, the creditors look to the personal assets of any of the owners of a:

a) corporation
b) partnership
c) a limited partnership
d) None of the above

116. In order to protect the public from fraudulent land sales, a developer involved in interstate land sales must:

I. provide each purchaser with a report of the details of the land, as registered with the Department of Housing and Urban Development
II. pay the prospective buyer's expenses to see the property involved

a) I only
b) II only
c) Both I and II
d) Neither I nor II

117. A salesman applicant can solicit listings and talk to prospects when he:

a) obtains a license
b) has filed license application
c) takes the exam
d) passes the exam

118. Charging interest in excess of the rate allowed by law is:

a) reversion
b) usury
c) acceleration
d) forfeiture

119. In looking at maps, East is usually:

a) at the top
b) at the bottom
c) to the right
d) to the left

120. Which is the most serious violation?

a) "Puffing" a property
b) Commingling
c) Conversion
d) Keeping $87 of own funds in trust account to cover bank charges

121. Real estate licenses are renewed on:

a) licensee's birthday
b) December 31
c) Either A or B
d) Neither A nor B

122. A broker's license may be revoked if he or she:

I. commingles client's money with his or her own
II. makes false statements concerning a piece of real property

a) I only
b) II only
c) Both I and II
d) Neither I nor II

123. A charge levied by a local government to finance street paving is:

a) an ad valorem
b) a zoning charge
c) an appurtenance
d) an assessment

124. Persons who must obtain a real estate license in order to sell real estate include:

I. homeowners who are selling their own homes
II. individuals who anticipate receiving a commission for selling another person's real estate

a) I only
b) II only
c) Both I and II
d) Neither I nor II

125. A purchase and sale agreement is also called:

a) an earnest money agreement
b) a listing agreement
c) an exclusive sale and listing agreement
d) None of the above

126. A deed of trust may be foreclosed:

a) judicially
b) non-judicially
c) Either of the above
d) None of the above

127. Washington is a:

a) lien theory state
b) title theory state
c) Both of the above
d) None of the above

128. Which of the following taxes are used to distribute the cost of civic services among real estate owners?

I. general real estate taxes
II. special assessments

a) I only
b) II only
c) Both I and II
d) Neither I nor II

129. Among the grounds for denial, suspension or revocation of licenses is the practice of discrimination which includes:

I. blockbusting
II. hiring sales personnel from a specific ethnic group

a) I only
b) II only
c) Both I and II
d) Neither I nor II

130. Escrow agents in Washington must be registered with the:

a) real estate division
b) insurance commissioner
c) escrow division
d) None of the above

131. Every broker must maintain:

I. a definite place of business
II. a special escrow account for monies belonging to clients

a) I only
b) II only
c) Both I and II
d) Neither I nor II

132. The real estate commission is composed of how many members?

a) Minimum of five
b) Six
c) Seven
d) Eight

133. A lease for one week is:

a) an estate at will
b) an estate at sufferance
c) an estate for years
d) a periodic tenancy

134. Adverse occupancy and payment of taxes for seven years may result in a claim of:

a) an easement by prescription
b) trespassing
c) accretion of land
d) prescriptive title

135. A deed description refers to a plat of the property recorded in the County Auditor's office. Under these circumstances:

I. the deed's description would be valid
II. the deed would have to be redrawn

a) I only
b) II only
c) Both I and II
d) Neither I nor II

136. Washington law stipulates which of these in connection with homesteads?

I. $25,000 is maximum exemption now allowed when a family head files a declaration of homestead
II. Real property must be free and clear of all encumbrances to be declared a homestead

a) I only
b) II only
c) Both I and II
d) Neither I nor II

137. On a $58,000 property, a husband but not the wife, signed a declaration of homestead. There is a balance of $42,000 on a first trust deed. A roofing contractor filed a lien. The lien was:

a) not enforceable—homestead protects from all liens
b) enforceable—wife did not sign declaration
c) enforceable—mechanic's liens take priority over homesteads
d) not enforceable—not enough equity above homestead entitlement

138. A person to whom real estate is devised by will acquires title by:

I. inheritance
II. law of remainderman

a) I only
b) II only
c) Both I and II
d) Neither I nor II

139. A tenancy for years is a:

a) life estate
b) fee simple estate
c) freehold estate
d) non-freehold estate

140. Which one of the following statements best describes a condominium?

a) It is an undivided interest in the whole
b) It is a separate interest in the whole
c) It is a separate interest in unit space and an undivided interest in the common area
d) It is an undivided interest in unit space and a divided interest in common area

1. c) 640 x 12 = $7,680 annual income; $7,680 divided by .07 = $109,714.28

2. d) Leverage is the effective use of borrowed money to finance an investment.

3. a) $35,200 divided by 1.10 = $32,000; the profit is $3,200

4. d) The NW¼ of Section 6 contains 160 acres. It is a square with ½-mile boundaries (2,640 ft.) A square acre has boundaries of 208.7 feet. Divide the 2,640-foot northern boundary by 208.7 for 12.65 lots.

5. b) The overwhelming number of defaults are for nonpayment.

6. b) This is the definition of market value.

7. a) Lenders can and do quote higher interest rates to borrowers with marginal credit. Clubs can refuse to rent their facilities to nonmembers; however, membership cannot be denied for discriminatory reasons.

8. b) A special endorsement is where the holder writes, "Pay to the order of a specific transferee." A restrictive endorsement is where the holder restricts future negotiation, as by writing, "Pay to the order of such and such bank, for deposit only."

9. d) The newer the property, the more reliable the cost method because depreciation, which is difficult to measure, will not likely be as much of a factor.

10. c) Mortgages have redemption periods; trust deeds do not.

11. b) If there were no subordination agreement in the trust deed or mortgage that secures the land loan, as a developer/builder you would not be able to obtain construction financing. Construction lenders insist on a first lien position.

12. d) This is the definition of a budget mortgage or trust deed. Most security agreements are of this type.

13. b) A quitclaim deed warrants nothing and conveys only the interest the grantor has, which may be none, at the time of the conveyance.

14. b) A contract is "executory" when in the process of being performed; an "executed" contract is one that has been performed.

15. c) An easement is a non-financial encumbrance. On the other hand, a lien is a financial encumbrance.

16. c) If the crops remain rooted to the land after being sold by contract, legally they no longer belong to the land; they have been constructively severed. Alternatives (a) and (b) refer to actual severance.

17. d) Actual fraud is intentional deceit; constructive fraud is an act that does not reach the degree of intentional misrepresentation but does not meet an accepted standard of behavior at law. Constructive fraud can result from negligence.

18. c) The exact wording in a granting clause should reveal the type deed being used. For instance, a warranty deed will specifically say "grant" or "grant and convey" — a quitclaim deed, on the other hand, will say, "the grantor remises, releases and quitclaims."

19. a) The broker must reveal a family relationship with the buyer. Where no such disclosure is made, courts have set transactions like these aside.

20. d) The four unities to a joint tenancy are: 1) time, 2) title, 3) interest and 4) possession.

21. d) A building code refers to construction standards; a list of nonconforming uses would be irrelevant to a determination of a lot's potential uses because it refers to uses contrary to zoning ordinances that existed at the time the ordinances were enacted.

22. b) Jones would be bound by her representations to the sellers. An exclusive agency listing permits the seller to sell the property without liability for a commission.

23. d) Refer to page 45 in "Fundamentals of Washington Real Estate."

24. b) Recordation of any document serves constructive notice of its existence and its contents.

25. c) Severalty refers to sole ownership.

26. c) When a broker acts in excess of the authority given him by the seller, any damage he causes third persons is his responsibility.

27. b) GNMA is a federal agency that functions in the secondary market, with primary responsibilities in the area of special assistance loan programs of federally aided housing programs and the management and liquidation functions of loans that formerly belonged to the FNMA.

28. d) Washington has no licensing requirement for appraisers. Membership in a private appraisal organization is not required either.

29. b) The Federal Home Loan Mortgage Corporation (FHLMC) is primarily involved in buying and selling conventional loans made by savings and loan associations.

30. c) As the broker is the principal's employee, he must obey instructions. If the instructions are to violate the law, he must terminate the relationship.

31. a) Orientation is the placement of a structure on a lot with regard to its exposure to the sun, wind, privacy from the street and protection from outside noises.

32. a) If a borrower defaults in connection with a senior lien, the junior lienholder(s) will want to be notified. They can assure themselves of such by recording a request for notice of default.

33. c) $27,000 divided by .30 = $90,000 gross income; $90,000 less $27,000 = $63,000 net income; $63,000 divided by 12½% = $504,000 value

34. b) Exciting the imagination of the reader is an important advertising objective. On the other hand, many brokers believe including rather than hiding the sales price is the best policy.

35. b) Equitable title refers to all of the rights of ownership, including the right to possess, except legal title.

36. a) A mechanic's lien's priority is determined by the date the work is started and not the date it is recorded.

37. c) There is a statutory period of one year following the sheriff's sale. The equitable redemption period precedes the sheriff's sale.

38. b) A tenant in common's interest will pass to devisees named in the will or to natural heirs (intestate successors) in the absence of a will.

39. c) Amortized payments include both principal and interest.

40. d) Cities, counties, state and federal agencies all have standards which must be met by developers of subdivided lands.

41. a) The cost to replace new usually reflects the upper limits of a property's value; the present value is the depreciated value. The difference between the two is the accrued (accumulated) depreciation.

42. a) Divide a rental's selling price by the monthly rent to determine the monthly multiplier. Divide selling price by annual rent for annual multiplier.

43. b) Management is an operating expense; principal and interest payments are not.

44. a) The borrower has three full business days, which includes Saturdays.

45. d) The broker could not refuse to show a property for discriminatory reasons.

46. b) Summation is another name for the replacement cost method.

47. a) Divide price by annual rental. $72,900 divided by $7,680 = 9.49 annual multiplier.

48. a) The only way to estimate the value of amenities is by comparison against prices paid for properties with similar amenities.

49. a) A mortgage is given voluntarily; the other two liens are placed against the property without the owner's consent.

50. b) Zoning ordinances usually stipulate how far back buildings must be placed from property lines. Look up the definitions of the other three alternatives.

51. c) The salesperson works for and is accountable to the real estate broker.

52. a) The metes and bounds description can be very lengthy and frequently incorporates technical language familiar only to surveyors and engineers.

53. b) A patent is a government deed used to convey title to public lands.

54. d) Neither is true.

55. a) The trustor is the borrower.

56. c) This is the ethical thing to do.

57. b) Capitalization is the process of converting income into present value. There is no way to determine future value.

58. c) Economic obsolescence is a loss in value to causes external to the property.

59. b) Depth tables, like the 4-3-2-1 rule, are used to roughly approximate the value of added depth in a lot.

60. c) Both the owner's objectives and the size of the building will influence the nature and scope of the maintenance program implemented by the property manager.

61. a) The four agents in production are capital, labor, coordination and land. See Principle of Balance.

62. d) A conditional commitment is an FHA appraisal, and FHA will allow it to be used for six months. Do not confuse this with the generally-accepted theory that an appraisal is good only for the date stipulated in the appraisal.

63. d) A price paid or accepted under distress conditions cannot be relied on as an indication of the value of the property.

64. a) The buyer is the vendee, not the vendor. Under a contract for a deed, the buyer is considered a borrower and the seller a lender.

65. d) The encroacher may acquire a prescriptive easement or even title by adverse possession, but not license, which would be revocable by the property owner, or an easement by necessity which usually refers to landlocked land.

66. c) A $700 note is not the same as cash, and Jones should know it.

67. b) If a broker represents both parties to a transaction, the dual agency must be disclosed to both in writing. Failure to do so is grounds for license revocation. He could also lose his commissions.

68. b) If the property owner is not responsible for work being done on his property, he may be able to avoid liability for payment and defeat any subsequent mechanic's liens if he records a notice of nonresponsibility in a timely manner. He should also post the notice at the site.

69. c) He can appeal to the city council.

70. a) Appurtenances, such as easements and water rights, are incidental to the land and transfer with it when sold. Appurtenances are classified as real property.

71. c) A deed to an unlocated easement, which is an easement with an undetermined placement across the land, is valid. However, an unlocated easement can pose problems for the servient and dominant tenants.

72. c) The agency relationship is a fiduciary relationship which calls for unfailing loyalty and good faith.

73. a) An illusory agreement is one where the terms are vague and difficult to enforce. An agreement conditioned upon obtaining satisfactory leases is vague in that what constitutes a satisfactory lease, what the buyer will do to obtain them and by when they will be obtained is not clearly defined.

74. a) Seller is client (principal) because he has employed agent. Buyer is customer.

75. c) Multiple listing services expose the market to many more buyers, and the broker's expertise in financing is a definite advantage.

76. d) No policy protects against every claim.

77. d) A tender is an offer to make an offer good and is usually made in anticipation of default by the other party.

78. b) C, C, and R's are conditions, covenants and restrictions, and they are found in deeds.

79. b) Expiration of term terminates a listing. A broker's failure to spend time on a listing is not grounds for termination.

80. b) It is reasonable to presume a deed has been delivered and accepted if it has been recorded, an act usually performed by the grantee.

81. c) Sally could void the contract if she wished, or she could enforce it against Bob if that was preferable to her.

82. a) Tucker could void the lease if he wanted.

83. b) Title by adverse possession is title acquired by continuous use under claim of right or color of title.

84. a) The exchange of promises forms a bilateral contract.

85. d) This refers to the city planning commission.

86. c) Zoning is a valid exercise of the police power, which in any form is intended to contribute to the public's health, safety and welfare.

87. b) The seller defaults by refusing to sell, and the remedies available to the buyer are a specific performance suit or money damages.

88. c) The optionee does not hold an interest in the property and will not acquire one unless he exercises his option to purchase.

89. d) Capacity, mutual consent, lawful object, consideration and in writing are essential to a real estate contract.

90. c) A tender is an offer to make an offer good and usually takes the form of an offer to pay the promised money or an attempt to deliver the promised deed.

91. b) The seller employs the broker, so it is the seller who must sign. As a matter of practice, seller and broker usually sign.

92. d) The original lessee retains a secondary liability for payment.

93. c) The Statute of Limitations is a law requiring certain legal actions to be brought within a defined time limit.

94. c) A judgment is a general lien.

95. c) Property owners who would be affected by a violation can consent to the violation. The consent must be unanimous.

96. a) A life estate is a freehold estate; the other options are leases.

97. b) An increased risk calls for an increase in interest (capitalization) rate.

98. c) Mary Frank's presence implies agreement. When Stone does this, he earns a commission which Hugh and Mary Frank are responsible for paying.

99. b) Corner influence is the phenomenon which brings additional value to a retail business situated on a corner.

100. b) A forfeiture is the seller's remedy for buyer default on a land contract. Trust deeds and mortgages are foreclosed.

101. c) A Latin term meaning according to value. It refers to the way real property is taxed.

102. a) Under a net lease, the tenant pays the landlord a specified amount of rent and, in addition, some or all of the property's operating expenses, including property taxes, insurance and utilities.

103. d) The head of family may file a declaration of homestead to receive protection to the extent of $20,000.

104. b) The licensee is entitled to a hearing before the director of the Department of Licensing; he need not have been found guilty of a discriminatory act for a hearing to be scheduled.

105. c) One year from the date of exam.

106. c) From the proceeds of a sale, the first charge against the property to be paid is always the general property tax, which includes special levies.

107. b) A CPA is a certified public accountant.

108. d) A condominium is a form of subdivision. It can be a residential, industrial or commercial subdivision.

109. b) Washington is a community property state. Community property is the property owned jointly by a married couple.

110. d) An estate for years continues for a specific period. The period to period is most often the month-to-month, which will end with notice from landlord or tenant.

111. c) A deficiency judgment is not allowed with a mortgage unless provided for in the mortgage and is never allowed if non-judicial foreclosure is used with a deed of trust.

112. d) In a conspicuous place in the office where he works.

113. d) A section is 640 acres; a quarter section is 160 acres.

114. a) Excise tax is charged on all real estate sales; it is usually paid by the seller.

115. b) A partnership, also called a general partnership, places each of the partners in a position of joint and several liability for the partnership debts. Stockholders in a corporation and limited partners in a limited partnership have limited liability and cannot be sued by creditors.

116. a) The developer must provide each potential purchaser with a property report.

117. a) He or she must actually obtain the license.

118. b) Excess interest charges are usurious.

119. c) To the right.

120. c) Commingling is mixing funds, but the more serious offense is conversion, converting trust funds to personal use.

121. c) Licenses issued to natural persons are re-renewed on the individuals' birthdays; licenses issued to corporations and partnerships are renewed on December 31st.

122. c) Obviously both are dishonest acts that will result in license revocation.

123. d) An assessment is a nonrecurring charge against the property for a definite purpose, such as street paving, curbs or sewers.

124. b) With certain exceptions, a license is required when an individual represents others in the purchase, sale or lease of real estate. Principals can sell their own properties without a license.

125. a) Alternatives (b) and (c) are listings.

126. c) A deed of trust can be foreclosed outside of court (nonjudicially) or through the court (judicially).

127. a) Washington, like most states, views the mortgage and trust deed as a lien and not a conveyance of title to the lender.

128. a) General real estate taxes support community services, such as police, fire and education. Special assessments are levied to fund specific improvements, like street lighting.

129. c) Both are discriminatory acts. See definition of blockbusting.

130. a) Any person in Washington who wishes to engage in the business of performing for compensation the duties of an escrow agent in a real estate transaction, must be registered with the Real Estate Division.

131. c) The broker must have a place of business accessible to the public and maintain a trust account for money received from clients in trust.

132. c) Seven. Six commissioners and the Director of the Department of Licensing.

133. c) A lease for a definite period of time, regardless of how short or long a period, is an estate for years.

134. d) Prescriptive title is title acquired by long and continuous use. Sometimes called title by adverse possession.

135. a) Reference to a recorded subdivision plat map rather than spelling out the details of the description in the deed itself is acceptable.

136. a) $25,000 is the maximum protection, but the property does not have to be free of encumbrances.

137. c) The owners of the property are responsible for the work they request or allow to be done to it. They could not escape responsibility for payment by hiding behind a homestead.

138. a) An inheritance can be by will or, in the absence of a will, by intestate succession.

139. d) A tenancy for years, also called an estate for years, is a lease, which makes it a less-than-freehold estate.

140. c) Separate interest in the unit, with an undivided interest in the whole.

Sample Examination 3

1. Federal Reserve can create more or less money for home loans by all but:

   a) buying or selling U.S. Government bonds
   b) increasing or decreasing the interest rate on VA loans
   c) increasing or decreasing discount rate
   d) increasing or decreasing reserve requirements

2. A developer has obtained a large loan in order to finance the construction of a planned unit development.

   I. This is a short-term loan, and the developer has arranged for long-term financing in order to repay it when the construction is completed
   II. The borrowed money is disbursed in installments, and the lender inspects the construction that has been completed to date and ensures that all subcontractors and laborers have been properly paid before disbursing each installment of the loan

   a) I only
   b) II only
   c) Both I and II
   d) Neither I nor II

3. Life insurance companies are interested in mortgage loans as investments because of:

   I. yield
   II. security

   a) I only
   b) II only
   c) Both I and II
   d) Neither I nor II

4. The only listing where the broker does not have to show he is the procuring cause is:

   a) exclusive agency
   b) exclusive right-to-sell
   c) exclusive agency-net-listing
   d) open listing

5. A seller makes a counter offer which the buyer rejects. Seller than offers to accept buyer's first offer. Buyer is:

   a) still bound to counter offer
   b) bound by original offer
   c) under no obligation to seller
   d) None of these

6. A requirement of a borrower under an FHA insured loan is that he:

   I. pay the required MIP
   II. certify that he will occupy the premises if that is a condition of the FHA approval

   a) I only
   b) II only
   c) Both I and II
   d) Neither I nor II

7. A warranty deed usually obligates the grantor to the warranties of:

   I. seizin
   II. quiet enjoyment

   a) I only
   b) II only
   c) Both I and II
   d) Neither I nor II

8. The person who obtains a real estate loan by signing a note and a mortgage or trust deed is called the:

I. mortgagor
II. beneficiary

a) I only
b) II only
c) Both I and II
d) Neither I nor II

9. A man purchased an $18,000 house using $5,000 and a purchase money mortgage for $13,000. Two years later the property value doubled. Considering that he made no payments on the purchase money mortgage, what is each original cash dollar invested worth today?

a) $2.00
b) $4.60
c) $5.20
d) $2.30

10. When an existing contract is replaced by a new contract, this is referred to as:

a) rescission
b) novation
c) hypothecation
d) subordination

11. If one owns a single unit and shares ownership in common with others for purposes of a shopping center, office space or apartment buildings, the situation is called:

a) condominium
b) stock in cooperative
c) neighborhood development
d) None of the above

12. To establish income property value, you capitalize the net income. Provision can be made to allow for return of investment. This would be:

a) income taxes
b) interest
c) principal payments
d) depreciation

13. The main purpose of zoning laws is to:

a) determine lot setbacks
b) control county and city ordinances
c) regulate the use and control of private property
d) observe the flow of traffic

14. The function of real estate advertising is to:

I. communicate images
II. keep the name of the agency before the public

a) I only
b) II only
c) Both I and II
d) Neither I nor II

15. Two people own property with no rights of survivorship. They have:

a) concurrent ownership
b) joint tenancy
c) a leasehold
d None of the above

16. A 6-unit apartment has a gross income of $1,500 per month. Annual expenses, excluding depreciation, are $7,200. There is a 5% vacancy and uncollected rent rate. A buyer desires an 8% return on his investment. What price should he offer?

a) $142,550
b) $123,750
c) $ 96,500
d) $116,000

17. An investor buys a 24-unit apartment in 1979 for $410,000 and charges $185 rent for each apartment per month. There are no vacancies. In 1980, one year later, the investor raises the rent by 10% and also suffers a vacancy rate of 10%. The investor's effective gross income was:

a) 10% more in 1979
b) 10% less in 1979
c) the same each year
d) 1% less in 1980

18. What is the length of the North-South boundary of the shaded triangle of land?

6
ACRES
N
400 ft.

a) 653 feet
b) 1,300 feet
c) 1,250 feet
d) 1,600 feet

19. If the payments on a $4,800 loan are designed in 48 equal monthly principal amounts plus simple interest at 10% per annum, what is the total amount of the third payment?

a) $38.33
b) $40
c) $138.33
d) $140

20. A person holding title to real property in severalty would most likely have:

a) a life estate
b) an estate for years
c) ownership in common with others
d) sole ownership

21. A freehold estate is most nearly:

a) an estate for years
b) an estate at will
c) fee simple
d) leasehold estate

22. The seller will not authorize the broker to accept earnest money deposits. The broker should:

a) accept deposits as agent of purchaser
b) do as seller says
c) deposit earnest money in his personal account
d) None of the above

23. Stevens lists his home for sale with broker, Brandon. He tells Brandon to be sure to let prospective buyer know that there are some leaks in the roof that have caused a few spots of dry rot here and there. One of Brandon's salesmen negotiates a sale of the house but forgets to tell the buyer about the roof leaks and dry rot. The buyer, upon discovering the defects, could recover from:

I. Stevens
II. Brandon

a) I only
b) II only
c) Both I and II
d) Neither I nor II

24. Which of the following is not a security instrument?

a) Mortgage
b) Deed of trust
c) Option
d) Agreement of sale

25. The difference between an exclusive agency and an exclusive right to sell is:

a) the broker's promise to undertake and bear certain promotional expenses
b) the principal's reservation of the right to sell his or her own home
c) the principal's reservation of the right to pay broker no commission
d) the principal's reservation of the right to pay broker no commission should the principal sell the property

26. Which of these statements is true with respect to the appraisal of a one-family home?

a) Capitalization of net income is the most accurate
b) You should appraise it by at least three methods, total the results and divide by three
c) The reproduction cost method is valid on new property where replacement cost of the building and land value can be ascertained
d) Capitalizing the average rent of the neighborhood properties is accurate

27. That the maximum value of property tends to be set by the cost of acquiring an equally desirable substitute property is an example of:

a) Principle of Substitition
b) Principle of Conformity
c) Principle of Change
d) Principle of Anticipation

28. The following are samples of advertisements placed by a broker on some of his listings. Which would be subjects to the provision of the Truth-in-Lending Law?

a) "2 bedrooms, large lot, nothing down"
b) "3 bedrooms, den, $80,000 E-Z terms"
c) "3 bedrooms, 1 bath, $75,000, excellent VA/FHA financing"
d) "4 bedrooms, family room, owner will carry financing"

29. The S½ of the NE¼ of Section 7, T4S, R3E is ambiguous because there is no:

a) lot number
b) boundary line
c) survey map
d) base and meridian lines

30. In the absence of a special agreement to the contrary, such as a subordination clause, the mortgage having priority is normally the one:

a) for the greatest amount of money
b) that is a construction loan
c) that is obtained first
d) that is recorded first

31. A building that represents an improper improvement to its site illustrates:

a) economic obsolescence
b) incurable locational obsolescence
c) curable functional obsolescence
d) incurable functional obsolescence

32. Shelter, Inc., an investment corporation, doesn't declare rent received on some of their investments on their income tax return. This might result in a:

a) general involuntary lien
b) general lien
c) involuntary specific lien
d) specific voluntary lien

33. The lower the loan-to-value ratio, the higher the:

a) risk
b) equity
c) possibility of foreclosure
d) loan amount

34. Which of the following takes place in the event the value of a real property is more than the amount of the exemption for homestead and liens?

a) The homestead is terminated
b) The creditor is able to purchase the property for the value placed upon it when the homestead was originally recorded
c) The creditor with a judgment can foreclose and receive the amount due him above the exemption
d) The creditor could not have the property sold in order to satisfy the judgment because the amount originally did not exceed the homestead exemption

35. Broker Skripchek verbally agrees to split his commission 50-50 if broker Ortiz secures a ready, willing and able buyer for the property Skripchek has an open listing on. Ortiz sells it. Skripchek is paid but refuses to split commission:

a) Ortiz can get relief in civil court
b) Ortiz should file an injunction in federal court
c) Ortiz should file a lis-pendens in criminal court
d) Ortiz can do nothing

36. A borrower obtains a mortgage loan in order to make repairs on her home. The loan is not insured or guaranteed by a government agency, and the mortgage document secures the amount of the loan as well as any future funds advanced to the borrower by the lender. This borrower has obtained:

I. a wrap around mortgage
II. a conventional loan

a) I only
b) II only
c) Both I and II
d) Neither I nor II

37. Which of the following is not considered personal property:

a) an installment sales contract
b) mortgage
c) crops
d) standing timber

38. Which of the following would give you notice of Harriet Stowe's interest in a parcel of real estate?

a) Stowe's telling you that she bought the property without ever recording her deed
b) The recording of a deed to Harriet Stowe
c) The fact that Stowe is in possession of the property, although she never recorded her deed
d) All of the foregoing would give you notice

39. A commercial acre is most nearly:

a) any property used for commercial purposes which is 43,560 square feet or larger
b) the portion of a farm that is actually used for agricultural purposes
c) what is left of a developed acre after dedication of streets, alleys, etc.
d) a parcel of undeveloped land zoned for commercial purposes

40. A purchaser who will be financing with a VA loan would least likely finance through:

a) national bank
b) insurance company
c) mortgage company
d) None of the above

41. To be valid, a deed must have all but:

a) a granting clause
b) description of the property
c) signature of grantor
d) valuable consideration

42. A developer is going to finance some land he wants to buy. It would be in his best interests to include in the mortgage a:

a) subordination clause
b) subjacent clause
c) subrogation clause
d) severalty clause

43. A salesman made an offer to purchase real property listed in his broker's office. The seller accepted the offer and the transaction closed, and all parties seemed satisfied at the time. Later the seller wrote a letter to the director complaining that the salesman had neglected to inform him that he was a licensed real estate agent.

a) The seller should have known better
b) The salesman was not ethical but did not violate the real estate law
c) Both the broker and salesman are subject to disciplinary action
d) The salesman only is subject to disciplinary action

44. No suit or action regarding commissions can be brought by a salesman against a seller without:

a) informing his broker
b) proving he was a licensed salesman at the date of the sale
c) filing a lis pendens
d) None of the above

45. Which of the following could an owner expect if his home were properly insured with fire insurance indemnifying him?

a) Lose, but will definitely not gain
b) To gain but never lose
c) Always gain
d) To neither gain nor lose

46. The purchaser of a real property would be most concerned with:

a) effective age
b) future economic life
c) chronological age
d) actual age

47. In order to establish net income for capitalization purposes, which of the following would be deducted from effective gross income?

a) Taxes
b) Mortgage interest
c) Building depreciation
d) Capital improvements

48. Which of the following is a cost of ownership which is likely to be overlooked?

a) Amenities
b) Depreciation
c) Loan amortization
d) The loss of interest on the equity of the owner

49. With an amortized mortgage or trust deed loan:

I. unless otherwise provided, interest is usually charged in arrears, meaning at the end of each period for which interest is due
II. the interest portion of each payment remains the same throughout the entire term of the loan

a) I only
b) II only
c) Both I and II
d) Neither I nor II

50. John Jones owned a parcel of land around his copper mine. He sold the mine and property for $230,000, with the verbal understanding that copper already mined before the date of sale would not be included in the sale. That copper is considered by law as:

a) realty
b) personal property
c) a fixture
d) sub rosa

51. When a real estate transaction is to be closed in escrow:

I. the seller and buyer execute a separate escrow agreement
II. the buyer's purchase money, mortgage, and mortgage note are deposited with the escrow agent

a) I only
b) II only
c) Both I and II
d) Neither I or II

52. Able lists property for sale with broker Baker for $110,000. The broker obtains a prospective buyer, Charlie, at $113,500. He has his mother-in-law buy the property at $110,000, and she deeds the property to Charlie for $113,500. Able paid Baker a commission of 7% on the $110,000 deal. In addition to recovering the commission paid and the profit, Able could:

a) file a complaint with the housing authority
b) file a complaint with the real estate director
c) file an injunctive suit against Baker continuing to operate as a broker
d) picket Baker's office

53. A parcel of land which is referred to as the "servient tenement":

a) is the parcel benefited by the easement
b) has an easement appurtenant
c) changes when the title is transferred
d) is the parcel burdened by the easement

54. Accession is closest to getting title by:

a) will or inheritance
b) imperceptible and gradual accumulation of alluvion
c) deed
d) None of these

55. Broker Brown received from a prospective purchaser a signed earnest money and a $2,000 earnest money deposit, all in cash, at approximately 4:30 p.m. on Wednesday. Brown did not want to keep that amount of cash on his person overnight, but did not have enough time before closing to get to the bank where his trust account was. Fortunately, the bank in which he kept his personal account was nearby. He deposited the money there, withdrew it the next morning and deposited it in his trust account on his way to work.

a) Broker Brown operated in a reasonable and normal business manner
b) In a strict legal sense, Brown should not have deposited the earnest money in his own account, but under the circumstances, he followed the most prudent course of action and, therefore, there was no breach of any fiduciary obligation
c) His action constituted commingling of funds, a violation of the license law which could result in revocation, suspension, or cancellation of his license
d) Since there was no intent to misappropriate the funds and, in fact, no misappropriation occurred, and the funds were deposited in a recognized Washington state depository by the next banking day, Brown's actions did not constitute commingling

56. You list an old home on a corner in an older residential area. The home has an addition on the front which has been used as a small neighborhood grocery store, but which has been vacant for some time. Your prospect wants to re-establish the grocery business and wants to know if there is anything to prohibit it.

a) You can assure him it is permitted as it has recently been used as a grocery store
b) It is permissible as there is a similar store two blocks away
c) You should check with the zoning authorities as the business may have been a hold-over when area was rezoned
d) You can assure buyer it is O.K. as the seller would know if a business could not be started

57. In the market data approach to value, the probable sales price of a building may be estimated by:

I. capitalizing net income
II. considering sales of similar properties

a) I only
b) II only
c) Both I and II
d) Neither I nor II

58. The Martins listed their home for sale with Albert Realty for $85,000 on July 16, 1987. On September 15, 1987, Harry, a salesperson, brought the owners a signed offer to purchase at $82,500 and received a $2,000 earnest money deposit. In fact, it was a note in that amount. Albert did not learn about the note, in lieu of cash deposit, until ten days later. Harry was instructed to obtain cash but was unsuccessful. The deal was to be closed on December 15, 1987. It was not until April 2, 1988, that the Martins learned about the note and also that the buyers would not go through with the deal. Under these circumstances:

I. the broker cannot collect a commission
II. the broker's license can be suspended or revoked

a) I only
b) II only
c) Both I and II
d) Neither I nor II

59. Using the unit cost per square foot or per cubic foot computation, an appraiser would generally conclude that on a unit cost basis:

a) a small house would cost less per square foot than a large house
b) a large house would cost more per square foot than a small house
c) a small house would cost more per square foot than a large house
d) the cost of a small house and a large house per square foot would be the same

60. The degree, quantity, nature and extent of interest which a person has in real property is called an estate. Which of the following is an estate?

a) Easement
b) Sublease
c) Mortgage
d) Holder in due course

61. If property values decreased as the result of an airline company rerouting the flight patterns of its aircraft over a residential area, this loss of value would be termed:

a) physical deterioration
b) functional obsolescence
c) economic obsolescence
d) None of these

62. Under the 1974 RESPA (Uniform Settlement Procedures Act), a "Federally Related Mortgage" is made primarily for:

a) vacant residence lot
b) building a single-family residence on a lot owned by the borrower
c) purchase of a lot on which a mobile home is located
d) for the purchase of property, the primary purpose of which is resale

63. Which of the following items are usually not designated on the plat for a new subdivision?

a) Easement for sewer and water mains
b) Land to be used for streets, schools, and civic facilities
c) Numbered lots and blocks
d) Lot sizes

64. A man sells his home for $30,000. The loan balance is $26,500 and the costs of selling were: 7% commission, excise tax, revenue stamps, 2% prepayment penalty and miscellaneous costs of $715. His selling costs are what percentage of his equity?

a) 13.88%
b) 12.15%
c) 105%
d) 62%

65. An agreement of sale becomes enforceable when signed by the:

I. buyer
II. broker, as agent for the seller

a) I only
b) II only
c) Both I and II
d) Neither I nor II

66. You hold a trust deed and note which has been paid in full. You do nothing about it, and the lien remains of record against the property. The trustor should take which of the following steps?

a) Record a notice of non-responsibility
b) Record a notice of completion of payments
c) Make demand for a deed of reconveyance and sue to enforce it if it is not forthcoming
d) Record an affidavit of payment

67. John Steele and Henry Steele are unmarried brothers. John agrees to sell his summer cottage on Lake Bedford to Henry for $53,900. Henry gives John $250 in cash, and they shake hands on the deal in the presence of two friends. Under these circumstances:

I. Henry is obligated to pay the balance to John
II. John is obligated to deliver a deed to Henry

a) I only
b) II only
c) Both I and II
d) Neither I nor II

68. Which of the following is not relevant in appraising a home?

a) Circumstances of sale
b) Original cost to build 12 months previous
c) Square footage of improvements
d) Recent selling prices of comparables

69. Best definition of a voidable contract is:

a) one that is no contract at all
b) one that appears valid on its face but can be voided by either party
c) one that appears valid on its face but can be voided by damaged party
d) one missing just one of the elements of a contract

70. Which of the following is not one of the limitations imposed on the community's right to zone?

a) Zoning must be non-discriminatory
b) Zoning must be for overall public benefit
c) Zoning must be for a limited time period
d) There must be a need for the zoning

71. A commercial property is listed with Rockwell Realty at $70,000. Rockwell Realty negotiates with Woods who is familiar with the property and who agrees to buy the property at that figure. Rockwell Realty prepares an agreement of sale which is signed by Downes, the owner. Copies are then mailed to Woods for signature on March 31, 1987. The copies are received by Woods on June 3, 1987. He signs and mails the signed copies to Downes the same day. The copies are received by Downes on June 6, 1987. On June 4, 1987, Downes wired Woods, "Offer withdrawn — property not for sale." Under these circumstances:

I. there is an enforceable contract
II. Rockwell Realty is entitled to a commission

a) I only
b) II only
c) Both I and II
d) Neither I nor II

72. An offer can be terminated by:

a) revocation by offeree
b) rejection by offeror
c) seller making counteroffer
d) buyer inquiring of seller if he will consider other terms

73. Broker Carp Deem informs home owner Matt James of the prospective entry of a minority group into home owner James' neighborhood. Broker Deem, seeing that James is very upset, offers to buy James' house at a low price. Broker Deem is:

I. guilty of steering
II. protecting the best interests of the home owner

a) I only
b) II only
c) Both I and II
d) Neither I nor II

74. Street paving is:

a) a special assessment
b) a general tax lien
c) a special tax lien
d) financed by voluntary contributions in residential neighborhoods

75. Mr. Bravura has a home he wants to sell. There is a conventional loan against the property which has monthly payments that include 8% interest. The note contains an alienation clause. In a period of tight money, with no relief in the foreseeable future, which of the following would be true if the property is sold?

a) The seller would be required to refinance
b) The buyer may assume the loan at the same rate of interest and monthly payments
c) The lender would favor the buyer taking the title "subject to" the loan
d) The lender would benefit from the sale

76. The effect of the ILSFDA is to:

a) decrease speculation in real property
b) extend federal regulatory authority to cover both intrastate and interstate land promotions, where the land is undeveloped, at least one lot is less than five acres, and the mails are used to promote sales
c) authorize HUD to sue a developer for fraud if there are misrepresentative and deceptive unfair practices in the advertising of land
d) protect the public by insuring that the public cannot purchase undeveloped lots which will later dramatically decrease in value

77. Seller Brown has signed a listing with Broker Green. Brown agrees to pay a 6% commission. Green agrees to use diligence in finding a ready, willing and able buyer. This is an example of:

a) express bilateral executory contract
b) express bilateral executed contract
c) express unilateral executory contract
d) implied bilateral agreement

78. When employing the cost approach to appraisal, the improvements and the land are valued:

a) individually by one approach
b) separately by more than one approach
c) jointly by one approach
d) jointly by more than one approach

79. Deferred maintenance is best represented by which of the following?

a) A building which requires rehabilitation
b) The need for a larger size water heater
c) An apartment building which will require painting in the future
d) Installation of a new roof on the house

80. A "master plan" of the city or county would normally show:

a) existing pattern of the streets
b) flow of freeway traffic
c) bus and train depots and airline terminals
d) All of the above

81. Seller O'Peck sells land to Sam reserving for himself an easement for oil, minerals and gas. O'Peck shows up with oil drilling equipment. Sam refuses to allow him to come on the land.

a) Sam is right
b) O'Peck can drill
c) O'Peck can only slant drill from outside the boundary of Sam's property
d) O'Peck can drill but must do so more than 500 feet deep

82. In an installment sales contract, who has vested legal title?

a) Mortgagor
b) Mortgagee
c) Vendee
d) Vendor

83. An easement in gross must, as a minimum have:

a) at least one piece of property
b) two or more adjoining lots
c) two or more lots
d) three contiguous lots

84. Which of the following is correct regarding townships?

a) Township lines run east and west
b) Townships are numbered east and west of the meridian
c) Range lines parallel base lines
d) Range lines run east and west

85. Which of the following would be given the greatest weight in the selection of a property management company?

a) Personnel all having accounting degrees
b) Knowledge of supply purchasing and building repairs
c) History of successful management for organizations
d) Superior rent collecting record

86. Which has been the hardest to enforce regarding deed restrictions?

a) A certain minimum investment in any planned development
b) Size of improvements
c) Square footage of lots
d) Setback restrictions

87. When a certain degree of social and economic homogeneity is reached, the maximum value of property is said to have been reached. This most nearly refers to:

a) principal of conformity
b) principal of substitution
c) principal of balance
d) principal of diminishing returns

88. A broker shows property on an open listing agreement. He should:

a) write a memo to his office
b) introduce his customer to the seller
c) advise the seller of his buyer's identity by memo
d) None of the above

89. The money for all FHA loans comes primarily from:

a) individual savings accounts
b) U. S. Government bonds
c) FHA
d) FSLIC

90. Betty has given open listing(s) to Mark and to Mary on March 18, 1987. Mark shows the property to a prospect, Charles, on March 27, 1987. Mary negotiates a sale to Charles on May 31, 1987. Betty pays Mary the commission. Under these facts, which of the following would apply:

I. Mark can sue for conspiracy against Betty and Mary
II. Mark is entitled to one-half of the commission from Mary

a) I only
b) II only
c) Both I and II
d) Neither I nor II

91. Jones, broker, negotiates a deal between Smith, seller, and Adams, buyer, at $50,000. The parties sign an agreement to that effect. Adams requires a $48,000 mortgage, so Jones prepares a second agreement of sale reciting a consideration price of $55,000 which is signed by the seller and buyer. The second agreement is submitted to a mortgage company for a $48,000 loan. Under these circumstances:

I. Jones is guilty of a criminal act
II. Smith and Adams are guilty of a criminal act

a) I only
b) II only
c) Both I and II
d) Neither I nor II

92. A buyer purchases a parcel of property in "as is" condition. The sale closes. Buyer then discovers defective plumbing. What can the buyer do?

a) Recover from seller as the "as is" condition only covers conditions open to observation
b) Nothing unless he can prove broker knew of defective plumbing
c) Nothing since he purchased "as is"
d) Recover from broker as he was responsible for inspection of plumbing

93. Taking property into custody, or seizure of goods by due legal process is called:

a) an eviction
b) a forfeiture
c) an attachment
d) an action in trespass

94. A document detailing all documents in reference to a piece of land is called:

a) abstract judgment
b) abstract title
c) title insurance policy
d) deficiency judgment

95. The key elements of successful selling include:

I. timing
II. planning

a) I only
b) II only
c) Both I and II
d) Neither I nor II

96. A properly drawn earnest money, which is signed by the prospective buyer of real property and is to be submitted to the seller, constitutes a/an:

a) offer
b) binding, enforceable contract
c) valid contract
d) All of these

97. Mechanics' liens can be filed by:

a) architects
b) draymen
c) subcontractors
d) All of these

98. A title insurance policy usually includes:

I. a legal description of the insured parcel of real estate
II. the exceptions which are not covered by the policy

a) I only
b) II only
c) Both I and II
d) Neither I nor II

99. Depth tables are most commonly used on:

a) commercial land
b) residential improvements
c) waterfront homes
d) unimproved residential lots

100. "Portfolio" most nearly refers to:

a) warehoused mortgages
b) band of investment
c) Both
d) Neither

101. If a wife signs a listing to sell community real property, the listing is:

a) illegal
b) voidable
c) enforceable
d) void

102. An unlicensed person acting in the capacity of a broker or salesman is guilty of:

a) gross misdemeanor
b) misdemeanor
c) felony
d) violation of license law

103. An offer, together with cash deposit, was made on a parcel to the broker holding the listing. A copy of the earnest money receipt stating the offer must be given the offeror:

a) when seller has signed an acceptance of the offer
b) when the broker returns to his office and types up additional copies
c) immediately
d) when escrow instructions are completed to the satisfaction of the buyer and the seller

104. A real estate licensee should reveal that he has a license:

a) in any real estate transaction
b) in any real estate transaction except personal ones
c) as licensee deems necessary
d) it is not necessary for a licensee to reveal that he is licensed

105. Where must a non-resident broker maintain a place of business if licensed in Washington?

a) Washington state
b) Resident state
c) Both
d) Neither

106. Salesman sold a house and sale closed. Broker and salesman have no written agreements about paying at another time. Both are in town; so, allowing for checks to clear, commission must be paid:

a) within 30 days
b) immediately
c) on demand
d) on seller's request

107. The purpose of the Bulk Transfer Law is to:

a) ensure all applicable state and federal taxes are paid upon the sale of goods in the regular course of business
b) prevent secret or fraudulent sales in bulk by the vendor to the detriment of creditors and purchasers
c) require the seller to pay all lawful claims of creditors prior to transferring title to personal property
d) All of the above

108. Which of the following is not true regarding a metes and bound description?

a) Definite and stable starting points
b) Lines must all be adjoining
c) Must be a parcel which is completely closed
d) There must be a recorded map according to the Washington Platting Statute

109. Which of the following may be homesteaded?

a) A triplex, one-third of which is owner-occupied
b) A family dwelling that included 500 acres of land
c) A family dwelling with a fair market value of $150,000
d) Any of the foregoing may be homesteaded

110. A disagreement between two salesmen is adjudicated by the:

a) director
b) real estate commission
c) Both
d) Neither

111. The director can investigate the actions of a licensee:

I. on her own motion
II. on verification of a written complaint

a) I only
b) II only
c) Both I and II
d) Neither I nor II

112. Which of the following taxes is/are used to distribute the cost of civic services among real estate owners?

I. Personal property tax
II. Inheritance tax

a) I only
b) II only
c) Both I and II
d) Neither I nor II

113. Administration of the law governing licensing of real estate brokers and salesmen in Washington is the responsibility of the:

a) real estate division
b) state legislature
c) courts
d) real estate commissioners

114. The state of Washington is a "lien theory" state. This means:

a) first to record is first in right
b) liens recorded against a property can be foreclosed through the courts
c) a mortgage or deed of trust are liens and do not give lenders title to the property
d) All of these

115. A father conveys ownership of his residence to his son but reserves for himself a life estate in the residence. The interest which the son owns during the lifetime of the father is:

I. an estate of land
II. a remainder

a) I only
b) II only
c) Both I and II
d) Neither I nor II

116. The interest or value which an owner has in real estate, over and above the debts against it, is best described as:

a) value
b) fee simple
c) equity
d) estate

117. Which is an example of an involuntary lien?

a) Attachment lien
b) Deed of trust
c) Mortgage
d) None of these

118. If a man purchases a six-unit apartment building, one unit of which he plans to occupy, he would be subject to:

a) the Civil Rights Act of 1866
b) Title VIII of the Civil Rights Act of 1968
c) the Washington State law against discrimination
d) All of the above:

119. Which of the following municipalities or agencies usually makes levies for general real estate taxes?

I. School districts
II. Counties

a) I only
b) II only
c) Both I and II
d) Neither I nor II

120. In Washington, the transfer of title by a seller's assignment of real estate contract and deed requires:

I. payment of 1% real estate excise tax
II. payment of state documentary tax stamps

a) I only
b) II only
c) Both I and II
d) Neither I nor II

121. Rules and regulations adopted by government agencies:

I. are used to administer and enforce legislative acts
II. usually outline specific illegal acts and set down penalties for violations

a) I only
b) II only
c) Both I and II
d) Neither I nor II

122. A tenant told his landlord of a ceiling crack and feared falling plaster; landlord repaired it; plaster later falls causing the tenant damage.

a) As landlord was not obligated to repair ceiling, he is not liable for damages
b) Landlord was obligated to repair ceiling but is not liable to tenant for damages
c) Landlord was obligated to repair ceiling and is also liable for damages
d) Landlord was not obligated to repair it but, as he undertook it, he is liable for any damages resulting from his negligent workmanship

123. An excise tax is levied:

a) by the state
b) by counties
c) for the provision of police and fire protection services
d) None of the above

124. Where is notice of mechanic's lien filed?

a) Recorder's office
b) Office of the County Auditor
c) Either of the above
d) None of the above

125. To appeal a revocation of his license, a salesman:

I. should appeal to the Supreme Court
II. ask Attorney General to review revocation hearing

a) I only
b) II only
c) Both I and II
d) Neither I nor II

126. A policy manual is:

a) a book which describes the policies of the National Association of Realtors
b) an outline of the Code of Ethics
c) a floor schedule for salespersons
d) an outline of the procedures under which an office operates

127. Under which of the following circumstances could it be possible to sue and hold a homeowner personally liable for payment of an obligation?

a) The foreclosed property does not realize enough to satisfy the mortgage note given in part to pay for the home
b) The deed of trust foreclosure was brought by court action, and the home sold for the principal amount of the note given to secure money with which to pay doctor bills
c) The trust deed held by the bank was foreclosed by virtue of a power of sale provision and property did not realize enough to satisfy the note
d) An FHA-insured trust deed was foreclosed and home was sold in about 180 days, not brining enough to pay note and costs

128. The Washington Land Development Act applies to all the following except:

a) ten or more undeveloped lots of less than five acres offered for sale during one year, all the land being located in Washington and not covered by the ILSFDA
b) the annual sale of ten or more undeveloped lots of less than five acres offered for sale within Washington and already registered under the provisions of the ILSFDA
c) the annual sale of ten undeveloped lots, some of less than five acres, where all the land is within the boundaries of any Washington city
d) offering ten undeveloped lots for sale during one year, most of the lots being greater than five acres, where all the land for sale is located out of Washington state but advertised in Washington state

129. The successful bidder at a Sheriff's Sale receives:

a) a certificate of sale
b) sheriff's deed
c) bill of sale
d) equitable redemption

130. With regard to a warranty deed and a quit claim deed, all of the following are true, except:

a) a warranty deed gives some implied warranties, but a quit claim deed does not
b) a warrandy deed conveys after-acquired title, but a quit claim deed does not
c) a quit claim deed conveys the title presently owned as effectively as a warranty deed
d) both warranty deeds and quit claim deeds use the word "grant" in the granting clause

131. The real estate market is considered local in character because:

I. land is fixed, or immobile
II. most people are not mobile enough to take advantage of available real estate in other areas

a) I only
b) II only
c) Both I and II
d) Neither I nor II

132. A real estate license is not required for:

a) salesman selling for builder only
b) salesman selling lots to builders only
c) executor who sells for a commission or fee
d) salesman who only lists property and doesn't sell

133. Judgments for money that can become a lien on real property continue for ________ years from the date of entry of the judgment.

a) 3
b) 6
c) 7
d) 10

134. Most real estate syndicates in Washington are:

a) corporations
b) limited partnerships
c) joint ventures
d) real estate investment trusts

135. The oral will made at a deathbed, usually verified later by witnesses who testify as to its authenticity, is the:

a) witnessed will
b) holographic will
c) nuncupative will
d) None of the above

136. Who would benefit most from inflation?

a) Grantee
b) Mortgagee
c) Grantor
d) Lessee

137. "Racial steering" means to:

a) steer brokers to minority prospects
b) steer minority prospects toward a limited number of choices
c) steer minority prospects toward affordable property
d) prejudicial behavior among cows

138. In Washington State, a deed:

I. evidences title
II. passes title

a) I only
b) II only
c) Both I and II
d) Neither I nor II

139. The legal term used to describe the individually-owned spaces in a building, the land under the building, and certain areas of the property owned in common is a:

a) condominium
b) condominium unit
c) condominium common area
d) condominium project

140. In a suspension or revocation hearing, the accused licensee must:

a) appear
b) pay for a transcript
c) have 20 days notice
d) have 30 days notice

1. b) Interest rates on VA loans (1) are not controlled by the Federal Reserve and (2) have no effect on the money supply in any event.

2. b) Even large construction loans are disbursed in installments. Alternative I is incorrect as the buyers of the various units will arrange their own permanent financing.

3. c) The three significant characteristics of any investment include risk (security), yield, and liquidity. Risk is the most important consideration.

4. b) With an exclusive right to sell, the broker will be paid regardless. With an open or exclusive agency, the property could be sold without the broker receiving compensation.

5. c) The counter offer terminates the original offer.

6. c) FHA requires MIP for all loans and if the buyer is applying for an owner-occupied loan, he must certify he intends to occupy the property.

7. c) These are two of the five warranties. See the chapter on "Acquisition and Transfer of Land."

8. a) The mortgagor is the borrower.

9. b) The borrower invested $5,000 for $5,000 equity. When the value doubled to $36,000, the equity increased to $23,000 ($36,000 less $13,000 loan). $23,000 equity divided by $5,000 investment = $4.60.

10. b) Nova is Latin for "new."

11. a) This is a condominium interest.

12. d) The capitalization rate for buildings allows for a return on the investment (interest) and a return of the investment (recapture or depreciation). See income approach to value in the Appraisal chapter.

13. c) Zoning protects certain types of properties from the adverse influences of incompatible types of properties.

14. c) To create favorable images of the product in the mind of the customer and to keep the name of the (real estate) agency in front of the public.

15. a) Concurrent ownership is ownership by two or more persons at the same time.

16. b) $1,500 x 12 = $18,000 annual income; $18,000 less $900 (5% bad debt/vacancy) = $17,100; $17,100 less $7,200 operating expenses = $9,900; $9,900 divided by 8% = $123,750.

17. d) Annual 1979 rent = $53,280 ($185 x 24 x 12 mos.); $53,280 x 1.10 = $58,608 annual 1980 rent; $58,608 x .90 (10% vacancy factor) = $52,747; $53,280 (1979) less $53,747 (1980) = $532.80 (1%).

18. b) Exactly 1,306.8. The area of the triangle is 261,360 square feet (6 x 43,560). Determine the length of the north/south boundary by dividing the area of the triangle by half the base (261,360 divided by 200 = 1,306.8).

19. c) The principal payments are $100 each ($4,800 divided by 48 = $100). Thus, when the third payment is due, the debt has been reduced to $4,600. Interest is computed on the declining balance ($4,600 x .10 = $460) divided by 12 = $38.33 monthly interest. Total third payment = $138.33.

20. d) Severalty refers to sole ownership, as opposed to concurrent ownership.

21. c) The two freehold estates are fee simple and life. Alternatives (a), (b) and (d) are leases—less than freehold estates.

22. a) Requiring a good faith deposit from a purchaser is good business. If the seller will not authorize the broker to accept deposits on his behalf, the broker should probably collect a deposit anyway, but will do so as agent for the buyer.

23. c) Stevens is responsible for Brandon's acts (and the acts of his sales staff), and Brandon is also accountable for his acts and the acts of his sales staff.

24. c) Mortgages, trust deeds and contracts secure debts against real estate. Options do not.

25. d) Under an exclusive agency, the seller does not have to pay a commission if he or she sells the home.

26. c) The older the property under appraisement, the less reliable the replacement cost method is.

27. a) This defines the principle of substitution.

28. a) By stating, "Nothing down," the ad must also contain cash price, number of payments, amount of each payment, period of payment (e.g. monthly, annually, etc.) and the APR.

29. d) Every government survey description must refer to the appropriate meridian and base line.

30. d) First to record, first in right.

31. a) For example, a residence where there are largely commercial buildings is economically obsolete. Another instance is a $200,000 home in an $80,000 neighborhood.

32. a) IRS liens are general involuntary liens.

33. b) Equity is the difference bewteen the property's value and the debts owed against it. A low loan-to-value will result in a higher equity.

34. c) The court would order the sale and from the proceeds, the voluntary liens would be paid first, next the owner would receive the homestead exemption amount ($25,000 for a family in Washington) and then the creditors.

35. a) An oral agreement between brokers to split a commission is enforceable.

36. b) A conventional loan is any loan not insured or guaranteed by a government agency. The loan appears to have an open-end provision.

37. d) Alternatives (a) and (b) are contracts which are always personal property interests. Crops are generally thought to be the personal property of the grower, unless they have been constructively severed by contract in which case they become the personal property of the purchaser.

38. d) (a) is actual notice; (b) and (c) are constructive notice.

39. c) In subdivision developments, portions of the land are dedicated to the public. That portion of an acre that remains after dedications is referred to as a commercial acre.

40. b) Insurance companies do not make loans for residences direct to borrowers.

41. d) Valuable consideration is not essential to the validity of a deed.

42. a) A subordination clause will allow subsequent construction loans to assume a first lien position.

43. c) The broker is responsible for the salesperson's actions and, of course, the salesperson is responsible for his or her own acts. The licensed status disclosure must be made before a contract is signed.

44. d) Only the broker can sue a seller for a commission.

45. d) The purpose of insurance is to protect against loss, not to promote gain.

46. b) It is the property's future that is important, not its age.

47. a) From effective gross income, property taxes, hazard insurance, management expense, maintenance costs, utilities and reserves for replacement are deducted to arrive at net income.

48. d) If the owner's equity were not tied up in the property, it could be reinvested elsewhere for profit. As it is tied up in the property, it is considered a cost of ownership.

49. a) Interest is normally charged in arrears, meaning a monthly interest payment made on December 1st probably covered the month of November. Amortized payments usually don't change over the life of a loan; however, as the debt declines, the interest portion of each payment goes down, and the principal portion increases.

50. b) It has already been mined (extracted from the ground) and its status as personal property has been confirmed.

51. c) Buyer and seller issue separate instructions, called escrow instructions, to the escrow agent which define what each has agreed to and how they expect him to go about finalizing the sale. The buyer's required funds, as well as the promissory note and mortgage, are usually placed with the escrow agent until the transaction is closed.

52. b) Baker's behavior is a violation of license law.

53. d) The servient tenement is the parcel burdened by the easement.

54. b) Acquisition of real estate by accession results from additions to one's present real estate. Man-made additions are buildings and the like. Natural additions can be through gradual accumulation, usually by the action of water.

55. c) There are no circumstances under which commingling is acceptable.

56. c) There is a good chance the nonconforming use will not be permitted. A continuation of an accepted nonconforming use is far from assured when the property is sold.

57. b) Capitalization refers to the income approach to value.

58. c) That the deposit was in the form of a note should have been made clear to the seller before the offer was accepted. The broker is responsible for his agent's actions.

59. c) The small house would cost more per square foot or cubic foot than the larger house.

60. b) The two types of estates are title and leases (freehold and less-than-freehold).

61. c) Economic obsolescence because the force causing the loss in value is external to the property.

62. c) RESPA applies when a federally related mortgage loan is made to finance the purchase of real estate on which there is a one to four family dwelling, including a mobile home.

63. b) Public easements, lot sizes, lot and block numbers are included in a subdivision plat. See the plat under "Land Description" in your text.

64. c) Selling costs are $3,675 ($2,100 commission, $300 excise tax, $30 revenue stamps, $530 prepayment penalty and $715 miscellaneous costs). Equity is $3,500. $3,675 divided by $3,500 is 105%.

65. d) The contract becomes enforceable when signed by buyer and seller. Broker does not have authority to commit seller to a contract.

66. c) The trustor is entitled to demand release of the lien, which is called a deed of reconveyance.

67. d) Any contract for the sale of land must be in writing to be enforceable.

68. a) Circumstances of sale can affect price but not value. Cost to build 12 months previous would have little meaning but would not be totally irrelevant.

69. c) A voidable contract must either be voided or ratified by the damaged party. Ratification can occur if the damaged party does nothing.

70. c) Zoning does not have to be for a limited period.

71. c) For a contract to be formed, there must be an offer, an acceptance and notification of acceptance. By Washington law, when notification of acceptance is by mail, notice is deemed given on the postmark date, in this instance, the day before the offer to sell was withdrawn.

72. c) A counter offer terminates the original offer.

73. d) Broker Deem is guilty of blockbusting.

74. a) Special assessments differ from property taxes in that the latter are levied for support of the general functions of government, whereas special assessments are levied for the cost of special local improvements such as streets, sewers, irrigation and drainage.

75. d) The lender would insist the old loan be paid in full and would be able to reinvest money that had been earning 8% at a higher rate of interest.

76. b) This is a reasonably concise explanation of the effect of the Interstate Land Sales Full Disclosure Act.

77. a) "Express" means the terms of the agreement have been stated; "bilateral" refers to an exchange of promises; "executory" means the contract is in the process of being performed.

78. b) The improvements are appraised by the replacement cost method; the land value is usually estimated by the market data method.

79. c) Deferred maintenance refers to repairs that have been put off.

80. d) All of these would be contained in a master plan.

81. b) O'Peck has an implied easement.

82. d) Vendor has naked title; vendee has an equitable interest.

83. a) An easement in gross, unlike an easement appurtenant, does not serve another property. It serves a dominant tenant, either a natural person or a corporation like a utility company.

84. a) Township lines run east/west; range lines run north/south. Townships are numbered according to their placement north or south of the base line, not east or west of the meridian.

85. c) Obviously.

86. a) It is difficult, if not impossible, to require a minimum dollar investment in subdivision property.

87. a) This is the principle of conformity.

88. c) The broker must be prepared to show he was the procuring cause; the best way to do this is to advise the seller, in writing, that he introduced a specific buyer to the property.

89. a) Savings deposits in banks and savings and loans account for the majority of funds used for real estate loans.

90. d) When nonexclusive listings are involved, the agent that actually negotiates the sale is entitled to the commission.

91. c) All three are guilty of criminal fraud.

92. a) Hidden defects, like plumbing and wiring, must be disclosed. The caveat emptor doctrine (let the buyer beware) applies only to visible or obvious defects.

93. c) This describes an attachment, that legal action which precedes a judgment.

94. b) An abstract of title is a short account of what appears in the public records affecting title of a particular parcel of real property.

95. c) Timing and planning are important ingredients to successful selling.

96. a) It is an offer. There must be acceptance and notification of acceptance before a contract is formed.

97. d) All of these. A drayman is the driver who delivers supplies to the site.

98. c) The policy will identify the insured property with a legal description. It will also detail what is and is not covered.

99. a) Depth tables are mathematical devices used in appraisal of real estate to measure differences in value between lots of different depths and corner lots. The theory is the front of a lot is the most valuable part, and the value diminishes as you get farther away from the front. This is more true with commercial properties than with residential properties.

100. a) A portfolio is a list of an investor's loans, stocks, bonds, etc. A warehoused mortgage loan is one kept by a lender, as opposed to one that is sold in the secondary market. A warehoused loan, then, is one kept "in portfolio."

101. c) A listing employs a broker to find a ready, willing and able purchaser. The wife (and husband) could not be compelled to sell the property, but she could be forced to pay the commission.

102. a) In Washington, this offense is classified as a gross misdemeanor. Remember this answer.

103. c) Immediately. No exceptions.

104. a) Whenever an active licensee is involved in a real estate transaction as a buyer or seller, his licensed status must be revealed to the other party before any agreement is signed.

105. b) In his state of domicile—his resident state.

106. b) Immediately.

107. b) To prevent secret or fraudulent sales in bulk, such as inventory that might be subject to a creditor's lien.

108. d) The recorded map relates to the maps and plats (lot and block) description method.

109. d) A homestead is any home which is used as a personal residence.

110. d) Disputes between salesmen might be arbitrated by their broker(s), a local real estate board or even in court. The director and the real estate commission do not arbitrate disputes of any kind.

111. c) The director can investigate a licensee on her own initiative or upon receiving a written complaint.

112. d) General real property taxes, not personal or inheritance taxes, are used to support civic services.

113. a) This is the responsibility of the real estate division.

114. c) Washington is a lien theory state, which means mortgages and trust deeds give creditors liens, not title, to secured property.

115. c) The son is a remainderman. The interest held is an estate in remainder.

116. c) This is a description of equity.

117. a) Attachments are involuntary; mortgages and trust deeds are voluntary.

118. d) All three acts. There is an exemption under the 1968 act for owner-occupied multiple units, but it is limited to duplexes, triplexes and fourplexes.

119. c) School districts and counties provide civic services which are supported by property owners.

120. b) If a seller assigns his contract to an investor, he must also give a deed to that investor so that the latter will be in a position to deliver title to the vendee at a later date when the contract debt is paid in full. Whenever a deed is given, revenue stamps must be paid.

121. c) Rule making is legislation at the administrative level, within the confines of the granting statute. The statutes enacted by the legislature set the general standards, authorize the agencies to determine the content of the regulations and, in many instances, provide penalties for noncompliance with the rules.

122. d) Unless there was a provision to the contrary in the lease, the landlord was not obligated to fix the crack. But when he did, he placed himself in a position of liability for his work.

123. b) The excise tax is a state-authorized tax levied by individual counties.

124. b) Office of the county auditor. The mechanic's lien must be recorded to be effective.

125. d) License revocation appeals are made to superior court.

126. d) Self-explanatory.

127. a) A deficiency judgment against the debtor is possible if the property is judicially foreclosed (in court) and the sale proceeds are inadequate to satisfy the debt owed the lender.

128. c) The exception is a subdivision entirely within the boundaries of a Washington city.

129. a) A certificate of sale. One year later, at the conclusion of the redemption period, she will receive a sheriff's deed.

130. d) The warranty deed uses the word "grant"; the quitclaim deed uses words like "quitclaim, quit, release or remise."

131. c) Both of these facts give the real estate market a local character.

132. c) As long as the executor is selling the real estate as a part of his duties as executor, no license is required.

133. d) The statute of limitations for enforcement of a judgment is ten years.

134. b) The limited partnership is the most popular form of syndicate.

135. c) A nuncupative will is an oral will made in anticipation of impending death.

136. a) A grantee is a buyer. Inflation will increase the value of his property.

137. b) For instance, showing minority prospects only homes in neighborhoods populated by members of their minority group.

138. c) The deed both evidences and passes title.

139. d) The owner's separate space is the "unit," the shared areas are the "common areas" and the units and common areas combined are called the "project."

140. c) The accused is legally entitled to 20 days' notice of the hearing. He does not have to appear; the hearing will be conducted in any event. If his license is revoked, he may appeal to the superior court. Not until this time does he have to pay for a copy of the revocation hearing transcript.

Sample Examination 4

1. In general, a promissory note:

   I. is a negotiable instrument
   II. may be sold by the lender to a third party

   a) I only
   b) II only
   c) Both I and II
   d) Neither I nor II

2. Real estate investment trusts are all of the following, except:

   a) corporations
   b) partnerships
   c) investment conduits
   d) owned by 100 or more investors

3. Pedestrian traffic counts are most valuable to:

   a) planning commission
   b) commercial investor
   c) industrial investor
   d) local law enforcement agency

4. In times of local economic distress, lenders:

   a) increase their local lending activities to stimulate the economy
   b) increase their local lending activities to reflect the economy
   c) decrease their local lending activities to stimulate the economy
   d) decrease their local lending activities to reflect the economy

5. Seller Stevens lists his property with Broker Barker for sale at $90,000. It is an exclusive agency agreement with an expiration date of April 14, 1987. Many low offers were made through Broker Barker and other cooperating brokers. The seller refused to accept any low offers. On April 13, Broker Barker submits a full price offer of $90,000 from the Real Corporation. Stevens accepts and the sale is consummated. Barker is a major share holder of the Real Corporation. Which is true?

   a) The agreement of sale is fraudulent as broker did not reveal his interest
   b) Contract is valid if broker inserts this clause in the Agreement of Sale: "Real Corporation consisting of Real Estate Salesmen and Brokers"
   c) Contract is valid if broker inserts the same clause in the escrow instructions
   d) Contract is valid if broker waives all rights to a commission

6. An option differs from an offer because:

   a) the option can be revoked at any time upon written notification to optionee
   b) offer can be revoked at any time prior to notification of acceptance
   c) an offer needs consideration, an option does not
   d) offer and option are the same

7. The gross multiplier would be of least assistance in the appraisal of:

   a) apartment houses
   b) residential properties
   c) commercial properties
   d) public buildings

8. All of the following are recognized methods of appraising land, except:

a) abstraction
b) comparative
c) development
d) economic

9. A farmer is in need of additional working capital and wishes to encumber his crops. In order to complete the loan, he would probably be required to sign a:

a) release of crops
b) financing statement
c) assignment of crops
d) trust deed

10. All of the following relate to a will, except:

a) bequest
b) demise
c) bequeath
d) devise

11. Escheat most nearly means:

a) property reverts to the State
b) dies intestate
c) eminent domain
d) dishonesty

12. Actual fraud is best described as which of the following?

a) The suppression of that which is true, by one having knowledge or belief of the fact
b) A promise made without any intention of performing it
c) Any act fitted to deceive
d) All of the above

13. If there is no mention in the escrow instructions of a termination date, the parties to the escrow would have:

a) as long as either one wished
b) 30 days
c) 60 days
d) a reasonable time

14. In a bilateral contract, a promise is given in expectation of a return promise. The return promise is:

a) consideration
b) partial performance
c) an option
d) moral obligation

15. A light company lays and maintains concealed electrical wiring along an agreed-upon line with owner. It does so by right of:

a) eminent domain
b) condemnation
c) an easement
d) a sub-surface appurtenance

16. Harold Albertson owns a fee simple title to unit 12 and 4½% of the common elements. Albertson:

I. owns a life estate
II. may mortgage unit 12 without placing a lien on the titles of the other unit owners

a) I only
b) II only
c) Both I and II
d) Neither I nor II

17. A court order to make a buyer or seller do what he or she promised to do is:

a) Writ of Execution
b) Decree of Specific Performance
c) Abandonment of Homestead Declaration
d) Estoppel Certificate

18. Adams orally agreed to sell 40 acres of land to Bell at $100 per acre. Bell took possession, paid part of the purchase price, and made some improvements. Later, Adams sued to regain possession.

a) Adams will succeed
b) Adams will not succeed
c) Adams will succeed, but must pay for the improvements
d) The oral agreement must be reduced to writing

19. Owners of a home decided to build a six-foot fence around their lot since they own a dog and want him to have run of the property. Before building this fence, the owners should carefully check applicable:

a) private restriction
b) zoning regulations
c) esthetic requirements of non-coterminus land-owners
d) Both (a) and (b)

20. Which of the following group of characteristics best defines the value of property?

a) Transferability, cost, utility, scarcity
b) Utility, scarcity, cost, demand
c) Transferability, utility, scarcity, demand
d) Utility, cost, demand, transferability

21. The requirements of a warranty deed differ from the requirements of a land contract in which of the following ways?

I. Signatures of the principals
II. Designation of price

a) I only
b) II only
c) Both I and II
d) Neither I nor II

22. Under the allodial system, individual land owners have maximum rights, subject to certain government powers such as:

I. confiscation
II. eminent domain

a) I only
b) II only
c) Both I and II
d) Neither I nor II

23. A broker lists a piece of land and subsequently sells it. Three days before closing the agent finds several other comparable parcels of land being sold to the same purchaser that bought his seller's land but at substantially higher prices. Broker should:

a) advise his seller to file an interpleader action
b) advise his seller of his findings
c) make no effort to destroy the sale between a willing seller and a ready, willing and able buyer
d) ask the purchaser if he wants to list the properties

24. Regarding options, all of the following are true, except:

a) in a lease-option, the terms of the lease are sufficient consideration
b) after an option is executed, the optionee has certain rights to use the property
c) a lease-option can be assigned unless expressly prohibited
d) the option period must be stated

25. A broker shows property on an open listing agreement. He should:

a) write a memo to his office
b) introduce his customer to the seller
c) advise the seller of his buyer's identity by memo
d) None of the above

26. How many acres are in the NE¼ of the SE¼ of Section 20?

a) .75 acre
b) 2.5 acres
c) 10 acres
d) 40 acres

27. Under the terms of an exclusive right to sell listing agreement, an owner may:

a) revoke the listing but may be liable for damages
b) revoke the listing but may not be liable for damages
c) revoke the listing provided he sold the property himself
d) not revoke because this is a binding contract

28. Reference to an "elevation" sheet in a subsdivision would be which of the following?

a) An aerial photograph of the subdivision site
b) Drawings showing the front and side views of the finished houses
c) The interior of the house together with the framing
d) The topography of the site, indicating the slope and elevation of the streets, sidewalks and curbs

29. For 11 years Margo, with the permission of Sam, crossed over Sam's land to fish at a creek. Margo most likely has:

a) an implied easement
b) an easement in gross
c) an easement by prescription
d) a license

30. The most accurate, time-consuming and expensive way to appraise is:

a) quantity survey
b) unit-in-place
c) quality survey
d) cost-in-place

31. Which of the following best describes a life estate?

a) A homestead estate
b) An estate conveyed to A for the life of Z, and upon Z's death, to B
c) An estate guaranteed by law to a surviving spouse
d) An estate conveyed to A and the heirs of A's body, but if A dies without heirs, then to Z upon the death of A

32. In order to determine effective gross income, which of the following would an owner deduct from the gross income?

a) Income taxes imposed by the federal government
b) Principal and interest payments on the first loan
c) An allowance for vacancies and rent loss
d) Real property taxes

33. There is a clause in a lease that allows the tenant to remove fixtures at the end of the lease period. The fixtures would most likely be:

a) trade fixtures
b) domestic tools
c) manufacturing fixtures
d) Any of these

34. Because of the Statute of Frauds, an oral contract for the sale of real estate

I. cannot be used as a basis of transfer of ownership
II. is enforceable if one party breaches the terms of agreement

a) I only
b) II only
c) Both I and II
d) Neither I nor II

35. When the government takes your property for the beneficial use of the public, the procedure is called:

a) eminent domain
b) attachment
c) condemnation
d) police power

36. In zoning, a use established after passage of a zoning ordinance, and in violation of it, is called:

a) a non-conforming use
b) a variance
c) illegal
d) spot zoning

37. Mr. Mark sells his home for $71,500. He takes back a promissory note and trust deed for $65,000. Market value of the home is $69,000. He sells the $65,000 note to Matthews for $63,500, signing the note as follows:

I transfer this note and trust deed to Matthews without recourse.

Signed,

Luke Mark

In the event the maker defaults before payment of any principal, Matthews can:

a) foreclose for $65,000
b) foreclose for $63,500
c) sue Mark for any loss sustained as a result of the foreclosure
d) do nothing because he accepted the note without recourse

38. The mortgagor's right to re-establish ownership after delinquency is known as:

a) a statute of allowances
b) unjust enrichment
c) equity of redemption
d) acceleration

39. The earnest money deposit:

I. is made by the buyer upon signing the sales contract and evidences his or her intention to carry out the contract terms
II. is generally held by the seller under the terms of the typical real estate sales contract

a) I only
b) II only
c) Both I and II
d) Neither I nor II

40. The market approach to value is the method of appraisal in which the value of property is:

a) based on factual data related to the income yield of the property
b) based on sales of comparable properties
c) based on cost of duplicating the improvements on today's market
d) determined by capitalizing the annual net income

41. It is permissible for the broker to give a buyer permission, after the contract of sale is signed but before the deal is closed, to make minor repairs, do some interior painting or redecorating if:

a) he has received substantial earnest money deposit
b) receives an additional earnest money deposit
c) he feels the property would be improved
d) he received permission from the owner

42. James hired an appraiser for $100 to appraise Black's home. With whom should the appraiser discuss it?

a) Mr. James
b) Mr. Black
c) Either
d) Neither

43. In real estate, the value is created, maintained, modified and destroyed by the interplay of three great forces. Which of the following is not included among the three?

a) Social ideals
b) Economic adjustments
c) Governmental regulation
d) Private restrictions

44. Harris seeks to buy improved property owned by Farmer Norris and listed by Acme Realty. To close the deal quickly, Norris insists upon the use of an installment sales contract as the financing instrument. The terms are $50,000 cash price, $10,000 down, the $40,000 balance payable at $500 per month at 9½% interest, with a balloon payment after 24 months. Harris is to pay all related costs (recording fees, broker's commission, and cost of title insurance). Harris asked Norris and the broker what the annual percentage rate will be and is told to see an attorney.

After nearly two years, Harris applies to National Bank for a refinancing loan. Harris receives the loan, and later builds a triplex on his property. Never has Harris received a uniform settlement statement, a HUD information booklet, or an estimate of likely settlement charges. The deal is closed in a branch office of National Bank.

a) RESPA requirements have not been complied with by National Bank
b) Harris can sue Norris and the broker for failure to make the necessary disclosures as required by the Truth-in-Lending Act
c) Real estate contracts and refinancing loans do not evoke RESPA regulations. The Truth-in-Lending Act disclosure requirements apply to creditors, not farmers selling their own homes
d) Harris can sue Norris and the broker for failure to disclose the A.P.R., but only HUD can sue National Bank for failure to comply with RESPA requirements

45. "Points" in real estate financing are determined by:

a) American Mortgage Bankers Association
b) conditions in the money market
c) Federal Reserve bank
d) the seller and buyer

46. The answer to which of the following questions will benefit an appraiser the most in trying to determine the economic obsolescence of a commercial income property?

a) Can building be operated efficiently?
b) Are the tenants in the neighborhood prospering?
c) Should a fire escape be installed?
d) Are the rents that are being charged to tenants equitable?

47. There is going to be a multimillion dollar office complex built on a lot next to a lot that you own. Property values near the proposed office complex will tend to increase. This is an example of:

a) principle of anticipation
b) principle of conformity
c) principle of change
d) principle of balance

48. Half of a standard township contains how many square miles?

a) 10
b) 18
c) 30
d) 36

49. An owner told a broker that he would be pleased to obtain $35,000 for a house left to him by an uncle. The broker sold it the next day to a buyer who resold it at $45,000 within three weeks. The owner can:

a) recover the $10,000 profit from the first buyer
b) recover from the broker
c) file a complaint with the licensing department or director
d) do nothing

50. All of the following instruments are negotiable, except:

a) a check
b) a promissory note
c) a trust deed
d) a bank draft

51. Smith owns 40 acres of land on which he grows onions. He sells the crop of onions to Williams who agrees to take care of the harvest. Before the onions are harvested, Smith sells his land to Jones and the deed is recorded. The crop of onions belongs to:

a) Smith
b) Jones
c) Williams
d) Williams and Jones in joint tenancy

52. Which of the following does not result in the release of a lien or attachment?

a) Order by the levying officer
b) Release signed by the plaintiff
c) Court order
d) Judgment in favor of the plaintiff

53. Which is not an exercise of police power?

a) Eminent domain
b) Housing codes
c) Health regulations
d) Tax assessments

54. A property owner lists a home for sale with a broker. The owner tells the broker he noticed a few termites around some time ago but hasn't seen any lately. He instructs the broker not to tell any prospective purchasers about the termite infestation as he doesn't think it's a problem any longer.

a) The broker should not tell any buyers about the termites because she has no duty to do so, and it might spoil a sale
b) The broker should not tell any buyers about the termites because she has been instructed not to by the seller, and her fiduciary obligations to her principal require that she follow instructions
c) The broker should disregard the owner's instruction and tell everyone about the termites anyway because she has an obligation in law to disclose hidden defects
d) The broker should withdraw from the transaction if the seller insists upon keeping the existence of termites a secret

55. Real property taxes are an example of:

a) involuntary specific lien
b) voluntary specific lien
c) involuntary general lien
d) None of these

56. Commission on a lease is normally:

a) percentage of deposit money
b) percentage of first year's lease amount
c) percentage of first and last year's lease amount
d) percentage of entire lease amount

57. Jones agrees to buy Smith's property and they sign a valid contract. Smith refuses to perform one week later. Since Jones wants the property, his best course of action would most likely be:

a) rescission
b) money damages
c) specific performance
d) novation

58. A deed of trust can be foreclosed by use of which of the following?

I. Power of sale clause
II. Judicial action

a) I only
b) II only
c) Both I and II
d) Neither I nor II

59. Holdem Fence Company has changed its name to Keepemont Fence, Inc. It has sold a parcel of land it purchased when it was still the Holdem Fence Company. The deed shows the grantor as: "Keepemont Fencing, Inc., formerly the Holdem Fence Company." Why do they do this?

a) To avoid double taxation
b) To give proper constructive notice for public records
c) It's just good advertising
d) To comply with the Uniform Corporation Act

60. In the purchase of a property, a street assessment bond of $2,000 was assumed by the buyer. This obligation of the owner is most properly considered to be:

a) the financing of an improvement and will not have any effect on the value of the property
b) usable to offset future taxes
c) an improvement on personal property
d) a part of the cost of the property

61. Mr. Brown and Mrs. Brown held title to community property. Mrs. Brown wanted a niece to inherit her share of the property when she died but did not want to tell her husband. So she made out a proper warranty deed conveying her interest to her niece, with her signature duly acknowledged, and gave it to a close friend who agreed to hand it over to the niece after Mrs. Brown's death. Mrs. Brown died, and the friend carried out the instructions. The deed was:

a) invalid for lack of proper delivery
b) invalid as she could not deed her interest in community property
c) valid because the friend could testify to Mrs. Brown's intent
d) valid as deed was delivered to a close relative after grantor's demise

62. A judgment is a lien:

a) in all counties of state where judgment is rendered
b) in all counties where judgment is recorded
c) only in county where judgment debtor's property is located
d) only in county where judgment is rendered

63. In order to secure an enforceable option to buy, the optionee should:

a) actually pay a valuable consideration which is agreed to by the optionor
b) always pay the optionor at least $10 in cash
c) never give jewelry or other valuables as consideration
d) never give a note as the consideration

64. Mutual Bank seeks borrowers under a new "graduated payment" plan whereby the initial monthly payments are based on an interest rate of 8½%. The interest rate rises to 9% for the third through the sixth years of the loan, and the seventh through the thirteenth are based on a 10¼% interest rate. The bank plans to advertise this program. Which of the following is correct?

a) If any interest rate is mentioned, the annual rate must also be mentioned
b) If the amount of the finance charge is stated, the cash price, number of payments, amount of each payment, A.P.R., and the down payment required must all be mentioned
c) Nothing particular is required as this would be an unconstitutional infringement of the free speech
d) Any and all forms of advertising are covered by the Truth-in-Lending Act

65. Ethical standards which must be observed by brokers in real estate deals are determined by:

a) Better Business Bureau
b) local real estate board
c) National Association of Real Estate Boards
d) law

66. Which of the following companies would invest in long-term real estate loans?

a) Commercial banks
b) Insurance companies
c) Private parties
d) Credit unions

67. Where there is a confidential or fiduciary relationship or one party has some special knowledge which the other cannot gain, false statements which are innocently made without an intent to deceive the other party may constitute:

a) actual fraud
b) constructive fraud
c) mistake of fact
d) None of the above

68. A real estate contract or a land contract is described as a method of financing used as a substitute for the mortgage or trust deed methods of financing. So, a real estate contract can be:

a) the same as a mortgage
b) a security device
c) similar to a lease
d) a lease with option to buy

69. The main purpose of the FHA program has been to meet the housing needs of all citizens. In addition to this, these programs have accomplished certain secondary results. All of the following are secondary results, except:

a) a comprehensive system of valuing property and rating mortgage risk
b) minimum standards of construction
c) scientific subdivision planning to protect against neighborhood deterioration
d) long-term high interest rate mortgage loans

70. Banks, insurance companies, and other institutional investors in real estate need professional property managers because:

I. their holdings are often geographically diversified
II. their personnel are not skilled in real estate management

a) I only
b) II only
c) Both I and II
d) Neither I nor II

71. In the final correlation state of an appraisal, the estimate of value is developed:

a) by averaging the three indications of value
b) by according the greatest weight to the median value indication
c) by selecting the value indication closest to the value desired by the employer
d) by relating the value indication to the type of property being appraised and the quantity and quality of the available data

72. What is the most accurate method of determining the effective age of a house?

a) Check the plat
b) Assessor's records
c) Physical condition
d) Architectural style

73. Of the following statements regarding financing using government guaranteed or insured loans, all except one are correct.

a) VA loans allow the purchase of multiple dwelling units
b) FHA loans are available on two-family dwellings whether the buyer plans to live in one of the units or not
c) FHA loans are available if the buyer does not intend to live on the property
d) The VA will guarantee a loan of an applicant if it is his intention to rent the property at the time it is purchased

74. If real estate loan interest rates increase and the income of a property is fixed, the capitalized value of the property will:

a) increase
b) decrease
c) have no effect on a short term
d) remain the same

75. Your petition to the City Planning Commission for a variance is rejected; you may appeal to:

a) the City Engineer
b) the City Council
c) the City Assessor
d) No one; decision may not be appealed

76. A roof slopes 3 feet over a 9-foot span; it will slope how many feet over 40.5 feet?

a) 12 feet
b) 13 feet
c) 13.5 feet
d) 14 feet

77. A salesperson becomes involved in a sale which requires that the buyer "assume" the existing loan. From his standpoint, the sale would be easiest if the existing loan is:

a) A conventional loan
b) a private loan
c) a construction loan
d) an FHA loan

78. Which of the following is a disadvantage of real estate investment?

I. Difficult to invest without expert advice
II. Physical efforts may be necessary

a) I only
b) II only
c) Both I and II
d) Neither I nor II

79. An appraiser, in determining depreciation, will consider:

I. wear and tear from use
II. lack of modern facilities

a) I only
b) II only
c) Both I and II
d) Neither I nor II

80. Jones, a developer, platted a section of undeveloped property and subsequently offered each of 130 "homesites" for sale or lease to the public. Brochures were prepared and offered to members of the public by use of mass-marketing techniques, including mailing the promotional material directly to home owners. Pilgrim, in responding to a mailed solicitation, leased one of the lots. After making monthly payments for nine months, Pilgrim took a vacation and went to see his property. To his amazement, he found that his entire lot was part of a large lake. Pilgrim can:

a) force the grantor to drain the water from his property
b) do nothing since the ILSFDA does not protect tenants
c) rescind the sale or sue the developer
d) do nothing since the ILSFDA governs only lots of five acres or less

81. Provided there is no agreement to the contrary, all of the following can be assigned except:

a) an option
b) a lease
c) fire insurance
d) trust deed

82. The management fee for a condominium or cooperative:

I. is prorated among the occupants according to their interest in the property
II. should be expressed as a percentage of revenue

a) I only
b) II only
c) Both I and II
d) Neither I nor II

83. A 6-unit apartment has a gross income of $1,500 per month. Annual expenses, excluding depreciation, are $7,200. There is a 5% vacancy and uncollected rent rate. A buyer desires an 8% return on his investment. What price should he offer?

a) $142,550
b) $123,750
c) $ 96,500
d) $116,000

84. A purchaser of real estate is charged with knowledge of all recorded documents so he or she must have current title evidence to indicate the rights and interests revealed by public records. The purchaser is also charged with the responsibility to:

I. make improvements on the property
II. learn the rights of the parties in possession

a) I only
b) II only
c) Both I and II
d) Neither I nor II

85. Which of the following are the four elements of successful advertising?

a) Arouse interest, promote the manufacturer, create interest, stimulate desire
b) Attract attention, arouse interest, stimulate action, promote the product
c) Attract attention, promote the manufacturer, arouse interest, create desire
d) Attract attention, arouse interest, create desire, stimulate action

86. If personal property is included in the sale of real property, the following document is needed:

a) Bill of Sale
b) Estoppel Certificate
c) Inventory
d) None of the above

87. Purchaser Perkins entered a contract to buy a parcel of land for $65,000 and made an earnest money deposit of $6,500. He subsequently decided not to go through with the transaction. He notified Broker Barlow that he was unable to complete the sale but would be willing to forfeit $5,000 of the earnest money. Barlow did not relay this information to the seller, Smith, but instead returned $1,500 to Perkins and had Perkins complete the transaction with Smith. Barlow received a $4,000 commission on that sale. Simultaneously with the sale to Perkins from Smith, Barlow purchased the property from Perkins for $60,000.

a) Barlow's actions in this case were commendable because he was able to save a sale that might otherwise have fallen through
b) Barlow's actions were permissible because his contract with Smith had been performed before his dealings with Perkins, and Smith received exactly what he bargained for, $65,000
c) Barlow's actions probably constituted a technical violation of his fiduciary obligations, but since Smith received the full $65,000 bargained for, Barlow would be subject to no further liability
d) Barlow's actions were a breach of his fiduciary obligation and he would probably have to give up both his $4,000 commission and $5,000 secret profit received on acquiring the property

88. Uniform Settlement Statement must be provided:

a) 10 days before closing
b) three days before closing
c) on or before closing
d) at lease one day before closing

89. Written instruments affecting real estate should be recorded:

I. in the county where the real estate is located
II. to give actual notice of the owner's interest in the property

a) I only
b) II only
c) Both I and II
d) Neither I nor II

90. The Truth-in-Lending law applies to which of the following?

a) Loans made to partnerships
b) Loans made to government agencies
c) All loans made to individual borrowers
d) Purchase money loans secured by a first trust deed on the personal residence of the borrower

91. In order for a commercial bank to achieve liquidity and marketability of their loans, they would prefer:

a) short-term loans
b) long-term loans because property would tend to appreciate more
c) construction loans
d) secondary money market loans

92. An acquired legal privilege of right of use or enjoyment falling short of ownership which one may have in the land of another is known as:

a) a devise
b) an abstract
c) an easement
d) a riparian right

93. A salesman presents an offer to a seller. There is a large earnest money deposit, but it is in the form of a non-interest bearing note. The salesman should:

a) tell buyer he can't accept offer until there is a cash deposit
b) tell the seller before he signs anything that the deposit is on a note
c) do not mention it to the seller as he may not accept the offer
d) send the seller a letter

94. Mr. White owns a 20-unit apartment building and desires to know what his net cash flow will be on his original investment. This would be the amount remaining from his gross income after deducting:

a) operating expenses, vacancy factor and an amount to cover the federal income taxes attributable to this investment
b) operating expenses, an amount to cover the federal income tax attributable to this investment, vacancy factor, depreciation and interest and principal on existing financing
c) operating expenses, payments of interest and principal on existing financing, and vacancies
d) operating expenses, depreciation and vacancies

95. A rectangular shaped lot contained 16,800 square feet and was 140 feet deep. There was a lot on each side of this parcel, both of which were the same depth and contained 4,200 square feet each. The total frontage of all three parcels is which of the following?

a) 170 feet
b) 180 feet
c) 200 feet
d) Cannot be determined from the information given

96. A house sold for $40,950 which was 17% more than the owner paid for it four years ago. What did he originally pay for his home?

a) $35,000
b) $34,000
c) $49,300
d) $24,090

97. In arriving at an appraisal based on recent selling prices, an appraiser is more interested in the date the:

a) purchase contract was signed
b) deed was recorded
c) deed was signed
d) sale was given to escrow

98. If a group of investors were to form a real estate syndicate and wished to limit the liability of its members in order that they might attract capital, they would form a:

a) real estate investment trust
b) corporation
c) limited partnership
d) Any of the above

99. A broker has a written promise from a buyer of a $5,000 commission if he can secure certain acreage. The owner agrees to sell if he can keep one-fourth of the mineral rights and will pay the broker $5,000 commission. The transaction was closed. The seller knew of the broker's commission arrangement with the buyer. Which of the following is true?

a) Broker made a clever deal and was entitled to the extra earnings
b) Broker is subject to disciplinary action by the director
c) Since the seller knew of the fee paid by the buyer, it was ethical
d) Broker violated the Statute of Frauds

100. If a building is valued at $100,000 using an 8% cap rate, what would it be valued at using a 10% cap rate?

a) $ 80,000
b) $120,000
c) $102,000
d) Not enough info to answer

101. According to Washington recording statutes:

a) a deed must be recorded
b) a deed must be acknowledged
c) Both
d) Neither

102. If no special provision is included in the lease regarding permanent improvements made by a tenant on leased property, such improvements:

I. are called fixtures
II. remain the property of the tenant after the lease expires

a) I only
b) II only
c) Both I and II
d) Neither I nor II

103. The instrument used to remove the lien of a deed of trust from the record is called a:

a) redemption of equity
b) satisfaction piece
c) certificate of no defense
d) deed of reconveyance

104. A homeowner may be allowed certain protection from judgments of creditors as a result of the:

I. homestead exemption
II. inchoate right of dower

a) I only
b) II only
c) Both I and II
d) Neither I nor II

105. Many states determine water use by allocating water to users who hold recorded beneficial-use permits. This type of water-use privilege is called:

a) the doctrine of riparian right
b) the doctrine of highest and best use
c) the doctrine of prior appropriation
d) None of the above

106. In the event a trust deed is foreclosed in court, the action:

a) is not recognized in this state
b) provides for a one-year period in which to redeem
c) bars the possibility of a deficiency judgment
d) provides the same redemption period as in the case of a trustee's sale

107. Which of the following liens would be given higher priority?

a) The current real estate tax
b) A mortgage dated last year
c) A judgment rendered today
d) A mechanic's lien for work started before the mortgage was made

108. An ALTA Policy of Title Insurance extends the coverage under the Standard Policy to include all of the following, except:

a) unrecorded mechanic's liens
b) unrecorded physical easements
c) rights of parties in possession
d) effects of zoning

109. Those exempted from the real estate examination are in part:

a) any person who purchases property or business opportunity for his own account or in any way disposes of the same
b) any authorized attorney in fact or attorney at law
c) any escrow agent, receiver, trustee in bankruptcy, executor, administrator, guardian or any person acting under a court order
d) All of the above

110. A broker is allowed to hold an uncashed check for several days under which of the following circumstances?

a) By instruction of the seller after acceptance of the offer
b) By instruction of the buyer until acceptance of the offer
c) Both (a) and (b)
d) Neither (a) nor (b)

111. A broker is alleged to have deposited a client's earnest money deposit in his personal checking account. If true, he is guilty of:

a) conversion
b) collusion
c) commingling
d) None of the above

112. The Real Estate Commission is responsible to:

I. prepare and administer the real estate exam
II. set licensing fees

a) I only
b) II only
c) Both I and II
d) Neither I nor II

113. A person who owns an undivided interest in common in a parcel of real property, together with a separate interest in space in a residential, industrial or commercial building on such real property is said to have an interest in a:

a) community apartment project
b) planned development project
c) condominium project
d) stock cooperative

114. The real estate cycle:

I. is generally slower to adjust to economic fluctuations because it is based on building activity
II. always corresponds to the overall business cycle

a) I only
b) II only
c) Both I and II
d) Neither I nor II

115. The return on investment that a real estate investor expects is generally higher than the interest the investor would earn from a savings account because:

a) banks are more risky
b) the real estate investment involves a lower degree of risk
c) the real estate investment involves a higher degree of risk
d) None of these

116. In an inflationary economy, which of the following would generally be considered the best investment?

a) Government bonds
b) A promissory note well secured by a first lien mortgage
c) Ownership of realty
d) Security investment

117. One thousand dollars was placed in a Broker's Trust Account. After the offer had been accepted by the seller and all the other conditions were met, the buyer said there was a provision in the contract which "gave him an out" and he demands his money be returned to him. The seller agrees to rescind the contract provided he can keep half the deposit. This is unacceptable to the buyer who wants his entire deposit returned to him. The seller rejects this and further indicates that he now wants to retain the entire amount. The broker should:

a) return the deposit to the buyer
b) leave the money in the trust account
c) give the money to the seller
d) give one-half the money to the seller

118. A deed made and delivered but not recorded is:

a) invalid as between the parties and valid as to third parties with constructive notice
b) valid as between the parties and valid as to subsequent recorded interests
c) valid as between the parties and invalid as to subsequent recorded interest without notice
d) invalid as between the parties

119. A store tenant firmly attaches appropriate appliances for his restaurant business on the leased premises. These appliances are:

I. trade fixtures
II. part of the real estate once they are installed

a) I only
b) II only
c) Both I and II
d) Neither I nor II

120. Which type of deed limits the covenants of the grantor when he conveys real estate?

a) Quitclaim
b) Special warranty
c) General warranty
d) None of these

121. The most commonly used deed in the state of Washington is the:

a) warranty deed
b) special warranty deed
c) quitclaim deed
d) sheriff's deed

122. The Bulk Sales Law applies to the sale of business opportunites. As a potential buyer of a business opportunity, you would be least concerned with:

a) cost of goods sold
b) inventory
c) cash on hand
d) gross receipts

123. "Under all is the land. Upon its wise utilization and widely allocated ownership depend the survival and growth of free institutions and of our civilization." This quotation comes from:

a) the United States Government
b) Washington License Law
c) Thirteenth Amendment to the Constitution
d) the Realtor's Code of Ethics

124. A valid listing on community property should be signed by:

a) husband
b) husband and wife
c) seller and mortgagee
d) broker and salesman

125. Mrs. Smith, in her husband's absence, files a declaration of homestead on their family dwelling. The declaration of homestead is:

a) valid
b) voidable
c) void
d) illegal

126. Who benefits by recording a deed?

a) Mortgagee
b) Trustee
c) Grantee
d) Optionee

127. Which of the following would be considered to be personal property?

a) Iron ore deposits
b) Appurtenances to the land
c) Fructus naturales
d) Crop mortgage

128. The description of land sold under an agreement of sale should:

a) give the house number and street
b) give a full legal description
c) describe the improvements
d) be handwritten and signed

129. The Statute of Frauds in Washington requires all of the following to be in writing to be enforceable, except:

a) an agreement for the leasing of real property for more than one year
b) an agreement that employs a broker to solicit, sell, lease or exchange real property
c) an agreement that, by its terms is not to be performed within one year of the execution of the agreement
d) a partnership agreement between two or more parties to engage in the sale or exchange of real property

130. WLTA title insurance:

a) is a standard policy
b) is an extended coverage policy
c) protects against all unrecorded matters
d) None of the above

131. Which of the following essentials for acquiring title by adverse possession is not necessary in acquiring an easement by prescription?

a) Open and notorious use
b) Color of title
c) Hostile to interests of owner
d) All of these are essentials to claiming a prescriptive easement

132. An escrow agent must place trust funds in a bank no later than:

a) the next banking day after receiving them
b) three banking days after receiving them
c) seven banking days after receiving them
d) None of the above

133. George, owner of a tract of land, occupied ten feet over on Sally's land upon the erroneous belief as to the true boundary. During this adverse occupation, Sally notified George that he was a trespasser. The period for adverse possession passed, and Sally now sues George.

a) George now owns the subject ten feet
b) Sally continues to own the land since she gave effective notice to George
c) George must pay Sally the reasonable value of the ten feet
d) George can occupy only one-half of the ten feet, or five feet

134. When a tenant holds possession of a landlord's property without a current lease agreement and without the landlord's approval:

I. the tenant is maintaining a tenancy at sufference
II. the landlord may file a suit for possession

a) I only
b) II only
c) Both I and II
d) Neither I nor II

135. Jack Gregory is an appraiser for a large appraisal company. He has been hired to appraise a large office complex. He must have:

a) a commercial appraisers license
b) an appraisers license
c) membership in M.A.I.
d) None of the above

136. RESPA specifies various duties that a lender must comply with when a borrower seeks a loan to purchase a home. The duties include all of the following, except:

a) ensuring that closing takes place in a licensed escrow office, attorney's office, or real estate broker's office
b) providing the borrower with an estimate of those charges which will be paid by the borrower in connection with the loan application (loan origination fees, credit report charges, and A.L.T.A. fees)
c) disclosing the existence of any business relationship where the lender requires the borrower to use the services of a particular attorney, title insurer, or settlement agent
d) permitting the borrower, upon request, to inspect the uniform settlement statement at least one business day before closing

137. Upon failure to pass the examination, an applicant may not:

a) apply again
b) ever engage in real estate again
c) buy or sell real estate
d) None of these

138. A secretary in a real estate office may:

a) discuss listings
b) solicit listings
c) Both (a) and (b)
d) Neither (a) nor (b)

139. With respect to mortgages and trust deeds, Washington is considered to be:

a) a title theory state
b) a lien theory state
c) a statutory theory state
d) None of the above

140. The tax on a given piece of property is always determined by multiplying the tax rate by the:

a) sales price
b) book value
c) mortgage loan value
d) assessed valuation

1. c) In general a promissory note is negotiable and can be sold by the lender (payee) to a third party called a holder in due course.

2. a) To qualify as an REIT, the association must be unincorporated.

3. b) Investors in commercial property, such as shopping centers, are very concerned with pedestrian counts for the proposed project.

4. d) Decrease their lending activities to reflect the economy.

5. a) To fulfill his fiduciary obligation, the broker must reveal his role as buyer in writing before seller acceptance.

6. b) An offer can be revoked prior to notification of acceptance. An option is irrevocable.

7. d) Public buildings do not generate income.

8. d) Refer to "site valuation" in your appraisal chapter. There is no such thing as an economic method of appraising land.

9. b) A financing statement, required under the Uniform Commercial Code, establishes a creditor's security interest in a chattel. The financing statement constructively severs the crops from the land.

10. b) To "demise" is to give a lease.

11. a) When property escheats, it reverts to the state, as when the owner dies intestate and without heirs.

12. d) Actual fraud is any willful effort to deceive.

13. d) In the absence of an agreed closing date, a "reasonable time" to close is allowed, which would be determined by a court in the event of a dispute.

14. a) Bilateral contracts are formed when there has been an exchange of promises.

15. c) The utility line is laid across the owner's land under a right called a gross easement.

16. b) This is a condominium interest, and the owner can mortgage his separate interest without affecting the other owners.

17. b) Specific performance is a legal remedy by which a party to a contract is ordered by a court to perform the contract exactly as agreed, or as nearly as possible.

18. b) Partial performance, by Bell taking possession and making improvements removes the contract from the Statute of Frauds and makes an otherwise unenforceable contract enforceable.

19. d) Zoning affects a building's use, height, position on a lot and off-street parking. It can also limit the height of a fence. Needless to say, private restrictions can affect the height, physical make-up or positioning of the fence.

20. c) The elements of utility, scarcity, transferability and demand are essential to the creation of market value.

21. c) Only the grantor signs the warranty deed, whereas vendor and vendee sign the land contract. Also, the warranty deed need not mention the purchase price, whereas price is an essential part of the land contract.

22. b) The allodial system is one of individual ownership, as opposed to the feudal system where the government owns the land. Under the allodial system, property ownership is limited by three government powers: police power, eminent domain and taxation.

23. b) The broker has a duty to call the findings to his seller's attention, though little could be done about it as there is no evidence of fraud.

24. b) Until the optionee has exercised his option to buy, he has no rights or interest in the land.

25. c) The broker must be prepared to prove he was the procuring cause, and he does this by advising the seller in writing of names of buyers he has shown the property.

26. d) Forty acres

27. a) The seller has the power to revoke the agent's authority but not the legal right to unilaterally rescind the contract. He may be liable for damages.

28. d) Statement of fact.

29. d) Since access to the stream was with Sam's permission, Margo has a license.

30. a) The most accurate, time-consuming and expensive way to estimate the replacement cost is the quantity survey method.

31. b) "A" holds the life estate; "Z's" life is the designated life; "B" is the remainderman.

32. c) The allowance for bad debts and vacancies is deducted from gross income to arrive at effective gross income.

33. d) Tenant-installed fixtures are usually regarded as the tenant's personal property and removable at the lease's conclusion.

34. a) Oral contracts for the sale of real estate are unenforceable.

35. c) The right is eminent domain; the process is condemnation.

36. c) Violation of a zoning ordinance is illegal. A variance is an inconsistent use established after enactment of a zoning ordinance with the permission of the authorities.

37. a) Matthews can foreclose for the full amount of the note ($65,000). The discounted amount is irrelevant.

38. c) Equity of redemption is the right to redeem after delinquency but before the sheriff's sale. Right of redemption is the right to redeem after the sheriff's sale.

39. a) The earnest money deposit is a show of good faith by the buyer; it is usually held in trust by the broker or an escrow agent.

40. b) It is a comparison of prices, amenities and other data of similar properties which provide indications of what the property under appraisement might be worth.

41. d) He should get the owner's permission in writing.

42. a) James is the employer; the appraiser is the agent and should not discuss the appraisal with anyone other than his employer.

43. d) Private restrictions may affect value, but they are not a major force.

44. c) Truth-in-lending requirements are not directed at farmers selling their own properties. National Bank does not have to comply with RESPA because the loan is for a refinance, not a purchase.

45. b) Points are sometimes called prepaid interest and are conditioned upon the state of the money market.

46. b) All four questions should be answered by the appraiser, but the economic status of the neighborhood is an external force that could affect the value of the property. If the effect is unfavorable, it would be a form of depreciation classified as economic obsolescence.

47. a) The anticipation principle explains that value is created by the anticipated benefits of owning a property in the future.

48. b) A township contains 36 square miles; half a township has 18 square miles.

49. d) In the absence of fraud or collusion on the part of the broker and buyer, the deal will stand.

50. c) A negotiable instrument is a written promise or order to pay money, as is the case with checks, notes and bank drafts. A trust deed is a security agreement.

51. c) Williams. When the crops are sold, they are constructively severed and are the personal property of Williams.

52. d) The judgment would replace the attachment as a lien. Thus the lien of the judgment would replace the lien of the attachment.

53. a) Eminent domain is the government's right to take rather than regulate property.

54. d) The broker cannot disobey her principal, nor can she practice dishonesty while complying with the client's instructions. She should withdraw.

55. a) Property taxes are involuntary and specific.

56. d) The commission is computed as a percentage of the total of the lease payments.

57. c) A suit for specific performance is an effort to force completion of the transaction.

58. c) A deed of trust can be foreclosed judicially (in court) or non-judicially (out of court) at the lender's option. This is not true of the mortgage, which may only be foreclosed through the courts.

59. b) If they didn't do this, a casual look at the records would appear to reveal a break in the chain of title, which would be a cloud on the title.

60. a) The $2,000 assessment bond is used to finance improvements and does not affect the property's value.

61. a) A deed cannot be delivered after the death of the grantor. There was no proper delivery.

62. b) The judgment will lien properties in any county in the state where the abstract of judgment is recorded.

63. a) One of the requirements of a good option is that the optionee (person securing the option) give a valuable consideration for it.

64. b) If the amount of the finance charge is mentioned in the ad, the cash price, downpayment, number of payments, amount of each payment, the period of each payment (e.g. monthly, quarterly, etc.) and the annual percentage rate must also be included in the ad.

65. d) Ethical standards which must be adhered to are prescribed by law; ethical conduct which should be practiced is set by a variety of real estate boards or associations for their members, the most notable being the National Association of Realtors' "Code of Ethics."

66. b) Insurance companies historically make long term real estate loans through loan correspondents.

67. b) Constructive fraud is often a result of a misuse or breach of a fiduciary relationship.

68. b) The real estate contract serves as a security device.

69. d) FHA insured financing has resulted in long-term low interest rate loans.

70. c) Both of these are reasons institutional investors seek representation from professional property managers.

71. d) The appraiser selects the value indication that is most suitable for the type property being appraised and makes certain adjustments based on the quantity and quality of the data used to arrive at the value indication.

72. c) The effective age, as opposed to actual or chronological age, is determined by a phyical inspection of the structure(s).

73. d) The VA will not approve a loan if the veteran does not intend to occupy the property when the loan is made.

74. b) Decrease, because the net earnings will be reduced by the amount of the increased interest.

75. b) You may appeal to the city council.

76. c) For each three feet of the roof span, the roof slopes one foot. Divide 40.5 by three.

77. d) FHA loans are assumable, while the others might not be. Also, FHA assumption fees are small.

78. a) Real estate investments are complex. Without expert advice the potential for loss is high. Real estate investments are often made without physical involvement on the part of the investor.

79. c) Wear and tear is the most visable form of depreciation (physical deterioration) and outdated facilities represent functional obsolescence.

80. c) The Interstate Land Sales Full Disclosure Act applies whether the property is for lease or for sale. Obviously the promotional materials were fraudulent and Pilgrim is entitled to sue or rescind or both.

81. c) Alternatives (a), (b) and (d) are ordinary contracts and can be assigned. Fire insurance policies are personal contracts made by an insurer with a particular insured person. Such policies, therefore, cannot be assigned without the consent of the insurer.

82. c) Both. It is prorated according to each occupant's percentage of interest and is usually expressed as a percentage of revenue.

83. b) $1,500 x 12 mos. = $18,000 annual gross income; $18,000 x .05 = $900 bad debt/vacancy; $18,000 less $900 = $17,100 effective gross income; $17,100 less $7,200 = $9,900 net income; $9,900 divided by .08 = $123,750.

84. b) Before making a purchase, a buyer must (1) search the records and (2) inquire as to the rights of the parties in possession.

85. d) A.I.D.A. Attention, Interest, Desire, Action.

86. a) A bill of sale transfers title to personal property; a deed transfers title to real property.

87. d) He would also be subject to license disciplinary action.

88. d) If requested by the borrower, the Uniform Settlement Statement must be provided at least one business day before closing.

89. a) Written notices affecting property should be recorded in the county in which the real estate is situated, but they give constructive, NOT actual, notice of their contents.

90. d) Certain disclosures, like the finance charge and the APR must be made to purchasers of residential dwellings, but not to the government, to businesses or ALL purchasers.

91. a) Short-term loans repay quickly and can be reinvested quickly.

92. c) An easement is a non-possessory right to use another's land, but does not amount to ownership.

93. b) Notify the seller before he accepts the offer. This is best accomplished by making a note of such in the offer itself.

94. c) The cash flow is the gross income less bad debt/vacancy, less operating expenses and debt servicing costs (principal and interest payments).

95. b) 16,800 + 4200 + 4,200 = 25,200 sq. feet. 25,200 divided by 140 ft. depth = 180 foot frontage.

96. a) $40,950 divided by 1.17 (117%) = $35,000.

97. a) When referring to comparable sales, the appraiser is concerned with the dates the purchase agreements were signed. It is on these dates the buyers and sellers agreed the properties were worth the indicated amounts.

98. d) REIT's, limited partnerships and corporations are all syndicates that offer their investors limited liability. General partnerships, on the other hand, do not afford this kind of protection.

99. b) The broker must disclose to seller and buyer that he is representing both parties to the transaction and that he is being paid by both. This is a dual agency.

100. a) $100,000 value times 8% cap rate = $8,000 net income. $8,000 net income divided by 10% cap rate = $80,000 value.

101. b) The deed must be acknowledged; it should be recorded.

102. c) Ordinarily a tenant may remove fixtures he installed during the tenancy, provided repairs are made for any damage caused by the removal. Tenant installed fixtures are called domestic, trade, industrial or agricultural fixtures, depending on the purpose they serve.

103. d) A deed of reconveyance is signed by the trustee and recorded, thus releasing the lien of the trust deed. A mortgage is released with a satisfaction piece or satisfaction of mortgage.

104. a) Homestead protection in Washington is limited to $25,000 net equity.

105. c) The doctrine of prior appropriation.

106. b) It is treated as a mortgage and allows for a one year statutory redemption period.

107. a) General property taxes always enjoy the highest priority when the property is sold.

108. d) No title insurance policy protects against value lost to any governmental action, such as rezoning or condemnation.

109. d) All of these individuals are exempt from the exam and licensing requirements while acting in their respective capacities.

110. c) In both instances the broker would be able to hold an uncashed deposit check; otherwise, it must be deposited in the trust account by close of the next banking day.

111. c) By mixing funds, he commingles; if he were to then spend the money, the offense escalates to conversion—a more serious offense.

112. a) The real estate commission prepares and administers the exam; the legislature sets licensing fees.

113. c) This is a condominium interest.

114. c) The real estate market tends to follow the overall business cycle, but its reaction to changes is generally sluggish.

115. c) Real estate investments are certainly higher risk than savings account deposits.

116. c) Real estate values tend to increase with the inflationary pace. Investments in interest-yielding areas like bonds, notes or securities are not significantly affected by the forces of inflation or recession.

117. b) If the buyer and seller cannot resolve the matter between them, the broker should interplead the funds, which means turn their disposition over to the court.

118. c) The deed is valid, but if not recorded it is known only to the grantor and grantee. The grantee's interest could be diminished or even defeated if he did not serve constructive notice of his interest by recording the deed.

119. a) Trade fixtures, which are removable by the tenant at the lease's conclusion.

120. b) A special warranty deed limits the covenants; a quitclaim deed has no covenants.

121. a) Warranty deed.

122. c) Cash on hand belongs to the owner of the business and would not be included in the sale.

123. d) The NAR's Code of Ethics.

124. b) As equal partners in the community property estate, both husband and wife should sign the listing.

125. a) Valid. The husband, wife, or single head of family can sign the homestead declaration.

126. c) The grantee is the buyer, the recipient of a deed.

127. d) Any mortgage is a contract, and contracts are personal property.

128. b) This is the most certain way to identify the property being sold.

129. d) A (general) partnership agreement does not have to be in writing to be valid. A limited partnership agreement does.

130. a) WLTA is the standard policy, which is normally paid by the seller.

131. b) To acquire title, an adverse possessor must be acting under color of title or claim of right. A landowner seeking a prescriptive easement, rather than title, does not need color of title.

132. a) The end of the next banking day.

133. a) George owns the land. His use was hostile, open and notorious and continuous for the prescribed period.

134. c) The tenant's occupancy is referred to as a tenancy at sufferance, and the landlord could proceed to evict by filing an unlawful detainer action.

135. d) There are no licensing or organization membership requirements for appraisers in Washington.

136. a) It does not matter where the closing takes place.

137. d) An applicant can take the exam until he passes.

138. a) A secretary can discuss listings to the extent that he or she can release factual information. He or she cannot solicit, negotiate or in any way perform acts that require a license unless a license is first obtained.

139. b) Washington is a lien theory state, as are most states.

140. d) Assessed valuation is appraised value for taxation purposes.

Washington Broker's Exam

National Section

1. On a listing contract, whose name should appear?

   a) Listing salesman's
   b) The branch office's
   c) The broker's
   d) The selling salesman's

2. Which one of these is not essential to a contract?

   a) Duress
   b) Offer and acceptance
   c) Legal object
   d) Capacity of parties

3. Most real estate brokerage agency agreements are created by:

   a) express written agreement
   b) implied agreement
   c) ratification
   d) estoppel

4. All of the following might legally terminate a listing with a broker, except:

   a) bankruptcy of the client
   b) inability of the broker to find a buyer within a reasonable amount of time
   c) a fire which destroys the listed property
   d) an economic depression

5. Brown executes a deed to Smith and records it; later he seeks to set it aside claiming there was no delivery to Smith. He probably would be unsuccessful in his effort because:

   a) Smith took possession of the property
   b) delivery is presumed from recording
   c) a deed is valid without recording
   d) recording established priority of the lien

6. There are several requirements necessary in a valid escrow for real estate title transfer. One is:

   a) a current beneficiary statement
   b) a valid and enforceable written contract
   c) a title insurance policy
   d) the absence of any conditions in the escrow instructions

7. Although a broker produced a ready, willing and able buyer with an offer on the exact terms of the listing, the owner refused it. Therefore, the buyer:

   a) could sue for specific performance
   b) could sue seller for damages
   c) would have no recourse against seller
   d) could sue the broker

8. All of the following are liens, except:

   a) unpaid real property taxes
   b) an easement appurtenant
   c) installment payment on an assessment bond
   d) recorded abstract of judgment

9. An officially-appointed group that studies city growth and recommends zoning policies is called a:

   a) city growth board
   b) master zoning board
   c) city policy commission
   d) planning commission

10. All of the following are real property, except:

    a) note and mortgage on a residence
    b) window shutters
    c) easement for ingress and egress
    d) sprinkler system in a factory

11. John Jones owned a parcel of land around his copper mine. He sold the mine and property for $230,000 with the verbal understanding that copper already mined before the date of sale would not be included in the sale. That copper is considered by law as:

a) realty
b) personal property
c) a fixture
d) sub rosa

12. All of the following instruments would be negotiable, except:

a) a personal check
b) a promissory note
c) a bill of exchange
d) a warranty or a grant deed

13. The type of deed which creates the least protection to the grantee is a:

a) quitclaim
b) general warranty
c) special warranty
d) deed to tenants in common

14. All of the following terms concern wills, except:

a) ambulatory
b) demise
c) codicil
d) holographic

15. A porch or balcony overhang beyond the established boundary of land is known as a/an:

a) easement
b) encroachment
c) right of way
d) lien

16. The right to possess property and have exclusive use of that property is best defined as:

a) equity
b) an estate in real property
c) sole proprietorship
d) ownership

17. A landlord rents a store to a men's clothier on a percentage lease. On which of the following is the percentage usually based?

a) Projected earnings
b) Gross effective income
c) Gross earnings
d) Net income

18. Which one of the following types of tenancies does not apply to a lessor-lessee relationship?

a) Tenancy at will
b) Tenancy in common
c) Tenancy for years
d) Tenancy at sufferance

19. A joint tenant cannot dispose of his interest in real property by:

a) lease
b) sale
c) gift
d) will

20. Which of these best describes a condominium?

a) Undivided interest in a common area and a separate interest in a unit space
b) Undivided interest in the whole
c) Separate interest in the whole
d) Divided interest in common areas and undivided interest in a unit space

21. The factor exerting the greatest influence on interest rates of a loan is the:

a) term of the loan
b) age of the property
c) credit rating of the borrower
d) availability of loan funds

22. Mortgage companies operating as correspondents:

a) do not service the loans
b) buy federally-insured loans
c) provide loans for the secondary market
d) All of the above

23. A land contract can be all of the following at the same time, except:

a) express
b) executory
c) unilateral
d) written

24. A real estate syndicate can operate as a:

a) partnership
b) real estate investment trust
c) corporation
d) Any of these

25. A contract signed under duress is:

a) void
b) voidable
c) illegal
d) unenforceable by the damaged party

26. An agency coupled with an interest is one:

a) that cannot be terminated before its expiration date
b) where broker makes a secret profit at the expense of his principal
c) where broker received interest-bearing note in payment of his commission
d) where a suit is filed for commission, which constitutes a lien on the real estate

27. All of the following are ways of acquiring an easement, except:

a) prescription
b) grant deed
c) statutory dedication
d) trust deed

28. An agreement of sale provided it was contingent upon the buyer's ability to obtain a $45,000 loan at 9% for a 30-year maturity. The buyer was unable to obtain a loan and sued to recover his deposit of $1,000. Under these circumstances:

I. it was incumbent upon the buyer to show that he was unable to procure a loan after a diligent effort
II. the buyer could withdraw from the agreement and recover the deposit

a) I only
b) II only
c) Both I and II
d) Neither I nor II

29 An assignment of a lease with an option to purchase:

a) transfers the option to the assignee
b) is prohibited
c) has no legal effect
d) is void

30. Riparian rights are:

a) absolute and exclusive rights to use of water to the middle of a stream
b) found in public records covering every property
c) listed in the grant deed
d) None of the above

31. A deed description refers to a plat of the property recorded in the County Auditor's office. Under these circumstances:

I. the deed's description would be valid
II. the deed would have to be redrawn

a) I only
b) II only
c) Both I and II
d) Neither I nor II

32. Property of a person who dies intestate, leaving no heirs, passes to the state by:

a) escheat
b) eminent domain
c) adverse possession
d) condemnation

33. Under a land contract, who retains legal title until certain specific conditions are fulfilled?

a) Vendee
b) Vendor
c) Public trustee
d) Recorder of deeds

34. An estate in fee would be:

I. a fee simple estate
II. a fee estate
III. an estate of inheritance

a) I only
b) I and II
c) II only
d) I, II and III

35. An assignment of a lease is the:

a) transfer of entire leasehold
b) transfer of less than whole leasehold period
c) subletting the leasehold
d) None of these

36. A standard title insurance policy covers all of the following, except:

a) matters disclosed by public records
b) conveyances executed by minors
c) zoning and government reservations
d) forgeries

37. Funds for real estate investment are principally obtained from:

I. savings of firms and individuals
II. the Eurodollar market

a) I only
b) II only
c) Both I and II
d) Neither I nor II

38. A deed restriction in a subdivision is normally put into effect by the:

a) FHA
b) developer
c) local building inspector
d) planning commission

39. A principal (owner) may have more than one agent under:

a) a multiple listing
b) an open listing
c) exclusive listing
d) exclusive right to sell listing

40. The only essential unity in a tenancy in common is:

a) equal right of possession
b) ownership to survivor
c) equal rights to heirs
d) None of these

41. The listing agreement most likely to be used by a multiple listing service is:

a) net
b) open
c) exclusive agency
d) exclusive right to sell

42. Mr. Louis was given real property for the term of his natural life. Which of the following statements is incorrect?

a) Louis has a freehold estate
b) Louis would have a fee simple estate
c) The duration of this estate is only for the length of the life of Louis
d) The estate can be encumbered by Louis, but only for the life of Louis

43. The FHA made major contributions to mortgage lending by:

I. providing underwriting standards
II. providing a secondary mortgage market so that funds available in capital surplus areas could be invested in areas of capital shortage

a) I only
b) II only
c) Both I and II
d) Neither I nor II

44. The Veterans Administration will guarantee loans wherein the purchase price exceeds the reasonable value if:

I. the veteran pays in cash from his own resources the difference between purchase price and appraisal (reasonable value) and the loan does not exceed the appraisal
II. the veteran signs the required certification

a) I only
b) II only
c) Both I and II
d) Neither I nor II

45. A valid earnest money agreement is:

a) an express, written, bilateral, executed contract
b) an implied, written, bilateral, executory contract
c) an express, written, bilateral, executory contract
d) None of these

46. A holder in due course must:

a) obtain a note before it is past due
b) pay consideration
c) have no knowledge of any defense of maker
d) do all of the above

47. Which of the following documents accompanies a deed of trust?

a) Deed
b) Abstract of title
c) Contract of sale
d) Promissory note

48. When one is a successful bidder at a mortgage foreclosure sale, one receives a:

a) certificate of sale
b) sheriff's deed
c) certification in lieu of foreclosure
d) quitclaim deed

49. A clause in a mortgage whereby the mortgagee waives his rights in favor of another party is known as a subordination. Under these circumstances:

I. the first lien holder is called an assignee
II. the first lien holder has no further security

a) I only
b) II only
c) Both I and II
d) Neither I nor II

50. An appraiser intends that the estimate of market value disclosed in his appraisal report be valid:

a) as of the date of the appraisal only
b) for a period of six months after the appraisal date
c) for a period of three months after the appraisal date
d) for a period of one year after the appraisal date

51. A listing contract provided that a commission would be paid to the broker, if (1) the sale was consummated or (2) if not consummated due to a title defect. A sale was made, but the buyer refused to close the deal. Under these circumstances:

I. the seller should sue the buyer for specific performance
II. the broker can recover a commission

a) I only
b) II only
c) Both I and II
d) Neither I nor II

52. A lease gives the tenant an option to purchase the property at $40,000. The owner receives an offer from a third party at $45,000.

a) Tenant can purchase property at $45,000
b) Tenant can buy at $40,000
c) Third party can buy it
d) Owner must pay tenant $5,000

53. The secondary mortgage market refers to:

I. sources of second mortgage loans
II. investors who provide mortgage funds by purchasing them from originators

a) I only
b) II only
c) Both I and II
d) Neither I nor II

54. A note made payable to the order of the broker is:

a) void
b) non-negotiable
c) negotiable
d) voidable

55. A requirement of a borrower under an FHA insured loan is that he:

I. pay the required MIP
II. certify that he will occupy the premises if that is a condition of the FHA approval

a) I only
b) II only
c) Both I and II
d) Neither I nor II

56. All of the following are encumbrances, except a/an:

a) note
b) easement
c) mortgage
d) judgment

57. A high quality expensive home erected in a neighborhood of houses costing half as much would suffer in value due to:

a) regression
b) supply and demand
c) progression
d) aversion

58. In arriving at capitalization rates, no provision is made for:

a) return of the investment
b) depreciation on the improvements
c) return on the investment
d) federal and state income taxes

59. Before beginning a subdivision, the subdivider must first:

a) consider site preparation
b) analyze the market
c) consider construction costs
d) evaluate directional growth

60. The type of structure that an owner can build can be controlled by:

I. zoning
II. deed restriction

a) I only
b) II only
c) Both I and II
d) Neither I nor II

61. In a house, a load bearing wall:

a) determines which way the house will face
b) is at right angles with the door
c) has no doors in it
d) must be recognized when remodeling is done

62. Which of the following types of depreciation would be the most difficult to correct?

a) Built-in obsolescence
b) Functional obsolescence
c) Economic obsolescence
d) Physical depreciation

63. If the title company discovers a delinquent sewer assessment, the party that would normally be required to pay for the portion that is in arrears is:

a) the buyer
b) the seller
c) both the buyer and the seller
d) to be settled by mutual agreement

64. If a non-veteran purchases a property encumbered by a VA guaranteed or insured mortgage, the loan:

I. must be repaid immediately
II. can be assumed by the purchaser

a) I only
b) II only
c) Both I and II
d) Neither I nor II

65. In searching the county auditor's records, a second mortgage can usually be distinguished from a first mortgage by which of these?

a) Recorded document's heading
b) Information contained in the note
c) Recorder's declaration
d) Time and date of recording

66. An appraiser, in determining depreciation, will consider:

I. wear and tear from use
II. lack of modern facilities

a) I only
b) II only
c) Both I and II
d) Neither I nor II

67. Ethics most nearly means:

a) observing usual closing hours of other businesses
b) belonging to the proper civic clubs and community projects
c) observing duties to clients, colleagues and public
d) None of these

68. Who usually pays the cost of recording a deed in a cash sale of property?

a) Buyer
b) Seller
c) Broker
d) None of these

69. In the absence of expressed provisions in the deed restrictions and plans, which of the following is part of a condominium unit?

a) Bearing walls
b) Central heating system
c) Elevator
d) None of the above

70. When at the commencement of a legal action, a plaintiff asks the court to confiscate certain property belonging to the defendant to act as security for the satisfaction of the judgment he's seeking, the plaintiff is asking the court to issue a:

a) garnishment
b) writ of possession
c) writ of attachment
d) None of these

71. Hathaway, a builder, has just completed a four-bedroom, one bath, 2,500 square foot home. It has already depreciated due to:

a) functional obsolescence
b) economic obsolescence
c) over-improvement
d) it has not depreciated

72. Which of the following is exempt from the Federal Fair Housing Law of 1968?

a) A broker selling vacant lots in a subdivision
b) A salesman selling a multi-family dwelling
c) An owner selling his unoccupied single-family dwelling
d) None of the above

73. Blockbusting is an acceptable practice:

a) only under the supervision of real estate licensees
b) only when approved by either HUD or the Justice Department
c) under no circumstances
d) only if the seller and buyer mutually agree

74. An appraisal involving the cost method would most likely always be used when appraising which of the following?

a) Single-family residence
b) Income property
c) Vacant lot
d) Public service properties

75. Mechanic's liens could be filed by a/an:

a) architect
b) subcontractor
c) materialman
d) All of the above

76. Creating an easement means:

a) restricting the style or cost of a house which can be built in a subdivision of lots
b) placing a dwelling over your property line onto another's property
c) giving someone the right, advantage or privilege to use your land
d) None of these

77. The quantity survey method, the square foot method and the unit-in-place method are terms most directly related to the field of real estate:

a) finance
b) management
c) appraisal
d) leasing

78. All of the following statements concerning condominium law are true, except:

a) the law does not provide for individual assessments and liens for real estate tax purposes
b) the unit ownership can be deeded for indefinite duration
c) the interest can be held in residential, industrial or commercial property
d) there is nonseverability of common and separate interests

79. A broker had an open listing on a house. To collect a commission he would have to prove which of the following?

a) He had a license
b) He had a ready, willing and able buyer
c) He was the procuring cause of the sale
d) All of the above

80. A property manager would realistically determine the rental charge per unit of space for income-producing property based on:

a) market data approach
b) a published schedule of rentals
c) the cost of construction per unit
d) a capitalization rate comparable to similar units in the vicinity

81. A binding sales contract is usually obtained when the broker or salesman has:

a) persuaded the prospect to sign an offer
b) convinced the seller that he should accept the offer
c) succeeded in getting both the buyer and the seller to escrow
d) advised the buyer that the seller has signed and accepted the signed offer

82. A contract authorizing the sale of real property signed by a minor is:

a) voidable
b) terminated
c) void
d) valid

83. Young signed an agreement of sale to purchase Bell's residence on December 13, 1987, the deal to be closed on January 3, 1988. Between January 2, 1988, and March 28, 1988, Bell tried to contact Young but was unsuccessful. On April 2, 1988, Bell sold the property to Hansen who recorded his deed the same day. On April 22, 1988, Young notified Bell that he was ready to close and learned the property had been sold to Hansen. Under these circumstances:

I. Young can compel Hansen to deed the property upon refunding Hansen's consideration price
II. Young has a valid right to join Hansen and Bell in an action to obtain title to the property

a) I only
b) II only
c) Both I and II
d) Neither I nor II

84. A mortgage company would give the least consideration to which of the following in granting a loan?

a) Borrower's income ratio
b) Value of the property in relation to the loan
c) Borrower's need for financial assistance
d) Amount of down payment

85. The capitalization approach to value would be widely used:

I. on residential property in a new subdivision
II. on leased property in a shopping center

a) I only
b) II only
c) Both I and II
d) Neither I nor II

86. If a purchaser desires to insure that there are no encroachments on the property, he should obtain a:

a) standard title insurance policy
b) survey
c) warranty deed from the seller
d) special warranty deed

87. Private restrictions can be created by:

I. deed
II. written agreement
III. general plans for the subdivision

a) I and II
b) I and III
c) II and III
d) I, II and III

88. The dominant tenement is the property:

a) upon which the burden is imposed
b) in whose favor the burden is created
c) the top story in an apartment building
d) owned by a person having the largest interest

89. Money realized in excess of indebtedness and foreclosure expenses at a mortgage foreclosure belongs to the:

a) bank
b) county auditor
c) mortgagee
d) mortgagor

90. The market approach to value is the method of appraisal in which the value of property is:

a) based on factual data related to the income yield of the property
b) based on sales of comparable properties
c) based on cost of duplicating the improvements on today's market
d) determined by capitalizing the annual net income

91. An area of land set off by municipal authorities for a specific use is called a:

a) cul de sac
b) subdivision
c) zone
d) territory

92. Marginal land is best defined as:

a) land that abuts a subdivision
b) the land is a subdivision that is left after dedication for streets, alleys, etc., has taken place
c) the land between the street and the setback line
d) land that barely produces enough income to pay for the cost of production

93. Title VIII of the Civil Rights Act of 1968 precludes:

I. discrimination in housing
II. discrimination in lending

a) I only
b) II only
c) Both I and II
d) Neither I nor II

94. The difference between police power and eminent domain can best be determined by:

a) whether or not the action was by sovereign power or by the statute
b) whether or not any compensation was paid to the owner
c) whether or not the improvements are to be razed
d) whether or not the owner's use was affected

95. The law guarantees a property owner his right to:

I. subjacent support
II. lateral support

a) I only
b) II only
c) Both I and II
d) Neither I nor II

96. In appraising, which approach to value tends to set the uppermost limit of value?

a) Market data
b) Summation
c) Income
d) None of the above

97. You would consider the following in determining net income for the capitalization method of appraising?

I. Payments on loan principal
II. Management costs
III. Interest payments

a) I and II
b) II only
c) II and III
d) I, II and III

98. Which of the following is covered by the Civil Rights Act, Title VIII?

a) Refusal to sell or lease on the basis of race, sex, religion, color or national origin where a broker's services are utilized
b) A lender quoting different rates to different people based on their credit rating
c) A private club refusing to rent to other than club members
d) All of the above

99. Any interest in or right to land held by third persons, adversely affecting the title, and possibly the value of property is an:

a) encumbrance
b) encroachment
c) appurtenance
d) escrow

100. Judgments are enforced by a process known as:

a) execution
b) enforcement
c) attachment
d) Any of these

Supplement Section

101. A person who has not had the required two years salesman's experience in Washington State, and has never been a salesman at all, may take the broker's examination after satisfying the director that he is:

a) qualified by reason of practical experience in a business allied with or related to real estate
b) of the right political party
c) a successful businessman
d) a college graduate

102. Which of the following is required to have a real estate license?

I. Resident manager of an apartment building
II. Property manager specializing in handling store buildings in business districts

a) I only
b) II only
c) Both I and II
d) Neither I nor II

103. The broker has earned his commission when:

a) the agreement of sale has been signed by both parties
b) the deed is recorded
c) the deed is signed
d) the deed is delivered

104. If an owner refuses to pay the broker an earned commission, the broker may properly seek relief by:

a) filing a mechanic's lien
b) bringing a formal complaint with the division of real estate
c) bringing a court action
d) bringing a quiet title action against the seller

105. A salesman's commission is paid by the:

a) seller
b) buyer
c) broker
d) escrow

106. The Statute of Frauds in Washington requires all of the following to be in writing to be enforceable, except:

a) an agreement for the leasing of real property for more than one year
b) an agreement that employs a broker to solicit, sell, lease or exchange real property
c) an agreement that, by its terms, is not to be performed within one year of the execution of the agreement
d) a partnership agreement between two or more parties to engage in the sale or exchange of real property

107. Unpaid real property taxes constitute a lien:

a) prior to a mortgage
b) concurrent with a mortgage
c) after a mortgage
d) None of the above

108. In Washington, a judgment may be recorded:

a) in the county where the judgment is given
b) in the county where the defendant's property is located
c) in any county
d) None of the foregoing

109. The most commonly used deed in the State of Washington is the:

a) warranty deed
b) special warranty deed
c) quitclaim deed
d) sheriff's deed

110. The State of Washington is a "lien theory" state. This means:

a) first to record is first in right
b) liens recorded against a property can be foreclosed through the courts
c) mortgages or deeds of trust are liens and do not give lenders title to the property
d) All of these

111. Smith is engaged solely in the business of appraising real estate. Smith is required to have:

a) the designation of MAI
b) an appraiser's license or certificate
c) a real estate broker's license
d) None of the foregoing

112. Who receives the interest paid on funds deposited in a broker's trust account?

a) Seller
b) Broker
c) State of Washington
d) None of these

113. A trust fund account maintained by a licensed broker need not:

a) provide for withdrawal of funds without previous notice
b) have a regular specified minimum balance
c) designate the broker as trustee
d) be the subject of a record showing deposits and withdrawals

114. John and Mary purchase a new home and an escrow is opened. Mary's parents demand that the escrow agent give them details of the transaction in case the children need advice. The escrow agent should:

a) comply since they are Mary's parents
b) give them the information only if the seller agrees to it
c) not give them the information since escrows are confidential
d) obtain permission from the escrow officer

115. If the broker of an office dies:

a) any qualified representative can go in and take over the broker's position
b) any qualified representative can go in and take over the broker's position for six months
c) any qualified broker could take over for not more than six months
d) the director may issue a temporary broker's permit to a qualified representative of the deceased, which shall not be valid for more than four months

116. The excise tax on real estate is not required to be paid on a:

a) real estate contract
b) purchaser's assignment of contract
c) seller's assignment of contract
d) statutory warranty deed

117. A condominium owner would own the following in fee simple.

a) The common hallways
b) The individual unit occupied by him
c) The common laundry area
d) All of the foregoing

118. Who administers the Washington Land Development Act?

a) Bureau of Land Management
b) Department of Natural Resources
c) Land Use Association
d) Real Estate Division

119. Washington law stipulates which of these in connection with homesteads?

I. $25,000 is a maximum exemption now allowed when a family head files a declaration of homestead
II. real property must be free and clear of all encumbrances to be declared a homestead

a) I only
b) II only
c) Both I and II
d) Neither I nor II

120. A homestead will defeat which of the following?

a) Mortgage
b) Mechanic's lien
c) Both
d) Neither

121. Among the grounds for denial, suspension or revocation of licenses is the practice of discrimination which includes:

I. blockbusting
II. hiring sales personnel only from a specific ethnic group

a) I only
b) II only
c) Both I and II
d) Neither I nor II

122. Broker secures a signed open listing in which owner inserted that sewers were in and connected. Broker thought there were no sewers in this block, checked it out, and found he was right. Broker showed house to buyer who did not ask about sewers and broker did not volunteer information. Buyer discovers absence and complains to the director. Which is true?

a) Broker had a right to rely on the listing even though he knew it was incorrect
b) Broker owed a duty to tell buyer, even if not asked
c) Buyer was at fault. He could have checked with the city
d) No provision at law covers this situation

123. An oral lease for five years is unenforceable under:

a) the Statute of Frauds
b) the Statute of Limitations
c) an act of Congress
d) the common law

124. In a contract for the sale of real property, the party who sells the property is known as the:

a) vendor
b) obligor
c) vendee
d) obligee

125. In listing property for sale, which item is not necessary for a valid exclusive listing agreement?

a) Date of listing
b) Address of property
c) Legal description
d) Listing period

126. How many days does a subcontractor have to file a mechanic's lien if a notice of completion is filed?

a) 10
b) 30
c) 60
d) 90

127. If a buyer wants to know how to take title to a parcel of land, tell him to:

a) ask the escrow officer
b) seek the advice of an attorney
c) rely upon the suggestion of the seller
d) consult his broker

128. In order to apply for and obtain a Washington non-resident broker's license, the nonresident broker must:

a) maintain a definite place of business in this state
b) retain in this state all funds arising from transactions within this state until such funds are distributed to the proper parties involved
c) Both A and B
d) Neither A nor B

129. A broker's license may be issued to a corporation provided:

I. All of its officers are licensed as brokers
II. One active officer, at least, is a licensed broker

a) I only
b) II only
c) I and II
d) Neither I nor II

130. A broker may split fees with which of the following?

a) Out of state broker
b) Any of his or her employed salespersons
c) Either A or B
d) Neither A nor B

131. The County Assessor must, according to law, assess property at:

a) loan value
b) market value
c) full cash value
d) liberal loan value

132. If a debtor owns three pieces of real estate and a judgment is entered against him, it will be a lien against:

a) the property first acquired
b) the property last acquired
c) all three properties
d) homestead property only

133. At the closing of a deal, which item is generally charged to the seller?

a) Recording deed
b) A.L.T.A. policy
c) Revenue stamps
d) Survey

134. When a land contract is signed, the seller has:

I. equitable title
II. naked title

a) I only
b) II only
c) Both I and II
d) Neither I nor II

135. The sale of subdivided lands is regulated by:

a) state
b) cities and counties
c) federal law
d) All of these

136. When a notice of completion is filed of record, contractors and laborers have:

a) ninety days to file a mechanic's lien
b) one hundred eighty days to file liens
c) thirty days to file liens
d) one hundred twenty days to file liens

137. When is the excise tax paid?

a) When the deed is delivered
b) When the land contract is recorded
c) When the land contract is signed
d) When the purchaser takes possession

138. Seller signs a non-exclusive listing agreement with a broker. Seller then sells the property himself and so notifies the broker. The listing agreement is:

a) voidable
b) enforceable
c) terminated
d) None of the above

139. Which of the following actions on the part of a real estate broker or salesman could result in revocation of his license?

I. Failing to submit to an owner, before his acceptance of an offer, all formal written offers received from property listed for sale
II. Quoting to prospective buyers of a property a sale price other than the one stipulated by the owner

a) I only
b) II only
c) Either I or II
d) Neither I nor II

140. If a broker places trust funds obtained from clients in his general operating account, he is guilty of:

a) conversion
b) collateral transfer
c) commingling
d) fraud

141. Under which of these conditions can the director investigate the actions of a licensed real estate broker or salesman?

I. On his own motion
II. On receipt of a verified complaint in writing

a) I only
b) II only
c) Both I and II
d) Neither I nor II

142. The commission shall be responsible for:

a) holding educational conferences
b) preparation of examinations not less than twelve times per year
c) administration of the examinations not less than twelve times per year
d) All of the above

143. Which of these statements concerning a salesman's legal status as a licensee is (are) correct?

I. He's an agent of his broker
II. A salesperson can be held liable for any misstatement made during a real estate deal, even though not a party to the sales agreement

a) I only
b) II only
c) Both I and II
d) Neither I nor II

144. If there is a violation of the Federal Fair Housing Law of 1968, the complainant takes action by:

a) filing a complaint with the Washington State Human Rights Commission
b) bringing suit in a U.S. district court
c) complain to HUD
d) Any of the above

145. An earned real estate commission must be disbursed by the broker to the salesman immediately except:

a) where there is written agreement between salesman and broker to pay at some other date
b) if broker is out of town when payable, providing disbursed within seven days of that date
c) if commission is from a rental property and paid as part of the rental payments
d) All of the above are exceptions

146. The description of land sold under an agreement of sale should:

a) give the house number and street
b) give a full legal description
c) describe the improvements
d) be handwritten and signed

147. Title VIII of the Civil Rights Act of 1968 is also called the:

a) Open Housing Act
b) Federal Fair Housing Law
c) Equal Opportunity in Housing Act
d) Washington Discrimination Law

148. Place the following steps in a mortgage foreclosure in the proper order.

I. Sheriff's Sale
II. Acceleration of the Note
III. Statutory period of redemption

a) I, II, III
b) II, III, I
c) II, I, III
d) III, II, I

149. All of the following are true concerning a deed of trust foreclosure, except:

a) the deed of trust must contain a power of sale clause authorizing a trustee's sale
b) the trustee may issue a deficiency judgment
c) the buyer at the trustee's sale receives a trustee's deed
d) the debtor must be given a notice of default

150. Which of the following are true concerning a homestead in Washington?

I. The exemption is limited to a maximum of $25,000
II. It must be declared prior to the beginning of execution proceedings
III. The exemption may be claimed by a head of household on land that the owner resides on or intends to reside on

a) I only
b) I and II only
c) I and III only
d) I, II and III

1. c) The listing is an employment contract employing the broker to act as agent for the seller in procuring a buyer for the property.

2. a) Duress, if present, can void a contract. If someone has been subjected to duress in order to induce him or her to enter a contract, that person may void the contract.

3. a) Real estate brokerage agency agreements are created by express contract. In Washington, a listing agreement creating an agency for the purposes of selling real estate must be in writing in order to be enforceable.

4. d) The depression would undoubtedly make it more difficult to sell the property, but the agency (listing) agreement would remain binding on both parties.

5. b) When a deed is recorded, it is presumed delivery has been made.

6. b) A written contract between the parties is necessary for a valid escrow.

7. c) The listing agreement is not an offer to sell. It is merely an employment contract with the broker. The prospective purchaser makes an offer to buy, which the seller can then accept or reject. Unless it is accepted, there is no contract between buyer and seller and no recourse for buyer. In the above case, the broker would have recourse against the seller for his commission as the broker performed his contract.

8. b) A lien is a financial encumbrance. Since an easement is a right to use the real property of another, it does not constitute a financial interest in real property.

9. d) This is the definition. Such a group will adopt a "master plan" for the locality.

10. a) Notes and mortgages are personal property.

11. b) Because it was removed from the ground prior to the sale, it became the personal property of the individual who owned the land when the copper was extracted.

12. d) A deed to real property is not negotiable. When the ownership is transferred, a new deed is given.

13. a) A quitclaim deed has no warranties.

14. b) Demise is to convey an estate, generally by a lease. The other terms refer to a will. Do not confuse demise with devise, the latter meaning to give real property by will.

15. b) Improvements intruding on the land of another are encroachments.

16. b) An estate in real property is defined as the right to possess property and have exclusive use.

17. c) The percentage is based on the tenant's gross receipts.

18. b) Tenancy in common is a form of concurrent ownership.

19. d) A joint tenant cannot dispose of his interest in real property by will.

20. a) A condominium owner owns his own unit separately and the common areas in conjunction with the other owners.

21. d) Supply and demand.

22. c) Mortgage companies sell all their loans while retaining the servicing rights. They do not buy, they sell federally insured loans.

23. c) A land contract, or installment sales contract, is never unilateral. Both parties have obligations to perform under a land contract. The purchaser (vendee) pays money while the seller (vendor) gives up possession and ultimately delivers the deed.

24. d) A syndicate is a pooling of funds by a group of individuals. The syndicate may take the form of a partnership, a real estate investment trust or a corporation.

25. b) A contract signed under duress is voidable.

26. a) An agency coupled with an interest is the one type of agency that the principal does not have the power to terminate by revocation prior to the end of the term.

27. d) A deed of trust, like a mortgage, is a financial lien and does not create an easement.

28. c) The contract was contingent upon buyer obtaining a loan under specific conditions to finance the purchase. If the buyer is unable to obtain a loan after making a good faith effort, the contingency is not met and the contract does not "ripen" into an enforceable obligation.

29. a) To assign is to transfer all rights and interest that the assignor has in the contract but not necessarily the legal burdens. The option also transfers with the lease unless the agreement provides otherwise. The assignor remains secondarily liable on the contract.

30. d) Riparian rights are those of the property owner which allow him reasonable use of surface water on his property. They are not necessarily of public record, nor are they absolute rights.

31. a) As long as the property can be identified with sufficient precision, the description will be valid.

32. a) Property reverts or escheats to the state when someone dies with no will and no heirs.

33. b) The vendor or seller holds title until full purchase price has been paid. The vendee has equitable title (the right to possess and use) until the contract is fulfilled.

34. d) An estate in fee is the largest estate. It is freely transferable, free from conditions. It is also called a fee simple estate or estate of inheritance.

35. a) When one assigns his leasehold interest, he transfers the entire interest to a third person.

36. c) No policy protects against government actions that damage an owner's land value or title, such as down-zoning or condemnation.

37. a) There are more residential loans made than any other type, and the funds for these loans primarily come from savings deposits.

38. b) The developer is the seller—the grantor. He will invariably draft a set of restrictions—called a declaration of restrictions— to assure uniformity of property use in his subdivision. He does this to satisfy prospective purchasers that there will be ongoing homogeneity and continuity of land use in the development throughout their period of ownership.

39. b) Under an open listing, the owner may list the property with as many brokers as he or she so desires.

40. a) The only unity in tenancy in common is equal right of possession.

41. d) The listing most likely to be used is an exclusive right to sell.

42. b) Louis has a life estate that will end at his death. A fee simple estate is perpetual and would pass to Louis' heirs when he died.

43. a) FHA's underwriting system has proven its effectiveness and is copied by lending institutions everywhere. However, the FHA does not provide mortgage money for any purpose. It insures loans; it does not make or buy them.

44. c) The VA will guarantee this loan but requires the buyer to certify that he is aware he is paying more than the VA's appraised value.

45. c) A valid earnest money agreement is express (terms spelled out, written), bilateral (exchange of promises), executory contract (in the process of being performed).

46. d) The holder in due course obtains a negotiable instrument in the ordinary course before it is due, in good faith and for value, without knowledge that it has been previously dishonored and without notice of any defect or set-off at the time it was negotiated to him.

47. d) The promissory note is secured by a deed of trust or mortgage, depending on what the lender and borrower decide.

48. a) A certificate of sale is awarded at the sheriff's sale; a sheriff's deed is received following the period of redemption if there is no redemption.

49. d) The first lien holder still has his mortgage as security; he has simply subordinated his lien position.

50. a) An appraisal report sets forth the views, experiences, and conclusions of the writer. The final estimate of value is true as of a certain date. It can be made for any date in the past but not for any period in the future. The date of inspection is usually the date of valuation unless otherwise called for by the property owner, his attorney, or a court of law. An appraisal as of a previous date is called retrospective value.

51. a) The deal did not consummate. The reason was not due to a title defect. The buyer simply backed out. Broker is not entitled to a commission. Seller could sue buyer for specific performance.

52. b) The option gives the tenant the right to purchase the property for $40,000 before the expiration of the option.

53. b) The secondary mortgage market refers to the transaction between lenders, not to the source of funds for second mortgages. Second mortgage loans are made at the primary market level.

54. c) The note would probably be a negotiable instrument.

55. c) FHA requires MIP for all loans, and if the buyer is applying for an owner-occupied loan, he must certify he intends to occupy the property.

56. a) A note is a written instrument evidencing a creditor/debtor relationship. It does not represent a right or interest in anyone's real property.

57. a) The value of the better house will decline toward the value of the cheaper homes. This is regression.

58. d) The interest rate portion of the overall rate is the provision for a return on the investment; the return of the investment—called recapture of the invested sum—is a way of allowing for depreciation of the improvements. The value of the property is not affected by income taxes to be paid by an investor and no allowance for them is reflected in the capitalization rate.

59. b) Without a market for the proposed new houses, the other considerations would be of little importance.

60. c) Both public (zoning) and private (deed) restrictions may affect the use to which a property owner may put his land.

61. d) A load bearing wall carries part of the weight of the structure and should not be removed during remodeling without provision for some other method of support.

62. c) Forces outside the property itself are usually impossible for the property owner to correct.

63. b) Generally, it is the seller's responsibility to discharge all encumbrances against the property and deliver clear title to the purchaser, but either party could pay the assessment (the government doesn't care who pays it). If the owner of the property refuses to pay, the county could force a sale of the property to satisfy its specific involuntary lien.

64. b) All VA loans can be assumed, even by non-veterans, though the original veteran borrower retains secondary liability in the event the new borrower fails to make the payments.

65. d) Ordinarily (absent a subordination clause), the priority of a mortgage can be ascertained by comparing its recording date against that of other recorded instruments.

66. c) I is physical deterioration and II is functional obsolescence, two of the three types of depreciation.

67. c) Ethics guide a licensee in his day-to-day business practices.

68. a) If the buyer wants to make his deed a matter of public record—and he should—he assumes the cost of recording it. The cost is minimal.

69. d) The unit is the owner's separate space. The bearing walls, central heating systems, and elevator are part of the common area.

70. c) The writ of attachment is sought so as to place a lien on the property of the defendant pending the outcome of the lawsuit. A writ of attachment is a lien.

71. a) Functional obsolescence is a loss of value resulting from such things as poor design, or outmoded design according to modern tastes. Residential styles today would dictate that a home of this size with four bedrooms have more than one bathroom.

72. c) One exemption would be if no broker were involved, the owner owned no more than three such dwellings, and the owner did not sell more than one such dwelling in any two-year period in which he or she was not the most recent occupant. However, there are other federal, state, and local laws prohibiting discrimination which do not provide for such an exemption.

73. c) Blockbusting is an illegal and discriminatory practice whereby some person induces a property owner to enter into a real estate transaction from which the first person may benefit financially, by claiming that an inevitable influx of minority families into the neighborhood will cause property values to decline.

74. d) Since public service properties do not generate any income and there are few, if any, properties to compare against, the cost method is the only appraisal technique available. The cost approach can be used when appraising residences and income property—but never land, of course—though the comparison method is usually used for homes and the capitalization method for income properties.

75. d) Anyone who contributes services, labor or supplies in connection with a construction project and goes unpaid, is entitled to file a mechanic's lien.

76. c) However, title to the land is not granted when an easement is created, only use rights regarding the land.

77. c) These are the three methods used in the cost approach to estimate replacement cost.

78. a) The individual units are assessed and taxed separately. Alternative (d) means an owner cannot sell his space and interest in the common areas separately.

79. d) If the listing was an exclusive right of sale, the broker would not have to prove he was the procuring cause—the person responsible for making the deal. However, with the more limited protection provided by the open listing, he must do all of these.

80. a) Realistically, the rent that could be charged would be determined by the market, the rents being charged for similar property in the area.

81. d) The buyer must be notified that the seller has accepted his offer; then the deal is binding.

82. a) A minor has the right to void his contracts during his minority or within a reasonable time after attaining majority. The contract is not void because the minor may enforce it. However, it may not be enforced against the minor.

83. d) One of the conditions of the performance of this real estate transaction was that the deal be "closed" by January 3. Since Young was unable or unwilling to perform either on the third or within a reasonable period of time thereafter, the deal is canceled. Bell is free to sell to someone else.

84. c) Whether or not the borrower needs a loan to finance the purchase is not relevant to the mortgage evaluation; only his ability to pay back the loan and the quality of the property he is buying are at issue.

85. b) The income (capitalization) approach is normally used for income property and is impractical when appraising residential property.

86. b) A survey will establish the true property lines. The standard insurance policy does not insure against matters that only a physical inspection would reveal.

87. d) Private restrictions can take any written form, though most often they are incorporated into deeds or the declaration of restrictions (general plans for subdivision) filed by the developer.

88. b) The dominant tenant is benefited in that the owner of the servient tenement must pay the taxes on the land which the dominant tenant is entitled to use for his own purposes. The tenement is the property; the tenant is the property owner.

89. d) The borrower (mortgagor) is entitled to any money paid at the foreclosure sale which exceeds the accrued debts against the property.

90. b) Sales of comparable properties are the market data or comparison approach.

91. c) This is a definition of zoning.

92. d) This is a definition of marginal land.

93. c) The Civil Rights Act prohibits discriminatory practices when selling, renting, advertising or financing housing.

94. b) The use of property is affected by both government powers, but only when the right of eminent domain is exercised is compensation to the property owner involved.

95. c) A property owner has the right to have his land undisturbed and supported in its natural state.

96. b) Summation is another name for cost approach.

97. b) Payments on the loan principal and payments of interest on the loan are not considered in determining the net income for the capitalization approach.

98. a) Alternative (a) would be an obvious violation of the Act. A lender, however, is entitled to charge a higher interest rate when lending to a poor credit risk. The restriction of lodgings owned or operated by a private club to members only is also permitted, even if discriminatory.

99. a) This is a good definition of an encumbrance.

100. a) When a judgment is rendered, a lien is created on the debtor's property. If payment of the debt is not forthcoming, the creditor can ask the court to order the sale of the property to satisfy the debt. The court's order is called a writ of execution.

101. a) Some examples are: the practice of law, or three years' experience closing transactions for an escrow company. He must also satisfy the other requirements.

102. b) The manager of an apartment complex in which the manager resides is not required to be licensed.

103. a) The broker has earned his commission when the agreement of sale has been signed by both parties.

104. c) In this case, the broker may seek relief by bringing a court action. He sues to enforce the terms of the listing contract.

105. c) A salesman's commission is paid by the broker.

106. d) A general partnership agreement is not required to be in writing by the Statute of Frauds.

107. a) Regardless of the date of the recording of a mortgage, general property taxes are always the first liens to be satisfied from the forced sale of property.

108. c) A judgment, once recorded, is good for ten years from the date of the original judgment. Within the ten-year period, the judgment is effective in any county in which it is recorded.

109. a) The warranty deed is the most commonly used deed in Washington. Here, the seller warrants good title and promises to defend it against all adverse claims.

110. c) In Washington, mortgages and trust deeds are nothing more than liens, securing a borrower's promise to repay a debt. During the period of indebtedness, the borrower, not the lender, has title to the property.

111. d) A real estate appraiser is not required to hold a license or be a member of any organization.

112. d) The funds are maintained in non-interest bearing checking accounts.

113. b) Since only monies of others are to be placed in the trust account, it is not necessary that the broker maintain a minimum balance.

114. c) Escrows are confidential. The escrow agent owes a fiduciary obligation to John and Mary and the seller—no one else.

115. d) The temporary broker's permit makes it possible for a qualified representative of the deceased to manage the affairs of the office until a permanent solution is found, like selling the business or locating a licensed broker to take over. However, the death of the original broker terminates all existing listings, and they must be renegotiated by the holder of the temporary broker's permit.

116. c) When the contract rights of the seller are sold and transferred to another, the excise tax is not required.

117. d) Title to a condominium, including the separate space and common areas, is generally held in fee simple. However, an individual could be granted a lesser estate, such as a life estate.

118. d) The Land Development Act of 1973 is consumer legislation intended to put complete, truthful information about lots in a development in the hands of purchasers before or at the time of sale. The Act is administered by the Division of Real Estate.

119. a) Property does not have to be clear of all liens and encumbrances before a homestead may be filed.

120. d) Debts secured by mortgages or mechanic's liens are not subject to the homestead exemption.

121. c) Both I and II apply.

122. b) Silence about a known defect is a form of misrepresentation. The broker's obligation requires that he disclose all facts detrimental to the property, known to him, which would not be revealed by a physical inspection.

123. a) A contract that cannot be performed within one year is subject to the Statute of Frauds and must be in writing. A lease for five years cannot be fully performed within one year and therefore must be in writing.

124. a) The parties are vendor (seller) and vendee (buyer). They become grantor and grantee when the deed changes hands.

125. b) In the State of Washington, the legal description is not absolutely necessary as long as the property is adequately described. As a practical matter, the adequate description most often used is the legal description. The street address is not adequate.

126. d) A subcontractor has 90 days to file a mechanic's lien if a notice of completion is filed.

127. b) Advice on how to take title is legal advice which should be given by an attorney.

128. b) The nonresident broker must maintain a definite place of business in his own state but not in Washington.

129. b) A license may be issued to a corporation or copartnership if a qualified individual is designated to act as its broker. In the case of a corporation, this individual must be an officer; in the case of a copartnership, a general partner.

130. c) A broker may share commissions with brokers licensed in any state, U.S. possession or Canada, as well as his or her own salespersons.

131. b) By law, the assessor must assess property at one hundred percent of its true and fair market value. Theoretically, this is true. Practically speaking, during times of rapid appreciation in property values, the assessed value of property will not reflect actual selling prices.

132. c) A judgment lien is a general, involuntary lien, affecting all properties owned by a debtor in the county where the judgment was rendered, as well as any he acquires subsequent to the judgment.

133. c) The buyer will record his deed and bear the cost of doing so. He also is generally responsible for the A.L.T.A. title insurance policy—the extended coverage policy that covers the new lender. If the purchaser wants a survey to confirm the property's actual boundaries, he must pay for it. Revenue stamps, however, are customarily a charge to the seller.

134. b) All that the seller retains is legal title (also called naked title) to the property. The right to possess and profit from the property passes to the buyer.

135. d) The state regulates through the Washington Land Development Act, the federal government under the Interstate Land Sales Full Disclosure Act, while cities and counties exercise regulatory control by approving or denying proposed subdivisions, zoning ordinances, etc.

136. a) From the time the notice of completion is filed of record, laborers and contractors have 90 days to file their claims (mechanic's liens).

137. b) The excise tax must be paid before the contract is recorded.

138. c) Sale of the property listed under an open listing by the owner would terminate the agency relationship between the seller and broker.

139. c) A licensee is required to present all written offers to the seller for acceptance or refusal. Answer II would indicate dishonesty, bad faith, untrustworthiness or incompetence on the part of the licensee. All of the above would be grounds for revocation.

140. c) Commingling is the mixing of funds.

141. c) The director may, on his own motion and shall, upon a verified written complaint, investigate the activities of a licensee.

142. d) The commission has the authority to hold educational conferences and is charged with preparing and administering examinations at least once a month.

143. c) A salesman is his broker's agent and he can be held personally responsible for misstatements made by him in the course of real estate transactions.

144. a) Since Washington has a stringent anti-discrimination law, complainants would seek redress by filing a complaint with the Washington Human Rights Commission.

145. d) All three are exceptions to the general rule that commissions are payable to salespersons or associate brokers immediately upon receipt of the funds by the broker. Note that the agreement to pay at some other time must be written.

146. b) A requirement for a land sale contract is that the property be properly described. The street address is not an adequate description.

147. b) Title VIII of the 1968 Civil Rights Act is that portion of the Civil Rights Act which addresses discrimination in housing. It is called the Federal Fair Housing Law.

148. c) The correct order would involve acceleration of the note, sheriff's sale, confirmation of sale, period of redemption and sheriff's deed if there were no redemption.

149. b) In order to get a deficiency judgment, the creditor must foreclose the deed of trust through the courts like a mortgage.

150. c) The homestead need not be declared at all for property on which the owner lives; in other cases, it must be declared prior to the sheriff's sale.